Complete Guide to Microsoft® Excel Macros

AF544997

Complete Guide to Microsoft® Excel Macros

Charles W. Kyd
and Chris Kinata

PUBLISHED BY
Microsoft Press
A Division of Microsoft Corporation
One Microsoft Way
Redmond, Washington 98052-6399

Copyright © 1992 by Charles W. Kyd and Microsoft Corporation

All rights reserved. No part of the contents of this book may be reproduced or transmitted in any form or by any means without the written permission of the publisher.

Library of Congress Cataloging-in-Publication Data

Kyd, Charles W.
Complete guide to Microsoft Excel macros / Charles W. Kyd, Chris Kinata.
p. cm.
ISBN 1-55615-250-7 : $29.95
1. Integrated software. 2. Microsoft Excel (Computer program)
I. Title.
QA76.76.I57K83 1991
650'.028'55369--dc20 89-13914
CIP

Printed and bound in the United States of America.

1 2 3 4 5 6 7 8 9 AGAG 6 5 4 3 2 1

Distributed to the book trade in Canada by Macmillan of Canada, a division of Canada Publishing Corporation.

Distributed to the book trade outside the United States and Canada by Penguin Books Ltd.

Penguin Books Ltd., Harmondsworth, Middlesex, England
Penguin Books Australia Ltd., Ringwood, Victoria, Australia
Penguin Books N.Z. Ltd., 182-190 Wairau Road, Auckland 10, New Zealand

British Cataloging-in-Publication Data available.

Apple® and Macintosh® are registered trademarks of Apple Computer, Incorporated. Lotus® and 1-2-3® are registered trademarks of Lotus Development Corporation. IBM® is a registered trademark of International Business Machines Corporation. Microsoft® and Multiplan® are registered trademarks and Windows™ is a trademark of Microsoft Corporation. OS/2® is a registered trademark licensed to Microsoft Corporation.

Companies, names, and data used in this book are fictitious unless otherwise noted.

Acquisitions Editor: Marjorie Schlaikjer
Project Editor: Jack Litewka
Technical Editor: Mark Dodge

Contents

Acknowledgments

Editor Jack Litewka, for helping resolve the angels-on-the-head-of-a-pin controversy, and for the bison on the wall of the cave.

Technical editor Mark Dodge, an Excel expert himself, for astute testing of the seemingly innumerable macros in this book, for his labors in "typesetting" them for publication, and for being persistent about the Bard in the Woods.

Proofreaders Shawn Peck and Jennifer Harris, who patiently suffered the explanation of how the FORMULA formula contained a FORMULA function.

Dan Williams, John Dauphiny, Matthew Crinklaw, and Jerry Fisher from the group of people at Microsoft who prepare and support Microsoft Excel, for reviewing the manuscript at various stages, for offering many helpful suggestions, and for answering numerous obscure questions.

Introduction

The first time you looked at the documentation for Excel's macros, you might have been appalled: Microsoft Excel has over 300 macro functions! Perhaps you thought "Who would ever want to do so much with macros that they would need to learn about them all?"

Soon, however, you might have started to change your mind. Perhaps you put together a macro to print dozens of reports from different worksheets while you relaxed over lunch. Perhaps you developed convenient utilities for working with charts and worksheets that saved you hours each week. Perhaps you learned that you can expand Excel's range of worksheet functions with your own custom functions.

Whether or not you've had such experiences, you need to know this: Microsoft Excel macros offer so many benefits that you can't afford to ignore them. With the power of macros, however, comes what can at first seem a bewildering complexity.

To find your way through the wilderness, follow what is probably the most important advice offered in this book: *Learn only what you need to know.* Most people use automobiles to get from place to place with hardly a thought about how this all happens, trusting that someone has (usually) figured everything out. Adopt the same attitude when studying macro programming, and focus only on what gets you closer to your destination. Over time, you'll accumulate a wide experience of the terrain.

Section One, "Getting Started," introduces command and function macros, programming style, and ways to recover from errors.

Section Two, "Basics," provides a grounding in how to use macros to work with text and references and how to control the flow of execution in a macro program.

Section Three, "Creating a User Interface," presents methods for making your macros more interactive by adding custom dialog boxes and menus.

Section Four, "Special Topics," discusses the fine points of using macros to prepare charts, text files, and printed reports.

Section Five, "Platform-Specific Topics," discusses the process of translating Lotus 1-2-3 macros into the Excel environment and how to use the SEND.KEYS function, available only in the PC versions of Microsoft Excel.

Finally, Appendixes A and B present tables of the standard worksheet and macro functions available to macro programmers, listed first by category and then in alphabetic order.

About this book

This book explains how to use Microsoft Excel macros running under Microsoft Windows, OS/2, and the Macintosh. It is possible to write one book for these three platforms because the various versions of Microsoft Excel are nearly identical. However, there are differences in terminology and in the way key sequences are described. Rather than referring to the complete product names for Microsoft Excel, we'll say *on the Mac* or *in Windows* or *in OS/2*. Or, if the OS/2 and Windows versions work in the same way, we'll say *on the PC*.

Occasionally we'll present tips that apply only to one of the platforms or present either the Windows or the Macintosh version of a screen display.

The term *spreadsheet* was in wide use before the advent of desktop computers. Originally, it referred to a paper form containing rows and columns that accountants and bookkeepers filled out by hand. Then, in the early 1980s, computerized simulations of the traditional spreadsheet became available. In this book, *spreadsheet* refers to the general category of manual and computerized documents laid out in rows and columns.

When you choose New from the File menu, Microsoft Excel presents a dialog box requesting you to select one of the three types of Excel documents: Worksheet, Chart, or Macro Sheet. In this book, each of these terms refers to a specific type of Excel document. Also, we use the term *sheet* to refer to both the worksheet and macro sheet formats because they contain rows and columns, and we use *document* for worksheets, macro sheets, and charts.

Filenames

The file-naming convention in the Windows and OS/2 versions is more restrictive than in the Macintosh version, so we'll specify filenames in eight or fewer uppercase letters, plus an extension that describes the type of file: XLS for a worksheet, XLM for a macro sheet, and XLC for a chart.

Menu commands

Where we might say *choose Arrange All from the Windows menu,* we'll often say *choose the Windows Arrange All command* instead. This syntax is close to the way the documentation presents menu commands and is procedurally advantageous because you go to the Windows menu first and then drag down to the Arrange All command.

Key sequences

You can issue a command or take an action in Microsoft Excel in so many ways that it would really bog things down to list them all. For example, if you wanted to recalculate a document, you could

- Choose Calculate Now from the Options menu
- In the Windows and OS/2 versions of Excel, press the Alt, O, and N keys
- In any version of Excel, if in the Options Workspace dialog box the Alternate Menu or Help Key is the slash key, press the /, O, and N keys
- Press Alt (or the / key if available), and then use the Right direction key to activate the Options menu, use the Down direction key to activate the Calculate Now command, and finally press Enter
- Press Ctrl-= on the PC, Control-= or Command-= on the Mac
- Press F9 if you have an extended keyboard

Because the third method is consistent and available in all versions of Excel, this is how we'll usually specify menu command key sequences. If you expect to use more than one version of Microsoft Excel, it's convenient to use key sequences common to all platforms. If you expect to use only one version, it doesn't matter which method you use: Simply refer to the documentation, and use key sequences that are easy for you.

Where we do cite key sequences, we enclose them in square brackets and indicate the pertinent platform, as in [PC—F9 or Ctrl-=; Mac—Command-=]. If we cite a key sequence without specifying a platform, the key sequence refers to all platforms, as in [F9] or [F9; Mac—also Command-=]. On the Mac, because the Control and Command keys usually produce the same result (if the keyboard has the Control key), we typically mention only the PC version of the Control key: *Ctrl.*

Also, on the Macintosh the Enter and Return keys sometimes don't produce the same results. The Enter key, which is part of the numeric keypad on the extended keyboard, enters data without moving the selection. The Return key, above the Shift key, enters data and moves the selection down one cell (if, in the Options Workspace dialog box, the Move Selection After Return check box is set). Extended keyboards on the PC, on the other hand, have two Enter keys and no Return keys. Because it usually doesn't matter whether you press Return or Enter on the Macintosh, this book generally refers to the Enter key. Where it does matter, we will be specific.

Syntax for arguments to macro functions

We use a slightly different way of listing the arguments for Excel's worksheet and macro functions than does the Microsoft Excel Function Reference. For example, the BORDER function takes the form

BORDER(outlineN,leftN,rightN,topN,bottomN,shadeL, outlineColorN,leftColorN,rightColorN,topColorN,bottomColorN)

Each argument name ends with an abbreviation that expresses the type of value the argument is supposed to take according to the following table:

Value type	Abbreviation
Number	N
Text	T
Logical	L
Reference	R
Error	E
Array	A

Each argument in the BORDER function (with the exception of *shadeL*) takes a numeric value, which in the case of the first five arguments specifies the type of line used in the border (from 0 through 7) and in the case of the last five arguments specifies the color of the border (from 0 through 16). Where we cite the syntax for a function (in an indented setoff line), we use italics to indicate optional arguments. For a complete list of the macro functions and the arguments each takes, see the Microsoft Excel Function Reference or Appendix B of this book.

Disk Available

Coauthor Charles Kyd has produced a disk that contains 25 working macros, most of which are taken from his own toolkit. For ordering information, write to The Kyd Group, 15009 8th Place West, Lynnwood, WA 98037, or call 206-742-7120 or 800-999-4KYD.

SECTION ONE

Getting Started

1

An Introduction to Macros

Microsoft Excel is a powerful spreadsheet and charting program that can solve countless problems. To fully realize the potential of this popular program, you need to master its macro language.

Macros are small programs that you design and write to accomplish a specific task. They are the power tools of Microsoft Excel. Macros allow you to automate, simplify, explain, and document everything from simple everyday tasks to complex interactive applications. They let you manipulate Microsoft Excel's enormous capabilities to suit your situation.

If you're familiar with macros used in other spreadsheet programs, the macros in Microsoft Excel might look somewhat strange to you. Most other spreadsheets, including Microsoft Multiplan and Lotus 1-2-3, use *keystroke* macros. These macros consist of columns of text that tell their spreadsheets which keys to activate to perform an action. For example, in Lotus 1-2-3 the macro command to adjust the width of the current column to 20 characters is

```
/WCS20~
```

which lists the keystrokes you would type to initiate the command

```
/Worksheet Column Set 20 (Enter)
```

Microsoft Excel, on the other hand, uses *procedural* macros. These macro functions are formulas that tell the spreadsheet what procedures to follow. For example, in Microsoft Excel the macro command to adjust the width of the selected column to 20 characters is

```
=COLUMN.WIDTH(20)
```

Obviously, procedural macros are intrinsically easier to read and understand.

For most purposes, procedural macros offer more power and convenience than do keystroke macros. Also, procedural macros are formulas (rather than text). This fact offers a distinct advantage when you're debugging a macro. When the statements in a procedural macro run correctly, they usually return the value TRUE; otherwise, they return either an error value or FALSE. Therefore, if a macro isn't running correctly, a glance at the results of each formula in the macro can quickly pinpoint the problem.

Another advantage of procedural macros becomes apparent when you use a macro recorder. Most of us can't record a macro without taking frequent false steps; for example, we'll choose a command or select a cell, change our minds, and then choose another. Because a keystroke macro recorder records each keystroke, it faithfully records all our false steps, which we must then tediously delete from the recorded macro. But because Excel records only completed procedures, the resulting macros tend to require hardly any cleanup at all.

In this chapter, we'll stand back and take a broad view of macros—the advantages and disadvantages they present, the different types of macros, and how to decide whether you should create a macro in the first place. We'll also outline the various types of macro functions you can use to create your own macros.

The advantages of macros

Users who get hooked on macros love them because of the great customizing power macros offer. The following list presents some of the many advantages of using macros and how these advantages help to adjust Microsoft Excel's features according to your needs.

Faster operation

At their best, macros can do in minutes what might take hours to do with standard worksheets and processes. Many businesses, for example, use simple macros to create templates for standard forecasts and analyses—they retrieve appropriate data from old worksheets, enter proper dates and formulas into new worksheets, and format the templates correctly. Without these macros, people might spend an hour or more doing repetitive formatting work before beginning to enter new data.

Less human involvement

Sometimes macros can't do a job any faster than you can, but they save you time and money because they relieve you from having to do the job yourself. Macros that manage the printing of charts and worksheets are a good example. Without print macros, you can spend hours or even days printing reports; as each report is printed, you rush to the computer to print the next report, unable to do anything else with the computer. A simple macro, however, can automate the entire job. Although the macro doesn't speed the actual printing of a worksheet, it can load each worksheet, calculate it, print it, close it, load another, and so on—all without human intervention. Print macros can run during a lunch hour or overnight, letting you do something more enjoyable.

Also, you might perform certain tasks only a few times a year. For example, you might calculate income quarterly, analyze inventory semiannually, and enter audit adjustments yearly. Because these events happen infrequently, it's easy to forget how you did the procedure the last time. The process of developing a system of macros to automate a task offers a range of ways to document a task, explaining what step comes next, why that task is necessary, where the needed data must come from, and where the data must go. Also, you can create a user interface for a system of macros, presenting customized help screens, menus, messages, and dialog boxes for entering data more easily.

Fewer errors

Everyone makes errors. We might enter data from the wrong column, put data in the wrong place, invert numbers, or forget to enter all the data. A macro, however, doesn't make these kinds of errors when it updates a worksheet. You can also write macros that manage the input of data, verifying the validity of the data before it actually becomes part of a worksheet. Of course, macros can also generate errors; but such errors are usually obvious and easy to fix, and once fixed, they should be gone for good.

Saved keystrokes

Because you can assign unique key sequences to your macros, you can assemble series of often-used commands in a macro, called by a few simple keystrokes. Used once, the macro may not save much time, but over the long haul, the savings add up. For example, a macro we'll develop in Chapter 2 recalculates a selected range of cells. Another macro in that chapter lets you jump quickly back and forth between two cells in your worksheet, speeding data entry.

Enhanced features

The first time you used Excel you were probably impressed with its capabilities. Eventually, however, you might need some feature that the program can't deliver. For example, Excel doesn't have statistical functions for smoothing or deseasonalizing time series data or finding the mode in a collection of measurements. Its date functions don't work with dates before 1904. However, you can create special *function macros* to add new functions to Excel.

When you need to enter a complex formula over and over in a worksheet, it often makes sense to hide the formula's complexity in a function macro. By substituting a simple reference to the function macro for the complex formula, you can make your worksheets easier to create, edit, and document.

Wider calculation options

Many worksheets contain complicated formulas that take a long time to recalculate. If these formulas don't need to be recalculated frequently, you might want to replace them with values generated by a macro. Doing so can shorten recalculation time significantly, reducing your worksheet's memory requirements. For example, we once created a worksheet that calculated monthly cost of sales by looking up in a large database the cost of each item sold. These hundreds of lookup formulas slowed recalculation considerably. Writing a macro to calculate costs on a monthly basis made it possible to keep the worksheet quick and efficient during the remainder of the month.

The disadvantages of macros

Macros aren't a panacea for problems in a worksheet or chart. It takes time to create a macro, as well as a sense of judgment to determine whether one is needed at all. The following four subsections discuss the downsides of using macros and explain how a misdirected or poorly documented macro can impede an already efficient worksheet.

Development time

Macros require an investment of time to learn and to write—time that you might otherwise direct toward more productive work. If you spend hours researching and refining a macro that saves only a fraction of a second every time you use it, where's the advantage?

When a macro works perfectly, the job is still half done. You need to document the macro, explaining what each line or section of programming does and, if a system of macros is to be used by others, perhaps even preparing help screens or printed information explaining how to use the system. The process of documenting a macro takes time when you know what's going on, and much more time after you've forgotten. If you don't document a macro when you understand it, you'll have trouble supporting it weeks or months later, and others will find it nearly impossible to understand.

Work to support

It's the rare macro that never needs support. Changes in procedures, databases, personnel, software versions, and so on can require changes in your macros.

Two spreadsheets rather than one

Unlike most other spreadsheet programs, Microsoft Excel requires that macros be written on a special macro sheet rather than on a worksheet. Although this approach offers many advantages, it does require that you manage two sheets rather than one. When you create the macro sheet, you need to invent a reasonable name for it. When you first open the worksheet, you need to remember to open the macro sheet. (Later we'll show you how opening a worksheet can automatically open a macro sheet.) After the macro sheet is open, it clutters your screen and consumes extra memory.

Extra recalculation steps

When you use a command macro to update a worksheet or chart, you can easily forget to run the macro. More than once, we've completed an analysis, recalculated the worksheet, printed its results, and then realized that we'd forgotten to run a macro to update vital information.

A closer look at macros

In the chapters ahead, you'll become very familiar with the many details involved in designing, writing, and debugging macros for Microsoft Excel. Let's take a closer look at the environment in which a macro operates, the two different classes of macros, and the functions available for macro programming.

Worksheets and macro sheets

A macro is a set of instructions that performs a task. In most spreadsheet programs, you enter macros as text in a standard spreadsheet. In Microsoft Excel, however, you enter macros as a series of special formulas on a macro sheet. (The other two types of sheets are worksheets and charts.) Three important benefits result from this macro-entry procedure. Entering macros as a series of formulas helps you develop and debug macros easily. Entering macros on a separate macro sheet allows you to use one macro with many other worksheets or charts.

To open a new macro sheet, open the File menu, choose the New command, select Macro Sheet, and press Enter. When you do this, you'll notice that the new macro sheet looks much like a standard worksheet. It also performs as a worksheet does except for significant differences in three areas: display options, calculation method, and formulas available.

Display options

The columns of a macro sheet are wider than those in a worksheet. This is because new macro sheets default to the display of formulas, and new worksheets default to the display of the results of formulas. To see this for yourself, enter the formula *=1+2* in cell A1 of both a macro sheet and a worksheet. After you do so, the macro sheet displays *=1+2* in a wide column and the worksheet displays *3* in a narrow column.

You can easily switch the formats of these two displays. First activate the macro sheet, choose Display from the Options menu, and deselect the Formulas option. Then activate the worksheet, call up the Display dialog box again, and select the Formulas option. After you do so, the worksheet displays *=1+2* in a wide column and the macro sheet displays *3* in a narrow column.

The macro sheet displays formulas by default for a good reason. This setting allows us to read the macro formulas that we enter, but it also creates certain side effects that you need to keep in mind. The primary consideration is that this setting overrides the effect of number and alignment formatting. For example, if you enter the date 1/1/89 into a macro sheet in its default setting, the sheet displays the serial date number 32509 instead. And if you try to center an entry within a cell, the entry continues to be left-aligned.

Use Ctrl-` (backquote) to alternate between the display of formulas and values [Mac—also Command-`].

Pressing this key combination is equivalent to opening the Options menu, choosing Display, and selecting or deselecting the Formulas option. Or you can set up two windows on the same macro sheet by opening the Window menu, choosing New Window, and setting one window to the display of formulas and the other to the display of values.

Another side effect of this setting causes some inconvenience when you document macros. If the text that you enter into a cell is too long to fit within the visible portion of the cell, the display text will not extend beyond the cell's boundaries as it does when formulas are not displayed. You'll have to adjust the column width; or you'll have to open the Format menu and choose Justify to wrap long text blocks into more than one cell.

Calculation method

A worksheet normally uses one of two calculation methods. With automatic calculation (choose Options Calculation and select the Automatic option), a worksheet recalculates each time you enter a value. (Note: *Options Calculation* is a short form for *open the Options menu and choose Calculation.* We'll use this menu-command short form throughout this book.) With manual calculation (choose Options Calculation and select the Manual option), you need to choose Options Calculate Now to recalculate your worksheet [F9 or Ctrl-=; Mac—also Command-=].

A macro sheet uses neither of these calculation methods. Instead, a macro fully recalculates only when you run it. More specifically, a macro recalculates in the manner described for each of the following kinds of values or formulas.

Constant values. When a macro finds a cell that contains a constant value (including a number, text, or a blank), it skips over that cell to the next cell. Consequently, macros can contain blank cells and comments within the macro itself, without adverse effect.

Value-returning formulas. A formula in a macro that returns a value recalculates under two circumstances—when you enter it and when you run it. By recalculating when you enter the formula, Excel helps you minimize errors. Suppose, for example, that you want to return the name of the active worksheet and you think that GET.DOCUMENT(1) is the function you need.

To test this assumption, enter *=GET.DOCUMENT(1)* and then press Ctrl-` (backquote) to view the values in the macro sheet. When you do so, the formula displays the name of the active spreadsheet (which is your macro sheet at this point). If you want to recalculate a value-returning function that you've entered previously, simply select the cell, click on the formula in the formula bar [PC—F2; Mac—Command-U], and press Enter.

Array formulas. Although it's uncommon to use array formulas in a macro, Microsoft Excel does have special rules for dealing with them. If a macro encounters the top-left cell of an array, it recalculates the array and then continues calculation below the bottom-left corner of the array. If a macro first encounters any other cell in the array, it skips over the array without calculating it.

Other macro formulas. Macro formulas that don't return values recalculate only when you run the macro. When you enter these macro functions, they return a value of FALSE. Then, if you used them correctly, they return a value of TRUE when you run the macro.

Formulas available

A third difference between worksheets and macro sheets is in the functions they can use. Worksheets can use only worksheet functions whereas macros can use both worksheet and macro functions. We'll discuss macro functions in greater detail at the end of this chapter.

The two types of macros

In Microsoft Excel, macros come in two types—command macros and function macros. Command macros are usually initiated by you when you press a unique key sequence that has been assigned to the macro. Command macros simulate the actions you take—using Microsoft Excel's menu and keyboard commands, as well as scrolling, moving, and resizing windows. You might use command macros to print or modify a worksheet, to generate a graph, or to save data on a disk.

Command macros are used so frequently that Excel offers a special tool called the Recorder for recording action sequences. As you perform operations on a worksheet, the Recorder reads, remembers, and translates these operations into macro programming code, which is stored on a macro sheet that you can later examine and modify.

Function macros expand the range and power of the standard functions available in Microsoft Excel; they are the equivalent of creating new functions. Function macros are executed not by your action but when they are calculated in a worksheet or a macro sheet. Standard functions, such as SUM and NOW, that you might use in a worksheet formula are the building blocks of a function macro. Function macros return the results of calculations performed on the data given them. For example, a meteorologist could use a function macro to change Fahrenheit to Celsius. An investor could use a function macro to find the theoretical value of a stock option. Or a gambler could use a function macro to calculate the odds for a poker hand.

Perhaps the best way to get a feel for the differences between command and function macros is to quickly create a few macros yourself. In this chapter, we'll create three macros—one command macro for adding borders to a selected range and two function macros for converting temperature measurements from Fahrenheit to Celsius and back again.

Don't confuse function macros with macro functions, which are the functions available in Excel that can be used in macros but not in worksheets.

You use macro functions (as well as the standard functions) to create both command macros and function macros.

Creating a command macro

To create a command macro, you can either enter formulas by hand or use the Recorder. We'll use the Recorder to create the following command macro, which outlines a selected area of a worksheet. In preparation, start Microsoft Excel and select several cells in the empty worksheet presented. Then

1. Press /*MC* (the equivalent of choosing Macro Record) to call up the Record Macro dialog box.

   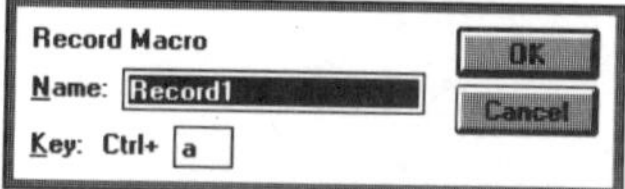

   Press Enter to accept the proposed macro name, which is probably *Record1*, and shortcut key, which is probably *a*. (If not, it's because you've already recorded a macro. Simply remember the name and letter proposed, or enter any name and letter you want.) A new macro sheet appears (although it might be hidden behind the default worksheet), and the Recorder begins translating your subsequent commands into macro code.

2. Press /*TBO* (the equivalent of choosing Format Border and selecting the Outline option). Press Enter to draw the outline.

3. Press /*MC* (the equivalent of choosing Macro Stop Recorder) to stop the Recorder.

The macro is created! To use the macro, select another range of cells in the worksheet and press Ctrl-a on the PC or Command-Option-a (or Control-a, if you have an extended keyboard) on the Mac. (If step 1 proposed a shortcut key other than *a*, use it instead.) When you do so, the macro outlines the selected range.

A closer look at the macro

Let's investigate. To view both the worksheet and the macro sheet, arrange their windows by choosing Window Arrange All. After you do so, the display should resemble Figure 1-1, allowing for the type of computer and display you're using. (To view the results in this figure, we removed the gridlines in the worksheet by choosing Options Display and deselecting Gridlines, and in the macro sheet we expanded the width of column A.)

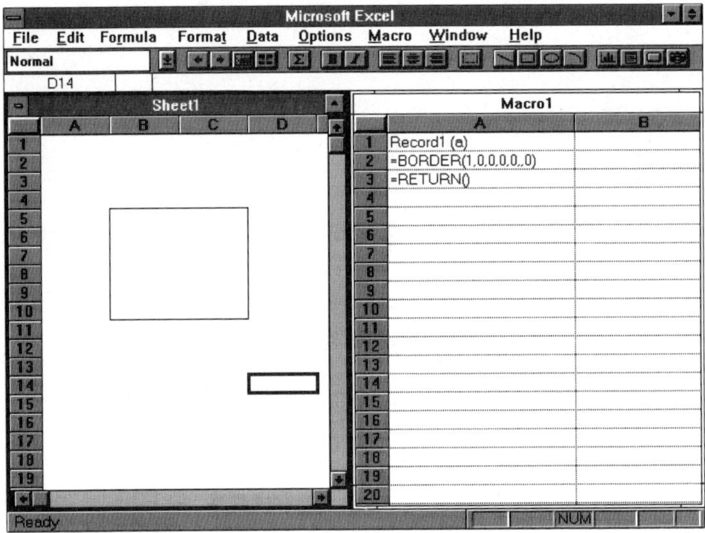

FIGURE 1-1.
The recorded macro on the macro sheet on the right draws a border around any selected range of cells.

The macro, named *Record1,* is listed in column A on the macro sheet.

	A
1	Record1 (a)
2	=BORDER(1,0,0,0,0,,0)
3	=RETURN()

The first line of the macro is, of course, the name proposed in the Macro Record dialog box. The next cell (A2) contains the BORDER macro function generated by setting options in the Border dialog box; it takes the following arguments.

```
=BORDER(outline,left,right,top,bottom,shade,outlineColor,leftColor,rightColor,
    topColor,bottomColor)
```

A *1* as the first argument means that the Outline option is set to a thin border; the next four *0*s mean that the left, right, top, and bottom areas of the range have no border; the sixth argument isn't specified, which means that shading isn't changed if present; and *0* as the seventh argument means that the color of the outline is set to Automatic. (Refer to the Microsoft Excel Function Reference for more information on the BORDER macro function.)

In cell A3, the Recorder entered *=RETURN()* as the last line of the macro when you stopped recording it. A RETURN statement tells Excel that the macro is done and to return control to the user (or to the macro that called this macro, as we'll discover later).

Finally, activate the macro sheet by choosing Formula Define Name, and select *Record1* to look at the name and key sequence assigned to the macro, as shown in Figure 1-2. If you wanted to do so, you could change the assigned name and key sequence, but the title of the macro in cell A1 of the macro sheet would remain *Record1* until you changed that too.

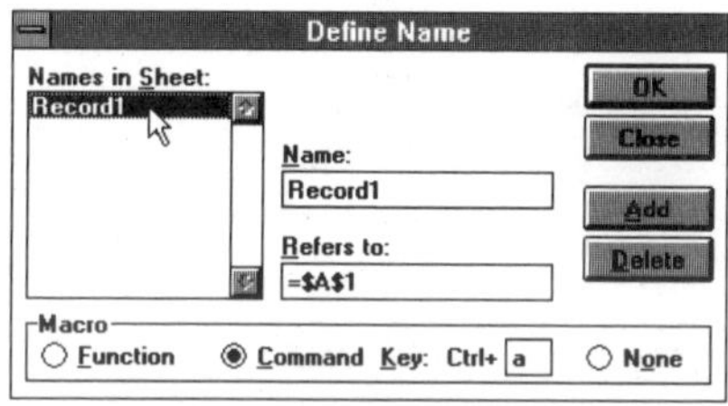

FIGURE 1-2.
The Define Name dialog box, with the name of the Record1 *macro selected.*

Modifying the macro

Simply because you can write a macro to do something doesn't necessarily mean that you *should* write one. The command macro that we just completed is a case in point.

The macro draws a border around a selected range of cells. Running this macro requires only a few keystrokes: Command-Option-a or Ctrl-a. However, with Excel's slash commands, you can outline a range with only five keystrokes: */TBO* and Enter. Using the macro saves only a few keystrokes and a fraction of a second—not a large return on the time you invested to create the macro.

Keep this point in mind when you see macros described in computer books and magazines or sold in your local software store. Because many of them compete with the convenience of a slash command or the power of a formula stored in the worksheet itself, many of these macros never should have been written.

If the macro is such a waste of time, why did we create it in the first place? One excellent reason for creating this macro is that we can make it much more useful if we modify it slightly. When you create your own macros, you'll often take a similar approach: using the Recorder to generate a macro that is close to the mark, and then fine-tuning the macro by hand.

In this case, we'll adjust the macro by changing the *outline* argument in the BORDER function to *0*. To do so, edit this macro as you would any other formula in Excel: Select cell A2 in the macro sheet, select *1* in the formula bar, and enter *0*. After you do so, your macro looks like this:

	A
1	Record1
2	=BORDER(0,0,0,0,0,,0)
3	=RETURN()

This macro works much like an additional option in the Edit Clear command might, removing all borders within a selected range, setting the outline color to Automatic, and leaving any shading unchanged. Depending on what borders and shading the area originally contained, this simple macro can save several seconds of adjusting the check boxes in the Border dialog box each time you want to clear borders.

Creating two function macros

Converting temperature measurements from Fahrenheit to Celsius and back again is a task that most of us learned in grade school and then forgot. Although this calculation isn't frequently used by most people, it is one that can quickly illustrate how function macros work.

In preparation, use the File New command to create a new, empty worksheet and macro sheet [Shift-F11 and Ctrl-F11, respectively].

Save the worksheet as *DEGREES.XLS* and the macro sheet as *DEGREES.XLM*. (On the Mac, you could save the sheets as *Degrees Worksheet* and *Degrees Macro*, for example, but because the PC file-naming convention is more restrictive, we'll standardize on filenames that work with both machines.)

Next, format both sheets to make them easier to read. To make border formats easier to see, choose Options Display and deselect the default Gridlines option in each sheet.

Entering the first function macro

Microsoft Excel doesn't permit using the Recorder to create function macros; it really wouldn't make sense to use the Recorder, in any case, because function macros contain only formulas for calculating and returning values. To build the *FtoC* (Fahrenheit-to-Celsius) macro, enter the following formulas.

	A	B	C
1	**function**	**FtoC**	**Fahrenheit to Celsius**
2		=ARGUMENT("temp",1)	Get the temperature.
3		=RETURN((temp-32)*5/9)	Convert and return Celsius.

Most function macros begin with one or more ARGUMENT functions. This macro function assigns to a range, a named range, or a defined name the data the worksheet passes to the macro. (Recall that a range is a series of cells on a worksheet or macro sheet; a named range is a range you give a name through the Define Name dialog box; and a defined name is a value, an array of values, or a formula stored in a worksheet or macro sheet but not in a cell. You use the Define Name dialog box to create these manually.) Here the value representing a temperature in Fahrenheit is assigned to a temporary value named *temp*.

The number following the range name in the ARGUMENT function tells the macro the type of data you're passing. In this case, using the number *1* means that the *FtoC* function macro should expect a number rather than text or an array. If a value other than a number is passed to the function, *FtoC* returns the #VALUE! error value.

The RETURN function in cell B3 returns the converted temperature measurement by applying the value stored in *temp* to the formula.

Before using this function macro, let's format it. While it's not required that you format your macros in the way we do, you'll find that setting macros off from each other in some way makes your macro sheets much easier to read. Select cells A1:C1, choose Format Border, set the Outline option, and then click on the Bold icon in the Toolbar. Select cells B2:C3, choose Format Border, and set the Left option, as shown in Figure 1-3. Drawing these borders provides a pattern for the macro as a whole and helps distinguish the various parts of the macro from each other.

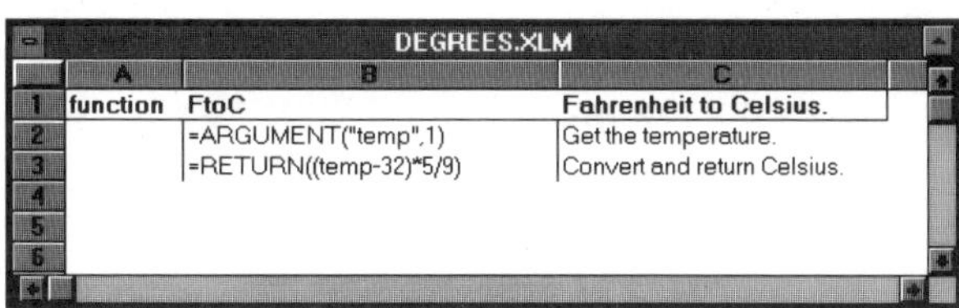

FIGURE 1-3.
The FtoC *function macro after entry and formatting.*

Finally, you must name the macro and identify it as a function macro. It's usually a good idea to name the cell above the first formula of the macro, which makes it easier to insert rows above the first formula if needed. To name the macro, select cell B1, and choose Formula Define Name; the Define Name dialog box proposes *FtoC* as the macro name. Click on the Function option button, and then click on the Add button; the dialog box (before you click OK) should resemble the one shown here.

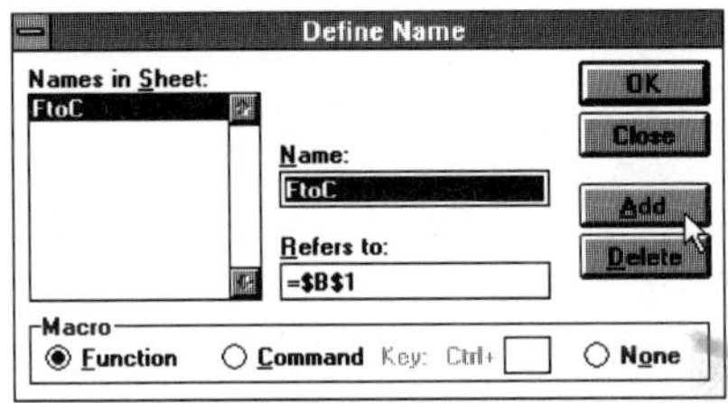

Entering the second function macro

To create the *CtoF* function macro for converting Celsius to Fahrenheit, let's work with a copy of the first macro. Copy the range A1:C3, select cell A5, and choose the Paste command. Now edit the formulas shown in italics below:

	A	B	C
5	**function**	**CtoF**	**Celsius to Fahrenheit**
6		=ARGUMENT("temp",1)	Get the temperature.
7		*=RETURN(temp*9/5+32)*	*Convert, return Fahrenheit.*

To name this macro, select cell B5, choose Formula Define Name, click on the Function button, and then press Enter.

Using the macros

To use the macros, activate the DEGREES.XLS worksheet, and enter the following formulas in the cells listed.

	A	B
1	Degrees Fahrenheit	212
2	Conversion:	=DEGREES.XLM!FtoC(B1)
3		
4	Degrees Celsius	37
5	Conversion:	=DEGREES.XLM!CtoF(B4)

First, enter the value *212* in cell B1 of the worksheet. Then, in cell B2, enter a formula that takes that value and uses the function macro you created to convert the Fahrenheit value to a Celsius value. Follow the same pattern for the formula that calls the *CtoF* macro in the second part of the worksheet.

Formulas that call function macros have four distinct parts:

1. The name of the macro sheet that contains the function macro. (On the Mac, names of macro sheets that contain spaces must be enclosed by single quotes.)
2. An exclamation point.
3. The name of the function macro.
4. A list of one or more arguments passed to the function macro, enclosed in parentheses.

Figure 1-4 shows both the worksheet and the macro sheet displayed simultaneously, with the correct conversions returned from the function macros.

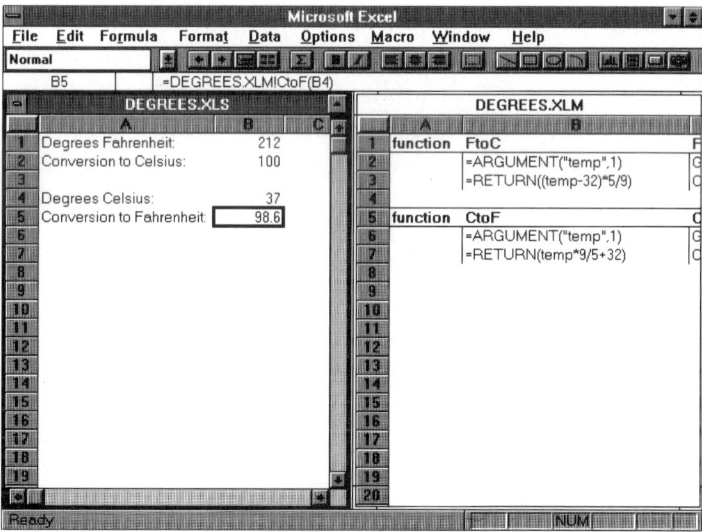

FIGURE 1-4.
The FtoC *and* CtoF *macros after entry and formatting.*

Macro functions available in Microsoft Excel

In addition to the worksheet functions with which you are probably already familiar (what we will call the *standard functions*), Microsoft Excel offers a large range of programming functions that pertain only to writing macros (what we will call the *macro functions*). These functions can be divided into several categories, according to their use; if you keep these categories clearly in mind, you'll be able to quickly find and use the macro functions you need.

We can separate all macro functions into those usable in command macros, those usable in function macros, and those usable in both. (Remember that a function macro is not the same as a macro function. A *function macro* is a macro that returns a value to a worksheet or a macro sheet. A *macro function*, on the other hand, is a built-in function used in command macros and function macros.)

Macro functions available only to command macros

Macro functions usable only in command macros are those that perform actions that can be done only by you or that cannot be executed from within a function macro. These functions fall into the following categories.

Command-equivalent functions. Command-equivalent functions achieve the same result as choosing a command from a Microsoft Excel menu. For example, the COLUMN.WIDTH() function is equivalent to choosing Format Column Width and entering a number in the resulting dialog box. Because command-equivalent functions often require many parameters (corresponding to the many options that can be set in their dialog boxes), using the Recorder is particularly convenient for entering these formulas.

Menu commands followed by an ellipsis (...) call up dialog boxes. When you want to call up the dialog box itself, rather than specifying the options set in the dialog box, you can use a form of a macro function that is followed by a question mark. If you use the COLUMN.WIDTH? function in a macro, for example, the macro will bring up the Column Width dialog box and stop, waiting for the user to enter a value and press Enter.

Action-equivalent functions. Action-equivalent functions correspond to actions you take without choosing commands, such as using the mouse to select a cell, entering a formula in a cell, using the scroll bars, or activating, moving, and resizing a window.

User-interface functions. User-interface functions let you customize a worksheet or a system of macros. They display messages, create customized dialog boxes and menu commands, permit the entry of data through input boxes, read and write data to text files, and even start other applications.

Functions available to both command and function macros

The following two categories of macro functions do not cause actions. As a general rule, both command macros and function macros can use these functions.

Control functions. Control functions divert a running macro to a location other than the next cell in a column. For example, the GOTO function continues execution of the macro in any specified cell. Other control functions include FOR, NEXT, and RETURN.

Information functions. Information functions return values that you can then use in a macro. For example, the GET.CELL function returns information about the formatting, location, or contents of a cell in a worksheet. The FILES function returns the filenames contained in a specified directory or folder.

Functions available only to function macros

With only three exceptions, you can use in command macros any of the functions in the control and value-returning categories described above. Command macros can use the control functions ARGUMENT and RESULT only if they are to be used as subroutines. Command macros cannot use the value-returning function CALLER, which only function macros can use. Function macros can use relatively few of these functions. (Chapter 3 provides a list of command macros.)

Help with writing macros: Appendixes A and B

Although the preceding categories help to explain the nature of Microsoft Excel's macro functions, they provide little help when you're actually writing macros. Suppose, for example, that you're writing a macro that opens, updates, and closes several files. You'd probably want to use the macro functions OPEN, a command-equivalent function; DIRECTORY, an action-equivalent function; and both FILES and GET.DOCUMENT, information-returning functions; but you would need to know that these functions exist in the first place.

The appendixes in this book provide a handy resource for mastering macro programming functions. Appendix A groups all macro functions by their purpose. For example, its categories include File Operations, Printing, Editing Operations, and so on. Appendix B provides an alphabetic list of all macro functions.

Keeping macros in perspective

You can get a wonderful feeling of accomplishment and power when you see a macro zipping around a worksheet, creating all sorts of amazing effects. That is, until you realize that you have a more important job to do than to watch flashing pixels on the monitor. Macros can save time and money—and they're fun and challenging to use—but you should also consider whether a given task is really worth the time a macro programming project can take.

In many cases, you'll find that writing a macro does not always simplify a problem. Part of good management is recognizing this and pursuing other options. Let's consider some of the available alternatives to macro programming.

Templates

Many people use macros to set up the skeleton of a worksheet, but often you can achieve the same end by creating your own worksheet templates. To begin, delete the data from copies of worksheets you frequently create. To display current dates in the worksheet, write formulas that refer to a date cell you can easily update, and then save the worksheet as a template. To perform a new analysis, simply open the template, adjust the date, and add your data.

Command shortcuts

Depending on your computer and keyboard, pressing the Alt, F10, or slash (/) key activates the menu bar in Excel. In this book, we specify key sequences with the slash key (set in the Options Workspace dialog box) because it is shared by every version of Excel and is found on every keyboard. This allows you the option of issuing all your menu commands without a mouse. Figure 1-5 provides a short list of some of the shortcut keys we use frequently. Look under "Keyboard" in your Microsoft Excel Quick Reference for a complete list of shortcut keys.

Menu Selection	Shortcut
Edit Paste Special, Values	/ESV [Mac—also Command-Shift-V]
Edit Paste Special, Formats	/EST [Mac—also Command-Shift-V]
Format Border, Outline	/TBO [Mac—also Command-Option-0]
Format Number, General	Ctrl-Shift-~ (tilde)
Format Number, $#,##0. 00_);($#,##0. 00)	Ctrl-Shift-$
File Save As	/FA [Mac—also Command-Shift-S]
Formula Define Name	/RD [Mac—also Command-L]
Formula Goto	F5 [Mac—also Command-G]

FIGURE 1-5.
Some frequently used shortcut keys.

Using styles instead of formatting macros

Prior to Excel version 3, the process of applying character, border, font, number, and alignment formats was tedious. In version 3, you can define your own styles and combine them with templates, or you can merge style sheets from other worksheets and macro sheets.

Formulas and name definitions

During the past several years, we've seen hundreds of examples of function macros in books, magazines, and newsletters. At least half of these produced an answer that simple formulas or name definitions could have produced easily and quickly. Whenever you see the need for a short function macro, particularly one that you don't think you'll need to use in more than one worksheet, think about inventing a formula or name definition that you could use instead. (Chapter 7 discusses defined names.)

Worksheet parameters

We've seen many worksheets that needlessly use command macros to adjust formulas or data. For example, a consultant we know of uses a command macro to copy a new client's name and address to the top of a half-dozen reports in a standard worksheet. Instead, he could enter the name once in a parameters section at the top of his worksheet and then reference the name with text formulas wherever he wants the name to appear. By changing the name in the parameters section and then recalculating the worksheet, he would update the name throughout his worksheet.

A company we know of uses a command macro to copy one of three formulas onto a worksheet that analyzes sales commissions. Instead, it could enter a number for the type of commission in a parameters section of the worksheet and then use a CHOOSE function to return the correct formula for the parameter it enters.

For example, assume that the range name *type* can have the value 1, 2, or 3, depending on the type of commission. The following formula performs one of three calculations, depending on the value of the *type* parameter:

```
=CHOOSE(type,sales*type1Pct,(sales-costs)*type2Pct,(sales-badDebts)
    *type3Pct)
```

This formula, though long, is probably easier to enter and support than a macro performing the same calculations would be. Sometimes *not* writing a macro saves more time than writing one.

2

Command Macros

When most people talk about using macros to customize their worksheets, they're talking about command macros. Command macros are initiated by the user and cause some sort of action. Function macros, however, are initiated by a reference in a worksheet, simply calculating and returning values to that worksheet.

Command macros can print worksheets, generate mailing labels, transfer data, run other applications, automate procedures, and support dozens of keyboard shortcuts. They can update, format, copy, move, save, delete, run, sort, search and replace, and so on.

As we discussed in the previous chapter, you can create a command macro by recording a series of command-equivalent and action-equivalent actions and by entering the corresponding formulas into a macro sheet by hand. In practice, you'll generally use a combination of the two methods. In this chapter, we'll cover each method in depth as well as develop a few macros that you might find useful.

Creating command macros with the Recorder

No matter how expert you become with macros, you'll use the Recorder constantly. It's fast, powerful, and easy to use. Although the Recorder can be easy to use, it can also cause confusion because two commands on the Macro menu are able to start it running: Record and Start Recorder. The Record command is useful when you want to create a command macro quickly and easily, without having to worry about what is happening behind the scenes. When you want more control over the recording and placement of macros on the macro sheet, you'll find that the Start Recorder command gives you that control.

Recording with the Record command

If you've worked through the example in Chapter 1 for creating a macro that adds an outline border around a selected area, you already know the basics of using the Recorder. The overall process for using the Record command is simple in structure.

1. Choose Macro Record, and in the Record dialog box give the new macro a name and keyboard shortcut key.
2. Take the actions you want recorded.
3. Choose Macro Stop Recorder.

Of course, after you've recorded a macro in this way, you'll often find it helpful to format and document the resulting macro, or hand-edit the macro functions in it in some way.

We can use the following example to investigate the process of using the Record command in more detail. The *Recalc* macro recalculates a selected range of cells and is most useful for worksheets containing a large number of complicated formulas. If a worksheet is small, you can choose Options Calculation and set the mode of recalculation to Automatic, which causes the worksheet to recalculate every time you enter a value. As the worksheet accumulates formulas, however, recalculation becomes sluggish, and at some point you find that it's more efficient to switch to manual recalculation. When using manual recalculation, you recalculate all the open sheets by choosing Options Calculate Now [F9; Mac—also Command-=], or recalculate the active document alone by holding down the Shift key while choosing Options Calculate Document [Shift-F9; Mac—also Shift-Command-=].

As you add even more formulas, recalculating a complete document can take a long time. You can, however, use the *Recalc* macro to recalculate only a selected area of a worksheet at a time, thereby saving time. After you start Excel, create the macro by following these steps.

1. Choose Macro Record [/MC] to start the Recorder. The Record Macro dialog box appears.
2. Type *Recalc* as the macro name in the Record Macro dialog box (as shown in Figure 2-1), type *r* as the shortcut key, and press Enter.

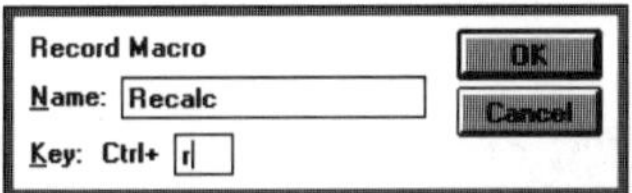

FIGURE 2-1.
Using the Macro Record dialog box to set the name and the shortcut key of the Recalc *macro.*

3. Choose Formula Replace [/RE] to activate the Replace dialog box.
4. In both the Replace and the With fields type an equal sign (=), as shown in Figure 2-2, and then press Enter to replace all equal signs with equal signs.

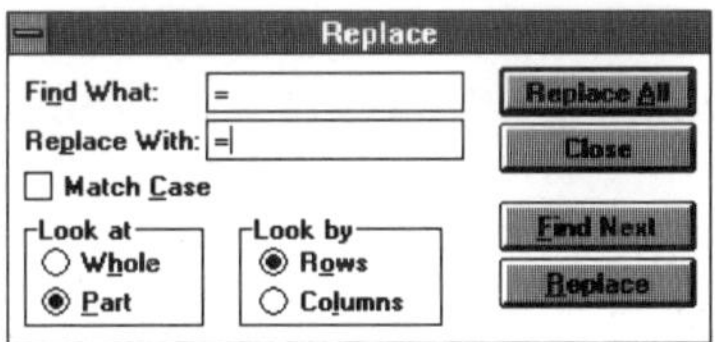

FIGURE 2-2.
Using the Replace dialog box to replace all equal signs with equal signs.

5. If Excel issues a *No Match* error message, telling you that no equal signs exist in the selected range, press Enter.
6. Choose Macro Stop Recorder [/MC] to stop the Recorder.

If you activate the Macro1 window, you'll see the macro shown in Figure 2-3 on the following page. To use it, simply select a range in a worksheet that you want to recalculate and then press Ctrl-r [Mac—also Option-Command-r].

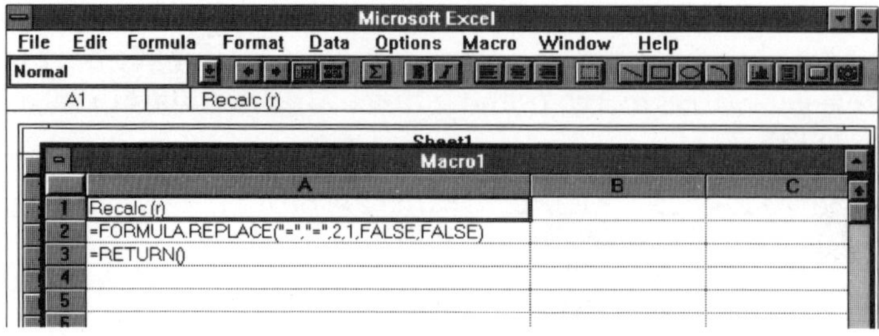

FIGURE 2-3.
The Recalc *macro, as recorded.*

Why does this macro work? Excel recalculates any cell that has been edited, so it displays the correct value after you've entered a formula in the cell. This recalculation occurs even if you simply click in the formula bar for a selected cell and press the Enter key. By replacing an equal sign with an equal sign, we never change a formula, but by running this macro, we force the recalculation of every cell in the selected range that contains a formula.

When you first started the Recorder, the Record command began by taking two steps behind the scenes. First, it checked to see whether a macro sheet was open, and if a macro sheet wasn't already open, it opened one. Second, it assigned the range name *Recorder* to column A of the new macro sheet (or the next empty column of the macro sheet if already open). This range name tells Excel where to put the macro it records. If a macro sheet is already open, the Recorder uses the next empty column. In other words, as you create one macro after another, the Record command records your macros column by column along the top row of the macro sheet—somewhat akin to hanging socks from a clothesline.

Using the Control key on the extended keyboard.

Excel supports the use of the Control key as a replacement for the Command-Option key sequence when initiating command macros. On the PC, this key is labeled *Ctrl*. Because the use of the Control keys on both machines is similar, from now on we'll simply use the PC name for the key when running a command macro.

To see the range names defined on the macro sheet, click on it and then choose Formula Define Name [Ctrl-F3; Mac—also Command-L]. If you select *Recalc,* you'll see that it's defined as *=$A$1.* If you select the name *Recorder,* you'll see that it's defined in the Define Name dialog box as *$A:$A,* as shown in Figure 2-4.

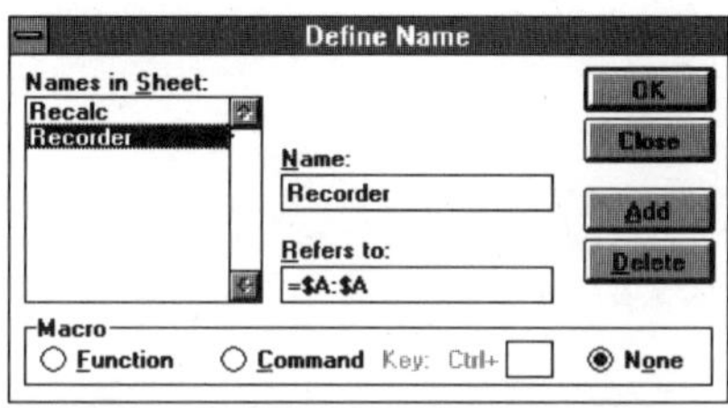

FIGURE 2-4.
The Define Name dialog box.

Recording with the Start Recorder command

The Start Recorder command seems very similar to the Record command. Here is the overall method for using the Start Recorder command.

1. Set the location for recording the macro by selecting a cell or range on a macro sheet and choosing Macro Set Recorder.
2. Start the Recorder by choosing Macro Start Recorder.
3. Take whatever actions you want included in the macro.
4. Stop the Recorder when you're done by choosing Macro Stop Recorder.
5. Give the macro a name and a shortcut key by choosing Formula Define Name and entering the appropriate information.

More steps are required when using this method than when using the Record command, but as we'll see, the Start Recorder command offers much more control over the process. To illustrate this control, suppose we want to create a macro that inserts in the active cell a SUM formula that totals the column of data above the cell. To begin, create a new worksheet by choosing File New [Shift-F11], and save it as TEST.XLS. Next create a new macro sheet [Ctrl-F11], and save it as SUM.XLM. Then choose Window Arrange All to arrange the sheets side by side. Now do the following.

1. In the worksheet, enter a column of numbers to sum, as shown in Figure 2-5 on the following page.

	A	B
2	2	
3	4	
4	6	
5	8	

FIGURE 2-5.
Enter these numbers in TEST.XLS.

2. In the macro sheet, enter the name of the macro, *Sum,* and its shortcut key, *s,* as shown in Figure 2-6.

	A	B
1	Sum (s)	Sum and format a column of numbers.

FIGURE 2-6.
The heading of the Sum *macro.*

3. To tell the Recorder where to put the recording, select cell A1 and choose Macro Set Recorder. When you do so, Excel defines *Recorder* as the entire column, or *=$A:$A.* (However, if you select an area that contains more than one row, Set Recorder defines only the selected area as the *Recorder* range.)
4. Choose Macro Relative Record to tell the macro to record relative addresses rather than absolute ones. (We'll discuss this command in detail a little later.)
5. Before you start to record the macro, select cell A6 on the TEST.XLS worksheet, the cell in which you want to put the SUM formula.
6. Choose Macro Start Recorder [/MS]. The significant difference between this command and Macro Record is that the latter would have first requested a macro name and a shortcut key and then entered that information on the macro sheet. The Start Recorder command, however, does not take any of these actions. It simply displays *Ready Recording* in the status bar at the bottom of your screen, waiting to record your macro starting at the first empty cell in the range defined by *Recorder.* In this instance, the first cell in the range is A1 and contains the name of the macro, *Sum,* so the first line of the macro will appear in cell A2.

7. To begin the macro, enter

   =SUM(

   in cell A6 of the TEST.XLS worksheet, press the Up direction key once to select the bottom cell of data, and while holding down the Shift key to extend the selection, press the Up direction key three more times to select the data above cell A6; when you've selected the entire range of numbers, the range in the formula should read *A2:A5*. To complete the formula, type

)

   and press Enter.
8. Choose Macro Stop Recorder [/MC].
9. To name the macro, select cell A1 on the macro sheet and choose Formula Define Name. When the Define Name dialog box appears, *Sum* appears in the Name field. Select Command, type *s* as the shortcut key, and press Enter.

Figure 2-7 shows the newly created *Sum* macro. To see more of the macro, change the widths of columns A and B and the Normal style font to whatever you like. If you follow these directions, and your recorded macro contains the formula

=SELECT("R[1]C")

in cell A3, it's because the Move Selection After Enter option is set in the Options Workspace dialog box; simply unset the option, and then delete the row.

	A	B
1	Sum (s)	Sum and format a column of numbers.
2	=FORMULA("=SUM(R[-4]C:R[-1]C)")	
3	=RETURN()	

FIGURE 2-7.
The Sum *macro.*

Although this macro in its current form is limited, it works correctly. To test it, enter data in the range B2:B5 of the TEST.XLS worksheet, select cell B6, and then press Ctrl-s.

Let's improve on this macro, and as we do so, we'll learn more about the power of the Start Recorder command.

Define the starting location of each macro as the cell above the first formula in the macro.

You can define a macro as a range of cells or as a single cell; either way, Excel will start the execution of the macro at the first cell of the range. Defining the macro as a range of cells is unnecessary because the execution of the macro proceeds to the first encountered RETURN, regardless of the definition. (Other formulas and events, such as an error in the macro, can stop execution. We'll discuss these later—notably in Chapter 9, "Controlling Program Flow.")

If you define the macro as a single cell, assign the name to the cell above the first macro formula, in the row where we put the name and the description of the macro. If you do this, you'll be able to easily open new rows above the first formula in the macro, without having to redefine the starting point of the macro each time.

The Absolute Record and Relative Record commands

In step 4 of the macro, you chose Relative Record rather than Absolute Record, setting the Recorder to record relative references rather than absolute references. To understand what these two commands do, let's go over the difference between absolute and relative references.

An *absolute reference* sticks to the referenced cell like glue. No matter where you copy the formula that uses the reference, the reference always specifies the original cell. To specify an absolute reference, you put a dollar sign before each part of the reference. For example, the formula *=$B$2* contains an absolute reference to cell B2, in the A1 style for specifying references. (In the R1C1 style, this formula would be *=R2C2*.) If you were to copy this cell to every cell of your worksheet, your worksheet would be filled with the formula *=$B$2*, referring always to cell *B2*.

A *relative reference,* on the other hand, doesn't refer to a specific cell at all. Instead, it points to the cell that is the specified distance from the cell containing the reference. Suppose, for example, that you enter the formula *=B3* into cell A1. This formula performs much like the knight in a game of chess—referring to the cell that is two rows down and one column to the right of cell A1. If you copy this formula to cell B1, the reference changes to *=C3*—still two rows down and one column to the right. One benefit of using R1C1-style references is that they make relative references much easier to see. In that style, the formula =B3 in cell R1C1 (cell A1) would be entered as *=R[2]C[1]*, using square brackets instead of dollar signs.

Therefore, when you choose Relative Record from the Macro menu, you're telling Excel that you want to record all references as relative references. You would do so when you create macros, like the one in Figure 2-17 on page 45, that use the active cell as a starting point—wherever that cell might be.

On the other hand, choose Absolute Record when you want the macro to act on the same cells every time the macro is run. For example, a macro that creates a template for financial reporting probably warrants use of absolute recording. No matter which cell is active when you start the macro, you'll want to enter the title of the report in cell A1, for example, column titles in row 2, and so on.

Excel uses the absolute recording method as its default method. Therefore, when you first pull down the Macro menu, you see the Relative Record command, which is probably dimmed, however, as you cannot choose the command until the *Recorder* range is set. If you choose Relative Record, the Macro menu then displays the Absolute Record command, offering you the opportunity to switch back again. You can switch between relative and absolute recording as frequently as you want while you're recording a macro.

Adding to the end of a macro

It would be nice to have the *Sum* macro draw a border between the formula and the data that it sums, thus making it easier to distinguish between the data and the sum. Let's modify the macro to add a border above the cell into which the formula is entered.

1. Select cell A6 in the worksheet.
2. Start the Recorder again by choosing Macro Start Recorder [/MS].
3. To create a top border in cell A6, choose Format Border, select Top, and then click OK [/TBT and Enter].
4. To stop the Recorder, choose Macro Stop Recorder [/MC].

Now the macro appears as shown in Figure 2-8.

	A	B
1	Sum (s)	Sum and format a column of numbers.
2	=FORMULA("=SUM(R[-4]C:R[-1]C)")	
3	=BORDER(0,0,0,1,0,,,,,0)	
4	=RETURN()	

FIGURE 2-8.
The Sum *macro after adding a border.*

As you added the border, the RETURN function was replaced by the BORDER macro function. This feature of the Start Recorder command permits appending new macro formulas to the bottom of an existing macro until you stop the Recorder.

The BORDER function takes the following form:

```
=BORDER(outlineN,leftN,rightN,topN,bottomN,shadeL,outlineColorN,
    leftColorN,rightColorN,topColorN,bottomColorN)
```

In this book, we'll use the convention of appending to each argument name an abbreviation that expresses the type of value the argument is supposed to take. The following table lists the abbreviations.

Value type	Abbreviation
Number	N
Text	T
Logical	L
Reference	R
Error	E
Array	A

Each argument in the BORDER function except *shadeL* takes a numeric value, which in the case of the first five arguments specifies the type of line used in the border (from 0 through 7), and which in the case of the last five arguments specifies the color of the border (from 0 through 16). In the formula used in the macro, only the top border is set to a thin line, and all the rest are turned off. (For a complete list of the macro functions and the arguments each takes, see the Microsoft Excel Function Reference or Appendix B of this book.)

Finally, when you stop the Recorder, a new RETURN function becomes the last line of the macro.

Adding to the middle of a macro

This macro is still too limited. When run, it enters a formula that sums only the four cells immediately above the active cell. Instead, we want the macro to return the sum of all contiguous data in the column above the active cell—that is, the sum of every cell above the active cell until the first empty cell is reached. To accomplish this, do the following.

1. Insert two rows between row 1 and row 2 of the macro sheet by selecting rows 2 and 3 and choosing Edit Insert. The macro should look like the one shown in Figure 2-9.

	A	B
1	Sum (s)	Sum and format a column of numbers.
2		
3		
4	=FORMULA("=SUM(R[-4]C:R[-1]C)")	
5	=BORDER(0,0,0,1,0,,,,,0)	
6	=RETURN()	

FIGURE 2-9.
Inserting two blank rows.

2. To tell the Recorder where to record the inserted macro functions, select cell A2 and choose Macro Set Recorder [/MT].
3. Check whether you're still recording relative references; when you pull down the Macro menu, the bottommost command should be Absolute Record. If it's Relative Record, choose the command.
4. To record the new commands, select A6 of the worksheet and then choose Macro Start Recorder [/MS].
5. Press the Up direction key once to select the bottom cell of the data to be summed. Press Ctrl-Up direction [Mac—Command-Up direction] to select the top cell in the data to be summed.
6. Excel issues the message *Recorder range is full,* because the Recorder has run out of empty cells into which to insert new formulas. Click OK or press Enter to clear the message and stop the Recorder.

Figure 2-10 lists the updated macro. The macro formulas in A2:A3, marked by italics, record the actions we've taken; they activate the top row of data in the column of the cell containing the SUM formula. Unlike the Record command, the Start Recorder command does not delete existing macro commands (other than moving the Return command, of course). This allows us to add one cell or hundreds of cells to the middle of a macro without having to be concerned about erasing other macro formulas.

	A	B
1	Sum (s)	Sum and format a column of numbers.
2	*=SELECT("R[-1]C")*	
3	*=SELECT.END(3)*	
4	=FORMULA("=SUM(R[-4]C:R[-1]C)")	
5	=BORDER(0,0,0,1,0,,,,,0)	
6	=RETURN()	

FIGURE 2-10.
The Sum *macro after adding two lines.*

This macro isn't functional yet. If you want to see what happens when you run the macro, select cell A6 and press Ctrl-s. The macro dutifully selects first cell A5 and then cell A2 at the top of the column, where it enters the SUM formula. At this point, Excel beeps and stops the macro without adding the border, displaying the message *Can't resolve circular references.* If you look at the formula in cell A2, it reads

```
=SUM(A1:A16382)
```

The macro stopped because the FORMULA function in cell A4 of the macro entered into the active cell (A2) a SUM formula containing a relative reference to the cell four cells above the active cell, which wrapped above cell A1 back to the bottom of column A. A circular reference was created, because the SUM formula uses data that includes its own cell.

What we need to do is edit the FORMULA function to use the references found in cells A2:A3 of the macro, instead of selecting them beforehand.

(Incidentally, the new Last Cell in the worksheet is now A16382 or B16382 because the formula in A2 refers to cell A16382; deleting the formula doesn't reset Last Cell to A6. Saving the worksheet takes forever, and the resulting file is perhaps 200 times the size of the original file. If you save, close, and load the file again, Excel resets Last Cell to A6.)

Editing a recorded macro

Rare is the recorded macro that doesn't need editing. At times, this is simply a matter of deleting rows of macro functions created when false steps were taken while the Recorder was running. At other times, as is the case in our example, it isn't possible to create the macro you want simply by recording actions. When you use the Recorder, creating macros is a mechanical process, but when you edit them, it's a creative one. In fact, one of the best ways to learn about macro programming is to edit recorded macros.

Figure 2-11 on page 36 presents the final version of the *Sum* macro, after all the formulas indicated by italics have been entered or edited and comments added. Actually, almost all the formulas in the new *Sum* macro have been entered by hand or edited from the original recorded versions; most could not have been entered by using the Recorder in any case. To update the macro, simply open new rows and enter the new formulas.

There's a daunting amount of new information in this macro. We'll discuss the functions in much greater detail in the coming chapters, but for now let's look over the macro line by line.

How the *Recorder* range affects the recording of a macro.

When you select a cell or a range of cells on a macro sheet and choose Macro Set Recorder, the command defines the *Recorder* range. If you select a range, that range becomes the definition of *Recorder*. If you select a single cell, the definition becomes the range from that cell through the bottom of the column. If the selected cell is in row 1, the entire column is used. Here are some examples.

You select	*Recorder* is defined as
Cell A3	$A$3:$A$16384
Range A3:A5	$A$3:$A$5
Cell A1	$A:$A

After you choose the Start Recorder command, where the Recorder places recorded functions depends on how *Recorder* has been defined.

- If the first cell in the *Recorder* range is empty, recording starts in that cell and proceeds down until it either reaches a non-empty cell or the end of the range; in either case, Excel displays a dialog box message that says *Recorder range is full.*
- If *Recorder* contains more than one column, and the Recorder hits the bottom of a column, it uses a GOTO function to continue the macro at the top of the next column. (The GOTO function, discussed in Chapter 9, simply directs the macro to continue execution at some other cell on a macro sheet.)
- If the first cell in *Recorder* is not empty, the Recorder looks for the last RETURN function in the range, replacing it with the first newly recorded function. For example, if your two macros are in the same column, and *Recorder* encompasses them both, the Recorder will start recording at the second RETURN. If there is no RETURN in *Recorder*, the Recorder looks for the last non-empty cell and puts the first recorded function in the first cell after it.

Therefore, the best general practice for using the Set Recorder command is usually to select only the empty cell in which you want the first recorded action to go. This way, the Recorder won't put newly recorded macro functions in surprising places.

	A	B
1	**Sum (s)**	Sum and format a column of numbers.
2	*=REFTEXT(ACTIVE.CELL())*	Get ref of active cell, as text.
3	=SELECT("R[-1]C")	Move into bottom cell of data.
4	=SELECT.END(3)	Select top cell of data.
5	*=ROW(ACTIVE.CELL())*	Get row number of top cell.
6	*=SELECT(TEXTREF(A2))*	Return to cell where SUM goes.
7	*=ROW(ACTIVE.CELL())*	Capture row number of this cell.
8	*=DEFINE.NAME("up1","=R[-1]C")*	Define relative range name "up1".
9	*=FORMULA("=SUM(R["&A5-A7&"]C:up1)")*	Enter SUM formula.
10	*=BORDER(,,,1)*	Add top border to this cell.
11	=RETURN()	Quit.

FIGURE 2-11.
The final version of the Sum *macro, with formatting.*

As before, you use this macro by selecting the cell below the column of data to be summed (let's assume it was A6 in the SUM.XLS worksheet) and then pressing Ctrl-s. The formula in cell A2 in the figure,

=REFTEXT(ACTIVE.CELL())

contains two macro functions: ACTIVE.CELL and REFTEXT. The ACTIVE.CELL function returns the location of the currently selected cell as a reference; the REFTEXT function converts this reference into a text string. Figure 2-12 shows the macro when values are displayed instead of formulas: Choose Options Display and deselect the Formulas option [Ctrl-\`; Mac—also Command-\`].

	A	B
1	**Sum (s)**	Sum and format a column of numbers.
2	TEST.XLS!R6C1	Get ref of active cell, as text.
3	TRUE	Move into bottom cell of data.
4	TRUE	Select top cell of data.
5	2	Get row number of top cell.
6	TRUE	Return to cell where SUM goes.
7	6	Capture row number of this cell.
8	TRUE	Define relative range name "up1".
9	TRUE	Enter SUM formula.
10	TRUE	Add top border to this cell.
11	TRUE	Quit.

FIGURE 2-12.
The Values view of the Sum *macro.*

As you can see, the text returned by the formula is in the form of an external reference, the first part of which is the name of the worksheet separated by an exclamation point from the location of the active cell, expressed in R1C1 style. This reference is used later in the macro, when we want to return to this cell. (Incidentally, we see the benefit here of defining the starting point of the macro in cell A1 instead of cell A2; if cell A2 is the starting point and you opened a new row above cell A2, the definition of the starting point of the macro as set in the Define Name dialog box would change to cell A3, and you'd have to go back and correct it.)

Cells A3:A4 contain the macro formulas recorded in the last section (as shown in Figure 2-11). The formula in cell A3,

```
=SELECT("R[-1]C")
```

moves the active cell into the first cell of the block of data we want the macro to sum. The formula in cell A4,

```
=SELECT.END(3)
```

is the equivalent of holding down the Ctrl key [Mac—also the Command key] while pressing the Up direction key to find the top of a column of data. This is why we first entered the formula in cell A3: You must first move the active cell into the block of data to find the top of the block.

The formula in cell A5 is

```
=ROW(ACTIVE.CELL())
```

It returns the row number of the active cell, as you can see in Figure 2-12; we'll use this number later to set the upper end of the range we want to sum.

The formula in cell A6 is

```
=SELECT(TEXTREF(A2))
```

It uses the text version of the external reference deposited in cell A2 of the macro. The TEXTREF function converts the text back into a reference, and the SELECT function selects the cell specified by the reference. The effect of this is to select again the cell that was selected when you first ran the macro. If you had used the formula *=SELECT(A2)* instead, the macro would have selected cell A2 on the macro sheet.

The formula in cell A7 is

```
=ROW(ACTIVE.CELL())
```

It returns the row number of the active cell, as you can see in Figure 2-12; we'll use this number later to set the lower end of the range we want to sum.

The formula in cell A8,

```
=DEFINE.NAME("up1","=R[-1]C")
```

is the equivalent of choosing Formula Define Name, entering the range name *up1*, and assigning it the relative reference *=R[–1]C*; this makes *up1* refer to the cell above the active cell. Defining this name has the side effect, of course, of affecting the entire worksheet; you could use *up1* in other formulas. Also, if the *up1* name was already defined, the formula replaces the prior definition with the one specified. (We'll learn how to use DEFINE.NAME nondestructively in Chapter 7, "Working with References and Names.")

The *up1* name then becomes an important part of the next formula, in cell A9:

```
=FORMULA("=SUM(R["&A5–A7&"]C:up1)")
```

This looks complicated, so let's break it down. The FORMULA macro function enters the specified text in the active cell; this text is an expression that uses the *&* operator to assemble three smaller text strings into one string. (We'll discuss techniques for manipulating strings in Chapter 6, "Working with Text Formulas.") The first string,

```
"=SUM(R["
```

is simply the beginning of the SUM formula and a relative address in R1C1 style. The second part of the expression,

```
A5–A7
```

uses the row number of the cell into which we want to enter the SUM formula and the row number of the top end of the range containing the data we want to sum. As you can see by looking at Figure 2-12, when the row numbers are substituted in the expression, the expression converts to 2–6, or –4. The third part of the expression,

```
"]C:up1)"
```

completes the formula, using the *up1* range name defined in cell A8 of the macro. All together, the expression evaluates to

```
=SUM(R[–4]C:up1)
```

The value of specifying the lower end of the range with a relative reference now becomes apparent: You can use it on a column of any size in the worksheet, and you can insert new rows between the bottom cell in the data and the cell containing the SUM formula without affecting how the SUM formula will work.

For example, suppose we had used a simple relative reference (as in the starting point of the range) instead of *up1*, which contains a relative reference. The resulting version of the SUM formula would be

```
=SUM(R[–4]C:R[–1]C)
```

Inserting a new row immediately above the SUM formula would give the appearance of the row being included in the range being summed, but this range would remain unchanged, and the new row would not be included in the calculation. Figure 2-13 demonstrates the effect of inserting a new row above the row containing the SUM formula, with ranges displayed in the R1C1 style. Notice that the range specification in cell R7C1 (A7 in the A1 style) has changed and that cell R6C1 is not included in the calculation.

Values View

	1
2	2
3	4
4	6
5	8
6	20

Formulas View

	1
2	2
3	4
4	6
5	8
6	=SUM(R[-4]C:R[-1]C)

	1
2	2
3	4
4	6
5	8
6	10
7	20

	1
2	2
3	4
4	6
5	8
6	10
7	=SUM(R[-5]C:R[-2]C)

FIGURE 2-13.
The effect on the range specification in the SUM formula of inserting a new row above row 6, in the R1C1 style.

In contrast, Figure 2-14 shows the effect of using the *up1* name in the formula: Because *up1* is still defined as *=R[–1]C,* adding a new row doesn't change the range specification in the SUM formula, and the new row is included in the calculation.

	1
2	2
3	4
4	6
5	8
6	10
7	30

	1
2	2
3	4
4	6
5	8
6	10
7	=SUM(R[-5]C:up1)

FIGURE 2-14.
Using up1 *in the range specification includes the new row.*

The formula in cell A10 (as shown in Figure 2-11) is

```
=BORDER(,,,1)
```

It presents an interesting twist on the formula that was recorded in cell A5 of Figure 2-10: If the formula specifies a value (0 through 7) for every argument in the BORDER function, the corresponding border is set for every argument. However, if an argument to the BORDER function isn't specified, the border that was there before (if any) remains.

Finally, the formula in cell A11,

```
=RETURN()
```

ends the macro and returns control to the user.

You could enhance the *Sum* macro still further. For example, you could change the expression that sets the range of the SUM formula so that it starts one cell above the top cell in the column of data; this would let you add new rows both above the column and between the column and the SUM formula itself. You would do this by subtracting 1 from the second part of the text expression in cell A9 of the macro.

```
A5–A7–1
```

If you did this, it might also be a good idea to have the macro add a bottom border to that cell, to mark the top end of the range.

Creating command macros without the Recorder

Creating command macros by hand really isn't much different than editing a recorded macro, except that there aren't any macro formulas to edit! The overall process is simpler, although you don't have the convenience of having the Recorder present the correct name and syntax for each macro formula recorded. To create a command macro without the Recorder, do the following.

1. Enter the macro formulas that you want to be in the macro, documenting and formatting the macro in whatever way you want.
2. Use the Define Name dialog box to give the macro a name and a shortcut key.

You enter formulas exactly as you would in a worksheet, except that you have all the macro functions, in addition to the standard functions, from which to choose. You can use the Paste Function command, available on the Formula menu, to enter any of these functions. When you choose the command, you'll see the Paste Function dialog box shown in Figure 2-15.

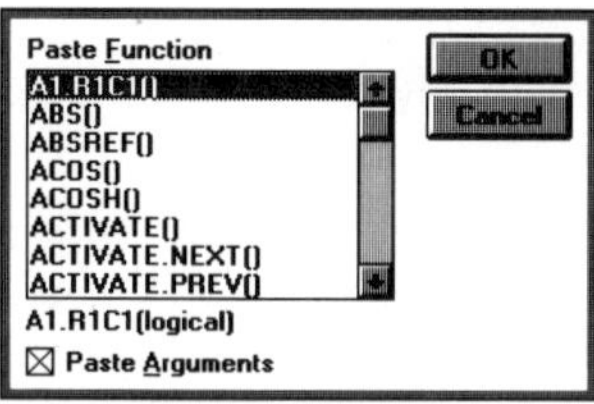

FIGURE 2-15.
The Paste Function dialog box.

The Paste Arguments option at the bottom of the dialog box is particularly handy, because without extensive practice it's difficult to remember the order of arguments of the 300 or so macro functions available in Excel. For example, if you clicked on the Paste Arguments option, selected the BORDER function, and clicked OK, the following text would be entered into the active cell.

```
=BORDER(outline,left,right,top,bottom,shade,outline_color,left_color,
    right_color,top_color,bottom_color)
```

Unfortunately, the list doesn't tell you the type of variable expected for each argument: number, text, logical, reference, error, or array value. (As mentioned earlier, in this book we use internal capitals instead of underscores and append a letter signifying the type of the argument.) Most often, however, given the cue, it's not difficult to remember the expected data type.

As you enter formulas, you can also have Excel check your spelling. To do this, enter the formula in lowercase letters and then verify that Excel changes the reserved words into uppercase on the macro sheet. For example, if you enter *=return()* in a cell of a macro sheet, Excel displays *=RETURN()*, thus confirming that it recognizes the function you entered. On the other hand, if you enter *=retrn()*, the program does not recognize the function and displays *=retrn()*.

Defined names are also case sensitive, and you can use the same technique to check their spelling. Because worksheet and macro functions always appear in uppercase, you'll find that defined names stand out more if you enter them in a mixture of uppercase and lowercase. For example, define a name as *thisRange* rather than *thisrange* or *THISRANGE*. When you enter the name in lowercase letters, the program changes them to whatever combination of uppercase and lowercase letters was set in the Define Name dialog box.

Naming command macros

You define macros through either the Record Macro dialog box, or through the Define Name dialog box, which you'll use when you create a macro from scratch. When you name macros, it's generally best to assign the name to the cell above the first formula in the macro, where we put the name of the macro. Doing so allows you to insert rows for new macro formulas above the first formula, as we did in the *Sum* macro earlier in this chapter.

Figure 2-16 shows the Define Name dialog box for macro sheets, which is very much like that displayed for worksheets but which adds a Macro group box at the bottom.

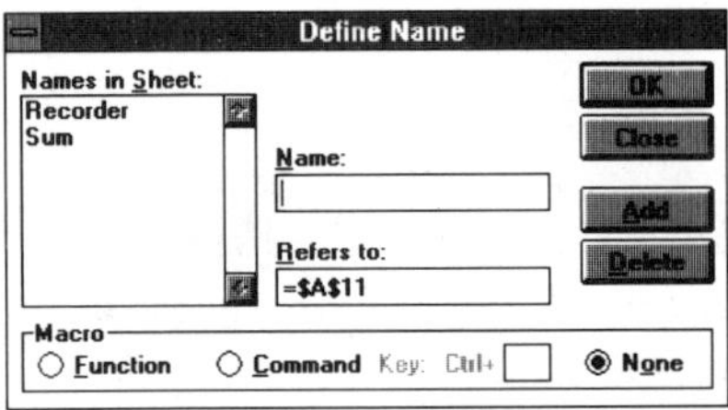

FIGURE 2-16.
The Define Name dialog box for macro sheets.

If you have selected the cell containing the name you've entered above the first cell of the macro, the name is proposed in the Name field of the dialog box; you can edit or change the name. Also, the reference of the active cell is entered in the Refers To field; you can change the reference, or click on a cell in the macro sheet to enter the reference in the field.

Click on the Function button in the Macro section to specify a function macro, or the Command button to specify a command macro. If you wish, you can enter a shortcut key, or leave the Key field empty if you don't want the command macro to have an associated command key. (If a command macro doesn't have a command key, you can run the macro by calling it from another macro, or through the Run dialog box, discussed next.)

Command keys must be letter keys. Because Excel distinguishes between uppercase and lowercase letters, you can define a total of 52 shortcut keys. On the Macintosh, the command key can be any uppercase or lowercase letter except *e, i, n*, or *u*, because these lowercase keys are used with the Option key to enter various types of diacritical marks, such as accents.

If the Caps Lock key is turned on when you use a command key, Excel recognizes the *lowercase* shortcut key. To use an uppercase key, you must always hold down the Shift key. Therefore, lowercase command keys are a little easier to use than uppercase keys. Be aware of the Caps Lock key when you assign a key, however; if the Caps Lock key is on, you'll assign the uppercase letter.

The third option in the Macro section of the Define Name dialog box is labeled None. If you select this button when you name a macro, you cannot use a command key to execute the macro, and when you choose Macro Run, the macro is not listed in the Run dialog box. You can, however, execute such a macro by choosing Macro Run and then entering the macro name in the Reference field.

We'll call a macro marked in this way a "None" macro, but it could actually be used as either a command or a function macro. You can use "None" macros as subroutines that are called by another macro, but the behavior of a macro called as a subroutine changes depending on whether it was called by a command or function macro. (We'll explore this subject in more detail in the next chapter.)

After you name a command macro, you can easily modify its command key or its associated reference. To do so, simply call up the Define Name dialog box, select the macro name you want to modify, make the needed changes, and then press Enter.

Managing macro names and shortcut keys

After you create more than about 15 command macros, each with its own command key, finding unassigned keys becomes more and more difficult. Here are three ways that will help you keep track of your macros.

1. Always document the command key that you assign to each macro. A good place to put this information is in a list near cell A1 of a given macro sheet, so you'll see it when you open the macro sheet.
2. You can look at a list of the currently defined macros in all open macro sheets in the Run dialog box (choose Macro Run). The dialog box lists the name of each macro and its associated command key. Choose Cancel after you find the information you need, or you can run a macro from the dialog box.
3. You can enter a list of the currently defined names for the active macro sheet (not for all open macro sheets) into the active macro sheet by selecting an empty area, choosing Formula Paste Name, selecting Paste List, and then clicking OK.

Running command macros from the Run dialog box

When you choose Run from the Macro menu, you'll see the dialog box shown in Figure 2-17 on page 45. As mentioned before, the list of macros in the Run dialog box shows the command key assigned to each macro on every open macro sheet, expressed as external references. These names are listed alphabetically, first by macro sheet name, and then by macro name.

A macro for keeping track of macros and command keys.

The following steps show how to create this macro quickly—recording these steps as a macro or entering the macro shown in the table below. (If you record the macro, first be sure that you're recording relative references.)

1. Select a cell three rows below the last row of the macro sheet. To do this quickly, press Ctrl-End to select the bottom-right cell, press Home to move the active cell to column A, and then press the Down direction key three times.
2. To paste a list of all defined names into the macro sheet, choose Formula Paste Name, select Paste List, and press Enter.
3. Press Tab three times, thus moving the active cell to the top of the column listing the command keys.
4. To sort the table alphabetically by command key, choose Data Sort and press Enter.
5. Choose Macro Stop Recorder.

The resulting macro, with formatting and documentation, follows.

	A	B
1	**NameList (n)**	Inserts a list of names.
2	=SELECT.LAST.CELL()	Find a blank area
3	=SELECT("R[3]C1")	below the last cell.
4	=LIST.NAMES()	Paste the name list.
5	=SELECT(,"RC[3]")	Move to the column containing the keys.
6	=SORT(1,"RC",1)	Sort the list.
7	=RETURN()	

The only difference between this macro and what you probably recorded is in cell A3; where we forced the selection of the cell three rows below the active cell in column A.

By reviewing this list, you can easily find keys you haven't used yet. Unfortunately, the Paste Name command returns only the names defined in the active macro sheet. Therefore, if you have more than one macro sheet open, you can run the macro on each open macro sheet, copy the lists to one worksheet, and then sort the combined lists.

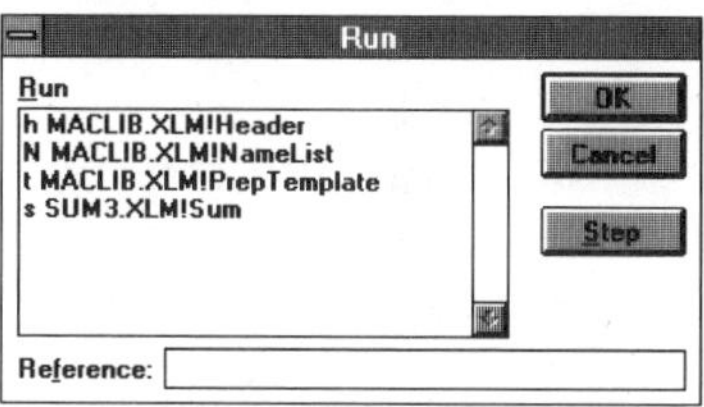

FIGURE 2-17.
The Run dialog box.

When you first begin to use macros, the Run dialog box might seem to be excess baggage; to run a command macro, after all, you need only use its command key. However, the Macro Run dialog box can be very useful at times. For example, the list in the dialog box not only alerts you to duplicate command keys but also helps you identify unused letters for assignment to new macros.

If two macros are assigned the same command key, using the key runs only the first one in the list having that command key. You'll usually discover this when you use a command key you thought performed an expected task, and something else happens instead. You can call up the Run dialog box and check the list for duplicate command keys, a common occurrence when more than one macro sheet is open. However, you can still run the second macro from the Run dialog box by selecting the macro from the list and pressing Enter or by double-clicking the macro's name.

When you write a macro it's sometimes a good idea to run a short section of it to see whether it actually performs as expected. Even if you haven't named the macro and assigned a command key yet, you can select the cell in which you want execution to begin and choose the Macro Run command. Because the Run dialog box displays the reference of the selected cell, all you need do is press Enter to start execution at that point in the macro. In other words, by pressing only four keys [/MR and Enter], you can execute any part of any macro, even if the macro has never been named. If you want, you can also click in the Reference field of the dialog box and then select a cell, as with other input fields in Excel; after the reference of the cell appears in the field, press Enter.

Finally, if you assigned a "None" macro type (that is, one that has not been explicitly assigned a function or command macro), you can run it in much the same way as you would by providing a cell reference. Because you haven't made it a command macro, it *won't* appear in the Run dialog box. Simply press /MR, type the macro name in the Reference field, and press Enter. If any sheet other than the one containing the macro is active when you run the macro, remember to enter the name as an external reference (the name of the macro sheet, an exclamation point, and then the macro name).

When I press Ctrl-a to run a command macro, my computer only beeps. Why?

This is one of the most common problems that new users of macros experience. Your computer beeps because it doesn't recognize the command key you used. This is usually caused by one of the following:

- You forgot to name the command macro.
- You didn't assign a command key when you named the macro.
- You assigned a different command key than the one you used. (Note: Because Excel distinguishes between uppercase letters and lowercase letters in command keys, this can be a particularly difficult type of error to recognize. For example, you could press Ctrl-a and get a beep because the computer is expecting you to press Ctrl-A.)

The solution to all these problems is to activate the macro sheet, choose Formula Define Name, and review the entries in the dialog box, changing them if necessary.

3

Function Macros

Like a standard worksheet function, a function macro accepts data in the form of the arguments supplied, performs calculations on the data, and returns data in the form of numbers, text, logical values, references, error values, or arrays. You can write function macros to look up and calculate values, manipulate text, process arrays, and more.

In contrast to command macros, function macros do not perform actions on the desktop: *You* initiate a command macro, whereas a worksheet initiates a function macro. For this reason, you can't use the Recorder to create a function macro; in fact, function macros are prohibited from performing any of the actions that the Recorder would recognize.

Excel's standard worksheet functions and macro functions are the building blocks of function macros. (Again, you use macro functions in a function macro.) Although you can use all the standard worksheet functions in function macros, you can use only a limited number of macro functions, simply because most of the macro functions emulate menu commands and actions taken on the desktop and can be used only in command macros. Appendix A lists all of the macro functions available in Excel, indicating which can be used in command macros and which can be used in function macros.

Later in this chapter, we'll cover the types of macro functions you can use in your function macros, but let's first use an example to familiarize ourselves with the elements of a function macro.

Creating a function macro

The process for creating a function macro is very similar to creating a command macro by hand.

1. Enter the macro as a series of standard functions and macro functions, either by entering the functions and operators by hand or by using the Formula Paste Function command.
2. Define the macro by using the Define Name dialog box.
3. Use the new function macro as you would a standard function, either in a worksheet or in another macro.

Entering the macro

The function macro in Figure 3-1 converts a column number between 1 and 256 to a corresponding column reference between A and IV. This function macro parallels the COLUMN standard function, which takes a reference and returns its column number. (The COLUMN function can also extract an array of the column numbers used in a range, but our macro doesn't address this issue.) The *ColLet* macro is useful in two ways: It solves a column-reference calculation problem that you might experience occasionally, and more important, it exemplifies elements central to most function macros.

	A	B	C
1	fnc	**ColLet**	Converts column number to letter.
2		=RESULT(2)	Return only text values.
3		=ARGUMENT("colN",1)	Allow only numeric input.
4		=CELL("address",INDEX(1:1,colN))	Convert col # ref to $A$1 ref.
5		=LEFT(up1,3)	Get first 3 chars of ref.
6		=SUBSTITUTE(up1,"$","")	Remove every "$".
7		=RETURN(up1)	Return column letter.

FIGURE 3-1.
The ColLet *macro.*

To enter the macro, open a new macro sheet [Ctrl-F11], and enter the text and formulas shown, adjusting the column widths as needed. Document and format the macro as shown, and then save the macro sheet as COLLET.XLM.

Before we define the macro and use it in a worksheet, let's go over the macro, describing its parts. A function macro usually contains four elements, three of which are built-in macro functions.

RESULT function

The RESULT function, an optional element, specifies the type of data the function macro returns. If you omit this function from the macro, Excel assumes that the macro can return either a numeric, textual, or logical value. The parameter value *2* in cell B2 specifies that the function macro can return only textual values, according to the following table.

Code	Data type
1	Numeric
2	Textual
4	Logical
8	Reference
16	Error
64	Array

As we'll see later when we discuss the RESULT function in greater detail, you can add these numbers to specify that the macro can return more than one type of result. For example, if a function macro is to return both numbers and text, you could use *RESULT(3)*, which is the sum of data types *1* and *2*.

ARGUMENT function

The ARGUMENT function defines a variable (really, a defined name on the macro sheet containing the function macro) for storing a value passed to the macro, and it specifies a permissible data type for the value. Because each ARGUMENT function can assign only one name to each value passed to the macro, you must include a separate ARGUMENT function for each argument you want to use. (You can pass up to 13 separate values to a function macro; however, a single array can count as 1 value.)

Each argument you define can be used repeatedly in the formulas of the macro following the ARGUMENT formulas. When you call the function macro from the worksheet, the arguments to the new function must be entered in the same order in which they appear on the macro sheet. For example, if you create a function macro named *Wait* on a macro sheet named MACRO1.XLM, which takes three arguments (*time, tide,* and *man*), the function when used in a worksheet would have to take the form

```
MACRO1.XLM!Wait(time,tide,man)
```

The *ColLet* macro stores the column-number value in a variable named *colN*. The parameter value 1 specifies that only numeric input is allowed, according to the data-type table shown on the previous page. If you use *ColLet* in a worksheet, passing anything but a number, the function returns the error value *#VALUE!*.

Calculation

After you indicate the data type needed for the result and define the arguments used in the function, the next step is to perform calculations on the arguments given. You can use any of the standard worksheet functions and many of the macro functions to produce the function macro's result. Although *ColLet* in Figure 3-1 uses three rows (rows 4, 5, and 6) to determine the result, your function macros can contain as many rows of calculations as you want. (Note: As a practical consideration, you might want to keep your function macros short to minimize calculation time.)

In *ColLet* the calculation is done entirely with standard worksheet formulas. The formula in cell B4 contains an INDEX function and a CELL function:

```
=CELL("address",INDEX(1:1,colN))
```

The INDEX function takes the range reference *1:1* (indicating all of row 1) and returns the reference corresponding to the cell indexed by the value stored in *colN*. If *colN* were 4, for example, the reference returned would be *$D$1*, and a *colN* value of 27 would return *$AA$1*. The CELL function takes this cell reference and returns the address of the cell as a text string, from which we can extract the column letter.

The formula in cell B5 uses the defined name *up1*:

```
=LEFT(up1,3)
```

To define the name, select cell B5, choose Formula Define Name, enter *up1* in the Name field, and enter *=B4* in the Refers To field. This creates a relative reference that you can use anywhere in the macro sheet to refer to the value stored in the cell above the cell in which the name is used.

The LEFT function returns the three leftmost characters of the address returned by the CELL formula in cell B4. Because column references consist of either one character or two, the left three characters of the value returned by the CELL function will be of the form *n* or *$nn*, where *n* is a column-letter reference. In our two examples, the strings returned would be *D* and *$AA*.

The SUBSTITUTE function in cell B6,

```
=SUBSTITUTE(up1,"$","")
```

takes the result of the formula in cell B5 and removes any dollar signs in the string, by substituting "" (quotation marks surrounding nothing—a so-called *null string*) for the dollar signs. In our two examples, only the column letters *D* and *AA* would remain.

RETURN function

Function macros must end with a RETURN function, but unlike command macros, in function macros the RETURN function requires an argument. In cell B7 of the macro, the RETURN function uses the *up1* name to reference the result of the SUBSTITUTE formula in the cell above, thus passing that result to the worksheet and ending execution of the macro.

Why do I get an *Error In Formula* message when I press Return at the last line of the following function macro?

	A
1	=ARGUMENT("a")
2	=ARGUMENT("b")
3	=ARGUMENT("c")
4	=RETURN(a+b+c)

The letters *R*, *r*, *C*, and *c* are reserved because they are used in RC (row-column) referencing. (Chapter 7, "Working with References and Names," discusses both R1C1 and A1 referencing in detail.)

To work around this situation, you can append a period or an underscore after the name: For example, the names *c_* and *R.* are acceptable range names. Longer, more descriptive names, however, are more in accord with better programming style.

Naming a function macro

To name this function macro, first select the cell containing the name of the macro (cell B1), and then choose Formula Define Name [PC—Ctrl-F3; Mac—Command-L]. Because cell B1 contains text—the name of the macro, *ColLet*—this text is proposed as the name to be defined. Excel proposes as the starting point of the macro the reference for cell B1 in the Refers To field. At this point, the dialog box should look like the one shown in Figure 3-2 on the following page. Finally, select the Function option and press Enter.

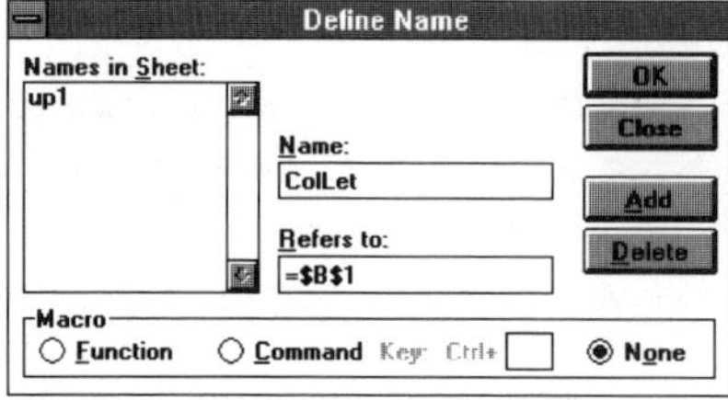

FIGURE 3-2.
Naming the ColLet *macro.*

When you assign a name to a function macro, do *not* use a name that is also the name of a worksheet or of a macro function.

A name used by both a function macro and a worksheet or a macro function might generate an error message or cause execution of the *function* rather than the macro. For example, you could create a new function macro called *Match,* possibly getting an *Error In Formula* message when using the function in a worksheet. The error message would occur because MATCH is the name of a standard worksheet function.

The following are some function names that are easy to use in macros: QUIT, HALT, ROW, COUNT, TIME, CLEAN, EXTRACT, and SAVE. Each name could be perfect for a given macro, but each could cause many problems before you discover the error and change the name of the macro. To eliminate this problem, change the name of your function macro to a name Excel doesn't use. One simple way of doing this is to put an underscore after the name, changing *Match* to *Match_;* or you can modify the name slightly, changing *Match* to *MyMatch,* for example.

Using a function macro

To test the *ColLet* function macro shown in Figure 3-1 on page 48, open a new worksheet and enter the values and formulas shown in Figure 3-3.

Notice that the worksheet uses a linking formula, one that refers to a cell or cells located on a separate sheet—in this case the COLLET.XLM macro sheet. You can enter a function macro on a worksheet much like you enter any formula. The reference must include the filename of the macro sheet in which your function

	A	B	C
1	Column	Column	
2	number	letter	Notes
3	-1	=COLLET.XLM!ColLet(A3)	
4	0	=COLLET.XLM!ColLet(A4)	
5	1	=COLLET.XLM!ColLet(A5)	
6	26	=COLLET.XLM!ColLet(A6)	
7	27	=COLLET.XLM!ColLet(A7)	
8	256	=COLLET.XLM!ColLet(A8)	
9	257	=COLLET.XLM!ColLet(A9)	

FIGURE 3-3.
Testing ColLet *in a worksheet, displayed in Formulas view.*

macro resides, an exclamation point, and the macro name. But unlike other references, the formula also includes in parentheses the arguments you want to pass to the macro.

In addition to entering the macro by hand, you can also use the Formula Paste Function command, as mentioned in Chapter 1. If you call up the Paste Name dialog box and scroll to the bottom of the list of macros, you'll see the dialog box shown in Figure 3-4:

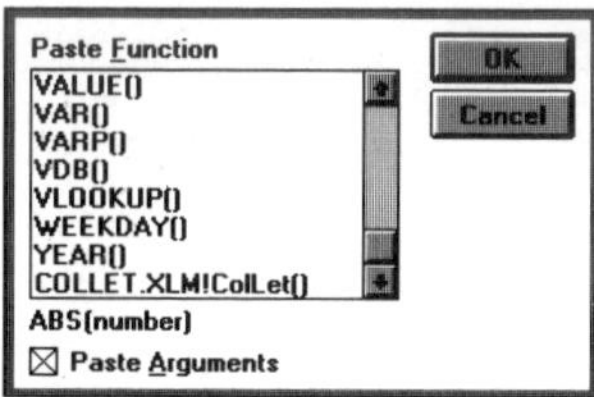

FIGURE 3-4.
The Paste Function dialog box, listing the new function.

If you select the *ColLet* function and click OK (or simply double-click the function name), the function is entered in the active cell in the worksheet, with the insertion point positioned between the parentheses, ready for you to enter the function's arguments. You can also select the Paste Arguments option at the bottom of the dialog box to add the list of arguments the function takes.

In this case, you can enter the formula in cell B3. With the Paste Arguments option selected, the argument *colN* appears and is highlighted between the parentheses of the function. Simply click on cell A3 to enter the reference to replace the function's single argument. Now select the range B3:B9 and choose Formula Fill Down to enter the formula into the rest of the cells in the range.

Figure 3-5 shows the same worksheet in Values view, so you can see the results returned by the macro for the values given, with notes added in the third column.

	A	B	C
1	Column	Column	
2	number	letter	Notes
3	-1	#VALUE!	Negative columns not allowed.
4	0	A	Minor error.
5	1	A	Good result.
6	26	Z	Good result.
7	27	AA	Good result.
8	256	IV	Good result.
9	257	#REF!	Maximum of 256 columns.

FIGURE 3-5.
The same worksheet shown in Figure 3-3, with added notes and displayed in Values view.

Because the macro references cells in an actual row of the macro sheet, *ColLet* returns error values for negative column values and for those values greater than 256 (the maximum available in Excel). The macro does, however, return an incorrect result for the column value 0. It does so because using an INDEX value of 0 returns an array of the complete row or column, and then the CELL function returns the address of the first cell in this array (cell A1). If this minor quirk causes a problem, insert a new row 6 in the macro and enter the following:

```
=IF(colN=0,RETURN(NA()))
```

This formula returns the error value *#N/A* if *colN* equals 0.

Functions available to function macros

You can use all the functions available to worksheets in creating function macros, but you can use only a limited number of the macro functions available to command macros. The reason for this is fairly straightforward: Worksheets are for performing calculations, not for manipulating other worksheets, the Excel environment, and so on. To write function macros effectively, therefore, you need to know which macro functions are permitted.

Generally speaking, when creating function macros, you can use any macro function that does not perform an action. If you do include an action-equivalent macro function in a function macro, it will be ignored when the macro is executed. (Appendix A lists the macro functions that you can use in function macros.)

Although we haven't discussed many of these functions yet, the group of macro functions you can use in function macros separates into two parts.

- Functions that return information about cells, open documents, files, windows, and so on. Again, these macro functions manipulate data rather than take actions on the desktop, so they are permitted in function macros. Included are those functions which take, process, or return references. (See Chapter 7.)
- Functions that perform control and branching operations within any macro. (We'll discuss many of these functions in Chapter 9, "Controlling Program Flow.")

Without using the lists presented in the appendixes or ones similar to them, you can never be quite sure whether an error in a function macro was caused by using a macro function improperly or whether you shouldn't have been using the function in the first place. If a formula doesn't work in a function macro, you can check the appendix to see if you're using an illegal macro function.

In the next section, we'll take a close look at the four macro functions that are most closely associated with function macros. We've already encountered two of these functions—ARGUMENT and RESULT. The third, CALLER, offers a way to customize your macros so that they are able to operate differently depending on how they are called in a worksheet or macro sheet. The fourth, VOLATILE, aids in the recalculation of custom functions in a worksheet.

The RESULT function

RESULT is an optional function that indicates the type of value a function macro will return. If you're like most macro programmers, you'll seldom use RESULT because most of your function macros already return numeric, textual, or logical values by default. If, however, you want a function to return a cell reference or an array, then RESULT is required. Its primary use is to provide a level of error checking in a function macro: You want to be sure that the result of the calculations inside the macro is of a certain data type.

The RESULT function takes a single numeric argument and must be the first formula in the macro. Its syntax is

```
=RESULT(typeN)
```

The value given as the *typeN* argument is a code that represents one or more data types. The list on the following page (repeated from earlier in this chapter) presents the possible code numbers and the types of values they represent.

Code	Data type
1	Numeric
2	Textual
4	Logical
8	Reference
16	Error
64	Array

You can specify a single data type by using one of the code numbers listed; you can specify a combination of data types by adding code numbers together. For example, if you want a function to return numbers, text, or logical values, you use the data-type number 7 (equal to 1+2+4). The data-type number 24 specifies that the returned value can be a cell reference (8) or an error (16).

When the calculations in the function macro have been made, Excel tries to convert the result to the data type specified in RESULT. This is often called *coercion*. For example, if the formulas you use to calculate a result create a number, but you've specified a *typeN* value of 2 for text, Excel converts the number to text. If the number can't be converted to the specified type, the function returns *#VALUE!*.

Using RESULT to return cell references and array values

The main use for the RESULT function is in macros that return cell references or array values. When used in these function macros, RESULT is not optional. To return a cell reference, you would enter *=RESULT(8)* as the first formula in your macro.

To use a reference returned by a function macro, you must call the function macro from within a larger formula. For example, suppose a function macro named *Macro1!SumIt* takes as an argument the value in cell A8 of a worksheet to calculate the cell reference of an area on the worksheet that you want to sum. You would need to enter the formula

```
=SUM(Macro1!SumIt(A8))
```

If instead you were to enter

```
=Macro1!SumIt(A8)
```

in cell A1, the value appearing in the cell would be the value contained in the cell pointed to by the reference returned by *SumIt*. If you then referenced that cell from another cell containing a SUM formula, the SUM formula would return not the sum of the *reference* stored in the cell, but the *value* stored in the cell.

To return an array value, you would enter *=RESULT(64)* as the first formula in the macro. Figure 3-6 illustrates a simple macro, *DateArray*, that takes no arguments but returns to the worksheet the array of date values calculated by the formulas contained in the range B10:B12 on the macro sheet. The figure also shows both the Values and Formulas views of a worksheet that uses this function macro.

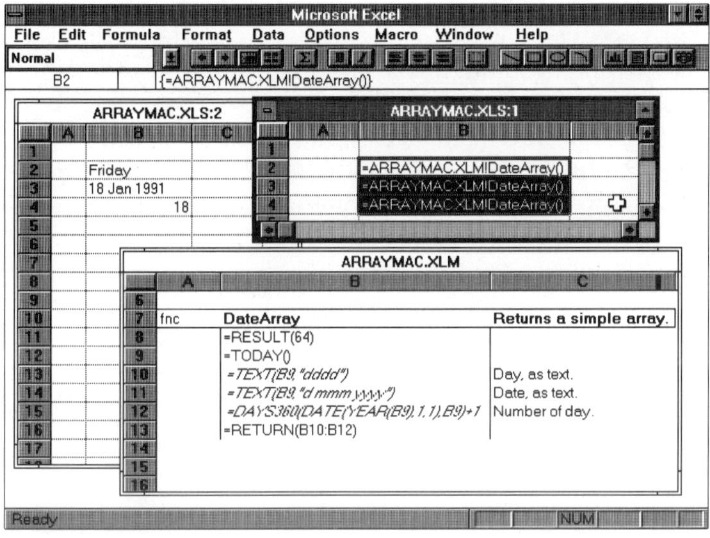

FIGURE 3-6.
The DateArray *macro.*

To produce the results in the worksheet, enter

```
=ARRAYMAC.XLM!Array()
```

as an array formula in the range B2:B4. To enter an array formula, select the range, type the formula, and then enter the formula by pressing Ctrl-Shift-Enter [Mac—also Command-Return]. The Formulas view in Figure 3-6 shows that Excel fills every cell of the array with the same formula. To indicate that the formula is an array, Excel encloses it in braces when it appears in the formula bar, as shown at the top of the figure.

If a formula is capable of performing calculations on an entire array, you can use the result of an array-returning function without actually entering the formula as an array. For example, you can find the sum of an array returned by a function macro by entering a formula such as

```
=SUM(Macro1.XLM!ArrayFnc(thisRange))
```

as a normal formula in any cell. You can write similar formulas using functions such as COUNT, MAX, and AVERAGE.

You can use TYPE instead of RESULT to verify the data type of a result and to create your own error values.

Although you can use RESULT to force the conversion of a result to a particular data type, using RESULT does not always offer the most direct approach. For example, you might use =RESULT(1) if you want a macro to return only numeric values and #VALUE! otherwise. Rather than using the RESULT function, you can send a clearer message to the user of the function by testing the type of the result with the TYPE function. Suppose that *thisRange* contains the result you want the function macro to return. The last line of the macro might appear as

```
=RETURN(IF(TYPE(thisRange)=1,thisRange,"Error! Why isn't this a
        numeric value?"))
```

You could also use RESULT if you want numeric values to be returned as text. You can use a RESULT(2) formula, which would return both textual and numeric values as text. However, a more direct method is to concatenate a null string to the result to be returned, which forces Excel to treat the result as a text expression. Using this method, the RETURN formula might appear as

```
=RETURN(thisRange&"")
```

The ARGUMENT function

The ARGUMENT function performs two tasks: It defines a name for a value passed to a function macro, and it defines the data type of the value. (Note: You can also use ARGUMENT in command macros.) Except for a RESULT formula, no other formulas should precede ARGUMENT in a function macro. The ARGUMENT function takes one of the following forms:

```
=ARGUMENT(nameT,dataTypeN)
```

or

```
=ARGUMENT(nameT,dataTypeN,ref)
```

As the name of the first argument suggests, *nameT* must be text; after Excel executes this formula, you can see the definition assigned the name in the Define Name dialog box. The argument *dataTypeN* has the same meaning as it does for the RESULT function, and it takes one or the sum of the same data-type numbers. If not specified, Excel assumes a data-type number of 7, indicating text, numbers, and logical values.

To understand how the ARGUMENT function *really* uses the data-type numbers (both individually and in combination), you can use the following function macro to exhaustively test the various data types passed to it.

	A	B	C
1	fnc	**TestArgs**	Returns definition of argument.
2		=ARGUMENT("dataTypeN")	Get data type.
3		=ARGUMENT("thisArg",dataTypeN)	Get argument in this data type.
4		=RETURN(GET.NAME("thisArg"))	Return definition of "thisArg".

The *TestArgs* macro takes two arguments. The first argument, *dataTypeN*, specifies the data type of the second argument, *thisArg*, the definition of which is returned to the worksheet as text. Name this macro *TestArgs* and save the macro sheet as ARGS.XLM. Next create the sample worksheet shown in Figure 3-7 on the following page. Cells B3:D3 contain the data to be passed through *TestArgs*, and cell B6 contains the formula

```
=ARGS.XLM!TestArgs($A6,B$3)
```

Select cells B6:B15, and choose Edit Fill Down. Now select cells B6:D15, and choose Edit Fill Right. In cell E6, enter the formula

```
=ARGS.XLM!TestArgs($A6,$B$3:$D$3)
```

Finally, add the *dataTypeN* numbers in cells A6:A15, add the table headings, and format the worksheet as shown.

Of course, you can enter any values you want in the range B3:D3, to see what effect a value has on the definitions returned in the table. Let's make a few observations, based on the results returned in this table.

This table shows that you *can* add cell-reference-type numbers to other data-type numbers, but it's pointless to do so because cell references take precedence over other data types.

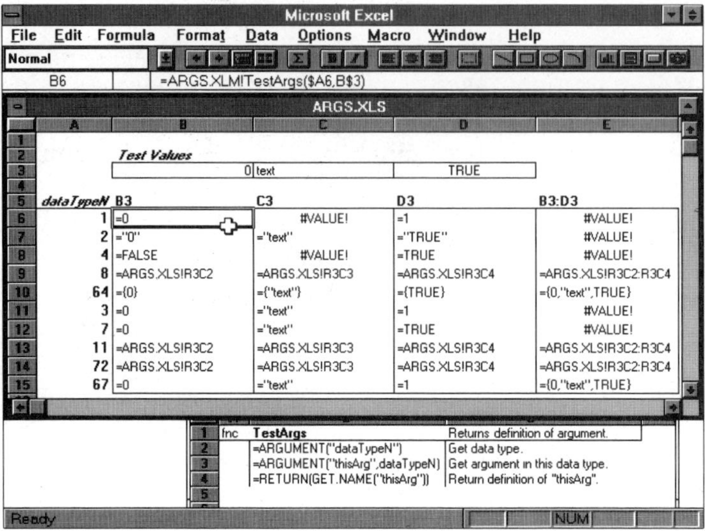

FIGURE 3-7.
A worksheet for experimenting with the data types passed through an ARGUMENT function.

dataTypeN	**The ARGUMENT function...**
1 (numbers)	Passes only numeric data to a function macro. If text, returns #VALUE!.
2 (text)	Passes text as text. Converts numeric data to text.
4 (logicals)	Passes the value TRUE to a function macro for all numeric values except 0, for which it sends the value FALSE. Passes the #VALUE! error for text.
8 (references)	Whether you indicate single cells or ranges, passes the indicated area to the macro as a cell reference.
64 (arrays)	Converts text or numeric values in the indicated cells to an array of the same values.
3 (numbers, text)	Passes text to the function macro as text, and numbers as numbers. FALSE becomes 0, and TRUE becomes 1.
7 (numbers, text, logicals)	Passes text to the function macro as text, numbers as numbers, logical values as logical values. The default for the ARGUMENT function.
11 (numbers, text, references)	References take precedence over text and numbers. If you include 8 in *dataTypeN*, the function macro stores only references.
72 (references, arrays)	References take precedence over arrays.
67 (numbers, text, arrays)	Text and numbers take precedence over arrays.

Error values

You might have noticed that the data-type value 16 is missing from the table above. It might seem that data type 16 is excess baggage. If the *dataTypeN* argument does include data type 16, a function macro returns the appropriate error value (*#N/A, #DIV/0!, #NUM!, #REF!,* or *#VALUE!*) passed to it. If *dataTypeN* does not include data type 16, and the formula passed an error value to the macro for any reason, the function macro returns an error value anyway. Because it passes error values in either case, what difference does this data type make?

The answer is this: If you don't include data type 16 in *dataTypeN*, and the formula calling the function macro passes an error value to the macro, the function macro will *always* return the same error value that the formula passed. But if you do include data type 16 in *dataTypeN*, the function macro can "trap" the error and return a customized error value or text string.

Arrays and cell references handle errors differently. If the formula that calls a function macro passes a cell reference to cells that contain error values, function macros that use both the reference-type and array-type numbers can test for these indirect error values even though the ARGUMENT function did not include an error-type number. That is, if the formula resembles =Test!Test(A1:A5), you don't need to add data type 16 to the array-type or cell-reference-type numbers.

On the other hand, you'll have problems if the formula that calls the function macro sends an error value directly. That is, if the formula resembles =Test!Test(#REF!), you'll be unable to trap the error in your macro unless *dataTypeN* adds data type 16 to the array-type or cell-reference-type numbers.

Variations of the ARGUMENT function

You can use the ARGUMENT function in two distinct ways: It can assign a value directly to a name, or it can assign a value to one or more cells in a macro sheet. The first approach—assigning a value directly to a name—ignores the last argument in the ARGUMENT function. When ARGUMENT is used in this way, it requires only two arguments: *nameT* and *dataTypeN*.

At times, however, you might want to place one or more values passed to a function macro in a range on the macro sheet. Using this approach, you add a third argument, *ref*, which is the reference to the range in the macro sheet where the value(s) will be stored. If supplied, Excel assigns *nameT* to the range in the macro sheet containing the value(s).

For example, this approach is useful if you want to pass an array of values to a function macro and need to change at least one of the values during the execution of the macro. If you use the first approach instead, assigning the array constant to a defined name stored in the macro sheet, Excel doesn't permit alteration of the elements in the array. However, if you place the array of values in a range of cells on the macro sheet, you can use the SET.VALUE function (discussed in Chapter 7) to modify these values. The INDEX function is very useful for getting at the individual elements in the array.

One caveat, however: When the ARGUMENT function passes a value directly to a range on a macro sheet, it erases any other data or macros that might exist in the referenced area. Therefore, when you use the *ref* argument of an ARGUMENT function, be very careful that the argument refers to an unused area of the macro sheet.

Maintaining formulas on a macro sheet outside macros.

Sometimes it's useful to store formulas in a range on a macro sheet that the other macros on the sheet (or, through external references, any other worksheet or macro sheet) can use. Because these formulas are on a macro sheet rather than a worksheet, you must take special steps to recalculate them, as no formula on a macro sheet is recalculated unless it is within a macro that Excel is executing. Here are two ways to do the recalculation.

- If your formulas are in a column, turn the column of formulas into a macro. To do so, assign a range name to the cell above the column and enter the formula *=RETURN()* below the column. So when you call this "macro" as a subroutine, Excel recalculates all the formulas it contains.
- If the formulas are in a row, it's too much work to convert each cell in the row into a macro. Instead, you can create a macro that uses the FORMULA.REPLACE macro function to replace the equal signs in a given range with equal signs. Doing so constitutes a meaningless edit, but it forces Excel to recalculate the formulas.

One advanced use for these techniques is to create dynamic or configurable custom dialog boxes, discussed in Chapter 12. You can recalculate the table in the macro sheet defining a custom dialog box, which contains formulas that result in the parameters specifying the items in the dialog box.

The CALLER function

The CALLER function returns the reference of the cell or array that called the currently running macro. This function takes no arguments and takes the form

```
=CALLER()
```

If the currently running macro is a command macro started by the user, the "caller" is actually the user. In this case, CALLER returns the error value *#REF!*. But if either a command macro started by the user or a function macro calls another macro, whether a function or command macro, then that macro can use CALLER to return the name or reference of the calling function or command macro. Similarly, if you've assigned a macro to an object, such as a button (discussed in Chapter 12), CALLER returns a text string that identifies that object.

How then can you use CALLER in your macros? Suppose you create a function macro that returns monthly commissions for the manager of your East Coast region. When you hire a manager for the West Coast region, you'd like to use the same macro to calculate her commissions. But, unfortunately, some of her commission rates are higher and some are lower than in the East Coast region. Therefore, for the macro to return the correct commissions, it needs to know whether it was called by formulas in the worksheet titled EAST or the one titled WEST.

To find this information, first include the macro formula

```
=REFTEXT(CALLER())
```

This formula converts CALLER's cell reference to text in the R1C1 format. For example, if a formula in cell D5 of the EAST worksheet called the macro, this formula would return *EAST.XLS!R5C4* on the PC and *EAST!R5C4* on the Mac.

Assuming this formula is located in cell B10 of the macro sheet, you can capture the name of the worksheet itself by using the following formula in cell B11:

```
=LEFT(B10,FIND("!",B10)–1)
```

With this information, you can determine a conditional commission rate by using the simple formula

```
=IF(B11="EAST",.06,.08)
```

If you cover several sales regions, you can use a VLOOKUP formula to look up the name of the worksheet in a database range that contains the commission rates you require.

You can also use CALLER to return the size of an array that a function macro will build. Because CALLER returns the reference of the array that calls it, the two formulas ROWS(CALLER()) and COLUMNS(CALLER()) provide a function macro with the dimensions of the array.

If you put the CALLER function in a macro that is called by another macro (not by the user), it can't directly identify the name of the macro that called it, but it can help identify the macro if you name every cell that calls the macro with a variation of the calling macro's name. For example, suppose each of the three macros *GetJob, Update,* and *PrintIt* calls a macro that contains CALLER. Label the three cells that call the macro *GetJobCall, UpdateCall,* and *PrintItCall.* To identify these names in the called macro, use the formula

```
=GET.DEF(REFTEXT(CALLER()))
```

I'm trying to use the CALLER function to return the reference of the cell that initiated my function macro. However, rather than returning the cell reference, this function returns *0*.

A cell in a macro sheet or worksheet cannot store a cell reference alone, because the reference is always evaluated to the value stored in the referenced cell. Therefore, when your CALLER function returns *0*, it's returning the *value* contained in the cell that called the function.

To capture the cell address, you can use either of two methods. You can capture the reference as a defined name. For example, to capture the definition as *callRef,* you can use the formula

```
=DEFINE.NAME("callRef",CALLER())
```

You can also convert the reference to text by using the formula

```
=REFTEXT(CALLER(),FALSE)
```

To store the text in a defined name, use the formula

```
=DEFINE.NAME("callRefT",REFTEXT(CALLER(),FALSE))
```

This formula returns the cell address as an absolute reference in R1C1 format. To return the reference in A1 format, change FALSE to TRUE. Later in the macro, a macro function might need to use the cell address as a reference rather than as text. To convert the text back to a reference, use

```
=TEXTREF(callRefT)
```

where *callRefT* was set by the last formula.

Note: See Chapter 7 for definitions of DEFINE.NAME, REFTEXT, and TEXTREF.

This formula returns the name assigned to the cell that called the currently running macro. For example, it might return the name *GetJobCall.* To find the name of the calling macro itself, simply eliminate the text *Call* from the result of the previous formula. Supposing that this formula is located in cell B45, you can use either of the following formulas to find the name of the calling macro:

```
=SUBSTITUTE(B45,"Call","")
```

or

```
=LEFT(B45,LEN(B45)–4)
```

The first formula substitutes a null string for the text *Call.* The second formula drops the last four letters from the previous text, returning the name of the calling macro.

Recalculation and the VOLATILE function

Excel uses *sparse recalculation,* which means that formulas aren't recalculated unless it's necessary. In the case of function macros, however, your opinion of when recalculation is necessary can differ from Excel's "opinion."

To decide when recalculation is needed, Excel takes what seems to be a reasonable approach. When any value in a worksheet changes, Excel recalculates only those formulas that directly or indirectly reference the value. This approach works well for predefined functions. After all, the formula =SUM(A1:A3) needs no recalculation unless a value in the range A1:A3 changes.

Unlike predefined functions, you can change the definition of a function macro, and as a consequence, a formula that calls the macro *will return a different result.* Excel's sparse calculation method ignores this fact. Therefore, no matter how often you rewrite your macro, the program won't recalculate this formula unless a value changes in the range A1:A3.

To illustrate the problem, open a new worksheet and a new macro sheet. Enter the value *1* in cell A1 of the macro sheet. Enter *=RETURN(A1)* in cell A2. Select cell A1, and then activate the Define Name dialog box by pressing Ctrl-F3 [Mac—also Command-L]. Assign the name *Test* to cell A1 and designate it as a function macro. Then, assuming that the name of the macro sheet is MACRO1, enter the formula *=Macro1!Test()* into any cell in the worksheet.

When you enter this formula, it returns the value *1.* To illustrate the problem, enter 2 in cell A1 of the macro sheet. Your worksheet formula *should* return 2, but it doesn't. You can switch calculation methods from Manual to Automatic and back again. You can choose the Options Calculate Now command all day, but the formula won't recalculate.

You can force recalculation of the formula in four ways. The first is to edit the cell that calls the macro, which always forces a recalculation. To do so, you can select the formula, click in the formula bar, and then simply press Enter to finish your "edit." (This recalculation method works, but if you have 2500 formulas in your worksheet, it can get tedious!)

To understand the second method, remember that formulas recalculate when a change has been made in the worksheet. Therefore, if you can't change the values in a worksheet, change the worksheet itself. In other words, when you insert or delete *any* cell in a worksheet, Excel recalculates every formula.

When you use this method to force a recalculation, select a cell below the active area, choose the Edit Insert command [PC—Ctrl-+ (plus); Mac—Command-I] to insert a new cell, and then press Enter to accept the suggestion to Shift Cells Down. If the calculation mode is set to Automatic, the worksheet recalculates immediately after the cell is inserted. Otherwise, choose the Options Calculate Now command [PC—F9; Mac—Command-=] to recalculate.

The third method depends on the fact that Excel recalculates every cell in which Formula Replace replaces something. You can use this fact to force all formulas in your worksheet to recalculate. You do so by replacing all equal signs with equal signs. (See Figure 3-2 on page 52.)

The fourth method is to insert a formula containing the VOLATILE function immediately after the last ARGUMENT formula in the function macro you want to recalculate. This causes the recalculation of any formula in a worksheet that contains the function, regardless of whether that function's dependent values have changed. Because the recalculation of a large number of formulas containing custom functions can take a long time, it's often better to use one of the other methods.

Adding convenience to function macros

We can create function macros that have the calculating power we need, but sometimes they don't have the convenience we would like. This section offers some techniques that will increase the power of your macros and make them more convenient to use.

Eliminating the filename

Using the Formula Paste Function command eliminates the need to enter long macro sheet, macro name, and argument lists into worksheet formulas, but you still spend time issuing the Paste Function command, scrolling through the list, and selecting the function. Why can't you enter a function macro without the macro sheet name?

Actually, you can. Two methods are available to do this. In the first, you save the macro sheet containing the functions you want to behave like built-in functions in the Add-In format, discussed in Chapter 12.

In the second method, you can define names to simplify the way you enter function macros. Remember that Excel lets you assign names on one worksheet that refer to names on another worksheet. This means that you can assign simple names on a worksheet that refer to the names of function macros on a macro sheet. And *this* means that you can hide the complexity of those filenames, allowing us to work with simple names on our worksheets.

Using macro functions in a worksheet.

At times, you might want to use macro functions within a worksheet. For example, you might want to monitor the memory available to a large worksheet. The macro function GET.WORKSPACE(16) returns in kilobytes the amount of available memory, but you can't use this function directly within a worksheet. This is no problem, however, because you can create the following two-line function macro that returns the information to the worksheet:

	A	B	C
1	fnc	**MemFree**	Returns amount of memory free, in KB.
2		=RETURN(GET.WORKSPACE(16))	

To use this macro, first name it and define it as a function macro. Within a worksheet, enter an external reference to the macro, completing the reference with a set of parentheses. For example, if you entered the macro on a macro sheet named MEM.XLM, the formula

```
=MEM.XLM!MemFree()
```

returns the available memory. Because the amount of available memory is liable to change frequently, this function macro is a good candidate for adding the VOLATILE function if you want constant updating of the amount of free memory.

For example, suppose you had a function macro named *MyFnc* on a macro sheet named MACRO1.XLM. Open or activate any worksheet. Choose Formula Define Name to access the Define Name dialog box, and define the name *MyFnc* as follows:

=MACRO1.XLM!MyFnc

To enter the function in the worksheet, you can enter the formula

=MyFnc(*arguments*)

as you would any predefined worksheet function—but only on the worksheet on which *MyFnc* has been defined as above. This method makes macro names short, easy to enter, and easy to read. They look like the names of Excel's predefined worksheet functions. In fact, if you define the names in uppercase letters, someone who isn't an Excel expert wouldn't know whether a formula was using function macros or predefined worksheet functions. But because this uncertainty could create long-term confusion, we recommend that you use uppercase and lowercase letters for function macro names.

4

Macro Programming Style

When you first start to write macros, the errors you make tend to be small and obvious. You misspell the name of a function, perhaps, or a function macro returns an incomprehensible value because you switched the order of its arguments. These errors soon become less of a problem. You'll still make them, of course—you'll *always* make them from time to time. But when you do make this type of error, you'll learn to recognize what you did wrong and fix it more quickly.

Over the long run, however, other types of macro problems tend to become more pervasive. If you don't use good design techniques, your macro sheets might become like bad translations of old German philosophers: You'll know what each word means, but you won't understand the idea that the words are intended to convey.

You can learn as much from studying poorly designed macros as you can from studying expertly engineered ones; that is, you can learn much about what not to do. Figure 4-1 presents the top-left corner of one of the macro sheets in the macro library that accompanied an earlier version of Excel for the Macintosh, *Worksheet Auditor*. (On the PC, the file was called AUDIT.XLM.)

File Edit Formula Format Data Options Macro Window

Normal

B27 =IF(B24=7,GOTO(go.forward))

AUDIT.XLM

	A	B	C	D	E	F	G	H	I	J	K
1	auto_open	Trace									
2	=ADD.COMMAND(1,"Fo&rmula",E	=IF(GET.WORKSPACE(15)<>3,AP	14	8	6	200	96	Worksheet Auditor			
3	=ADD.COMMAND(5,"Fo&rmula",E	=GET.WORKSPACE(14)-128	11						1		
4	=IF(A2<>15,DELETE.COMMAND(	=SET.VALUE(E29,B3)	12	16	21	184	18	&Report Errors			
5	=IF(A3<>11,DELETE.COMMAND(	=FULL(FALSE)	12	16	39	184	18	&Map			
6	=ADD.COMMAND(1,"Fo&rmula",E	=GET.WINDOW(3)	12	16	57	184	18	&Trace Cell Paths			
7	=ADD.COMMAND(5,"Fo&rmula",E	=GET.WINDOW(4)	12	16	75	184	18	&Worksheet Analysis			
8	=RETURN()	=GET.WINDOW(5)	1	220	6			OK			
9	auto_close	=GET.WINDOW(6)	2	220	30			Cancel			
10	=DELETE.COMMAND(1,"Fo&rmul	=SIZE(350,295)				288	120				
11	=DELETE.COMMAND(5,"Fo&rmul	=MOVE(132,1)	1	216	6	64	21	OK			
12	=IF(A4=FALSE,DELETE.COMMAN	=SHOW.INFO()	2	216	30	64	21	Cancel			
13	=IF(A5=FALSE,DELETE.COMMAN	=DISPLAY(TRUE,TRUE,TRUE,FAL	14	8	6	200	108	Audit Report			
14	=RETURN()	=MOVE(1,1)	13	16	21	184	18	&Errors			
15	Auditor	=SIZE(139,295)	13	16	45	184	18	References to &Blank			
16	=DIALOG.BOX(C1:I9)	=ACTIVATE(A19)	13	16	69	184	18	&Circular References			
17	=IF(A16=FALSE,RETURN())	=ECHO(TRUE)	13	16	93	184	18	&Names with Bad Ref			
18	=MESSAGE(TRUE,CHOOSE(I3,"E	=SET.VALUE(cell.list.pos,0)		1	164	168					
19	=GET.DOCUMENT(1)	=FALSE	3		4	150		Find &Dependents			
20	=REFTEXT(SELECTION())	=cell.list.pos+1	3		28	150		Find &Precedents			
21	=IF(I3<>3,ECHO(FALSE))	=cell.list.pos	3		52	150		&Reset Active Cell			
22	=LEN(A19)+2	=SET.VALUE(OFFSET(ColumnJ,c	2	48	76	70		Cancel			
23	=NOT(GET.WORKSPACE(4))	=SET.VALUE(E18,IF(others,B3-34	5	16	102	136		Retrace Past Move			
24	=CHOOSE(I3,Report,Map,Trace,V	=IF(others,DIALOG.BOX(C18:I28)	3	12	116	72		&Backward			
25	=MESSAGE(FALSE)	=GOTO(CHOOSE(B24+1,done.t,d	3	88	116	68		&Forward			
26	=FORMULA.FILL("",J1:M50)	=SET.VALUE(others,FALSE)	5	16	144	136					
27	=GET.DOCUMENT(1)	=IF(B24=7,GOTO(go.forward))	3	12	156	72		&Next			
28	=ACTIVATE("Audit.xlm")	=IF(cell.list.pos>1,SET.VALUE(ce	3	88	156	68		Pre&v			
29	=ERROR(FALSE)	=GOTO(B31)		1	164	168					
30	=SAVE.AS(,0)	=IF(cell.list.pos<cell.list.size,SET	5	24	6	152					
31	=ERROR(TRUE)	=SELECT(TEXTREF(OFFSET(Colu	1	8	24	72		Goto			
32	=ACTIVATE(A27)	=GOTO(main.loop)	2	88	24	72		Cancel			
33	=RETURN()	=IF(B24=9,1,-1)	15	8	51	152	84		2		
34	Report	=SET.VALUE(I33,I33+B33)				312					

FIGURE 4-1.
A section of the auditing macro from an old version of the Excel Macro Library. It serves as an example of how not to write macros.

The most obvious problem in the collection of macros shown in Figure 4-1 is its lack of documentation and formatting. It is difficult to distinguish where one macro ends and another begins, much less their purpose. None of the cells that hold macro formulas is wide enough to permit easy viewing of its contents. The system was built for speed and size: In earlier versions of Excel, a macro sheet took up less memory if the macros on it were crowded as close to cell A1 as possible. This collection of macros would be difficult for most people to understand, maintain, and debug if the need should arise. In the long run, time spent carefully designing, formatting, and documenting macros is time subtracted from tedious backtracking and debugging.

The most important step you can take to avoid errors is to make everything as clear and consistent as possible—the programming, formatting, naming conventions, and documentation. In this chapter, we'll discuss the various methods you can use to organize your macros, how to format and document them in a clear way, and other means of minimizing the potential for errors.

Designing modular systems of macros

If you're writing a macro longer than roughly 20 lines, it's probably better to break it up into two or more modules. Develop a system of short macros rather than one long macro. That is, if several different operations are involved in the process of arriving at a particular value, you most likely will improve the clarity of your program by isolating some of those operations as subroutines.

Thinking in terms of short macros with quick paybacks allows you to understand and immediately use what you've completed, one piece at a time. For example, suppose you need a macro to open a worksheet; print many different ranges on it; close it; and then open, print, and close a hundred other worksheets. First write a macro that can print one range. Then write a macro that tells the first macro to print all the ranges on one worksheet. Then write a macro that opens one worksheet and starts your print routine. Keep building in this way until your project is finished.

The modular approach also has the benefit of offering *repeatable code*—that is, a macro procedure that you can apply to more than one situation. Instead of reinventing the wheel every time you need a particular procedure, you can develop a general-purpose routine that saves you time and effort in the long run.

Types of hierarchical structures

When you design a series of macros that are intended to work together, it's usually best to work from the top down. That is, first describe the broad functions that the system needs. Then break down each function into more detailed procedures. The larger a system of macros is, the more its structure should resemble that of a pyramid. Breaking down a design into separate logical steps keeps the macro manageable and minimizes the addition of unnecessary steps.

Keeping macros modular also helps to organize your thinking about a large project. For example, if you wanted to create a macro that formatted a large document that included a table, you might want to create two formatting routines, one for the table's headings and one for the table's columns. Each uses relative addressing, relative to the top-left corner of the table. Then you could create an executive macro that calls the other two routines:

	ExecutiveMacro	
	:	
	=HeadingMacro()	When done, move active cell back to top-left corner.
	=ColumnMacro()	When done, move active cell back to top-left corner.
	:	

Because *HeadingMacro* and *ColumnMacro* both move the active cell back to the top-left corner of the table, you don't have to worry about where on the worksheet each macro will do its formatting.

What unifies a system of macros? For a large printing macro, it could be an overall procedure, organized as follows:

```
PrintingMacro
=PrintRegionReports()
=PrintRegionSummaries()
=PrintTotalReport()
=RETURN()
```

Or you could create a menuing system containing a series of the possible commands corresponding to the purpose of your application. For example, in a database application you could use the techniques described in Chapter 12, "Taking Action Through Macros," to create a new menu bar that replaces Excel's menu bar, listing the following commands:

File	Edit	Search	Sort	Report
Open	Add Records	Name	Name	Mailing List
Close	Delete Records	Address	ZIP Code	Directory
Delete	Copy Records	ID Code	ID Code	
	Move Records		Order Entry	

The macro that handles menu command selections then calls one macro that services each command; each of these could then call other macros, which in turn break that task into still smaller tasks.

How far you go with this, of course, is intimately connected with the size and complexity of the application you're developing, who you're doing it for, and the way you want to structure the user interface (that is, the look and handling characteristics of the application).

There are other ways of making a macro system modular, rather than breaking macros into smaller chunks. You can think of other objects in an application as modules as well: database worksheets, template worksheets, charts, scratch worksheets and temporary files, lookup tables, and so on.

Using a single routine for common actions

Often you'll find that several different macros require a common operation. Rather than writing the same macro several times, you can call the common macro from all macros that need it. For this reason, it is to your advantage to build macro systems containing short macros that each perform one general-purpose task. Each task can then be performed separately and is clearly understandable.

Systems that make extensive use of general-purpose routines are often best designed from the bottom up. The macro sheet shown in Figure 4-2 is a simple example of this type of hierarchical structure. The two shorter macros, *MoveDown* and *MoveUp*, call the third macro, *MoveIt*. Both *MoveDown* and *MoveUp* describe the broad steps of the desired actions, and *MoveIt* is a command macro acting as a subroutine, performing the more detailed actions common to the other two macros.

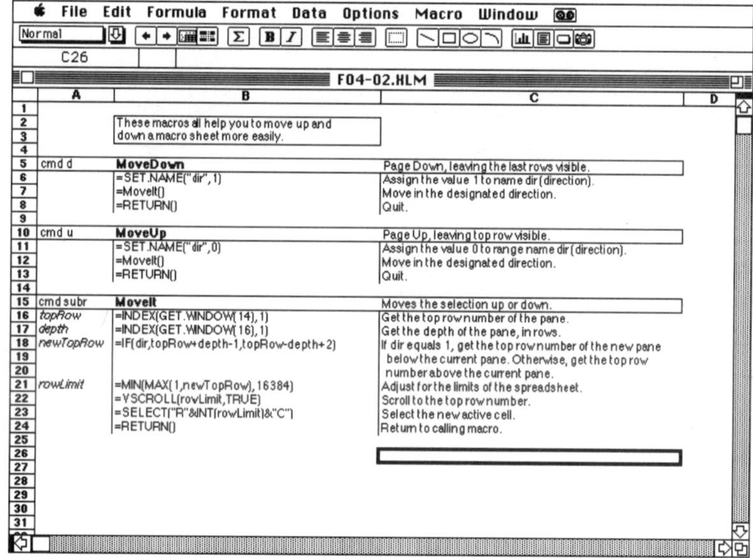

F04-02.HLM

	A	B	C
1			
2		These macros all help you to move up and	
3		down a macro sheet more easily.	
4			
5	cmd d	**MoveDown**	Page Down, leaving the last rows visible.
6		=SET.NAME("dir",1)	Assign the value 1 to name dir (direction).
7		=MoveIt()	Move in the designated direction.
8		=RETURN()	Quit.
9			
10	cmd u	**MoveUp**	Page Up, leaving top row visible.
11		=SET.NAME("dir",0)	Assign the value 0 to range name dir (direction).
12		=MoveIt()	Move in the designated direction.
13		=RETURN()	Quit.
14			
15	cmd subr	**MoveIt**	Moves the selection up or down.
16	*topRow*	=INDEX(GET.WINDOW(14),1)	Get the top row number of the pane.
17	*depth*	=INDEX(GET.WINDOW(16),1)	Get the depth of the pane, in rows.
18	*newTopRow*	=IF(dir,topRow+depth-1,topRow-depth+2)	If dir equals 1, get the top row number of the new pane
19			below the current pane. Otherwise, get the top row
20			number above the current pane.
21	*rowLimit*	=MIN(MAX(1,newTopRow),16384)	Adjust for the limits of the spreadsheet.
22		=VSCROLL(rowLimit,TRUE)	Scroll to the top row number.
23		=SELECT("R"&INT(rowLimit)&"C")	Select the new active cell.
24		=RETURN()	Return to calling macro.

FIGURE 4-2.
Two tasks that share a procedure.

MoveIt depends on the value assigned to *dir* (indicating direction) to determine the direction in which to move. If *MoveDown* and *MoveUp* were not structured in this way, each one would have required duplicating most of the formulas in *MoveIt*, increasing the size and complexity of the macro sheet by carrying the same procedure twice.

Managing macro libraries

If you aren't careful, you'll wind up with macro sheets sprinkled throughout your hard disk. Soon you won't remember what each one does or where it is when you need it. It's a good idea to maintain macro libraries—macro sheets that contain related macros. In this way, opening one macro sheet can make many related macros available to you.

How do you go about organizing the macros you create? You can organize them by function—for example, putting all your quick-and-dirty shortcut macros in one place. If you're developing a large application, on the other hand, you might need to put all of its parts on one macro sheet, and put all of its supporting documents in one directory. If memory is restricted on the machine for which you are developing an application, you might want to divide the various parts of a macro application over a series of small macro sheets, rather than require that a huge repository containing every routine be opened in order to perform one task.

Using a workspace to keep groups of documents together

When a worksheet always depends on a specific macro sheet, you can use a workspace to save both sheets. When you open the workspace, both the worksheet and the macro sheet open automatically. To use a workspace to save the sheets, simply choose File Save Workspace and follow the instructions in the dialog box. All open worksheets, macro sheets, and charts will be included in your workspace, so be sure that only those you want to include are open.

Saving macro libraries in the Add-In format

You can also use the Add-In format to save a macro sheet containing the macros you want to use. To save a macro sheet in the Add-In format, simply activate the macro sheet, choose the File Save As command, click the Options button, select the Add-In file format, and click both of the OK buttons.

When an Add-In macro sheet is opened, the function macros defined in it appear in the Paste Function dialog box as if they were one of Excel's built-in functions, instead of appearing at the end of the list. Also, Excel does not include the command macros defined in it in the Run dialog box; however, any shortcut key sequence you've assigned to a command macro still works. To call an Add-In macro, you simply leave off the filename; for example, if you had created a macro for returning the discount on a certain item given its inventory code, you might use the formula

```
=MACRO1.XLM!DiscountRate(invCode)
```

If the macro sheet was opened in the Add-In format, then the formula would appear as

```
=DiscountRate(invCode)
```

To open an Add-In macro sheet as a regular macro sheet again, choose File Open, select the name of the macro sheet, and then hold down the Shift key while clicking the Open button. When Excel opens the macro sheet, it is hidden; to unhide the macro sheet, choose the Window Unhide command.

The Excel Library contains a selection of command and function macros for performing a wide range of tasks. It also includes the Add-In Manager, which is useful for creating a set of macros that are opened whenever you or the user starts Excel.

Autoloading macro sheets

You can have Excel load macro sheets, worksheets, charts, Add-In macro sheets, and templates when the program is started by placing the desired files in Excel's startup directory. On the PC, this directory is called XLSTART, and it's placed within the directory that contains the Excel program itself. On the Mac, you use a folder called *Excel Startup Folder* within the System Folder on your hard disk.

Using an autoloaded system of worksheets and macro sheets is very useful when creating an Excel application for users who are not experienced with Excel. You can put in the startup folder an Add-In macro sheet containing an *Auto_Open* macro (discussed in Chapter 12), which is run when Excel opens the macro sheet. This *Auto_Open* macro can replace Excel's default menu commands with others, open templates, and effectively hide Excel itself from the user.

Macro formatting, documentation, and layout

Most people first write macros and add documentation and formatting after the macro is done—that is, if they do it at all. They document if there's time (there never is) and if there's nothing more interesting to do (there always is). A better way is to document and format as you write. This ensures that the job gets done, of course, but you'll also write better macros when you remind yourself through your documentation what you are doing and why.

It's true that documentation and formatting are often inconvenient and time-consuming, but they also offer many advantages. First, your own macros will look completely foreign to you several weeks after you write them. You'll be able to find your own errors and correct them if you document your macros carefully when the procedures are fresh in your mind.

Second, as you create new macros you'll often review related macros you created previously. By reading the comments next to each existing macro formula, you can often gain a point of reference for creating the new macros you need.

Third, as you read comments next to each macro formula, you'll occasionally notice comments that conflict with the formulas that they document, helping you identify errors that you might otherwise miss.

Fourth, you might need to write macros for others to use or macros that might be "inherited" by others who will fill your shoes. In this sense, accurate and detailed documentation is a service to others, as well as to yourself. If something changes in the way a macro must operate, clear and concise documentation helps another person make the necessary modifications without your involvement. A macro sheet such as the one shown in Figure 4-1 on page 70, on the other hand, might require your personal attention or, if you are no longer available, might be discarded in frustration. Proper documentation is, in effect, an investment in the future.

A macro formatting convention

There are many ways to format a single macro. Because Excel executes macro formulas in a strict top-to-bottom order and ignores text and empty rows within a macro, you have a great deal of freedom in arranging the macros, comments, and data on a macro sheet any way you want.

The worst case is to put macro formulas in one column, with no room made for comments, as shown in Figure 4-1. This figure shows macros lying in single columns, arranged in a side-by-side format, without any form of documentation beyond listing the name of the macro. Slightly better is putting all your macros in column A, one after another, because at least it's easier to insert and delete rows without interfering with the other macros on the macro sheet.

Figure 4-3 presents three macros that are similar to those we examined in Figure 4-2 on page 73 and that illustrate a convenient approach to formatting and documentation. (The Microsoft Excel Library contains a macro sheet template, called STRUCTM.XLT on the PC and *Structured Macro Template* on the Macintosh, that demonstrates a slightly different style and includes a handy macro for indenting macro formulas inside loops, discussed in Chapter 9.) This macro sheet uses three columns to present macros. To set up this macro sheet, open a new macro sheet and turn off the gridlines by choosing Options Display and deselecting Gridlines. Because the default Normal font for macro sheets is usually too large to display macros conveniently, reduce the font size to whatever works best for you. You can also set the column widths to whatever works best; a good starting place is to set column A to 6 and to set columns B and C to 20.

First of all, the titles of each macro contain a comment in column A indicating the type of the macro: function, command, subroutine, the associated command key, and so on. Column C contains a short description of the purpose of the macro. *MoveIt* is a command macro acting as a subroutine; it cannot be called by a key sequence because it uses an ARGUMENT formula that takes a number specifying the direction to move.

	A	B	C
1	cmd d	**MoveDown**	Page Down, leaving the last rows visible.
2		=MoveIt(1)	Move in designated direction.
3		=RETURN()	Quit.
4			
5	cmd u	**MoveUp**	Page Up, leaving top row visible.
6		=MoveIt(0)	Move in designated direction.
7		=RETURN()	Quit.
8			
9	cmd subr	**MoveIt**	Moves the selection up or down.
10		=ARGUMENT("dir")	Get the direction: 0=up, 1=down.
11	*topRow*	=INDEX(GET.WINDOW(14),1)	Get top row number of pane.
12	*depth*	=INDEX(GET.WINDOW(16),1)	Get depth of pane, in rows.
13	*newTopRow*	=IF(dir,topRow+depth-1,topRow-depth+2)	If dir equals 1, get top row number of new
14			pane below current pane. Otherwise, get
15			top row number above current pane.
16	*rowLimit*	=MIN(MAX(1,newTopRow),16384)	Adjust for limits of worksheet.
17		=VSCROLL(rowLimit,TRUE)	Scroll to top row number.
18		=SELECT("R"&INT(rowLimit)&"C")	Select new active cell.
19		=RETURN()	Return to calling macro.

FIGURE 4-3.
These macros illustrate effective documentation techniques.

In the *MoveIt* macro in Figure 4-3, column A beneath the title bar contains the labels assigned to the cells to the right in column B. By using column A for labels, you can take advantage of the Formula Create Names command to define all the labels in a macro quickly and easily. After entering names in column A and formulas in column B, you can select both columns A and B, choose the Formula Create Names command, select the Left Column option, and then click OK. When you choose the Formula Define Name command, you'll see all the labels entered in column A listed as names. If you select one of the names, the appropriate cell reference appears in the Refers To box.

What the labels refer to depends on the macro, of course; the cell to the right could be a constant value buried within the macro, or the result of a formula to be used in another formula elsewhere on the macro sheet. In other programming languages, the use of such a label is called a *variable.*

Column B contains the actual macro formulas. Above the formulas is the title of the macro. Assign the macro name to the cell that contains the title rather than to the first cell containing a macro formula. Doing so allows you to insert rows above the first macro formula or to delete the first row of formulas without having to change the cell to which you assigned the name.

Column C of each macro contains comments on the formulas in column B. If you find it's impossible to write an adequate description in the space available, you can break up the formula into sections that you can describe in short sentences or insert new rows to hold long comments. Remember that Excel ignores rows filled with anything other than a formula, so you can add as many rows as you want to explain each macro step, as shown in cells C14:C15 of Figure 4-3. Use this method sparingly, however, because it's difficult to follow macros that are frequently interrupted by blank rows, and each empty row within a macro slows its operation slightly.

You can also use the Formula Notes command to add a note to a prominent cell in the macro such as the cell containing the macro's title. Doing so lets you add more description to the macro without interfering with its operation. However, it's easy to overlook the notes, and you must make a special effort to look for and print notes after you print a macro. If the Note Indicator option is set in the Options Workspace dialog box, you'll see a red or black mark in the top-right corner of the cell containing the note. To view a note, simply double-click the cell, or choose the Formula Note command to see a list of all notes on the macro sheet.

Finally, you can add an outline border to the macro's title and left borders to columns B and C to make the structure of the macro stand out. To add an outline border to these sections, simply select them, type the slash command */TBO*, and press Enter.

Techniques for minimizing errors

This section presents techniques for preventing macro errors and for improving the clarity of your macros. First we'll discuss syntax errors, the most common type of error, and then we'll cover general tips for preventing the other types of macro errors.

Preventing syntax errors

If you're a beginning macro writer, you'll probably find that most of your macro errors are syntax errors. The following are some preventive measures for becoming syntax-error free.

Enter macros in lowercase letters

Always enter your macro formulas in lowercase letters. When Excel recognizes the names of built-in worksheet functions, macro functions, and references that you enter, it displays them in uppercase letters. Therefore, if you enter a function or cell address and it remains in lowercase letters, you'll know you made a spelling error.

Also, when Excel recognizes a macro name or defined name that you enter, it changes the format of the name to match the format in which it was originally defined. Therefore, if you capitalize the first letter of each macro name when you define it, as we do in this book, Excel uses that format for the name. If you later enter the name and it remains in lowercase letters, you either spelled it incorrectly or the name was not originally defined as you thought.

Use Formula Paste Function

When you first begin to write macros, it's a good idea to enter them in your macro sheet using the Formula Paste Function command with the Paste Arguments option selected. This practice aids in entering arguments in the correct order for the function. After Excel enters the argument list, you can simply double-click the name of each argument in the formula bar and enter a value, an expression, or a defined name that evaluates to an appropriate value for the argument.

Use the Recorder

When writing command macros, using the Recorder is a surefire way to avoid syntax problems with macro functions that perform actions in Excel's workspace. Excel not only enters the arguments in the correct order, it also supplies values for the arguments. Even when creating a macro that contains formulas that you can't enter with the Recorder, the Recorder is still helpful, because you can record a single-line macro in an area called *TestMacro,* for example, and cut the formula out and paste it into the macro on which you're working. This method works very well when you want a certain action to take place but you can't remember the name of the macro function that performs the action.

Enter RETURN in the middle of a macro to test part of a macro.

When you're writing a macro, you often need to test several rows in the middle of the macro. To start a macro elsewhere than its beginning, use the methods discussed in Chapter 2.

To designate where you want the macro to stop, simply insert a temporary row somewhere below this point and enter *=RETURN().* Then, after you've tested that section of the macro, delete the temporary row and continue programming.

Keep each line brief

In addition to writing short macros, it's best to enter short formulas within each cell of a macro. For example, in a given macro you could use the long formula

```
=SET.VALUE(INDEX(data,MATCH(MAX(data),data,0)),MIN(data))
```

But there are three very practical reasons for not doing so. First, combining several short macro formulas into one long macro complicates the debugging process considerably. With short formulas, you can switch from Formulas view to Values view to more easily find formulas that contain errors. If a long formula returns an error value, on the other hand, you have no way of knowing which part of the formula caused the error.

Second, using short formulas simplifies documentation, making it easier to describe in short sentences what each formula in the macro does.

Third, long formulas require extra space on the screen and when printed; they are often cut off by the right edge of the cell. If you print your macros in the three-column format described above, a succession of short formulas improves the readability of a macro dramatically.

A better way to arrange these formulas might be like this:

```
=MATCH(MAX(data),data,0)
=SET.VALUE(INDEX(data,up1),MIN(data))
```

where *data* is a range on the macro sheet and *up1* is a name for a relative reference to the cell above the active cell.

Use 0 for FALSE and 1 for TRUE.

One of the easiest ways to create long formulas is to use a series of TRUEs and FALSEs when specifying the arguments to a macro function. Because 0 evaluates to FALSE and 1 to TRUE, you can use these shorter values in your formulas instead. You can also use the Define Name command to assign the name *t* to the value *=TRUE* and assign *f* to *=FALSE,* but this technique can slow down a macro if used excessively. (See Chapter 16 for more information on making macros perform more quickly.)

Use named values instead of direct values

The formulas in macros often require the use of constant values. Most macro programmers insert the needed constants in each macro formula that needs them. This, however, is a bad practice; if a constant needs to be changed, every instance of the constant must be found and edited throughout the macro sheet.

Instead, you can enter the constant once in a macro sheet and use the Define Name command to assign a name to the constant, thereafter referring to the constant by its name rather than its value. There are two ways to do this. You can assign a name to the constant in the Define Name dialog box, but this requires opening the dialog box each time you want to find the value of a constant.

Alternatively, you can enter the constant in a cell on the macro sheet, enter the name of the constant in the cell to the left, and use the Create Names command (as described earlier) to assign a name to the cell containing the constant. When you refer to the stored value, you're actually referencing the cell. Using named references in this way can save time and increase the efficiency of your macros, especially if you use the same constant values repeatedly and want to change them globally later.

The use of named references also helps to document your macros. For example, if you wanted to use (in a series of function macros) the velocity of light in a vacuum, would *2.9997925E10* centimeters per second be clearer and easier to use than *lightSpeed*?

Use named ranges instead of direct cell references

It's always dangerous to link worksheets by using cell addresses rather than name definitions. If you were to enter a formula such as *=Sheet1!$A$3* in Sheet2 and then insert a row at the top of Sheet1, the formula in Sheet2 would not update to include the addition of the row. It would still refer to cell A3. However, if you assign a name such as *MyCell* to cell A3 and enter a formula such as *=Sheet1!MyCell* in Sheet2, the formula continues to reference the correct cell in Sheet1 wherever you move the name in the referenced worksheet.

Macros work in the same way. If you want a macro to refer to an area of a worksheet that might change its size or position, always define a name for this area of the worksheet and then refer to the area by name in your macro sheet.

Similarly, it is better to use names frequently within a single macro sheet, rather than using direct cell references in your formulas, for the same reasons it is better to use named constants. In Figure 4-1, for example, the extensive use of cell addresses rather than range names adds considerably to the task of deciphering the purpose and operation of a macro.

Test partial macros often

After you've written several lines of a macro, it's often a good idea to test them. By doing so, you'll catch errors early and save yourself the effort of rewriting many lines of a macro that might be built on error. Remember that you don't necessarily need to name a command or function macro in order to run one.

Normally you would run a command macro by using its shortcut key or by selecting its name from the list presented in the Macro Run dialog box. But what if you are in the middle of writing the macro and you want to test only a part of it? It's easy.

First, insert a row and add a RETURN function at the end of the segment you want to test, which you can delete as soon as you finish testing and are satisfied with the macro's operation.

Next, select the beginning cell of the segment, choose Macro Run [/MR], and press Enter. The selected cell is suggested in the Reference field of the Run dialog box as the starting cell of the "macro" to run, as shown below.

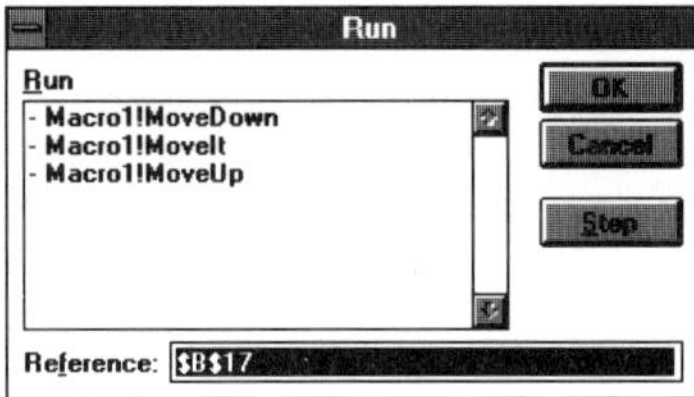

If the macro segment you are testing depends on the active cell being in a specific location, you can still use Macro Run. Select the cell that must be active when the macro is run, and choose Macro Run as before. Next, activate the macro sheet and click on the beginning cell of the macro you want to test: Excel enters the reference in the Reference field. Click OK or press Enter to run the macro from the indicated cell.

Test your assumptions

A computer consultant tells the story of a firm designing an expensive program for a large bank. The program worked well for several years until the day a clerk entered *Yes* in response to the prompt *Date:*. After six weeks of work, the consultant's team still hadn't corrected all the problems this trivial error caused.

The point is that whenever you write a macro, you make certain assumptions about the way it will be used. You have some idea of who will use it, how frequently it will be used, what type of data you will give it, and what conditions it will find. Your assumptions will usually be correct, but sometimes they'll be wrong. It's always a good idea to test the assumptions built into a macro when you can and then assume the worst. The following list presents some specific applications of this advice.

Use Input dialog boxes

The INPUT function (discussed in Chapter 11, "Presenting and Requesting Information") displays a dialog box that you can use to request data from the user. This function requires that you specify a data type or combination of types as you would when using the ARGUMENT and RESULT functions. Use this function to ensure that users enter the type of data you expect.

Test for errors

If your macro processes data that follows a particular format (for instance, a telephone number, social security number, or part number), be aware that a user might enter the data incorrectly. You can create a macro that validates the data and alerts the user if the format is incorrect.

Test boundaries

People often write macros to handle a certain amount of data and don't consider circumstances in which the amount of data might be abnormally large or small. How does your macro respond to a database that contains only one row of data or no data at all? If your macro prints expenses by department, can it handle the rare instance in which expenses equal zero? Can your macro process dates that occur after the year 2000? Is there a possibility of running out of memory while using your macro?

When you expect a *Yes* or *No* answer, provide for *Maybe*. That is, when your macro tests for one of two values, be sure it would also work correctly if a third value were to be entered. For example, you might assign the value 1 to a variable named *more* if the macro has more work to do, and you might assign 0 if the macro has finished its job. You can use an IF statement to provide an action for all possible values of *more*, as follows:

	A	B
82		=IF(more,DoMore(),CleanUpAndQuit())

If *more* equals 1, the macro branches to the *DoMore* macro; otherwise, it branches to the *CleanUpAndQuit* macro. Of course, if *more* does not equal 1, you expect it to equal 0. However, if *more* equals –1, the macro would still branch to the *DoMore* macro.

The macro would not run properly if your statements appeared as

	A	B
82		=IF(more=1,DoMore())
83		=IF(more=0,CleanUpAndQuit())

Here, if *more* equals any value other than 1 or 0, macro execution continues in cell B84.

The macro function CHOOSE can have problems similar to the Yes/No ones. For example, suppose the name *source* contains the value 1 to indicate an order from within your state, 2 to indicate an order from one of the other 49 states, and 3 to indicate a foreign order. And suppose you use the CHOOSE function to perform different actions depending on which value *source* contains. In this circumstance, be sure that you build your macro like this:

	A	B
45		=CHOOSE(source,InState(),OutOfState(),OutOfCountry())
46		*(action to take if* source *equals some other value)*

Most frequently, your macro will continue in cell B46 when *source* equals 0, meaning that someone didn't know where the order came from, or when it equals an error value. But this approach also protects you if someone decides to use the code 4 to indicate an order from a ship at sea.

5

Recovering from Errors

Despite all your precautions, your macro isn't working correctly. Now what? Don't panic! That's the first step. You've done something wrong. It's not the first time or the last time. It's certainly not the most serious thing you've ever done wrong, and it's probably one of the easiest to fix.

In this chapter, we cover the process of stopping a macro to find the source of an error, the use of Excel's Macro Debugger, and the common types of errors that are liable to occur.

Discovering errors

You discover an error during the execution of a macro in one of two ways: Either you notice that something is going wrong and want to stop the macro, or Excel encounters an error condition and stops the macro for you. The results in both instances are very similar.

To stop a macro during execution, press Esc [PC—also Ctrl-Break; Mac—also Command-. (period)]. When you stop the macro, Excel displays a dialog box like the one shown in Figure 5-1 on the following page.

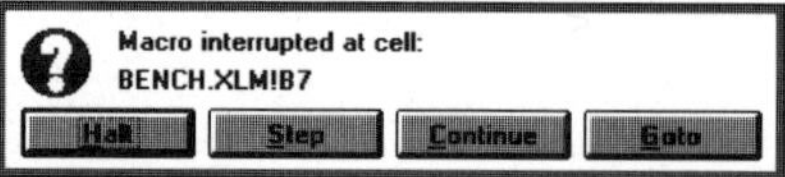

FIGURE 5-1.
This dialog box appears when you interrupt a macro.

If Excel encounters an error in a macro—a formula containing an argument that evaluates to an unacceptable data type, for example—it brings up an error dialog box that is almost identical to the one displayed when you stop the macro, as shown in Figure 5-2.

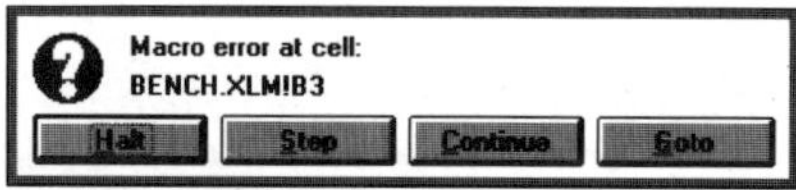

FIGURE 5-2.
This dialog box appears when Excel encounters an error.

In either case, both variants of the dialog box present buttons for halting the macro, stepping through the next formulas in the macro one formula at a time, continuing the macro, and jumping to the cell containing the formula that caused the macro to stop. To halt the macro, click Halt or press Enter. To resume execution of the macro, click Continue. To go to the cell that caused the error, click Goto.

If you click the Step button, you'll see a dialog box like the one shown in Figure 5-3, in which the Halt, Step, and Continue buttons are presented, although in a different order. The Single Step dialog box also displays the reference of the cell to be executed next and the contents of that cell. To step through the macro one instruction at a time, click the Step button repeatedly. As we discuss next, stepping through a macro can be a great way to debug a macro when something goes wrong.

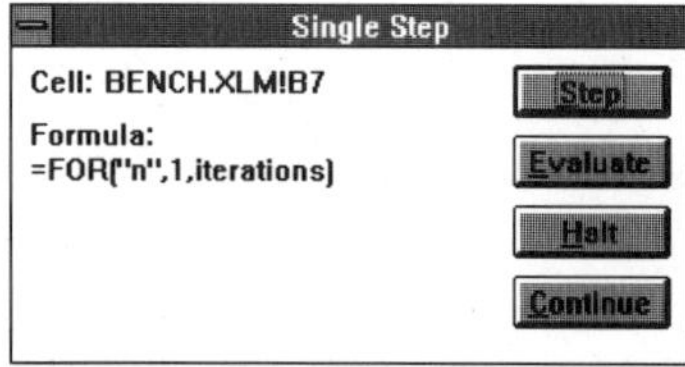

FIGURE 5-3.
The Single Step dialog box.

When you see Excel's error dialog box, it's often a good idea to do three things:

1. Note the reference of the cell that stopped the macro.
2. Halt the macro. (Although the error dialog box provides the opportunity to step through the macro at this point, we seldom choose this option because the first macro formula that Excel executes when you choose Step is the first formula *after* the one that caused the macro to fail.)
3. Switch to Values view of the macro sheet by pressing Ctrl-` (backquote) [Mac—also command -`] and look for error values in the cell that caused the error and in any cells referenced by the formula in that cell.

   At this point, you'll know where your macro went wrong, but you might not know why it did. The most common problems are incorrect syntax, incorrect cell references, and missing or incorrect data. As you research the problem, be open to all possibilities.

Viewing cells referenced in a formula.

If a cell containing a formula does not have an attached note, you can double-click the cell to jump to the cell named by the first reference in the formula. If the cell does have an attached note, Excel displays the Note dialog box.

Using the STEP function

The STEP function is probably the most valuable tool that Excel provides for debugging macros. This is particularly true because of the Evaluate button in the Single Step dialog box that appears when you use the STEP function.

Figure 5-4 on the following page presents the *Bottom* macro. This macro moves the active cell to the bottom row of the active window. Suppose, however, that you don't understand how this macro performs its calculation. You therefore decide to step through the macro one row at a time, watching its performance and trying to understand how it works.

To do this, insert a row in the macro where you want single-stepping to begin and enter the STEP function, as shown in cell B3 of Figure 5-4. When you run the

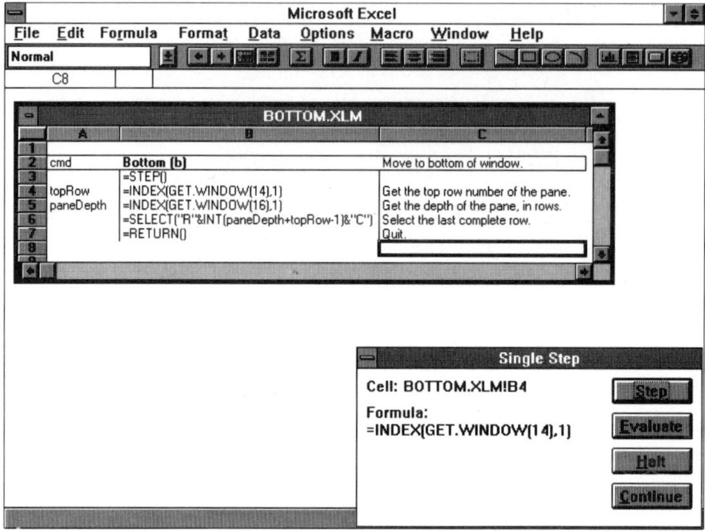

FIGURE 5-4.
When Excel encounters the STEP function in cell B3, it stops and displays the Single Step dialog box.

macro, the Single Step dialog box displays both the next cell that Excel will execute and the formula contained in the cell. You can step to the next cell in the macro, you can freeze the macro by clicking the Halt button, or you can move on without stepping by clicking the Continue button. Figure 5-4 really doesn't tell you much about how the macro operates. So you step to cell B5, and then to cell B6.

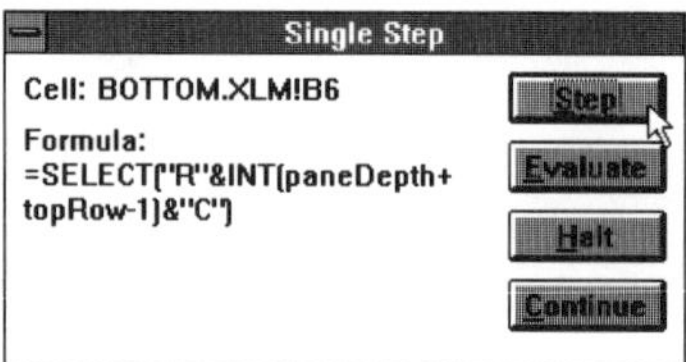

When you look at this dialog box, you suspect that this is the heart of the macro. This macro formula somehow converts *topRow* (cell B4) and *paneDepth* (cell B5) to a command to select the bottommost row. You begin to wish that STEP would provide not only the formula in a cell, but also its value. If it would do so, you could get a much better idea of how your macro works. This is the purpose of the Evaluate button. When you click the Evaluate button, the Single Step dialog box displays the intermediate values that produce the final result stored in the indicated cell.

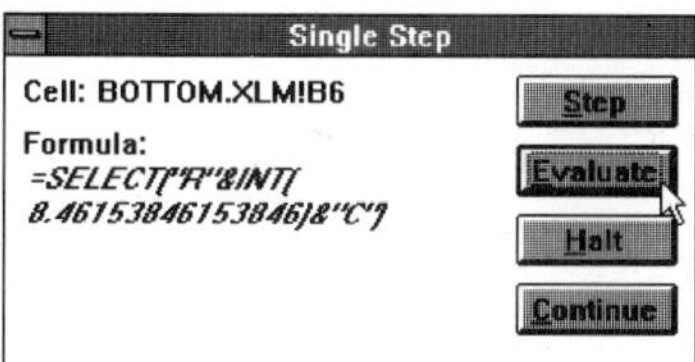

When you click the Evaluate button, Excel performs the first calculation, replaces the fragment of the formula that it evaluates with the results of the calculation, and then displays a revised formula in italics. Here, for example, it replaces *paneDepth+topRow−1* with *8.46…*, which is the row number at the bottom of the pane, plus the fractional amount of the next row showing in the pane.

If you click the Evaluate button again, you'll see this:

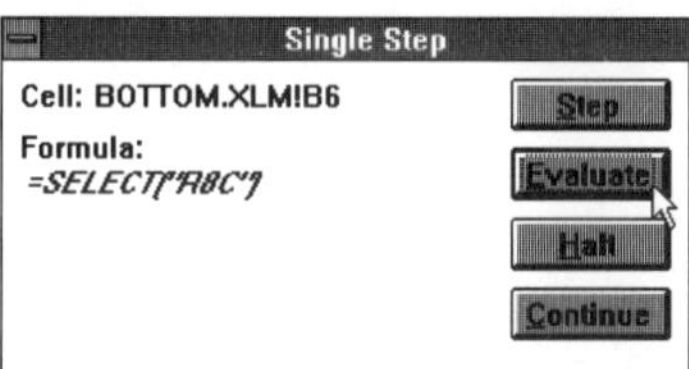

This time, Excel performs a text concatenation, replacing *"R"&INT(8.46…)&"C"* with *"R8C"*. This text represents the cell address (cell B8) at the bottom of the pane that the SELECT function should select.

For the third time, click the Evaluate button:

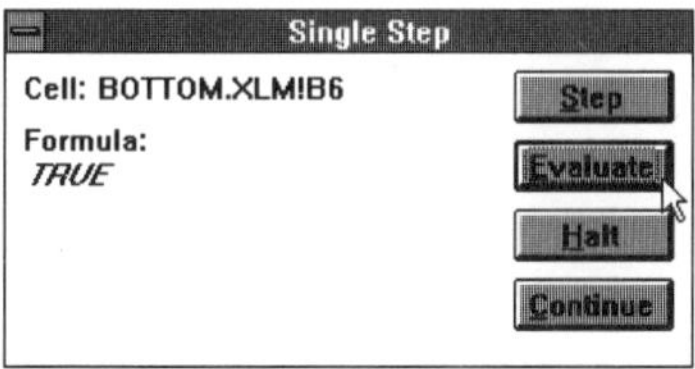

This time, the macro takes two actions. The macro actually performs the SELECT operation, selecting cell B8. It also displays the value *TRUE* in the Single Step dialog box, which is the value your macro displays if you switch to Values view after the macro is finished.

But then, just to see what happens, you click the Evaluate button one last time:

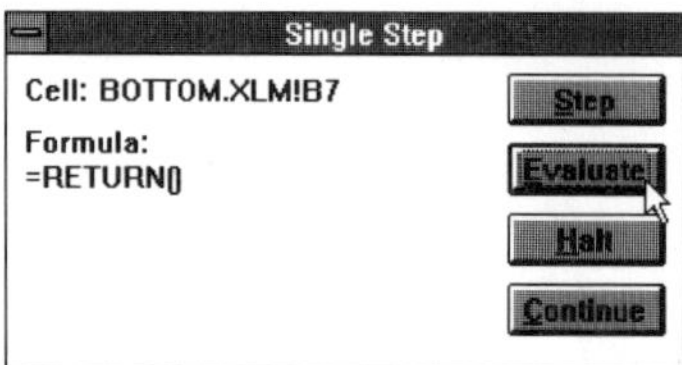

When you do so, you see that Excel displays the next macro step, which is what you would have seen if you had clicked the Step button rather than the Evaluate button back in Figure 5-4.

In other words, if you want to see the details of every calculation in every row of your macro, you can click the Evaluate button again and again. When you do, you'll probably learn more than you ever wanted to know about how a macro operates.

Using the STEP function in formulas

Most of the time, you'll use the STEP function as it's shown being used in Figure 5-4, by inserting a row and entering the function. Using this method, Excel single-steps the macro whenever it encounters the STEP function.

However, when you want better control of the STEP function, you can enter it within a formula, rather than by itself. For example, suppose you're working with a macro that changes all text in a selected range from uppercase to a mixture of uppercase and lowercase. To do so, the macro inspects each cell in the selected range and, if it's text, modifies it as needed. The macro works wonderfully until it reaches cell M205, for example, but you don't want to step through every cell that it modifies correctly until it reaches that cell. Instead, you could enter the following formula:

```
=IF(REFTEXT(ACTIVE.CELL(),TRUE)="$M$205",STEP())
```

This formula allows the macro to run unimpeded until it reaches the problem cell, and then it shifts into step mode.

Similarly, suppose a particular formula returns an error value occasionally, and you don't know why. The following formula shifts your macro into step mode when the error develops, allowing you to review the values returned by the macro formulas that lead up to the error:

```
=IF(ISERROR(B84),STEP())
```

At other times, you might want to insert a STEP formula in several places in your macro and then turn single-stepping on or off as needed. To do so, first define the name *stepIt*, to which you assign the value *1* when you want the STEP formulas active, and *0* when you want them inactive. Next, enter the following formula wherever you want to switch to single-stepping.

```
=IF(stepIt,STEP())
```

Creating one-line "micro-macros."

If you want to use the above formula repeatedly on a macro sheet without having to enter the formula over and over, you can use the Define Name command to assign a name to the formula in the Define Name dialog box—*doStep*, for example. Then, when you want to use the formula on your macro sheet, simply insert a new row and enter the following formula:

```
=doStep
```

When Excel executes this formula in a macro, it "looks up" the value of the name and executes the assigned formula, starting single-step mode if *stepIt* has been set to *1*. Of course, you can also apply this principle to create other kinds of one-line macros.

Monitoring values in a macro

When you're debugging a macro, you often need to monitor the values it generates—without slowing down the macro with a STEP command. Excel provides several tools to help you do this.

The Values view

One advantage in writing short macros is that you can monitor the results they produce by using the Values view of the macro sheet. You can use Values view in two ways. When your macro isn't running, you can press Ctrl-` (backquote) [Mac—also Command-`] to toggle from Formulas view to Values view. Press the key combination again to return to Formulas view.

You can use a similar technique to view values while the macro is running. Before you start the macro, you can use the Window New Window command to open a second window on the same macro sheet and then set one window to

Formulas view and the other to Values view. When you run the macro, you can monitor values by watching the window displaying the values. This technique is especially useful when you're single-stepping through a macro.

Using the SET.VALUE function

Occasionally, you'll need to monitor several values that are too far apart to appear at the same time on the screen. At other times, the values you need to monitor aren't normally displayed in the Values view of the macro sheet. In these circumstances, the SET.VALUE command can be a big help.

All you need do is set up a temporary area of the macro sheet to contain the values you want to monitor. If you want, add short labels for each value to remind you what they represent, and then insert rows where needed within the macro to enter the SET.VALUE formulas.

For example, suppose you set up a temporary viewing area at the bottom of a macro sheet. You want cell B232 to contain the row number of a cell address returned as text in cell B45, and you want cell B233 to display the name *testVal* defined in cell B128. You might therefore insert the following two formulas in the indicated cells:

	A	B
46		=SET. VALUE(B232,ROW(TEXTREF(B45)))
129		=SET. VALUE(B233,testVal)

To view the values in cells B232 and B233, you could simply scroll the window to this area before you run the macro, or you could open a second window on the macro sheet, which is set to Values view.

Using the MESSAGE function

When you run a macro, you often see a worksheet on the screen rather than the macro sheet. The MESSAGE function (discussed in greater detail in Chapter 11, "Presenting and Requesting Information") lets you monitor the operation of a macro even when you can't see the macro sheet at all.

The previous illustration, for example, used SET.VALUE to display two values in a macro sheet. Figure 5-5 shows that even if the rest of the screen is filled by a worksheet, you can still monitor the two values by using MESSAGE to display them in the status bar at the bottom of the screen. To do this, use string concatenation to combine several messages into one. (Chapter 7 contains a detailed discussion of string concatenation.)

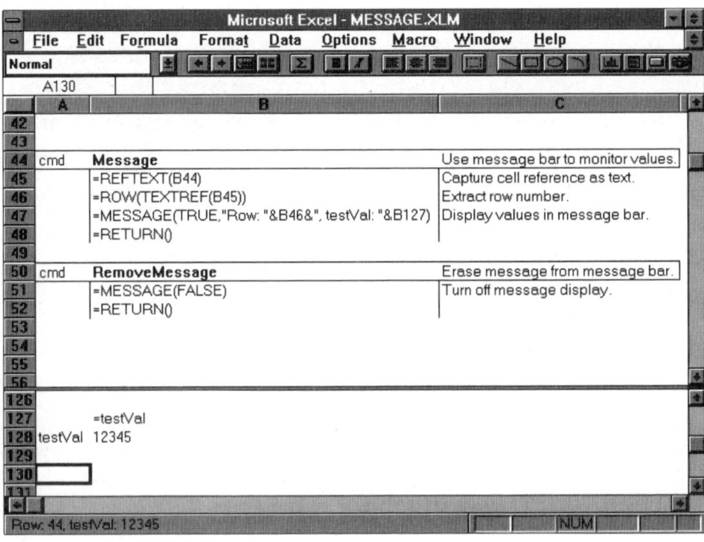

FIGURE 5-5.
You can use the MESSAGE function to monitor values in a macro when you can't see the macro sheet.

When using this technique, you're limited to about 50 characters of text. Also, Excel doesn't automatically clear the message when the macro ends. Therefore, you must use a macro to return the status bar to its normal state. To do this, you create a simple macro by entering the formula *=MESSAGE(FALSE)* followed by a RETURN function. You might think of entering the MESSAGE(FALSE) function at the end of the same macro used to display the message, but unless you had built an incredibly long macro, the message would be cleared so quickly you would never see it.

Using the Macro Debugger

One of the macros in the Excel Library is called DEBUG.XLA on the PC or *Macro Debugger* on the Mac. It provides three primary tools that are useful for debugging macros. With the Debugger, you can set what are called *debug points,* of which there are two types. When Excel encounters a *breakpoint,* the Debugger brings up a dialog box that lets you halt or single-step through the macro and also displays the values attached to certain names and references on the macro sheet that you specify. When Excel encounters a *tracepoint,* it displays the Single Step dialog box.

To use the Debugger, first open DEBUG.XLA or *Macro Debugger*. The Debugger contains an *Auto_Open* macro that adds a new command to the Macro menu, called Debug.

Next, activate the macro sheet you want to debug, and save a copy of it under a different name so that you're protected in the unlikely event that some obscure interaction between the Debugger and your macro corrupts the contents of your macro sheet. Be sure that document protection is off, because the Debugger alters the formulas on the macro sheet.

Finally, choose the Macro Debug command. The macro sheet replaces Excel's standard menu with the Debug menu bar, which contains three menus: Debug, Formula, and Display.

The Debug menu

The first choice, Debug, offers most of the commands you'll use for debugging a macro. We'll cover them in the order you'll most commonly use them.

Set Breakpoint

To use this command, select a cell in the macro that you want to be a breakpoint. When you choose the Set Breakpoint command, Debugger presents a dialog box requesting an identifying message.

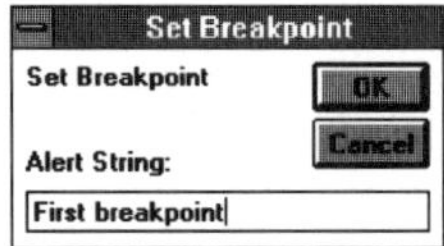

You can use this message to identify the area of the macro that is currently being executed. After you type the message and press Enter, Debugger modifies the formula to create a dialog box containing the message you've entered. For example, if the original formula had been

```
=SELECT("RC")
```

the new formula would be

```
=IF(DEBUG.XLA!breakpt(1),SELECT("RC"))
```

When you run the macro and Excel encounters this formula, it calls up an alert box similar to this:

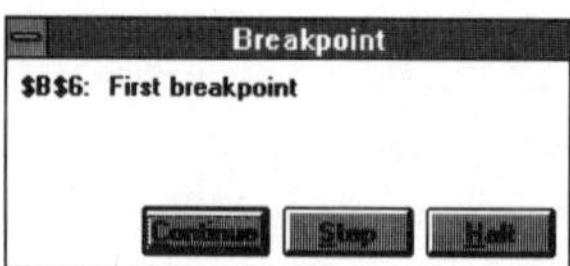

The Breakpoint dialog box displays the message, as well as the values of the specific macro cells or names that you had previously chosen with the Breakpoint Output command (discussed below).

At any breakpoint, you can choose to continue, single-step, or halt the macro. If you click the Step button, Excel presents the standard Single Step dialog box for you to step through the next formulas in the macro.

Breakpoint Output

When you choose the Breakpoint Output command on the Debug menu, the Debugger presents a dialog box that requests a list of cells and names that Debugger displays in the Breakpoint dialog box. You can enter a defined name or reference in the Breakpoint Output dialog box's Variable field, or you can click in a cell to enter its reference and then click the Add button to add the reference or name to the list, as follows:

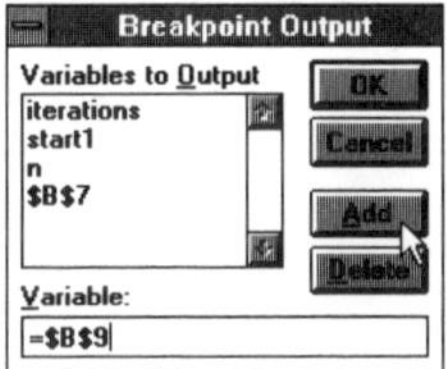

When you run the macro and Excel encounters a breakpoint given in this list, the corresponding Breakpoint dialog box looks like this.

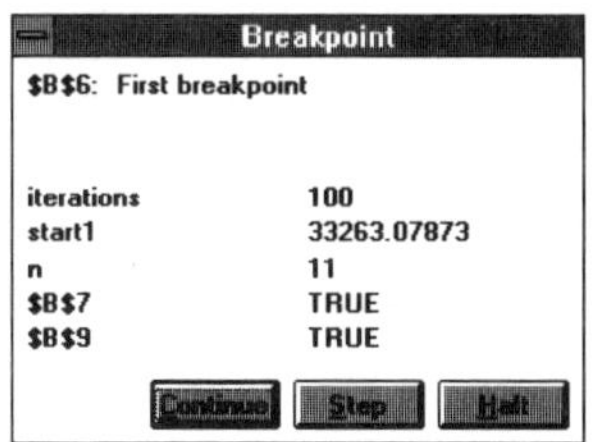

To delete a name or a reference, select it in the Breakpoint Output dialog box and click the Delete button.

Set Tracepoint

What the Debugger calls a tracepoint is simply a cell in the macro where the Debugger adds a STEP function to the contents of the cell. For example, if you set a tracepoint in a cell where the original formula was

```
=SELECT("RC")
```

the macro formula after setting the tracepoint would be

```
=IF(STEP(),SELECT("RC"))
```

Because execution of the STEP function in the first part of the IF function always evaluates to TRUE, Excel always executes the SELECT function in the second part of the IF function.

Run Macro

This command calls up the Run dialog box; you can use the command, or you can invoke the macro you want to test through the command's shortcut command key sequence.

Erase Debug Point

The Erase Debug Point command removes the modifications the Debugger has made to the selected cell, if any. To use the command, select a breakpoint or tracepoint in the macro and choose this command.

Exit Debug

This command serves two purposes. First, it changes all formulas that Debugger has modified back to their original forms. Second, it replaces the Debugger menu bar with the normal Excel menu bar.

The Formula menu

Because you can't use the normal Excel menus when you use Debugger, the Formula and Display menus offer certain commands from Excel's normal menus that you might need as you debug a macro. The Note, Goto, and Find commands are the equivalent of the same commands on Excel's normal menu bar. The Hidden Names command displays a dialog box listing the hidden names defined in the Excel workspace, if any, and their definitions.

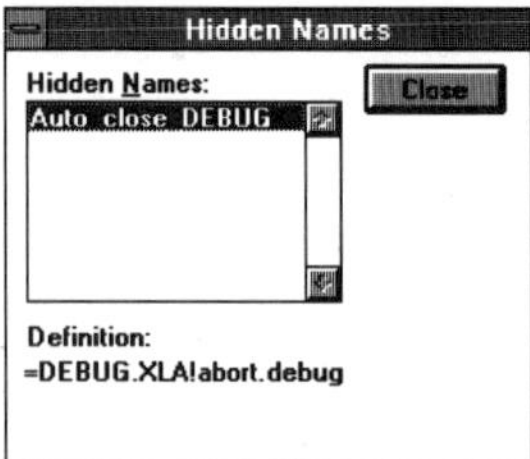

The Select Errors command is the same as selecting the Errors option in the Select Special dialog box. The Select Debug Points command is similar, but it selects all the breakpoints and tracepoints on the macro sheet.

The Display menu

The Formulas Values command is the equivalent of setting or unsetting the Formulas option in the Options Display dialog box. However, it's usually easier to press Ctrl-` [Mac—also Command-`] to toggle the display from Formulas view to Values view and back again. The Arrange All command is the equivalent of the same command on Excel's normal Window menu. Finally, the Show Info command is the equivalent of the same command on the Window menu.

Should you use Debugger?

As nifty as the Debugger is, it has a few drawbacks that might make you decide to use one of the other debugging methods described in this chapter. First, Debugger denies you access to almost all of Excel's menu commands, which can often seem restrictive. Second, because Debugger protects cells containing debug points, it doesn't let you fix the errors in those cells that the Debugger might help you find.

The third drawback is that the job of debugging can become more complicated rather than simpler when you're using a macro whose details you don't fully understand to help debug a macro you also don't understand. Fourth, and most important, the main benefits the Debugger provides are those that are easy to add by using the other techniques described in this chapter.

Nevertheless, the Debugger is worthwhile as a teaching tool. You can learn much about macro programming by documenting the Debugger and experimenting with the macros in it until you know how everything works. Be sure you work with a copy of the original version, however. To open the copy as a normal macro sheet instead of as an Add-In, hold down the Shift key while you double-click the name of the macro sheet in the File Open dialog box. Next, choose the Window Unhide command, select the macro sheet, and click OK. By the time you're finished with your explorations, you'll know more about macro programming than you ever thought possible.

Redisplaying the Debug menu if your macro changes the menu bar.

What do you do if you're debugging a macro that uses the techniques we describe in Chapter 12, "Taking Action Through Macros," to create or alter the menu bar? The Debugger contains a macro called *Restore,* which reconstructs the Debugger's menu bar. You can run this macro through the Run dialog box or by pressing Ctrl-Shift-r.

Common macro problems

When you look for bugs, it often helps to have a good idea of the kinds of problems you might find. Otherwise, you might stare for hours at an "obvious" bug before you ask yourself, "I wonder if this is the problem?" Let's take a short look at quick fixes to the most common problems that can occur in your macros.

The macro won't run at all

This is an easy problem to solve because there are only two possible causes: problems with the way the macro was defined or a problem with the macro that creates the illusion that the macro didn't run at all.

Problems with the macro's name and shortcut key sequence

This is by far the most common source of the problem. To investigate, first activate your macro sheet, choose Formula Define Name, and then select the name of the problem macro in the Define Name dialog box.

In the dialog box, check for the following:

- If you've called the macro as a subroutine from another macro, is the name of the macro correct?
- Is the reference specified in the Refers To field correct? This reference ought to be the cell containing the macro's name, above the first formula in the macro.
- For a command macro, is the shortcut key correct? (Be sure that you haven't entered an uppercase command key when you've been using a lowercase key.)
- Does the macro have a name? If you can't find the name, that's your problem! You (or someone) forgot to assign a name to the macro.

If two macros have the same shortcut key, Excel runs the macro whose external reference is listed first in the Macro Run dialog box. If the macro doesn't run when you press the shortcut key, you might be trying to run another macro that has its own problems or that did something other than what you expected to see.

Problems with the macro

Occasionally, a macro might start and then stop for some reason, making it seem that the macro never ran in the first place. To test this possibility, use the techniques described on page 82 (under "Test Partial Macros Often") of Chapter 4 to run the macro without using its name at all. If the macro runs using this technique, you know there's something wrong with the macro's name. If it doesn't run, you know there's something wrong with the macro.

The wrong macro runs

If the wrong macro runs, you have three possible problems. First, you might have duplicate shortcut keys. Second, the macro's name might have been defined by referencing the wrong cell on the macro sheet. And third, you've started the correct macro, but it might branch to the wrong macro for some reason. To test this last possibility, try running the macro without using its range name.

You can't enter a macro formula

This problem can be very frustrating. You type in a formula and press Enter. But rather than accepting your formula, Excel beeps at you and then selects some area of the formula. Now what?

Check parentheses and quotes

Every left parenthesis that you enter, of course, must have a matching right parenthesis. When you enter a left parenthesis in a formula, Excel momentarily puts in boldface the matching right parenthesis. If you suspect a missing parenthesis, you can use the direction keys to move the insertion point back and forth in the formula bar. (In Mac Excel, press Command-U to activate the Edit mode, which allows you to use the direction keys in the Formula bar.) When the insertion point crosses over a parenthesis, Excel displays both it and its mate in boldface. Similarly, every quotation mark in a formula should have a matching partner.

Matching parentheses is easy to do when you enter short formulas but is more difficult to do when entering long ones. The fact that you have a long formula with a parenthesis problem is probably a clue that you should split up the formula and distribute it over two or more cells. However, suppose that Excel won't let you enter a long formula because you need to add one more right parenthesis, and you can't figure out where it goes. Here are two tricks to help you solve this problem.

The first trick is to start over and enter the long formula in pieces, working from the inside out. For example, to enter the formula

```
=SET.VALUE(INDEX(data,MATCH(MAX(data),data,0)),MIN(data))
```

in pieces, enter the simplest function first:

```
=MAX(data)
```

and then edit this formula to surround it with the second function:

```
=MATCH(MAX(data),data,0)
```

and then edit that formula to surround it with the next function, and so on.

The second trick doesn't force you to start over; however, you still simplify the formula by working with it a piece at a time. To use this trick, first select the simplest complete function in your formula bar, and then press F9 [Mac—also Command-= (equal sign)], which causes Excel to calculate the function you selected and replace the function with its result.

Next, select the simplest expression that remains, and repeat the process. Repeat the process as often as necessary until Excel returns an Error In Formula dialog box, which tells you that the syntax is incorrect within the selected area. Because this area is the simplest piece of a simplified formula, you should have no trouble deciding how to fix the error.

To enter the complete formula, first press Esc to discard your edits and restore the original formula. Using what you've learned from collapsing the long formula into its values, correct the original formula and enter it again.

Check syntax

The term *syntax* means the way words are put together to form sentences and phrases. In macro programming, however, the term refers to the way that macro functions and their arguments are put together to form macro formulas.

You'll often have syntax problems: not providing a macro function with enough arguments or specifying the wrong type of argument. If you suspect that this is the case, turn immediately to the documentation (or to Appendix B of this book) to check the proper syntax of the function.

If you seem to have entered the correct number of arguments, and they seem to be in the correct order, pay particular attention to the types of arguments that you've entered. That is, be sure that for each argument you've entered text, references, or values where necessary, or that you've provided values that Excel can convert to the needed type, as shown in the following table.

from...to	**Number**	**Text**	**Logical**
Number	*no conversion*	Excel converts the number to text.	Excel converts 0 to FALSE and any other number to TRUE.
Text	Excel converts the text to a number if the text is in a valid number format.	*no conversion*	Excel converts only the values "TRUE" and "FALSE".
Logical	Excel converts TRUE to 1 and FALSE to 0.	Excel converts TRUE to "TRUE" and FALSE to "FALSE".	*no conversion*

For example, Excel refuses to accept the formula

```
=REFTEXT("Trash")
```

because the function expects you to provide a reference that it can convert to text.

Many functions require a cell address as an argument in the form of text, others require that a cell address always be in the form of a reference, and others allow either form.

For example, the reference argument in DEFINE.NAME allows a cell address to be either text or reference. SET.VALUE requires that its cell address be in the form of a reference only. And ABSREF requires that references be entered as text for the first argument and as a reference for the second argument. If you use the wrong type when you enter any of these functions, you're going to generate errors.

Here are some general guidelines to help you decide which type of argument to use.

- Cell addresses entered as text usually refer to the active worksheet. Usually, these addresses must be in R1C1 style rather than A1 style.
- Cell addresses entered as simple references (D3, for example) usually refer to the macro sheet. For cell references to apply to some other worksheet, enter them as external absolute references. For example, the reference Sheet5!$D$3 refers to cell D3 on the Sheet5 worksheet, and the reference !$D$3 refers to cell D3 on the active worksheet.
- Functions that can refer only to the macro sheet (SET.VALUE, for example) or only to the active worksheet (DEFINE.NAME, for example) have their own rules. To provide additional guidance, Chapter 7 discusses the use of cell references in macros.

Enter formulas in pieces

In the previous chapter, we recommend that you enter short formulas so that you can document and debug them easily. Another reason for doing so is that you'll often introduce syntax problems if you try to enter formulas that are long and complicated.

Spelling errors

As we mention earlier, you can minimize spelling problems by entering formulas in lowercase. When Excel recognizes the names of the standard functions and macro functions you type in, it displays them in uppercase. When Excel recognizes the defined names and macro names you enter, it displays them using the capitalization used when the names were defined. If you use the naming convention we use in this book, macro names will appear with initial caps (for example,

DoItNow), and defined names will remain in lowercase with internal capitals but without an initial cap (for example, *thisValue*)—and both take italics.

Eliminate the equal sign.

At times, you'll want to "turn off" a macro formula. For example, you might use *=ECHO(FALSE)* in a macro to freeze the screen and make the macro run faster. When you're debugging the macro, however, you want to watch Excel update the screen.

To turn off any macro formula, simply edit the formula and delete the = (equal sign), turning the formula into text. Later, when you want to turn the formula back on, simply insert the = (equal sign) again.

Names that duplicate functions

If your macro starts to behave so strangely that you wonder whether your computer is working properly, you might have assigned the name of an Excel function to one of your macros.

For example, suppose you have a macro system that updates many worksheets with data from one worksheet. Furthermore, suppose that because one of the macros in this system closes a worksheet after it's updated and then returns you to the worksheet with the data, you call the macro *RETURN*. Of course, as soon as you try to call this macro using the formula *=RETURN()*, the result will be different from the one you expect.

Specify names as text

In Excel, when you refer to the name of a range, rather than to its definition, you often must enter the name as text. If you forget this fact, you'll create bugs that will drive you crazy.

For example, to assign the value 3 to the name *test* in a given worksheet, you use the formula

```
=DEFINE.NAME("test",3)
```

To begin a FOR-NEXT loop using the name *count* as the counter, you use the formula

```
=FOR("count",1,10)
```

But if you forget to enter the quotation marks in these formulas, the results could surprise you.

If either of these names had not been defined previously, entering these formulas on a macro sheet returns a *#VALUE!* error. This error is bad enough, because when you're new to Excel macros these missing quotation marks are easy to overlook, and consequently there appears to be no reason for the error value returned. If, however, the names *test* and *count* had been defined previously, this macro error can generate bizarre results.

For example, suppose you had previously defined *test* as cell B3, and this cell contains the text *Income Statement*. Here's what happens if you use the following macro formula:

```
=DEFINE.NAME(test,3)
```

Because you did not enclose *test* in quotation marks, Excel thinks you want to define a name using the contents of the name *test* on the macro sheet. Therefore, because *test* contains the text *Income Statement*, the macro defines the name *Income_Statement* on the active worksheet and assigns it the value 3.

SECTION TWO

Basics

6

Working with Text Formulas

As you've already learned in the previous chapters of this book, in Excel you can manipulate text as well as numbers. Because you'll make extensive use of this capability whenever you write macros, this chapter explains text handling in greater detail.

Using text in formulas

Text is easy to manipulate—you simply string blocks of it together like boxcars on a railroad, joining each block of text with an ampersand (&). For example, to join the text *Hi* with the text *There*, enter the formula

```
="Hi"&"There"
```

to get the result

```
HiThere
```

To make the result more readable, you could insert a space between the words by using

="Hi"&" "&"There"

to get

Hi There

Of course, you can also use cell references to join (concatenate) your text. For example, suppose the following cells contained the data shown:

	A
4	Mom
5	="Dad"

You could enter the formula

="Hi"&" "&"there"&", "&A4&" and "&A5&"."

to obtain the result

Hi there, Mom and Dad.

Notice in this example that cell A4 contains the value *Mom* and that cell A5 contains the formula *="Dad"*, which evaluates to the value *Dad*. Either way works.

Manipulating numbers as text

First-grade students struggle with the concept that "two" is the name of that number and that "2" is its picture. Similarly, people who are new to spreadsheet programs often struggle to learn the difference between the number 2 and the textual character "2."

The reason this difference matters is that number formulas can only calculate values and textual formulas can only manipulate text. However, Excel can *coerce* numbers into text and back again, which makes the difference between values and text nearly transparent and often confusing.

To better understand how this feature works—that is, how this coercion takes place—let's take a moment to see how most spreadsheet programs convert numbers to text and back again.

In Lotus 1-2-3, as in most other spreadsheet programs, you must explicitly convert numbers to text before you can manipulate them in text formulas.

Suppose, for example, that cell A6 contains a formula that returns the number 5, and that you want to enter a formula that refers to this cell and that returns *The answer is 5*. Lotus 1-2-3 requires that you use a special function to change the number 5 into the text *5* before you can use the character in a text formula. For example, in 1-2-3 you would need to enter a formula like this:

```
+"The answer is "&@STRING(A6,0)
```

Here the @STRING function converts the value in cell A6 to text (also known as a *string* value), displaying the value with 0 decimal points.

However, in Excel you need merely enter this formula:

```
="The answer is "&A6
```

Both formulas convert the numeric value 5 to the text value *5* before they concatenate the text with *The answer is.* However, Excel transforms (that is, coerces) the number into text.

The same method works in reverse. For example, suppose that cell B3 contains the text *99*. To add 1 to this number in Lotus 1-2-3, you would enter the formula

```
@VALUE(B3)+1
```

But in Excel, you can enter this formula instead:

```
=B3+1
```

Both formulas evaluate to *100*. However, unlike 1-2-3 and most other spreadsheets, Excel does not usually require an explicit conversion from text to numbers. In a sense, the program does what you want it to do, not what you've told it to do.

Translating from text to numbers and vice versa

When Excel coerces a value into text, the program adds no special formatting. Particularly in macros, this lack of formatting is a desirable feature.

For example, suppose you want a macro to select an area in column A on the active worksheet that extends from the row that contains the active cell to the topmost row of the range name *bottom*. To make this occur, you could use these two macro formulas in the cells shown:

	A	B
10		=ROW(!bottom)
11		=SELECT("RC1:R"&B10&"C1")

Here cell B10 returns the row number of the topmost row in the range name *bottom* on the active worksheet, and cell B11 uses this value to calculate the range to select. If Excel added any formatting when it coerced the number into text in cell B11, the SELECT formula would return an error value.

However, you'll often need to format a number when you convert it to text. To do so, use the TEXT, DOLLAR, or FIXED function.

TEXT(valueN,formatT)

The TEXT function is the most useful of these functions by far. It converts the number given in *valueN* to text according to the number format specified by *formatT* in the same way that the Format Number command assigns number formats. There are, however, three exceptions.

- You cannot use TEXT to format a number as General. (Normal coercion does that, however.)
- You cannot use the asterisk (*) character to repeat symbols within the number format.
- You cannot use the color specifiers in the *formatT* argument. For example, the formula

  =TEXT(999,"[RED]#")

  doesn't carry its "redness" with it.

DOLLAR(valueN,*decimalsN*)

The DOLLAR function converts an expression that evaluates to a number, *valueN,* to a text string in the currency format. Excel rounds the number to the number of digits to the right of the decimal point specified by *decimalsN*; negative numbers round to the left of the decimal point. The default number format used is

$#,##0.00_);($#,##0.00)

FIXED(valueN,*decimalsN*)

The FIXED function is similar to DOLLAR, but it simply rounds the number to the specified number of decimal places to the right of the decimal point, adds commas where appropriate, and returns the result as text. For example,

=FIXED(–1003.14159,4)

evaluates to *–1,003.1416.*

VALUE(valueT)

Excel also includes the VALUE function, which converts text that looks like a number to a number. But as we've already seen, when you use the textual number as a value, the program coerces the text into a value anyway. Why, then, does this function exist?

There seem to be two reasons. First, the function is included for clarity. In a complex text formula, it might not be clear to people who read the formula that a numeric value is intended. Using the VALUE function leaves no doubt. Second, it is included in order to be compatible with spreadsheets such as Lotus 1-2-3 that require the VALUE function.

Suppressing text coercion

Occasionally, you might want to keep Excel from coercing text into values and vice versa. To prevent this coercion, use the T and N functions.

T(valueN)

In a sense, the T function tests whether *valueN* is text. That is, if *valueN* evaluates to text, the function returns that text. If it evaluates to any other type of value, such as numeric or logical, T returns a null string.

For example, suppose that cell A5 contains the number 5. We've already seen how the formula

```
="The answer is "&A5
```

would return *The answer is 5* because Excel coerces the number 5 into text. However, if you wanted to suppress this coercion, you would enter this formula:

```
="The answer is "&T(A5)
```

which would return this result:

```
The answer is
```

N(value)

The N function converts *value* to a number. As with the T function, you could consider it a way of testing whether *value* is already a number. If *value* is a number or a serial date, N returns that number; if *value* is TRUE, it returns the value *1;* if anything else, including text, it returns *0.*

For example, suppose cell B3 contains the formula

```
="99"
```

If you entered the formula

```
=B3+1
```

somewhere in a worksheet, the formula would evaluate to *100*, because Excel coerces the text value entered in B3 into the numeric value 99. However, if you entered the formula

```
=N(B3)+1
```

the formula would evaluate to *0.*

Searching for text

The functions FIND and SEARCH perform a very similar task: They both find one text string within another and return the position in the string where the beginning of the matching text was found.

FIND(findT,withinT,*startAtN*)

The FIND function finds *findT* within *withinT* and starts the search at character *startAtN* of *withinT*. The function is case sensitive, which means that the formula

```
=FIND("A","aaaa")
```

returns the #VALUE! error value because "A" does not equal "a". For example, cell A5 in the following macro fragment evaluates to *9*, and cell A6 evaluates to *13*.

	A	B
5		=FIND("!","COST.XLS!R5C3")
6		=FIND("C","COST.XLS!R5C3",A5)+1

In the example for cell A5, the FIND function finds the exclamation mark that separates the filename from the cell reference and returns its position as *9*. The formula in cell A6 uses this value to find the starting position of the column number within the reference. In other words, the second formula ignores the first "C" because it starts looking after the ninth character, the exclamation point.

SEARCH(*findT*,withinT,*startAtN*)

The SEARCH function is similar to FIND, but it is not case sensitive, which means that the formula

```
=SEARCH("A","aaaa")
```

evaluates to *1*. Unlike the FIND function, SEARCH can contain wildcard characters. The wildcard ? refers to any single character and * refers to any sequence of characters, as the following examples demonstrate.

	A	B	C
1		=SEARCH("C","Microsoft")	evaluates to 3
2		=SEARCH("o*t","Microsoft")	evaluates to 5
3		=SEARCH("o*t","Microsoft",6)	evaluates to 7
4		=SEARCH("o*z","Microsoft")	evaluates to #VALUE!
5		=SEARCH("c??s","Microsoft")	evaluates to 3

Extracting sections of text

Often in macros you need to extract a section of text from a longer section. To do so, you'll often use the FIND function along with the LEN, RIGHT, LEFT, and MID functions.

LEN(text)

The LEN function returns the number of characters in text. For example,

=LEN("1234")

evaluates to *4*.

RIGHT(text,*charsN*)

returns the *charsN* rightmost characters in *text*. For example,

=RIGHT("1234",2)

evaluates to *34*.

As an example of using both LEN and RIGHT in a macro, suppose you want to return all but the first character from a text string. This occasionally happens when an expression has been entered as a formula in a cell, and you want to eliminate the equal sign before it so that the expression alone remains. For example, suppose cell D4 on the worksheet contains the formula =D3*2. You could use the following sequence of macro formulas to extract the expression.

	A	B	C
4		=SELECT("R4C4")	selects cell D4
5		=GET.CELL(6)	evaluates to "=D3*2"
6		=LEN(B5)	evaluates to 5
7		=RIGHT(B5,B6-1)	evaluates to "D3*2"

MID(text,startN,*charsN*)

The MID function returns the *charsN* characters from *text* starting at character number *startN*. For example,

=MID("1234",2,2)

evaluates to *23*.

As an example in a macro, assume that in the file named *Budget* you define the range name *source* as A1:C5. The following macro fragment returns the cell reference assigned to that range name:

	A	B	C
7		=REFTEXT(!source)	evaluates to Budget!R1C1:R5C3
8		=FIND("!",B7)	evaluates to 7
9		=MID(B7,B8+1,999)	evaluates to R1C1:R5C3

Notice the argument *999* in the MID function. This is a convenient way to tell the program to return all text from *startN* through the end of the text.

LEFT(text,*charsN*)

The LEFT function is similar to RIGHT, but it returns the first *charsN* characters in *text*. For example,

=LEFT("1234",2)

evaluates to *12*.

Suppose that in the previous macro example you also wanted to return the filename. You could use the following formula, shown in cell B10.

	A	B	C
7		=REFTEXT(!source)	evaluates to Budget!R1C1:R5C3
8		=FIND("!",B7)	evaluates to 7
9		=MID(B7,B8+1,999)	evaluates to R1C1:R5C3
10		=LEFT(B7,B6-1)	evaluates to Budget

When I open a database created by another application, its date column contains text in the sequence "mmddyyyy". For example, it enters *03051992* for March 5, 1992. How can a macro substitute the correct date serial number for this text date?

The following routine returns the contents of the active cell (which contains the text date, we'll assume), reorders the numbers, and enters them into the active cell as a date serial number.

	A	B
5		=ACTIVE.CELL()
6		=FORMULA(DATE(MID(B5,5,4),MID(B5,1,2),MID(B5,3,2)))

Working with character codes

The operating system running on your computer uses numeric codes 1 through 255 to represent each of the 255 characters that a specified font can display on the screen or print on a printer. The first 127 of these codes correspond to the ASCII character set. Beyond code 127, however, the character assigned to each code varies with the font and operating system used: Windows uses the ANSI character set,

OS/2 uses the Code Page 850 character set, and the Macintosh uses a code system that is different from the others. Excel provides three functions that work with these codes: CHAR, CODE, and CLEAN.

CHAR(number)

The CHAR function returns the character assigned to the code number, which can have a value of any number from 1 through 255. You can easily use this function to generate a list of all characters that a given font can produce.

To generate the list, you first need to create a column of numbers that counts from 1 through 255. To do so, enter *1* in cell A1 of a new worksheet, click on the heading of column A to select the entire column, choose Data Series, enter a Stop Value of *255*, and then press Enter. Next, to generate the characters themselves, select cell B1, enter the formula *=CHAR(A1)*, and copy this formula to the range B2:B255.

Note: If you try this on a macro sheet, you'll get a list of small squares in column B—because the formulas need to be recalculated individually after you copy them. (This is why it was suggested that you use a worksheet.) To recalculate, select column B and replace equal signs with equal signs.

CODE(text)

The CODE function returns the numeric code of the first character in text. It is the complement of the CHAR function. To continue the previous example, if you enter into cell C1 the formula *=CODE(B1)*, the formula returns *1*, which is the code you started with in cell A1. If you then copy this cell to the range C2:C255, you'll have a column of codes from 1 through 255.

The first 31 codes are nonprinting codes used to control printers. You'll often see the boxes or bars these codes produce in documents prepared by word processors that you open in a worksheet.

CLEAN(text)

The CLEAN function removes nonprinting codes from text. Specifically, CLEAN always removes codes 1 through 31 and those characters above 127 that aren't defined in the specified font. For example, the formula

```
=LEN(CLEAN(CHAR(31)))
```

evaluates to *0* because CHAR(31) generates a nonprinting code, which CLEAN removes, leaving text with a length of 0.

You might use these functions in several ways. For example, you can use the CLEAN function in macros to remove nonprinting characters from documents created by word processors. Also, the formula

```
=CHAR(64+num)
```

allows macros to "count" from A through Z, where *num* can take the value 1 (for A) through 26 (for Z).

Adding and removing characters

Excel provides four functions that add, replace, or remove characters from text: SUBSTITUTE, REPLACE, REPT, and TRIM.

SUBSTITUTE(text,oldT,newT,*instanceN*)

The SUBSTITUTE function substitutes *newT* for *oldT* in *text*. If you specify an *instanceN*, the function replaces only that instance of *oldT*. Otherwise, it replaces every instance of *oldT* with *newT*. For example,

```
=SUBSTITUTE("COST.XLS","COST","SALES")
```

evaluates to *SALES.XLS*, and

```
=SUBSTITUTE("$A$1","$","")
```

evaluates to *A1*, turning an absolute reference into a relative reference.

You can use SUBSTITUTE to count the number of times that a character occurs in a block of text.

To do so, use the formula

```
=LEN(text)–LEN(SUBSTITUTE(text,character,""))
```

The SUBSTITUTE function in this formula erases every instance of the character by replacing it with a null string ("") in the text. Then the formula subtracts the length of the text after the erasure from the length before the erasure, returning the number of times that the character appeared in the text.

REPLACE(oldT,startN,charsN,newT)

The REPLACE function removes *charsN* characters from *oldT*, starting at *startN*, and then replaces them with *newT*. For example,

	A	B	C
1		=REPLACE("1234",3,1,"c")	evaluates to 12c4
2		=REPLACE("1234",3,2,"c")	evaluates to 12c
3		=REPLACE("1234",3,1,"cd")	evaluates to 12cd4

REPT(text,timesN)

The REPT function repeats *text timesN* times, returning a new text value. If *timesN* equals 0, REPT returns a null string, (""). If *timesN* is not an integer, REPT truncates the value. For example,

	A	B	C
1		=REPT("A",5)	evaluates to "AAAAA"
2		="A"&REPT("*",3)&"B"	evaluates to "A***B"

TRIM(text)

The TRIM function removes all spaces within the text, except for single spaces between the words. For example:

	A	B	C
1		=TRIM (" for whom the bell tolls")	evaluates to "for whom the bell tolls"

Changing capitalization

Excel provides three functions that change the capitalization of text: LOWER, UPPER, and PROPER. You'll use these functions when you need to clean up text imported from other applications.

LOWER(text)

The LOWER function converts text to lowercase. For example,

LOWER("ASCII")

evaluates to *ascii.*

UPPER(text)

The UPPER function converts text to uppercase. For example,

UPPER("Ascii")

evaluates to *ASCII.*

PROPER(text)

The PROPER function converts text to initial capital letters. For example, both

PROPER("ascii")

and

PROPER("ASCII")

evaluate to *Ascii.*

In the following example, a macro statement converts the text in the active cell to initial capital letters and then enters the revised text in the active cell.

```
=FORMULA(PROPER(ACTIVE.CELL()))
```

Comparing text

Excel provides two ways to test whether two strings are the same.

EXACT(text1,text2)
The EXACT function returns TRUE if the two text strings are exactly the same; otherwise, it returns FALSE. The EXACT function is case sensitive. That is,

```
EXACT("AAA","aaa")
```

evaluates to *FALSE*, because *A* is not exactly the same as *a*.

The other way to compare two strings for equality is to use a logical argument, which returns TRUE or FALSE. This method is not case sensitive. That is, the formula

```
="AAA"="aaa"
```

evaluates to *TRUE*.

In practice, we prefer the logical test over EXACT. That is, it's generally better to use a formula that takes the form

```
=IF(B5=B6,...)
```

rather than

```
=IF(EXACT(B5,B6),...)
```

because most text comparisons within a macro are case insensitive. For example, the filenames *SALES.XLS* and *sales.xls* are the same in Excel, as are the names *DATA* and *Data*.

7

Working with References and Names

The way that Excel manipulates cell references is one of its most powerful features. If you're new to Excel, references can also be one of the product's most mysterious features. In this chapter, we show you how to manipulate references, and then we discuss how you can use Excel's naming feature to assign names to formulas containing constants, references, and functions.

What is a reference?

The word *reference* has two uses in Excel. First, you can use it to specify the actual location of one cell or a range of cells on a worksheet or macro sheet. Second, it refers to the specific data type used for specifying locations on a worksheet or macro sheet, in the same way that text, numbers, and arrays are data types.

Excel can express the address of a cell or a range in either of two styles of reference. The *A1 style,* with which you're probably most familiar, assigns the letters A through IV to the columns 1 through 256 and numbers the rows from 1 through 16384. The *R1C1 style,* on the other hand, numbers both rows and columns. For example, the absolute references $B$5 and R5C2 both refer to cell B5. Similarly, the absolute references $E$2 and R2C5 both refer to cell E2.

The most significant difference between these two styles is in how relative references are expressed. In the A1 style, a relative reference expresses the resulting cell reference. For example, enter the formula *=E2* in cell D1. Although it's not clear from the entry, this relative reference specifies the cell one row below the current cell and one column to the right. To demonstrate that this is in fact what the reference does, copy cell D1 to cell F3. The formula changes to *=G4*, which is one row down and one column to the right of cell F3.

In the R1C1 style, on the other hand, relative references express the path or process to follow to arrive at the specified cell reference, not the result of the process. If you now switch to the R1C1 mode (choose Options Workspace, select R1C1, and press Enter), you'll see that both cells display the relative reference *=R[1]C[1]*.

Relative references in the R1C1 mode use positive numbers to describe cell positions below and to the right of the current cell and negative numbers to describe positions above and to the left of the current cell.

Why does Excel support both reference styles? So that it's compatible with both Lotus 1-2-3, which uses the A1 style, and with Microsoft Multiplan, a sheet that uses the R1C1 style. However, as you'll see in this chapter, a better reason for supporting both styles is that doing so gives you more power and convenience than you have by using only one style.

Choosing the correct form of a reference

Excel macros generally use references in either of two formats: R1C1-style references in the form of text, such as "R1C1" and "R[2]C[3]", and A1-style direct references, such as $A$1 and !D3. These formats are often called the *quoted* and *unquoted* styles of reference, which is not completely correct because an R1C1-text reference can consist of an expression that evaluates to text in the R1C1 style. For example, you could use the formula

```
=SELECT(rowRefT&colRefT)
```

where *rowRefT* has been assigned the value *R[–1]* and *colRefT* has been assigned the value *C[1]*.

References can also be either *internal* or *external*. An internal reference refers to a cell within the sheet containing the reference and contains only the cell address. For example, "R1C2" and $B$3 are internal references. An external reference includes the document name, an exclamation mark, and the cell address. For example, external references on the PC could be SALES.XLS!$A$1 or "DOC.XLM!R2C4", and on the Macintosh, "Sales!R[1]C[1]" or Documentation!$B$3.

If you precede a reference with an exclamation mark without specifying a filename, Excel assumes you mean the active sheet.

For example, the macro formula

```
=FORMULA("Hi There",B3)
```

enters the text *Hi There* in cell B3 of the macro sheet. The macro formula

```
=FORMULA("Hi There",!$B$3)
```

enters the text in cell B3 of the active sheet, as does the formula

```
=FORMULA("Hi There",!B3)
```

But if you edit your macro sheet in certain ways, you could accidentally change the cell to which the last formula refers.

When you use a reference in a macro, you must be careful to use the correct form. If you don't, you might see unexpected results. Following are some guidelines for using the correct form of a reference.

The terminology used in this book when discussing references.

To help keep things straight, we use:

- Two styles of reference—the R1C1 and the A1 styles.
- Two common formats for entering references as arguments in functions—the R1C1-text format and the A1-direct format.
- Two types of reference—internal and external.

Finally, you can express any reference as an absolute or a relative reference.

We use italics in this book to indicate text entries, entries the user makes in dialog boxes, and named references and arguments.

For example, the reference MYSHEET.XLS!R1C1 is an absolute external reference in the R1C1-text format, but MYSHEET.XLS!A1 is an external reference in the A1-direct format. Similarly, R[1]C[1] is an internal relative reference to the cell that is one cell down and one cell to the right of the active cell, but A1 is an internal reference in the A1-direct format. Because you can never tell whether a given reference in the A1 style is an absolute reference or a relative reference, we'll always use the R1C1 style when discussing relative references.

Referencing the active sheet using an absolute reference

To reference a specific cell on the active sheet, use an absolute reference in either the R1C1-text format or the A1-direct format preceded by an exclamation mark. For example,

```
=SELECT("R5C5")
```

and

```
=SELECT(!$E$5)
```

both select cell E5 on the active sheet.

Referencing the active sheet using a relative reference

To use a relative reference on the active sheet, you have only one choice: Use a relative reference in R1C1-text format. For example,

```
=SELECT("R[1]C")
```

selects the cell one row below the active cell, and

```
=SELECT("RC[-1]")
```

selects the cell one column to the left of the active cell.

Referencing the macro sheet

To enter in a formula a reference to a cell on the macro sheet that contains the formula, use an internal reference, as in

```
=SIN(B5)
```

or

```
=SIN($B$3)
```

That is, when you want a macro formula to reference a cell on its own macro sheet, never use a reference that contains an ! (exclamation mark) or a reference in the form of text.

Referencing named sheets

To reference cells on a named sheet, use external absolute references in either the R1C1-text or the A1-direct format. For example,

```
=FORMULA(1,"Sheet1!R3C1")
```

and

```
=FORMULA(1,Sheet1!$A$3)
```

both enter the value *1* in cell A3 of the document *Sheet1*.

The cell-reference table

The table in Figure 7-1 summarizes the range of choices for expressing cell references. To use this table, locate across the top the type of cell reference you need, and down the left side the sheet on which the referenced cell resides. The type of references you can use for this combination are listed at the intersection of the chosen column and row.

	Type of cell reference		
Residence of referenced cell	Absolute	Relative to active cell	Relative to formula position
On sheet containing the formula	$A$1 R1C1		A1 R[#]C[#]
On active sheet	!$A$1 !R1C1 "R1C1"	"R[#]C[#]"	*!A1* *!R[#]C[#]*
On named sheet	name.xls!$A$1 name.xls!R1C1 "name.xls!R1C1"	*"name.xls!R[#]C[#]"*	*name.xls!A1* *name.xls!R[#]C[#]*

FIGURE 7-1.
Cell references—by type, residence, and format—summarizing the forms of cell references you can use in macros. The italicized forms are dangerous to use in macros. (Also, Macintosh filenames do not include an XLS extension unless you add it.)

For example, suppose you want a macro to refer to a cell on the active sheet (the options in the second row of the table) and you want the cell relative to a cell on the active sheet (the options in the second column of the table). The box at the intersection of this row and column offers only one option, the form "R[#]C[#]".

Although this table offers 16 forms of cell reference to choose from, you can eliminate many of these—for two reasons. First, you should avoid the italicized forms of references because they are dangerous to use. (We'll explain the dangers shortly.) Second, if you set the workspace to the A1 style, you can ignore unquoted R1C1-style references. (Similarly, if you set your workspace to the R1C1 style, you can eliminate A1-style references.)

To give you a better idea of how these references work, let's take a closer look at each result in the table.

$A$1
R1C1
Each of these forms is an absolute reference to a cell on the sheet that contains the formula. When used in a macro, in other words, it refers to the macro sheet.

For example, if the workspace is set to the A1 style, the formula

```
=SELECT($A$1)
```

selects cell A1 on the macro sheet containing the formula. If the workspace is then set to the R1C1 style, Excel displays this formula as

```
=SELECT(R1C1)
```

A1
R[#]C[#]
When used in a macro, each of these forms is a relative reference to a cell on the macro sheet, relative to the formula that contains the reference. For example, if you enter

```
=SIN(B27)
```

in cell B26, the reference B27 refers to the next row down in the macro sheet. You'll generally use relative rather than absolute references in macros. The reason: When you edit macros by copying them, or when you copy complete macros to other macro sheets, you want Excel to adjust the references in these macros as needed. For example, if you copy the preceding SIN formula to cell B45, you probably want the formula to refer to cell B46. If you used an absolute reference the function would still refer to cell B27.

!$A$1
!R1C1
Each of these forms, which can be used in macro formulas only, is an absolute reference to a cell on the active sheet. For example, if the workspace is set to the A1 style, then

```
=FORMULA("=1+2",!$B$5)
```

enters the formula *=1+2* in cell B5 of the active sheet.

"R1C1"
This form is an absolute reference to cell A1 on the active sheet. When it's used with functions that can accept references expressed as text, it works in the same manner as the two previous forms. For example, the formula

```
=SELECT("R1C1")
```

selects cell A1 on the active sheet. You can't express a text reference in the A1 style.

"R[#]C[#]"
This form provides a reference on the active sheet that is relative to the active cell.

For example, the formula

```
=SELECT("R[1]C[1]")
```

selects the cell that is one row down and one column to the right of the active cell.

!A1
!R[#]C[#]
Each of these forms is dangerous to use because it references a cell on the active sheet that is relative to a cell on the macro sheet. This type of reference is particularly dangerous because if you edit it by copying it, the reference changes. For example, suppose you enter *=!D5* into cell B20 of a macro sheet. If you copy the formula to cell B19, it changes to *=!D4*, which is probably not what you intended.

name.xls!$A$1
name.xls!R1C1
Each of these forms is an absolute external reference to cell A1 on the named sheet. (Excel on the Macintosh doesn't use the XLS file extension unless you add it.) For example, the formula

```
=FORMULA("data",BUDGET.XLS!$B$5)
```

enters the text *data* in cell B5 of the BUDGET.XLS worksheet.

"name.xls!R1C1"
This form is an absolute external reference to a cell on the named sheet, expressed as text. For example, the formula

```
=FORMULA("data","BUDGET.XLS!R5C2")
```

also enters the text *data* in cell B5 of the BUDGET worksheet.

"name.xls!R[#]C[#]"
This form is dangerous to use because it references a cell on the named sheet that is relative to the active cell, a cell that could be on another sheet entirely. For example, suppose cell A1 is active in the document SALES.XLS. The formula

```
=FORMULA("data","BUDGET.XLS!R[1]C")
```

enters *data* in cell A2 of the BUDGET.XLS worksheet. If you had activated cell C5 on the SALES.XLS worksheet, the same formula would have entered *data* into cell C6 on the BUDGET worksheet.

name.xls!A1
name.xls!R[#]C[#]
Each of these forms is dangerous to use for the same reason as the previous form. These forms, however, reference a cell on the named sheet that is relative to a cell on the macro sheet.

Mixed references

You can also use references that refer to complete rows or columns, that mix absolute and relative references in the same reference, or that do both. Figure 7-2 provides a number of examples of these mixed references.

A1 style	R1C1 style	Refers to...
=A1	=RC	The current cell.
=$A1	=RC1	The cell in the current row of column A.
=A$1	=R1C	The cell in row 1 of the current column.
=$A2	=R[1]C1	The cell in the next row down in column A.
=B$1	=R1C[1]	The cell in the next column to the right in row 1.
=$A:$A	=C1	Column A only.
=A:A	=C	The current column only.
=$A:$C	=C1:C3	Column A through column C.
=$1:$1	=R1	Row 1 only.
=1:1	=R	The current row only.
=$1:$3	=R1:R3	Row 1 through row 3.
=$1:$16384	=R1:R16384	The entire sheet.
=$A:$IV	=C1:C256	The entire sheet.

FIGURE 7-2.
Examples of mixed references.

Notice that in Figure 7-2 all examples using the A1 style with relative references assume that the reference is used in cell A1. This information is important because without knowing this, we don't know what a relative reference in the A1 style actually does. For example, if you're told to copy an unspecified cell containing the formula *=A1* to cell B5, you won't be able to say what the formula will be in cell B5 until you know the address of the cell that originally contained the formula.

Constructing references

In macros you frequently need to calculate new cell references. For example, you might want to select the cell in column A that is one row below the top-left cell in the range assigned to the name *bottom*, which is defined in the active sheet. How should you construct a cell reference that you could use in combination with a SELECT formula to select this cell?

Following are two methods for doing this: You can use one when you want to use R1C1-text references and the other when you want to use A1-style references. Let's take a look at each.

Using R1C1-text references

One way to construct a new cell reference is to construct a quoted reference with string concatenation. For example, you could use these two formulas in the cells shown.

	A	B
4		
5		=ROW(!bottom)+1
6		=SELECT("R"&B5&"C1")

Here the formula in cell B5 takes the row number of the top-left cell in the range named *bottom* on the active sheet and adds 1 to that number, resulting in the number of the row that is one row below *bottom*. The formula in cell B6 coerces this value into text and then concatenates it with the remaining text to create an R1C1-text reference, which is then provided as the argument to the SELECT function.

Using the OFFSET function

Another way to construct a reference is to use an R1C1-text reference in combination with the OFFSET standard worksheet function, which takes the form

OFFSET(reference,rowsN,colsN,*heightN,widthN*)

This function returns a reference that is offset by *rowsN* rows and *colsN* columns from *reference*. You can use the optional *heightN* and *widthN* arguments to set the dimensions of the returned reference. To use OFFSET to construct the reference used in the previous example, you could use the following formula:

```
=SELECT(OFFSET(!$A$1,ROW(!bottom),0)
```

The first of these two formulas works in a manner similar to an absolute reference. It returns a reference that is offset from cell A1 by a specified number of rows and columns. Each row and column number is 1 greater than you would use with a true absolute reference. For example, the result of OFFSET(!$A$1,2,1) and the reference !R3C2 both refer to cell B3.

Choosing between R1C1-text and A1-style references

We've demonstrated that the references "R1C1" and !$A$1 perform in much the same way, and we've described how to construct new references based on each style. That is, you can use string concatenation with R1C1-text references, and you can use the OFFSET function with A1-style references. But which of these styles should you use?

One consideration is execution speed. It takes a slight amount of time for Excel to switch between one style of reference and another; therefore, minimizing these switches causes a macro to run a bit faster. (You can use a benchmarking macro, such as the one presented in Chapter 16, "Speeding Up Your Macros," to test procedures.) But because the difference in execution time is so slight for most purposes, the practical answer is that it doesn't really matter which style you use. In general, use the style that is easiest to understand for the task at hand.

Reference operators

When you write a formula such as *=1+2*, the plus sign is known as an *arithmetic operator*. Other arithmetic operators include those for multiplication (*), division (/), subtraction (–), and exponentiation (^). Similarly, Excel offers three operators for "adding" and "subtracting" references: range (a colon), union (a comma), and intersection (a space).

The range operator. You've already encountered the most common of the reference operators—the colon, also called the range operator. This operator tells Excel to produce one reference containing all the cells between and including the two references entered on either side of the colon. For example, in the reference $B$3:$D$5 the colon tells Excel to reference the range extending from cell B3 through cell D5.

You can also use a defined name on either or both sides of the expression, as long as the defined name evaluates to a reference. For example, in the reference *range1:range2*, the colon tells the program to reference the range extending from the name *range1* through the name *range2*. If either of these names is itself a range, the combined reference becomes the smallest rectangular area on the sheet that includes both ranges.

A good way to experiment with the reference operators is to enter an expression in the Formula Goto dialog box [F5; Mac—also Command-G], as shown:

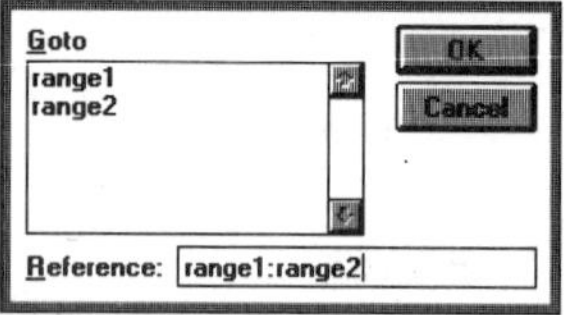

When you press Enter, Excel selects this range:

Also, as Figure 7-2 on page 126 illustrates, you must use the range operator to refer to entire rows or columns in the A1 style. For example, $B:$B specifies all of column B.

The union operator. The union operator, a comma, produces a reference that includes two or more references—but not the area between them. This is the same result you get by holding down the Ctrl key [Mac—also the Command key] to select a discontinuous set of cells or cell ranges. For example, in the reference

```
=SELECT(!$B$3,!$D$5)
```

the comma tells Excel to reference only cells B3 and D5. You can enter the following in the Goto dialog box:

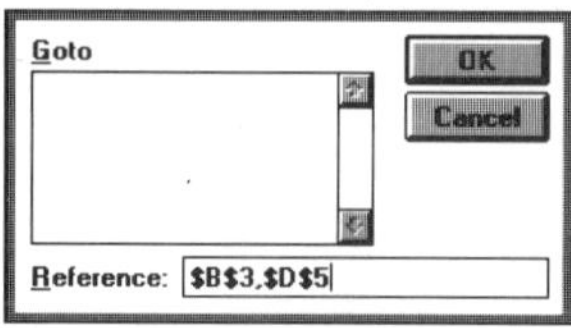

When you press Enter, Excel selects this discontinuous range:

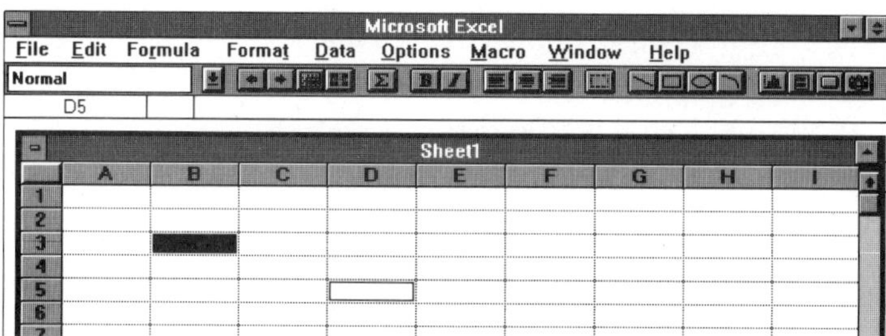

The intersection operator. The intersection operator, a space character, results in a range that is the area shared by two other ranges. If the two ranges have no cells in common, Excel returns the #NULL error value.

For example, suppose the name *range1* is defined as $C$3:$E$7 and *range2* is defined as $D$6:$F$8. If you enter *range1 range2* in the Goto dialog box and press Enter, Excel selects the range D6 through E7, as shown:

Because the Macintosh version of Excel allows you to use filenames containing spaces, take care not to create references that could be misinterpreted as using an intersection operator.

For example, consider the following formula:

=SUM(Our Sales!JanSales)

Should Excel sum the intersection of the range *Our* with the range *Sales!JanSales*? (This would probably result in a #VALUE! error because you can't intersect a reference on the active sheet with one on another sheet.) Or should it sum the range *JanSales* in the document *Our Sales*?

To specify that *Our Sales* is the full document name, enclose it in apostrophes (also called single quotes or foot marks).

=SUM('Our Sales'!JanSales)

To see a more practical use for the intersection operator, define the range B3:D3 as *sales* and the range C1:C10 as *january*. Then, when you enter either

=SELECT(january sales)

or

=SELECT(sales january)

the formula refers to the intersection of the two ranges, which represents, of course, the sales in January.

Combining reference operators. When you use arithmetic operators, you can use parentheses to force Excel to evaluate the parts of a formula in a specific sequence. For example,

=(2+3)*4

returns a different result than does

=2+(3*4)

Similarly, when you use reference operators you can use parentheses to combine references in a specific sequence. To illustrate why this can be important, define the following names and associated references.

Name	Reference	Meaning
range1	$3:$3	Row 3.
range2	$C:$C	Column C.
range3	$E$5	A single cell.

Now use the Goto dialog box to go to the reference *range1 range2:range3*. When you press Enter, you'll see the following result:

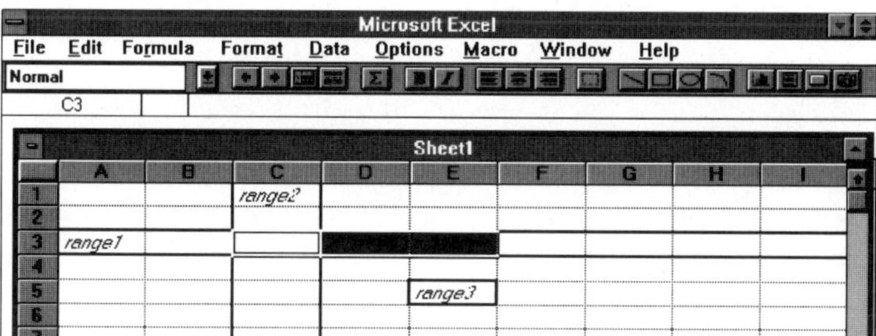

Here Excel selected the intersection of *range1* and *range2:range3*. (To see this more clearly, try entering both parts in the Goto dialog box separately.)

Next, use the Goto dialog box to go to the reference *(range1 range2):range3.* When you press Enter, you'll see this:

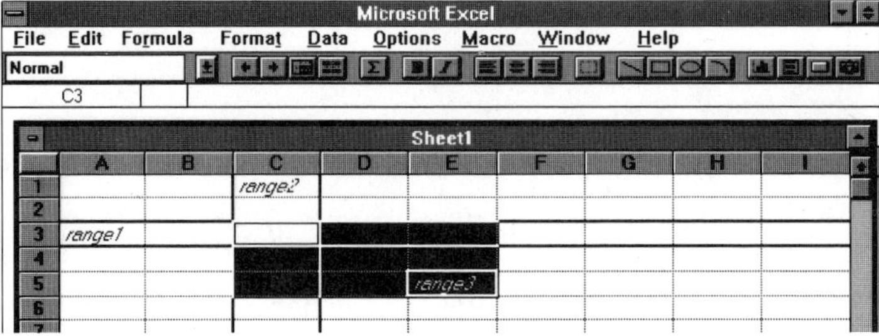

Here Excel selected the intersection of *range1* and *range2,* and then it selected the range between the intersection and the cell defined by *range3.*

If you don't use parentheses to control the evaluation of an expression, Excel evaluates operators in this order: range, intersection, union, and arithmetic operators. To nail down your understanding of the way Excel's reference operators work, try other combinations in the Goto dialog box, such as:

```
range1:range2:range3

range1:range2,range3

range1:range2 range3

range1(range2:range3)

range1,range2,range3
```

Standard functions for working with references

In addition to the OFFSET function, discussed earlier, Excel provides nine other standard worksheet functions for working with ranges; of course, you can use them in your macros.

COLUMN(*reference*)

This function returns the column number of *reference.* What Excel actually returns depends on the form *reference* takes; if the argument is omitted, Excel returns the column number of the cell containing the COLUMN function. If *reference* contains more than one cell, Excel returns a horizontal array of the column numbers in the range. For example, supposing you wanted a macro to assign the name *arrayCols* to an array containing the column numbers of the current selection, you could use this formula:

```
{=SET.NAME("arrayCols",COLUMN(SELECTION()))}
```

If you use this formula, don't forget to enter the formula as an array formula [Ctrl-Shift-Enter; Mac—also Command-Enter]. If the current selection was B2:D5, for instance, Excel would assign the array value {2,3,4} to the name *arrayCols.*

ROW(*reference*)

This function is exactly the same as COLUMN, but it returns the row numbers in *reference* instead of the column numbers.

COLUMNS(*array*)

This function returns the number of columns in *array; array* can be an actual array, an expression that evaluates to an array, or a reference to a range of cells.

ROWS(*array*)

Like COLUMNS, this function returns the number of rows in *array; array* can be an actual array, an expression that evaluates to an array, or a reference to a range of cells.

AREAS(*reference*)

This function returns the number of areas in *reference*—that is, the number of contiguous ranges in the specified reference. If the function returns a number greater than 1, you know the selected range is discontinuous. For example, in the macro fragment

	A	B
4		=SELECT((!$A$1:$C$3,!$D$4:$F$6))
5	*numAreas*	=AREAS(SELECTION())

numAreas becomes the value 2. The double set of parentheses is necessary to isolate the comma as a union operator. The inner parentheses group the two references and the comma, to tell Excel that the comma isn't separating two arguments in the SELECT function.

ADDRESS(rowN,columnN,*absN,a1L,sheetT*)

You can use this function to "manufacture" the reference of a cell, given only the row number (*rowN*) and the column number (*columnN*) of the cell for which you want the reference. The *absN* argument specifies whether the reference returned is absolute, relative, or a mixture of the two, according to the following table.

absN	**Type of reference returned**
1 or omitted	Absolute.
2	Absolute row, relative column.
3	Relative row, absolute column.
4	Relative.

The *a1L* argument specifies whether to return the reference in the R1C1 or A1 style; if TRUE or omitted, Excel returns the reference in the A1 style. The *sheetT* argument specifies the document name in an external reference. For example, the following macro fragment manufactures the cell reference shown in the Values view column and then selects it.

Formulas view	Values view
=ADDRESS(2,3,1,FALSE,"TEST.XLS")	TEST.XLS!R2C3
=FORMULA.GOTO(DEREF(up1))	TRUE

INDIRECT(refT,*a1L*)

The INDIRECT function returns the reference specified by *refT*. If *a1L* is TRUE or omitted, the reference is returned in the A1 style; if FALSE, Excel returns the reference in the R1C1 style. You can use this function to convert text stored in a cell to a reference, which Excel then uses to find the value stored in the cell. To continue our last example, you could use the following two formulas to first create an external reference to the cell TEST.XLS!$C$2 and to then return to the macro sheet the value stored in the cell. Supposing the cell contains the text *Test Text*, the INDIRECT function returns *Test Text* to the macro sheet.

Formulas view	Values view
=ADDRESS(2,3,1,FALSE,"TEST.XLS")	TEST.XLS!R2C3
=INDIRECT(up1,FALSE)	Test Text

One of the benefits of this method for getting at the contents of a cell external to the macro sheet is that it doesn't generate an actual external reference and link to another document.

INDEX(reference,rowN,columnN,*areaN*), form 1

This function returns the reference of the specified row and column within *reference*. If *reference* is a discontinuous range (that is, composed of more than one range), you can specify the *areaN* argument. The *reference* argument is like the one in the SELECT macro function: To use the union operator in it, you should enclose the list in parentheses. For example, the formula

```
=INDEX((TEST.XLS!$B$16:$B$24,TEST.XLS!$C$9:$C$12),1,1,2)
```

returns the reference TEST.XLS!$C$9, which is the first cell in the second area of the discontinuous range enclosed in the parentheses.

You can also use one or more named ranges as the *reference* argument. For example, if *range1* and *range2* are named ranges on the worksheet TEST.XLS, the formula

```
=INDEX((TEST.XLS!range1,TEST.XLS!range2),2,1,1)
```

returns an external reference to the first cell in the second row of *range1*. Notice that you cannot mix internal and external references when specifying a discontinuous area for the *reference* argument; remember that the comma here is the union operator, and the union of an internal and an external reference results in a #VALUE! error.

CELL(infoTypeT,*reference*)

This standard worksheet function returns various types of information about the top-left cell in *reference*, such as the reference of the top-left cell converted to text, the full pathname of the cell, and the formats attached to the cell. Compare CELL with the macro function GET.CELL, which provides more information. (GET.CELL is discussed later in this chapter.)

Macro functions for working with references

Excel provides a wide range of macro functions for changing reference styles in the workspace, finding the reference of the selected range, and converting between the various styles and forms of references.

A1.R1C1(logical)

The A1.R1C1 function is the equivalent of selecting or deselecting the R1C1 option in the Workspace Options dialog box, and it takes one argument: If TRUE, Excel expresses the row and column headings and references in the A1 style; if FALSE, Excel expresses them in the R1C1 style. If omitted, Excel switches from one style to the other.

ACTIVE.CELL()

The ACTIVE.CELL function takes no arguments, and it returns the reference of the active cell expressed as an external reference. If you use this function by itself in a macro, you'll generally get the contents of the active cell rather than the reference because Excel usually converts references to the values referenced. The exception is that Excel doesn't convert the reference returned by ACTIVE.CELL if you use the function as an argument in another function that expects the argument to be a reference. To work with the reference apart from what it refers to, use the REFTEXT function, described on the next page, to convert the reference to text.

SELECTION()

The SELECTION function, very similar to ACTIVE.CELL, takes no arguments and returns the reference of the selected range as an external reference.

ABSREF(refT,reference)

This function returns an absolute reference in the A1 style that is offset from the top-left corner of *reference* by *refT*. The *refT* argument must be in the R1C1-text format. If *reference* is an external reference, ABSREF returns an external reference. For example, the formula

```
=ABSREF("R[1]C[1]",TEST.XLS!A1)
```

returns the reference *TEST.XLS!$B$2*, which in this case is evaluated to the contents of that cell. If you use ABSREF in another function as an argument requiring a reference, Excel doesn't convert the reference to the contents of the referenced cell.

RELREF(reference,relToRef)

This function is the complement of ABSREF; it returns a relative reference in the R1C1-text format instead of an absolute reference in the A1 style. The relative reference returned is the distance in cells between *reference* and the top-left corner of *relToRef*. For example, if the range E5:F6 were selected with E5 being the active cell, the formula

```
=RELREF($G$7:$H$8,$E$5:$F$6)
```

would return *R[2]C[2]:R[3]C[3]* to the macro sheet.

DEREF(reference)

This function returns the values associated with the range specified by *reference*. A good use for this function is within another function that takes a reference as an argument; however, you want the function to use not the reference but a reference stored in the cell to which the reference refers. For example, suppose cell B2 contains the text *R2C3*. If you use the function

```
=FORMULA.GOTO($B$2)
```

in a macro, Excel selects cell B2. This isn't what you want. Instead, use the formula

```
=FORMULA.GOTO(DEREF($B$2))
```

Excel goes to cell B2 and uses the text value stored in it as the reference to select.

REFTEXT(reference,*a1L*)

This function converts *reference* to either an A1-text or R1C1-text absolute reference. If *a1L* is TRUE, Excel converts the reference to the A1 style; if FALSE or omitted, Excel uses the R1C1 style.

Examples of this function and of TEXTREF appear later in this chapter.

TEXTREF(refT,*a1L*)

This function is the inverse of the REFTEXT function. It converts a text reference to either an A1 or an R1C1 absolute reference. If *a1L* is TRUE, *refT* is assumed to be in the A1 style; if FALSE or omitted, *refT* is assumed to be in the R1C1 style. As with the other functions that return references, you'll usually get the value stored in the referenced cell unless you use the function as an argument in another function that takes a reference as an argument.

FORMULA.CONVERT(formulaT,fromA1L,*toA1L,toRefTypeN,relToRef*)

This function performs various types of reference conversions on the formula given in *formulaT* and returns the converted formula as text. The formula given as *formulaT* should be a complete formula in the form of text, including the preceding equal sign. The *fromaIL* argument tells Excel whether the references in *formulaT* are in the A1 (TRUE) or R1C1 (FALSE) style. The *toA1L* argument tells Excel whether to convert the references in the formula to the A1 style (TRUE) or to the R1C1 style (FALSE) or to leave the styles of reference in the formula unchanged. The *toRefTypeN* argument determines whether to return absolute, relative, or mixed references, according to the following table:

toRefTypeN	Type of reference returned
1	Absolute.
2	Absolute row, relative column.
3	Relative row, absolute column.
4	Relative.

If *toRefTypeN* is omitted, Excel doesn't change the reference type.

Finally, *relToRef* sets an absolute reference to which the relative references in the formula (if any) are relative.

GET.CELL(typeN,*reference*)

This function returns various types of information about the upper left cell in *reference*, only some of which pertains to working with references. If *reference* is omitted, Excel assumes the active cell. The *typeN* argument specifies the information returned, according to the following table:

typeN	Type of reference returned
1	Absolute reference of the cell, as text, in the current reference style for the workspace.
2	Row number of the cell.
3	Column number of the cell.
5	Value stored in the cell; the result of the cell's formula, if any.
6	Cell's formula, with references in the current reference style for the workspace.
32	Name of the sheet containing the cell.

One of the main benefits of this function is its ability to work with the absolute reference of the cell in the current reference style, set by the R1C1 option in the Workspace dialog box. For example, if you want a macro to find the formula stored in the active cell, and the workspace has been set to the A1 style, you could use the following formula:

```
=GET.CELL(6,ACTIVE.CELL())
```

Interestingly, if you enter this formula in a macro and immediately switch to Values view, you'll see the same formula again. This happens because the formula has returned the formula stored in the active cell at the moment you pressed Enter, which is the cell containing the formula itself.

Using references in macros

Often you'll need to change from one form of reference to another, from the R1C1-text format to an A1-style reference, from relative to absolute, and so on. This section explains how to make these changes easily.

Storing R1C1-text references

As you probably know, Excel cannot evaluate an R1C1-text format reference unless it's supplied as an argument to a function that takes such a reference. Instead, when a cell contains an unquoted reference, it returns the contents of the cell being referenced.

You can capture the reference of the current selection in two ways. First, you can assign the reference to a name. For example, you could use the following macro formula:

```
=DEFINE.NAME("range1",SELECTION())
```

Here the reference of the current selection is assigned to *range1* in the current sheet.

The main benefit of using this approach is that creating the name makes it available to your macro. However, this approach has two negative aspects if used frequently. First, DEFINE.NAME executes rather slowly, as macro functions go. Second, a sheet can quickly become cluttered with the temporary names used to store references unless you take steps to delete them before the end of each macro.

Alternatively, you could capture the current selection as text with the REFTEXT function. For example, you could use this formula:

```
=REFTEXT(SELECTION())
```

To use this reference later in the macro, you can refer to the cell that contains this formula. For example, if the previous formula is in cell B23, you could use the following formula to select the range stored in the cell:

```
=SELECT(DEREF(B23))
```

Here the DEREF function specifies that the selection is based on the reference stored in cell B23. If you had excluded the DEREF function, the SELECT function would have tried to select cell B23 on the macro sheet itself.

If your macro formula requires an A1-style reference rather than one in the R1C1-text format, use the TEXTREF function to perform the conversion. For example, to get the column width of the earlier selection, you could use this formula:

```
=GET.CELL(16,TEXTREF(B23))
```

Converting a formula to text

Let's say that one part of a macro assigns a reference to the name *ref* and that later you want to convert this reference to text. You have two choices. If you're sure that *ref* always contains only a reference, and never a formula, you can use this formula:

```
=REFTEXT(!ref)
```

However, if *ref* contains a formula, the REFTEXT function here returns a #VALUE! error value. To return the formula as text, you can use this formula:

```
=MID(GET.NAME("ref"),2,999)
```

The GET.NAME function in this formula returns the definition of *ref* as it appears in the Refers To field of the Define Name dialog box. The MID function eliminates the equal sign that precedes the definition.

Switching between A1 and R1C1-text format references

As described earlier, Excel provides two functions that let you switch between quoted and unquoted references. The REFTEXT function converts a reference to an absolute reference in the form of text. The TEXTREF function converts a text-format reference to an absolute reference.

When you use these functions, keep in mind that they convert relative references to absolute references. Generally, this is what you intend for your macros. At times, however, you'll want to switch from one form of reference to another without changing the mixed references encountered by your macro.

To convert an R1C1-text relative reference to an A1-style relative reference, you can assign it to a name. For example, the following formula assigns the formula "=R[1]C1" to the name *testRef* on the active sheet:

```
=DEFINE.NAME("testRef","=R[1]C1")
```

To demonstrate that *testRef* does contain the relative reference, choose Formula Goto, select *testRef*, and press Return. Doing so selects the cell in column A one row below the row containing the active cell.

To convert the reference in a name to an R1C1-text relative reference, use the GET.NAME function, which returns the name's definition as text. For example, the formula

```
=GET.NAME("!testRef")
```

returns the text *=R[1]C1*. On the other hand, the formula

```
=REFTEXT(testRef)
```

returns an absolute external reference. For example, if cell B4 contains this formula, the formula returns *R5C1*.

Using R1C1-text references in a function that takes a text argument

As you've learned, macro functions such as SELECT and FORMULA treat R1C1-text format references as references to the active sheet. However, other functions that can accept text arguments treat R1C1-text format references as regular text, not as a reference. For example, the formula

```
=ISBLANK("R1C1")
```

always returns FALSE, even when cell A1 on the active sheet is blank. The reason for this is that the string "R1C1" is not an empty string.

Similarly, the formula

```
=IF("R1C1"=1,TRUE,FALSE)
```

always returns FALSE because the text string "R1C1" never equals 1, and

```
=LEFT("R1C1",1)
```

always returns *R*, which is the first character of the text string "R1C1".

To get around this problem, put R1C1-text format references within a TEXTREF function, as follows:

```
=ISBLANK(TEXTREF("R1C1"))
=IF(TEXTREF("R1C1")=1,TRUE,FALSE)
=LEFT(TEXTREF("R1C1"),1)
```

Switching between R1C1-text and A1-text absolute references

To convert an R1C1-text format reference to an absolute reference in the A1-text format, convert the text to a normal reference using TEXTREF, and then convert the normal reference to a text reference using REFTEXT.

For example, to convert the text *R2C6* to the A1-text format reference *$F$2*, use the formula

```
=REFTEXT(TEXTREF("R2C6"),TRUE)
```

Similarly, to convert the text *R2C6:R3C7* to *$F$2:$G$3*, use

```
=REFTEXT(TEXTREF("R2C6:R3C7"),TRUE)
```

These formulas convert the text references in R1C1-text format to normal ones, and then convert these normal references to references in the A1-text format. (If you change TRUE in these formulas to FALSE, the formulas return references in the R1C1-text format.)

To convert references in the A1-text format to absolute references in the R1C1-text format, you use essentially the same approach. This time, however, use a TRUE argument with the TEXTREF function to tell it that you're passing A1-style references rather than R1C1-style.

For example, to convert *$F$2* to an R1C1-text format reference, use

```
=REFTEXT(TEXTREF("$F$2",TRUE))
```

Similarly, to convert the text *$F$2:$G$3* to *R2C6:R3C7*, use

```
=REFTEXT(TEXTREF("$F$2:$G$3",TRUE))
```

These formulas first convert text references in the A1 style to normal references and then convert the normal references back to R1C1-text references. (The TRUE arguments in these formulas tell the TEXTREF functions to expect A1-style references.)

Switching between A1 and R1C1 relative references

Generally, you'll find that REFTEXT and TEXTREF provide exactly the help you need to convert between A1 and R1C1 styles. At times, however, you might experience two problems with this technique. First, as mentioned previously, these functions convert all references to absolute. Second, the technique works only with references, not with formulas that contain references.

To convert relative references or formulas from one style to the other, the references or formulas must first exist as formulas in a cell. You use either GET.CELL(6) or GET.FORMULA to return the text of the formula in A1 or R1C1 style, respectively.

For example, suppose you enter the formula *=A1* in cell A2 of a macro sheet. To convert the reference A1 to R1C1 style, enter the following formula:

```
=MID(GET.FORMULA(A2),2,999)
```

The GET.FORMULA function returns the formula *=R[–1]C*. The MID function that surrounds this function drops the initial equal sign, returning *R[–1]C*. Alternatively, the following formula returns the reference in A1 style:

```
=MID(GET.CELL(6,A2),2,999)
```

The GET.CELL function returns the formula *=A1*, and the MID function returns *A1*.

Use the same approach to return formulas to either A1 or R1C1 style. For example, if the formula in cell A2 is =A1+$B$1, the previous formula containing GET.FORMULA returns R[-1]C+R1C2.

Entering references with the INPUT function

You can use the INPUT function to request a range from the user during the execution of a macro. However, because you can't actually store A1-style references in a macro sheet, you must take special steps to keep from losing the reference. To capture references in a macro, use

```
=REFTEXT(INPUT("Enter the reference",8,"INPUT Example"))
```

or

```
=SET.NAME("ref",INPUT("Enter the reference",8,"INPUT Example"))
```

The first formula captures the reference as a text reference in the cell containing the formula. To use the reference later, simply reference the cell. The second formula captures the reference as the name *ref*, which you can use in other formulas.

It's easy to enter a reference using the Input dialog box generated by either formula. Either use the mouse to select the cells you want to enter, or use the keyboard to enter one or more cell addresses or range names.

For example, let's say you want to create a macro formula that requests a range to be summed and then enters a SUM formula in the active cell, using the range requested. The following two formulas accomplish this task.

	A	B
5		=RELREF(INPUT("Select the cell(s) to add:",8),ACTIVE.CELL())
6		=FORMULA("=SUM("&B5&")")

The first formula captures as text the relative reference of the area selected with the Input dialog box. The second formula enters a SUM formula in the active cell, using the relative reference.

Working with names

One of the main reasons that Excel is more powerful than other spreadsheet programs is its great flexibility in assigning names to cells, ranges, constant values, and formulas. We'll cover the major capabilities that names provide and discuss their use in macros.

Defining names

A name is a label assigned to a formula, but the formula resides "inside" the worksheet or macro sheet rather than in a cell. This formula can consist of

- A single value, such as assigning *=3.14159* to the name *pi*
- A formula that evaluates to text, a number, or a logical value, such as assigning the formula *=TEXT(NOW(),"dddd")* to the name *thisDay*
- A reference, such as assigning *="R[-1]C"* to the name *up1*
- A complex formula containing references and functions, such as assigning *=SIN(2*CHOOSE(up1,left1,left2,left3))^2* to *sinFnc*

To use a name, you must define it of course by using the Formula Define Name command or the Formula Create Names command or by defining it in a macro (as we'll discuss later in this chapter).

Guidelines for names

The first character of a name must be a letter, underscore (_), or backslash (\). The other characters in the name can be letters, numbers, periods, underscores, or backslashes.

Excel does not let you create a name that it could misinterpret as a reference. If you tried to define names such as *A1, CC23,* or *R5C2,* Excel would return the message *That name is not valid.* Similarly, you can't define the name *C* or *R* because in the R1C1 style these letters refer to the current column or row. For example, when using the R1C1 style, the formula *=SUM(C)* returns the sum of all numbers in the current column.

Occasionally, however, you'll need to use a prohibited name. For example, you might want to create the names *A, B,* and *C*: Excel lets you define the first two names but not the last. Although no perfect way exists to get around this restriction, a partial solution is available: Add a period or an underscore to the end of the name you want to use. For example, although Excel doesn't let you define the names *Z1, C,* and *RC,* the names *Z1_, C_,* and *RC_* are perfectly acceptable.

Excel does not allow spaces to appear in a name. Instead, use an underscore, a period, or internal capitals (for example, *firstRange*). When you use the Formula Create Names command to create a name, Excel creates names from labels in rows or columns; if the text in a cell contains a space or other unacceptable character, Excel substitutes an underscore.

Although names can be as long as 255 characters, we recommend that you keep them as short as clarity permits. The longer names are, the longer will be the formulas that use those names, the more you will have to type when you use the names, and the less of the name you will see in dialog boxes such as the Define Name dialog box.

You can use any combination of uppercase or lowercase letters in a name, but the case of the letters affects only how the name is displayed. Excel ignores capitalization when it uses the name.

What you can assign to a name

Although names often refer to groups of cells in Excel, the names exist independent of those cells. In fact, names are so independent that it's often convenient to think of a name as a cell hidden within a regular macro sheet or worksheet.

For example, if you define the name *test* as *=$A$1*, and then enter *=$A$1* in cell B1, Excel makes no reference to *test* in this cell. Or if you enter *=test* in cell B1, the program makes no reference to cell A1. The cell address and the name are independent. (Of course, you can use the Formula Apply Names command to replace the references to cell A1 with references to *test*. Remember, however, that you can't easily reverse this process.)

To get a better idea of how names work, let's take a closer look at the different ways you can use them.

Absolute references to ranges

If you can think of a name as a hidden cell stored within a sheet, this "cell" has special features that do not apply to the actual cells in a macro sheet or worksheet.

Unlike sheets, names can contain A1 references. When you define the name *test* as *=$A$1*, the reference $A$1 is an A1 reference. If a name has been assigned to a simple reference (that is, it labels a range through an absolute reference), the name appears in the Goto dialog box. For example, names associated with the following definitions would appear in the dialog box:

```
=$A$1
=$A$1:$A$2
=$A$1,$A$3
=$A$1:$A$3 $A$2:$B$2
```

and so on.

Relative references to ranges

You can also define a name as a relative reference; when you use such a name, it is relative to the cell in which the name is used. For example, suppose you select cell B1 and then define *nextLeft* as *=A1*. If you enter the formula *=nextLeft* in cell D45, the formula returns the contents of cell C45.

Because the R1C1 style provides more information about the way relative references work, it's often helpful to switch to this style when you define relative references. (Choose Options Workspace and select the R1C1 option.) For example, entering *=RC[–1]* as the definition of *nextLeft* provides a clearer picture of the purpose of this relative reference than does the same reference in the A1 style.

If a name assigned a relative reference contains only a simple reference, rather than a formula that evaluates to a reference, such as

=OFFSET(A1,20,0)

the Goto dialog box lists its name as well. For example, names associated with the following definitions would appear in the dialog box:

=R

=R1C[1]

=RC:R[5]C[10]

and so on.

Names that reference names

Excel allows names to reference other names, both on the same sheet and on other sheets. For example, suppose your formulas frequently reference the range *costData* in the worksheet MYSHEET.XLS. To eliminate the need to type *MYSHEET.XLS!costData* each time you create a formula that uses this reference, you can define the name *data* as

=MYSHEET.XLS!costData

Referring to *data* each time is certainly easier than typing a long external reference.

The Goto dialog box does not display names defined using other names. Even so, you can go to the name by typing it into the Reference field and pressing Enter.

Complex formulas

When you use a name defined as a formula, it acts something like a one-line function macro, but it can reside on a worksheet as well as on a macro sheet. Each time a formula that uses the name is recalculated, the formula in the name definition recalculates as well. This lets you simplify sheet formulas by condensing calculations into a name.

For example, you could define the name *squareLeft* (in R1C1 style) as *=RC[–1]^2*. This name squares the value in the cell to the left of the cell containing the name. Therefore, if you enter

=3*squareLeft

in cell M80, the formula returns three times the square of the value in cell L80.

If you try to use the Goto dialog box to go to a name that contains a complex formula, Excel returns the message *Reference is not valid.*

Dynamic names

When you define a name in most other spreadsheet programs, the dimensions of the name are fixed until you either redefine the name or physically alter the sheet. For example, after *test* is defined as the range $A$1:$A$3, it doesn't change unless you or a macro explicitly changes it.

Often, however, you'll want to use names with range definitions that adapt to the changing conditions on a sheet. To do so, you can define a dynamic name, which is a name that uses a formula to calculate the range to which the name refers.

Let's suppose you enter daily sales into a database each day, entering the date in column A and the sales for that day in column B. You could define the name *lastFive* to always reference the last five days of sales. This information would allow you to use formulas such as =SUM(lastFive) and =AVERAGE(lastFive), which return the sum and the average of the last five days of sales.

Assuming you enter each day's sales in the row above the bottom border of your database, the following formula returns the reference of the last sales amount in the database:

```
=INDEX(Database,ROWS(Database)–1,2)
```

The following formula returns the reference for the sales amount four rows above this cell:

```
=INDEX(Database,ROWS(Database)–5,2)
```

The reference for the last five days of sales is equal to the range defined by these two references. Therefore, the definition of *lastFive* in the Define Names dialog box would be:

```
=INDEX(Database,ROWS(Database)–5,2):INDEX(Database,ROWS
 (Database)–1,2)
```

Macro functions for working with names

Although no standard worksheet functions are available for working with names, Excel offers several macro functions for this purpose: functions for creating and deleting names, returning information about names, and returning a name given its definition. One of these is the ARGUMENT function, which takes a value passed to a function macro and assigns it a name in the macro sheet. (We discussed the ARGUMENT function in Chapter 3, so we won't go into it here.) Two others are the FOR and the FOR.CELL functions, which we cover in Chapter 9, "Controlling Program Flow."

DEFINE.NAME(nameT,*refersTo,macroTypeN,shortCutT,hiddenL*)
DEFINE.NAME?(*nameT,refersTo,macroTypeN,shortCutT*)

Use this function to define a name on the active sheet. The *nameT* argument is the name, chosen according to the rules presented earlier in this chapter for defining names. The *refersTo* argument can be a constant number, text, or a logical value that is assigned to the name. This argument can also be a reference or a formula in the form of text, with references given in the R1C1 style. If omitted, Excel assumes the current selection.

When used on an active macro sheet, you can use DEFINE.NAME to define both command and function macros, by supplying a number specifying the type of the macro (1 for function macros, 2 for command macros, and 3 or omitted if *nameT* doesn't define a macro). If the macro being defined is a command macro, you can specify a single letter through the *shortCutT* argument.

Notice that the question-mark form of the DEFINE.NAME function doesn't contain the *hiddenL* argument, which does not correspond to an option in the Define Name dialog box. You can use this argument to hide names that you don't want to appear in the Paste Name, Define Name, or Goto dialog box. You can also use it for creating a name on a sheet that you expect others to use, but you don't want a user redefining the name. For example, if you inserted the formula

```
=DEFINE.NAME("macroVersionN","FormatMacro 2.01",,,TRUE)
```

in a macro that formatted a worksheet, the formula would define the name *macroVersionN* on the worksheet, assign it the current version number of the macro, and hide it from the users of the worksheet.

SET.NAME(nameT,*value*)

Use this function to define the name specified by *nameT* on the macro sheet, whether or not the macro sheet is active. If you omit *value,* Excel deletes *nameT.*

This function is less powerful than DEFINE.NAME because SET.NAME can't be used to define the text of formulas, values, or references as true formulas, values, or references. (For example, it can't define "=A1+1" as the formula =A1+1.) Also, SET.NAME can't be used to define command or function macros.

Excel supports a shorthand syntax for assigning values to names in a macro. This form is unusual because it deviates from the convention that only formulas preceded by an equal sign are executed by Excel. This syntax is easy to use, however, because it conforms to other programming languages, such as Basic, that support the definition and assignment of values to names. To use this syntax, you simply enter the name, an equal sign, and the value you want to assign to the name.

For example, inserting either

```
=SET.NAME("n",1)
```

or

```
n=1
```

achieves the same end. In either case, if you open the Define Name dialog box, you'll see the name *n* defined and assigned the value *1*. If, however, you inserted

```
n=$A$1
```

in the macro, Excel would first evaluate the reference and then assign *n* to whatever value was stored in cell A1.

NAMES(*documentT,typeN*)

This information function returns to the macro sheet a horizontal array of all names defined in *documentT*, in alphabetic order. If *documentT* is omitted, Excel assumes the active document. The *typeN* argument, if 1 or omitted, returns only unhidden names; if 2, returns only hidden names; if 3, returns all names.

You can use the INDEX function to return the *n*th name in the array, as in

```
=INDEX(NAMES(),5)
```

which returns the fifth name on the active sheet.

Finally, you can use the TRANSPOSE function to change a name array from horizontal to vertical. For example,

```
=SET.NAME("vertNameArray",TRANSPOSE(NAMES("MYSHEET.XLS",3)))
```

defines the name *vertNameArray* on the macro sheet and assigns to that name a vertical array of all the names, whether hidden or not, defined in the worksheet MYSHEET.XLS.

LIST.NAMES()

This function is the equivalent of choosing the Formula Paste Name command, selecting the Paste List option, and pressing Enter: It enters a list of all the names defined in the active sheet, except for hidden names, starting at the active cell. If the active document is a worksheet, Excel enters a table having as many rows as names defined on the sheet, and two columns. The first column lists the name as text, and the second column lists the definition of the name as text.

If the active document is a macro sheet, Excel adds two more columns: a column for the type of the name (1 for function macros, 2 for command macros, and 0 otherwise) and a column for the shortcut keys belonging to command macros.

Interestingly, the formulas pasted into the sheet are in text form. They look like standard Excel formulas, but they perform no calculations in the sheet. If you click in any of these cells or replace text in them, they become real formulas.

DELETE.NAME(nameT)

This function is the equivalent of using the Define Name command, selecting the name specified by *nameT*, and clicking the Delete button: Excel deletes that name from the active document.

GET.NAME(nameT)

This information function returns as text the definition of the specified name as it would appear in the Define Name dialog box; references are given in the R1C1 style. You can use the text form of an external reference to find the definition of a name on a certain sheet. For example,

```
=GET.NAME("salesTotal")
```

returns the definition of *salesTotal* on the macro sheet;

```
=GET.NAME("!salesTotal")
```

returns its definition on the active sheet; and

```
=GET.NAME("MYSHEET.XLM!salesTotal")
```

returns its definition on the macro sheet named MYSHEET.XLM.

GET.DEF(defT,*documentT,typeN*)

This information function, in a sense the opposite of GET.NAME, returns as text the first name listed in the Define Name dialog box matching the *defT* argument. You must use R1C1-style references in the text supplied for *defT*, but you can leave off the preceding equal sign. The *documentT* argument specifies the name of the worksheet or macro sheet on which the name is defined; if omitted, Excel assumes the active sheet. The *typeN* argument, if 1 or omitted, returns only unhidden names; if 2, returns only hidden names; if 3, returns all names.

CREATE.NAMES(*topL,leftL,bottomL,rightL*)

Additionally, Excel includes the CREATE.NAMES function, which is a command-equivalent function for the Formula Create Names command. The four arguments correspond to the Top Row, Left Column, Bottom Row, and Right Column options in the Create Names dialog box. You could, for example, use this function when developing a macro that formats and defines a series of names on a template worksheet.

SET.VALUE(*reference,values*)

This function puts one or more values in the cell or the range of cells on the macro sheet specified by *reference*. This function doesn't define names on the macro sheet, but it is used frequently with named ranges on the macro sheet and functions that use names—particularly SET.NAME and ARGUMENT.

You can use the SET.VALUE function only to put values in cells on the current macro sheet. For example, the following formula returns an error when you run the macro:

```
=SET.VALUE(ACTIVE.CELL(),99)
```

The formula returns an error unless the macro sheet containing the formula is active. To enter the value *99* into the active cell on any sheet, use the following formula:

```
=FORMULA(99,ACTIVE.CELL())
```

Keep in mind, however, that SET.VALUE and FORMULA are distinctly different. If the active cell of the current macro sheet contains a formula, SET.VALUE does not alter that formula. Instead, it merely changes the value that the cell displays. On the other hand, the FORMULA function replaces both the formula and the value in the active cell with the new formula or value that you specify.

Using names in macros

Following is a series of applications for working with names in a macro; we show these functions working together.

Determining the size of a named range

You can use the ROWS and COLUMNS functions to determine the dimensions of a given name, if that name evaluates to a reference. For example, assuming the name of a range on the active sheet is *data*, the formula

```
=ROWS(!data)
```

returns the number of rows in the range assigned to *data*, and

```
=COLUMNS(!data)
```

returns the number of columns in *data*.

Changing elements of an array stored as a defined name

Let's say that you've defined the name *array* on an active worksheet as *={1;2;3;4}*. You want to change the array to *={1;2;3;99}*. How does one go about doing this?

You can't directly modify the definition of a name. Instead, you must convert the array to text, use string functions to modify the text, and then redefine the name using the new text. The lines of macro code at the top of the facing page illustrate the procedure.

	A	B	C
5		=GET.NAME("array")	Returns "={1;2;3;4}"
6		=SUBSTITUTE(B5,"4","99")	Returns "={1;2;3;99}"
7		=DEFINE.NAME("array",DEREF(B6))	Redefines "array".

If the name you want to update is on the macro sheet instead of on the active sheet, the problem is more difficult—because you can't use SET.NAME to define a text string as anything other than text. (In the formula in cell B7 above, using SET.NAME would define *array* as the text *"={1;2;3;99}"*, not as the array constant {1;2;3;99}.) Therefore, if *array* is on the macro sheet, you must activate the macro sheet, use the above lines of macro code, and then reactivate the original active sheet.

However, there's an easy way to take this round trip. Use the formula

```
=FORMULA.GOTO(A1)
```

to go to cell A1 on the current macro sheet. After the macro has updated the name, use the formula

```
=FORMULA.GOTO()
```

to return to the selection in the sheet that was previously active.

Deleting temporary names on a sheet

You can use any name in any way that you want, of course. However, you might find it convenient to use names beginning with a character such as the underscore or period to solve two problems that you might experience.

First, sometimes macros must define names on a worksheet for the macro to use. Some of these names are temporary and some are permanent. When your macro creates a name, however, you must take care not to have it create a name that existed on the sheet previously. If it does, the definition your macro gives the name will undoubtedly be different than its earlier definition, probably wreaking all sorts of havoc on the sheet.

Second, after the macro has done its work, you might need to delete names created by the macro. When you do so, you must be careful to avoid deleting names that someone created in the worksheet previously.

To solve both these problems, you can begin these special-purpose names with an underscore or with any other text you're sure is unique, such as mac1. (Note: If you do this, never start a name with these reserved characters for any other purpose.) Doing so offers several advantages:

- You know that your macro can safely delete any name that begins with an underscore without corrupting any names required by the sheet.

- You can easily delete all such names in a macro without having to specify every name completely.

For example, the following macro deletes all names beginning with an underscore.

cmd	**DeleteTempNames**	Deletes all names starting with "_".
	=SET.NAME("arrayNames",NAMES())	Get an array of every name.
	=FOR("n",1,COLUMNS(arrayNames))	For the number of names...
thisName	= INDEX(arrayNames,n)	Find each name.
	= IF(LEFT(thisName,1)="_")	If it begins with "_", then
	= DELETE.NAME(thisName)	delete it.
	= END.IF()	
	=NEXT()	Next name.
	=RETURN()	

Entering arrays with SET.VALUE

Let's say you've defined the name *array* on a macro sheet as *{1;2;3;4}*, and you want to enter this array into the range D1:D4 of the macro sheet. But when you use the following command, the value *1* is incorrectly entered into all four cells:

```
=SET.VALUE(D1:D4,array)
```

How do you go about entering the correct values?

To use a name that references an array, you must enter the macro formula as an array. To do so, first edit the formula by clicking in it, then press Ctrl-Shift-Enter [Mac—also Command-Enter]. After you do so, the formula enters the values 1 through 4 in cells D1 through D4, respectively.

8

Navigating Worksheets and Macro Sheets

Suppose you want a macro to select the entire database beginning several rows below the active cell. How do you do it? Or suppose the active cell is at the top of a range of values and you want a macro to select the bottom value in the range. What macro functions should you use?

These are among the questions most frequently asked about Excel macros. This is no surprise. When you're new to Excel macros, it isn't easy to get around the worksheet.

Fortunately, it's easy to navigate the worksheet with macros, after you know a few basic principles. This chapter discusses how to get around the worksheet itself and how to get around ranges and values in the worksheet. Much of this chapter builds on the information presented in the last chapter—working with references and using names to refer to ranges on worksheets and macro sheets.

The SELECT and FORMULA.GOTO functions

The macro functions SELECT and FORMULA.GOTO are very similar, but they have several significant and useful differences. We've already made extensive use of the SELECT function in earlier chapters, but let's investigate it and FORMULA.GOTO in detail.

SELECT(*selectionRef,activeCellRef*)

The SELECT action-equivalent macro function has three forms. The first is for selecting cells on a worksheet or macro sheet; the second is for selecting objects on a sheet; the third is for selecting the items in a chart. Form 1 of the function takes two arguments: *selectionRef* specifies the selection, and *activeCellRef* indicates the location of the active cell within the selection. Both arguments can take A1-style references, absolute and relative R1C1-text format references, and references stored as names on the worksheet or macro sheet. If *selectionRef* is omitted, Excel uses the current selection; if *activeCellRef* is omitted, Excel makes the top-left corner cell in *selectionRef* the active cell.

FORMULA.GOTO(*reference,cornerL*)

The FORMULA.GOTO function corresponds to choosing the Formula Goto command [F5; Mac—also Command-G], entering a reference or name that has been assigned a reference, and pressing Enter. The *reference* argument specifies the reference to select, either as an external reference or in the R1C1-text format; it's optional if you've already used the function or the command. If the *cornerL* argument is TRUE, Excel scrolls the sheet so that the top-left corner of *reference* appears in the upper left corner of the window; if *cornerL* is FALSE or omitted, Excel scrolls only if the selected range is outside the currently displayed area on the sheet.

Similarities

Both the SELECT and FORMULA.GOTO functions select an area of a worksheet, and both frequently use the same type of references to specify the range to select. For example, the macros paired in the following table have exactly the same result. In the first row, they both select cell A1 of the active worksheet. In the second row, they both select the cell one row down and one column to the right of the first selection. In the third row, they both select the range B1:B3 of the active worksheet.

=SELECT("R1C1")	=FORMULA.GOTO("R1C1")
=SELECT("R[1]C[1]")	=FORMULA.GOTO("R[1]C[1]")
=SELECT(!$B$1:$B$3)	=FORMULA.GOTO(!$B$1:$B$3)
=RETURN()	=RETURN()

Differences

Using SELECT offers a limitation and an advantage in comparison with using FORMULA.GOTO. The limitation of SELECT is that it can select areas only on the active worksheet; any attempt to move between worksheets with a SELECT formula causes a macro error. The advantage lies in the *activeCellRef* argument, which allows you to specify the active cell within the selection. For example, the following formula selects the area B3:D9 on the active worksheet and makes cell C4 the active cell.

```
=SELECT(!B3:D9,!C4)
```

The Recorder uses the SELECT function when you select an area with your mouse. If you activate another worksheet and then select an area, the Recorder uses the ACTIVATE function and *then* the SELECT function.

Using FORMULA.GOTO offers two advantages over using SELECT. With FORMULA.GOTO, you can select areas on worksheets and macro sheets that are not on the active worksheet. For example, suppose the worksheet BUDGET is active and that the name *sales* is the defined range A5:M45 on the FORECAST worksheet. All the following macro formulas are able to select the *sales* range.

```
=FORMULA.GOTO(FORECAST.XLS!sales)

=FORMULA.GOTO("FORECAST.XLS!sales")

=FORMULA.GOTO(FORECAST.XLS!$A$5:$M$45)

=FORMULA.GOTO("FORECAST.XLS!R5C1:R45C13")
```

To use the SELECT function, on the other hand, first you need to activate the FORECAST worksheet and then make your selection, as in this short macro.

```
=ACTIVATE("FORECAST.XLS")

=SELECT("sales")

=RETURN()
```

The other advantage in using FORMULA.GOTO is created by a small quirk of the function. When you use a FORMULA.GOTO formula in a macro or choose the Goto command, Excel remembers the selection that was current before either command was carried out. To return to that selection, use a FORMULA.GOTO formula with no reference specified. For example, suppose you select the range A1:B3 in the worksheet SALES.XLS and then use the Goto command to select any cell on the FORECAST.XLS worksheet. The macro at the top of the following page returns you to the original selection.

```
=FORMULA.GOTO()
=RETURN()
```

The Recorder uses the FORMULA.GOTO function when you choose the Goto command from the keyboard.

Selecting in a worksheet or macro sheet

Getting around a worksheet using macros is as easy as doing so from the keyboard. Often, it's even easier. Following is a collection of formulas you can use to make navigation in a sheet easier. Many of these techniques use the GET.DOCUMENT function, discussed in more detail in Chapter 10, "Documents, Windows, and Workspaces," to return various pieces of information about the extent of the area on a sheet containing non-empty cells.

Home

To go to cell A1 from the keyboard, press Ctrl-Home [Mac—also Command-Home]. To select cell A1 on the active sheet from within a macro, use the macro formula

```
=SELECT("R1C1")
```

or

```
=SELECT(!$A$1)
```

Similarly, you can substitute any other reference to select any range on the worksheet.

The last cell

To go to the bottom-right cell of a sheet from the keyboard, choose the Formula Select Special command and then choose the Last Cell option [Ctrl-End; Mac—also Command-End]. To select the last cell on the active sheet, use the macro formula

```
=SELECT.LAST.CELL()
```

If you want to determine the reference of the last cell without selecting it, use two of the GET.DOCUMENT functions to assemble the reference of the last cell in the R1C1-text format, as follows:

	...earlier formulas	
lastRow	=GET.DOCUMENT(10)	Last-used row.
lastCol	=GET.DOCUMENT(12)	Last-used column.
lastRef	="R"&lastRow&"C"&lastCol	Assemble the reference.
	...later formulas	

The two GET.DOCUMENT functions return the row number and column number of the last used row and column on the active worksheet. Later in the macro, when you want to use this reference as part of a selection, remember to use the DEREF function. For example, you could use the following formula to select the last cell.

```
=SELECT(DEREF(lastRef))
```

You must use DEREF, of course, because Excel would interpret the formula

```
=SELECT(lastRef)
```

to mean that you want to select the cell named *lastRef* on the macro sheet itself, rather than on the active sheet. And because the SELECT function can't be used to switch sheets, Excel will return an error message if the macro sheet isn't active when it encounters the formula.

However, the DEREF function isn't necessary when you concatenate text to return an R1C1-text format reference within the SELECT function. For example, to select the range extending from the active cell to the R1C1-text format reference *lastRef*, you can use the following formula.

```
=SELECT("RC:"&lastRef)
```

Note: This function is the same as

```
=SELECT.SPECIAL(11)
```

which is discussed a little later in this chapter.

The active cell

You can select the active cell in several ways that are mostly equivalent.

SHOW.ACTIVE.CELL()

The SHOW.ACTIVE.CELL function corresponds to choosing the Formula Show Active Cell command [PC—Ctrl-Backspace; Mac—Command-Delete]. To use this function to select the active cell, use the following formula:

```
=SHOW.ACTIVE.CELL()
```

This formula is the exact equivalent of

```
=SELECT(ACTIVE.CELL())
```

Another way to select the active cell is to use the FORMULA.GOTO function in the following formula.

```
=FORMULA.GOTO(ACTIVE.CELL())
```

The only difference between this formula and the previous two formulas is how the window appears after Excel executes the formulas: The FORMULA.GOTO function puts the selected cell just inside the active window while the previous two functions put it in the middle of the active window.

The beginning of the current row

To go to the beginning of the current row on a sheet, press Home. To select the cell in column A that is in the same row as the active cell from within a macro, use the formula

```
=SELECT("RC1")
```

At times, the first several columns of the sheet will be blank. In this case, you might want to select the cell in the current row that's in the first-used column. To do so, use the following formula.

```
=SELECT("RC"&GET.DOCUMENT(11))
```

The GET.DOCUMENT function returns the number of the first-used column in a sheet. If the sheet is empty, the function returns a value of 0. To capture the reference without selecting it, you could use the following macro fragment.

	...earlier formulas	
firstCol	=GET.DOCUMENT(11)	First-used column.
firstRef	="RC"&firstCol	Assemble the reference.
	...later formulas	

The rightmost cell

To go to the end of the row containing the active cell, press End on the keyboard. To select this cell from within a macro, use the following macro fragment.

	...earlier formulas	
lastCol	=GET.DOCUMENT(12)	Last-used column.
lastRef	="RC"&lastCol	Assemble the reference.
	=SELECT(DEREF(lastRef))	
	...later formulas	

As in an earlier example, this formula depends on GET.DOCUMENT(12), which returns the number of the last-used column in the worksheet. For example, if column L is the rightmost column, the R1C1-text format reference returned by the DEREF function is *RC12*, which the SELECT formula selects.

The top cell of the current column

From the keyboard, no convenient way exists to select the top cell in the current column—but it's easy to do so with a macro. Simply use the macro formula

```
=SELECT("R1C")
```

If the first several rows of a sheet are blank, you might want to select the cell in the current column that is in the first-used row, rather than selecting row 1. To do so, use this macro formula:

	...earlier formulas	
firstRow	=GET.DOCUMENT(9)	First-used row.
firstRef	="R"&firstRow&"C"	Assemble the reference.
	=SELECT(DEREF(firstRef))	
	...later formulas	

The function GET.DOCUMENT(9) returns the number of the first-used row in the active sheet. If the sheet is empty, it returns a value of 0.

As always, if you want to capture the reference for this cell rather than select it, you can use *firstRef* in other formulas.

The bottom cell of the current column

Selecting the bottom cell in the current column is much like selecting the end cell in the current row. To do so, you could use the macro formula

```
=SELECT("R"&GET.DOCUMENT(10)&"C")
```

As mentioned earlier, the function GET.DOCUMENT(10) returns the number of the last-used row in the active sheet. As before, this function returns a value of 0 if the sheet is empty.

The beginning of the first unused row

When you're working with a database, you often want to begin the next entry in column A of the first empty row at the bottom of a worksheet. To find this cell, you can use the formula

	...earlier formulas	
lastRow	=GET.DOCUMENT(10)	Last-used row.
lastRef	="R"&lastRow+1&"C1"	Assemble the reference.
	=SELECT(DEREF(lastRef))	
	...later formulas	

This formula first adds 1 to the number of the bottom row of the worksheet, and then it concatenates the results to return an R1C1-text reference that the SELECT formula uses to select the desired cell.

You can often use and act upon an area of interest without actually selecting the area.

Why not simply select an area of interest? The main reason is that your macro usually runs more quickly if you can reference areas and act upon them without actually selecting them.

Unfortunately, however, Excel provides only a handful of macro functions that let you act upon referenced areas. These functions include COLUMN.WIDTH, DEFINE.NAME, FORMULA, FORMULA.ARRAY, FORMULA.FILL, NOTE, ROW.HEIGHT, and TABLE. Other functions such as the FORMAT functions, FORMULA.FIND, EDIT.DELETE, and so on, all require that you first select the area on which the functions act.

Selecting in a block of data

Selecting ranges of cells around a filled block of data on a sheet requires special techniques. Depending on the shape of the block of data and what you want a macro to do with the data, you can take two general approaches. One approach is to select the edges of the block of data, a method that we discuss below. The other approach is to select the entire block and treat it as a named range, a method we discuss a little later in this chapter.

A block of data

To select an entire block of data from within a macro, you can use the SELECT.SPECIAL function, useful for finding a wide range of items on a worksheet or macro sheet, such as the range occupied by a block of data or an array. This function takes the form

SELECT.SPECIAL(typeN,*valueTypeN,levelsN*)
SELECT.SPECIAL?(*typeN,valueTypeN,levelsN*)

The SELECT.SPECIAL function corresponds to choosing the Formula Select Special command, choosing an option in the dialog box that Excel presents, and pressing Enter. The *typeN* argument determines what you're looking for, according to the following table:

typeN	Item selected
1	Notes
2	Constants
3	Formulas
4	Empty cells
5	Non-empty cells around the active cell
6	Array of which the active cell is a part
7	Row differences
8	Column differences
9	Precedents
10	Dependents
11	Last cell
12	Visible cells in an outline
13	All objects

The *valueTypeN* argument applies only if *typeN* is 2 (for selection of constants) or 3 (for selection of formulas); with this argument you can select the data type of the cells to be selected, and it takes the same numbers as the *dataTypeN* argument in the RESULT function, as follows:

valueTypeN	**Data type selected**
1	Numbers
2	Text
4	Logical values
16	Error values

Finally, the *levelsN* argument applies if *typeN* is 9 (precedents) or 10 (dependents), and it determines the level of precedence or dependence to select: If 1, Excel selects only those cells directly precedent or dependent on the active cell; if 2, Excel selects all levels of cells.

To select a block of data surrounding the active cell, you would use a *typeN* value of 5, as follows:

```
=SELECT.SPECIAL(5)
```

This formula does in a macro what you would do manually by selecting Current Region in the Select Special dialog box. That is, the formula selects the rectangular range of cells around the active cell, bounded by any combination of blank rows, blank columns, and the borders of the sheet.

When you use this command, be certain that the "blank" rows and columns that surround the current region really are blank. If they aren't, you might see unexpected results. For example, if you select any cell in columns B through M in Figure 8-1 that contains numeric data and then use the Select Special command to select the current region, Excel selects the area shown. The reason the program fails to select one of the smaller blocks of data is that each small block is linked to the others by the cells that contain an *x*. In other words, if you select cell B10 and want to use SELECT.SPECIAL to select the block of data in the range B10:D13, you must first delete the *x* in cell E9.

Similarly, you can also get confusing results if a cell contains a formula that evaluates to a value that makes the cell appear empty. For example, if cell N8 in Figure 8-1 contained

```
=""
```

the selected range would extend from cell B2 through Q19.

	A	B	C	D	E	F	G	H	I	J	K	L	M	N	O	P	Q	R
1																		
2										88	15	4						
3										96	94	75						
4										50	31	67						
5									x	16	29	96			7	69	7	
6						52	72	97							92	15	42	
7						29	57	75							1	30	35	
8						96	4	36							51	65	28	
9					x	90	32	5	x									
10		32	6	72						55	81	67						
11		93	67	29						35	80	31						
12		38	87	37						53	63	20						
13		5	54	32						30	94	3						
14									x									
15							27	19	82									
16							46	93	32		5	42	94					
17							29	32	86		35	66	0					
18							25	40	92	x	95	79	16					
19											71	15	44					
20																		

FIGURE 8-1.
If you use SELECT.SPECIAL(5) with any cell containing a number in the shaded area selected, Excel selects the entire shaded area shown.

An edge of a block of data

In Chapter 7 we discuss the process of capturing the reference of a range without actually selecting it. When you're navigating around a block of data of unknown dimensions, however, such a process is no longer possible. Instead, you must first somehow find the edges of the block before you can capture the reference.

We can use Figure 8-1 again to illustrate. Let's say the active cell is somewhere inside the range B10:D13, an unknown distance from an edge in the block of data. You can use the SELECT.END function to find the boundaries of the range.

SELECT.END(directionN)

The SELECT.END action-equivalent function works in the same manner as when using Ctrl-direction key combinations from the keyboard to move the active cell to the edge of a block of data [Mac—also Command-direction key]. The *directionN* argument specifies the direction in which to search.

directionN	Direction to search
1	Left [Ctrl-Left arrow; Mac—also Command-Left arrow]
2	Right [Ctrl-Right arrow; Mac—also Command-Right arrow]
3	Up [Ctrl-Up arrow; Mac—also Command-Up arrow]
4	Down [Ctrl-Down arrow; Mac—also Command-Down arrow]

Specifically, when Excel encounters the SELECT.END function, it starts at the active cell and moves off in the specified direction, stopping when it reaches the end of the current region or the beginning of the next region. For example, if cell C11 in Figure 8-1 is the active cell, SELECT.END(1) selects cell B11, SELECT.END(2) selects cell D11, SELECT.END(3) selects cell C10, and SELECT.END(4) selects cell C13. If, however, cell D11 is the active cell, SELECT.END(2) selects cell J11—the first cell in the next region.

If you want to capture the references of the edges of a block of data on a worksheet or macro sheet, given that the active cell is in the middle of a region, you can adapt the following formulas:

	...earlier formulas	
	=SELECT.END(4)	Move down.
	=SELECT.END(2)	Move right.
botRightRef	=REFTEXT(ACTIVE.CELL())	Find the reference.
botRightRef2	=MID(botRightRef,FIND("!",botRightRef)+1,999)	Remove filename and "!".
	=SELECT.END(3)	Move up.
	=SELECT.END(1)	Move left.
topLeftRef	=REFTEXT(ACTIVE.CELL())	Find the reference.
rangeRef	=topLeftRef&":"&botRightRef2	Assemble the reference.
	...later formulas	

Cell *botRightRef* returns an external reference of the bottom right cell in the R1C1-text format. Cell *botRightRef2* removes the filename and the "!" in the external reference. Cell *topLeftRef* returns the reference of the top-left cell, and cell *rangeRef* takes the two pieces of text and assembles the complete reference.

When you use this technique, however, be certain that you use it only in purely rectangular areas; using this procedure in non-rectangular areas can result in an incorrect reference. For example, if G7 is the active cell when you run this procedure, Excel first moves down to cell G9, then right to cell I9, and captures the reference of the active cell in cell *botRightRef* and *botRightRef2*. Excel then executes the next formula, moving up until it reaches the upper limit of the worksheet, cell I1, and moving left to cell A1. The reference returned in *rangeRef* then becomes R1C1:R9C9.

The moral is: If you're not sure whether the block of data is rectangular, it would be better to first move from the active cell straight up and down, capturing the row numbers of the top and bottom rows in the block. Next, return to the original active cell and move left and right to capture the column numbers of the left and right edges of the block, and finally reassemble the row and column numbers into the range desired.

Areas in a block of data

After you've found the boundaries of a block of data, you can easily select areas within the block. For example, if *topLeftRef* contains the reference of the top-left corner of a range returned in the previous macro, and you want to obtain the reference of the cell that is offset by *rowNum* rows and *colNum* columns, the formula

```
=REFTEXT(OFFSET(TEXTREF(topLeftRef),rowNum–1,colNum–1))
```

returns the reference of the cell in the R1C1-text format. For example, if *topLeftRef* in Figure 8-1 is R10C2 (corresponding to cell B10), and you want the reference of the cell that is one cell down and one cell to the right (both *rowNum* and *colNum* set to 2), the formula would return R11C3.

You can also select entire rows and columns in the block of data. If *rowNum* is the number of the row you want to select in *rangeRef*, the formula

```
=REFTEXT(INDEX(TEXTREF(rangeref),rowNum,0))
```

returns the reference of the entire row. The INDEX function here, given a *columnN* argument of 0, selects entire rows in the supplied range. Similarly, the formula

```
=REFTEXT(INDEX(TEXTREF(rangeref),0,colNum))
```

returns the reference of an entire column in *rangeRef*, given the number of the desired column in *colNum*.

Selecting in a named range

In macros, you often need to select areas within a named range in the worksheet. To do so, you'll generally depend on the INDEX function, discussed in the previous chapter.

The top-left cell of a range

To select the top-left cell of a range is easy. If the worksheet contains a range named *data*, you can use the formula

```
=SELECT(INDEX(!data,1,1))
```

To convert this reference to the R1C1-text format, use the following formula:

```
=REFTEXT(INDEX(!data,1,1))
```

The bottom-right cell of a range

To select the bottom-right cell of a range, you can use the ROWS function to determine the number of rows in the range and the COLUMNS function to determine the number of columns. Doing so produces this formula:

```
=SELECT(INDEX(!data,ROWS(!data),COLUMNS(!data)))
```

Specific rows or columns

To select specific rows or columns in a defined range, use a variation of the preceding formulas. For example, to select column 2 of the range *data*, use either

```
=SELECT(INDEX(!data,1,2):INDEX(!data,ROWS(!data),2))
```

or

```
=SELECT(INDEX(!data,0,2))
```

The first of these formulas selects the column by specifying the range defined by the first and last cells in the column. The second formula uses the fact that if you enter 0 for the row or column argument of an INDEX function, Excel selects the entire column or row specified by the other argument.

Again, if you want to capture the reference produced by the INDEX function in the R1C1-text format, substitute REFTEXT for SELECT in the preceding formulas. For example, if *data* is defined as the range B3:D7, the following formula returns the reference of the third row of this range ("R5C2:R5C4"):

```
=REFTEXT(INDEX(!data,3,0))
```

An area from the active cell through a named range

Suppose you've defined a range named *end* on a sheet. To select an area from the active cell through *end*, use the formula

```
=SELECT(ACTIVE.CELL():!end)
```

Other ideas for getting around your data

At times, your macro must find data that is hidden throughout a sheet. In this circumstance, you must be creative in your macro programming.

Unlike the previous sections in this chapter, this section provides no general procedures to follow for finding your data. This is because you can search for many different kinds of data. Instead, we'll discuss several tools that you can use in your search.

Other uses for SELECT.SPECIAL

SELECT.SPECIAL is one of two powerful and convenient macro functions that Excel provides for selecting data in a sheet, the other being the FORMULA.FIND function, which we discuss a little later in this chapter. We've already encountered SELECT.SPECIAL earlier in this chapter.

Because SELECT.SPECIAL can select more than one area in a sheet, it offers special challenges. The first of these challenges is that of capturing the reference or references that it finds. Of course, capturing a normal reference is not a problem. You can either define the reference as a name or save it in the R1C1-text format with the formula

```
=REFTEXT(SELECTION())
```

However, Excel has a limit of 255 characters for the amount of text in a cell or in the definition of a name. Therefore, if a SELECT.SPECIAL formula creates a multiple selection containing many references, you might not be able to store the entire reference in 255 characters.

To get around this problem, select half the sheet, run SELECT.SPECIAL, capture the references, and then select the other half—and repeat the process. If the references are still too long, instruct your macro to divide the sheet into even smaller sections before running SELECT.SPECIAL.

After you capture the references for the selection, you'll probably want to reference each area within the selection.

To count the number of areas, use the formula

```
=AREAS(reference)
```

where *reference* can be a name, a union of names as in

```
=AREAS(!data1,!data2)
```

or the macro function SELECTION().

To select a particular area, use the *areaN* argument of the INDEX function (discussed in greater detail in the previous chapter). This function takes the form

INDEX(reference,rowN,columnN,*areaN*)

The *areaN* argument is a number from 1 through the number of areas in the selection. The lines of macro code at the top of the following page illustrate how AREAS and INDEX might be used together.

	...earlier formulas	
	=SELECT.SPECIAL(2,1)	Select cells containing constants.
	=DEFINE.NAME("_data",SELECTION())	Store the reference.
areasSelN	=AREAS(SELECTION())	Find the number of areas.
	=FOR("n",1,areasSelN)	
	= SELECT(INDEX(!_data,0,0,n))	
	...formulas for processing each area	
	=NEXT()	
	...later formulas	

The SELECT.SPECIAL formula selects all constants in the sheet. The DEFINE.NAME formula defines the selection as *_data* on the active sheet, and the AREAS formula finds the number of areas in the selection. The *_data* name begins with an underscore to specify a temporary name in a worksheet that is created by a macro. Later, when it's time to delete these temporary names, a macro can safely delete all names beginning with an underscore.

The FOR-NEXT loop looks at each area of the selection. (We cover FOR-NEXT loops in detail in the next chapter.) Because the row and column arguments both equal 0 in the INDEX function, that formula selects the entire area defined by the value of *n*.

I've created a worksheet that contains a lot of data and formulas. Now I want to create a version without numbers so that I can use it as a template for entering new data. How do I write a macro to do this?

Insert the following two macro formulas after the code in your macro that selects the area containing the numbers you want to clear.

```
=SELECT.SPECIAL(2,1)
=CLEAR()
```

The first formula selects all cells within the selection containing constant values. The second formula clears the formulas resulting in numeric values from the selected cells while leaving cell formats unchanged. (Using CLEAR on a worksheet with no argument is equivalent to using =CLEAR(3), which clears the formulas in the selection.)

Of course, the SELECT formula and the succeeding formulas within the FOR-NEXT loop could vary, depending on what you want to do with the data in each area now that you've found it. For example, rather than selecting each area with the SELECT function, you could capture the reference of the area with the formula

```
=REFTEXT(INDEX(!_data,0,0,n))
```

Or you could select a particular cell in each area with the formula

```
=SELECT(INDEX(!_data,rowN,colN,n))
```

Here *rowN* and *colN* are references to row and column positions within each area.

How do I use the SELECT.SPECIAL function to select cells containing 0 values?

The SELECT.SPECIAL function can't be made to select non-zero cells while ignoring cells containing 0. For example, let's say that the most important column in a variance-analysis worksheet calculates the relatively few variances that are in excess of 50 percent. When variances are less than 50 percent, the formulas in this column, which are number-formatted to display blank cells, return a value of 0.

If you're willing to change the variance formula slightly, you can make the selection easily. If *variance* represents the variance calculation, the current formula might be something like

```
=IF(ABS(variance)>.50,variance,0)
```

This formula returns the amount of the variance if its absolute value exceeds 50 percent; otherwise, the formula returns a value of 0. Instead, substitute the formula

```
=IF(ABS(variance)>.50,variance,"")
```

This formula returns a null string if the absolute value of the variance is less than or equal to 50 percent. When you use this formula, the only cells in the column that contain values are those whose values exceed 50 percent. This allows you to use the following formula to select all formulas that return values.

```
=SELECT.SPECIAL(3,1)
```

Using FORMULA.FIND

SELECT.SPECIAL selects all cells in a sheet containing the *type* of contents you specify, and FORMULA.FIND selects the first cell containing the *actual* contents you specify. For example, SELECT.SPECIAL could select all cells that contain constants, but FORMULA.FIND could select the first cell that contains a constant value equal to 193. The FORMULA.FIND function takes the form

FORMULA.FIND(text,inN,atN,byN,*dirN,matchCaseL*)

FORMULA.FIND is a command-equivalent macro function that performs exactly as the Formula Find command does; it selects cells in which the function has found *text*. If *inN* is 1, Excel searches in formulas; if 2, Excel searches in values; if 3, Excel searches in the notes attached to cells. The *atN* argument specifies whether *text* is the entire content of the cell (1), or either all or only part of the cell (2). The *byN* argument tells Excel to search by rows (1) or columns (2). The *dirN* argument specifies the direction of the search: either the next occurrence (1) or the previous occurrence (2). Finally, if *matchCaseL* is TRUE, Excel selects only those cells matching the case of *text*; if FALSE or omitted, Excel does not match the case.

You need to test for two conditions when you use this command in a macro. First, you check whether FORMULA.FIND has found any cells that meet the criteria. Second, because the function finds the same cells over and over forever, you need to know when your macro has found all the occurrences for which you're searching. The following lines of macro code check for both conditions.

	...earlier formulas	
thisText	="1"	Search text.
	=SET.VALUE(tempRef,"")	
	=ERROR(FALSE)	
findTest	=FORMULA.FIND(thisText,2,1,2)	
	=ERROR(TRUE)	
	=IF(NOT(findTest),NoMatch())	
	=IF(REFTEXT(ACTIVE.CELL())=tempRef,GOTO(doNext))	
tempRef	=IF(tempRef="",REFTEXT(ACTIVE.CELL()),tempRef)	Cell to store refs.
	:	
	...formulas that process the found cell	
	:	
	=GOTO(findTest)	
doNext	*...later formulas*	

thisText is the value for which you're searching. In actual practice, this formula will probably be more complex. The SET.VALUE formula initializes (clears) the value in cell *tempRef*, which will contain the reference of the first cell found by the macro, in the R1C1-text format.

The first ERROR formula turns off error checking, which suppresses the error dialog box that appears if no cells are found that meet the search criteria. The FORMULA.FIND formula searches for whole values that match the contents of *thisText*. The second ERROR formula turns error checking back on.

If FORMULA.FIND fails in its search, it returns the value FALSE. Because NOT(FALSE) equals TRUE, the first IF formula jumps to a macro called *NoMatch* whenever FORMULA.FIND fails in its search. *NoMatch* takes whatever action is appropriate to respond to the failed search.

The second IF formula checks whether the new active cell is the same as the first cell found in the search. If it is, the formula branches to *doNext*, which continues the macro.

Because the SET.VALUE formula sets the initial value of *tempRef* to a null string, the third IF formula replaces the string with the R1C1-text reference of the first active cell it encounters. From that point on, the text in this cell doesn't change.

After your other macro formulas do what you want with the active cell selected by the FORMULA.FIND function, the final GOTO formula loops back to *findTest* for another search. Notice that if the macro actually reaches this cell, the FORMULA.FIND function has found a cell that meets its criteria. Therefore, there's no reason to loop back to the first ERROR formula.

Both SELECT.SPECIAL and FORMULA.FIND search the entire sheet if a single cell is selected when Excel executes these functions.

Therefore, if your macro determines the area to search, it's always a good idea to check for a single-cell range immediately before using either of these functions. To do so, use the formula

```
=IF(ROWS(SELECTION())*COLUMNS(SELECTION())=1,
    HandleOneCell())
```

where *HandleOneCell* is a macro routine set up to deal with a single-cell range. This section might arbitrarily increase the selection to two cells, issue an Alert dialog box, or take some other action, depending on the purpose of your macro.

9
Controlling Program Flow

Some of the real power of macro programming comes from the ability to use macro functions to control program flow. For example, a simple macro can open, print, and close one worksheet. By looping, however, a macro can open, print, and close hundreds of worksheets. Or a short macro can check one cell for a certain value or condition. But by nesting loops, the macro can check every cell in every worksheet on a hard disk.

Branching in macros

Under normal conditions, macros follow Alice's advice: They start at the beginning, and when they get to the end, they stop. However, it's often necessary to interrupt or break the linear order of execution into smaller pieces to reduce redundancy in a system of macros, to save time, or to change the order of execution based on a decision or option chosen.

For example, suppose you have two macros, each of which opens a different worksheet and sets a print area. After the print areas are set, each macro uses virtually identical commands to print the document, reset the print area and page setup, and close the worksheet. Rather than writing the same code twice, you could have each macro jump to a macro subroutine that contains the code common to both routines.

Excel offers several ways to redirect the order of execution within and among the macros on a macro sheet. For example, the GOTO function simply tells Excel to continue execution not with the formula in the cell below the formula being executed but at another location on a macro sheet; the *ref()* syntax provides a method for creating macro subroutines—probably the most powerful control structure available to you; and several methods are available for branching based on a decision, such as the two forms of the IF function and the CHOOSE function.

The GOTO function

Use the GOTO function for jumps, either to a routine on the same sheet as the GOTO formula or to a routine on another macro sheet. This function takes the form

GOTO(reference)

The *reference* argument specifies the cell at which you want macro execution to continue and can be a direct cell reference, a named reference, or an external reference to a routine on another macro sheet. For example, if cell B23 has been assigned the name *endProcessing* on a macro sheet called PROCMAC.XLM, the following three formulas transfer control to the same routine:

```
=GOTO(B23)
=GOTO(endProcessing)
=GOTO(PROCMAC.XLM!endProcessing)
```

The first two formulas redirect program flow to cell B23 on the current macro sheet. The third formula can be used on any macro sheet, but if the specified macro sheet isn't already open, Excel stops the macro and presents the message *Illegal reference argument*. Also, if *reference* is a range of more than one cell, Excel directs the flow of execution to the top-left cell in the specified range.

The dangers of overusing the GOTO function

The GOTO function allows you to redirect program flow to any cell in any open macro sheet. However, if you use this ability extensively, there's a real danger that your macros will become hopelessly complicated. The technical term for this condition is *spaghetti code*, the antithesis of clear, modular macro programming.

If you write spaghetti code, you'll find it difficult to debug or modify a macro because changes in one macro often change the behavior of other macros, which causes changes in still other macros, which can affect the original macro, which... You get the idea.

How should you use the GOTO function so that you avoid spaghetti code?

Probably the best answer is to avoid using the function wherever possible, using one of the other control structures described in this chapter instead.

Using subroutines

The GOTO function tells your macro to go somewhere, without telling it to return. Calls to subroutines tell your macro to go somewhere, perform a task, and come back when finished.

Using subroutines provides many benefits. It lets you create macros in short modules, the purpose of which you can easily define and understand. It lets you more quickly identify sections of a macro that you need to debug or update. It lets you save time by reusing routines in more than one macro. And it lets you create complex macro systems from libraries of routines that are general and that have been tested thoroughly over time.

The way to call a subroutine is to use the *ref()* syntax. In this syntax, you put either a direct or a named reference to a single cell before a pair of parentheses, as follows:

```
=B19()
=ProcessRecord()
```

Obviously, although both forms of reference work, the second is self-documenting and much clearer.

When you use the *ref()* syntax to call subroutines, be careful to include the parentheses. The formula

```
=NextRecord()
```

(with parentheses) calls the subroutine at the cell associated with the name *NextRecord*. The function

```
=NextRecord
```

(without parentheses) returns the value associated with the name *NextRecord*; if the value associated with *NextRecord* is a reference, the value stored in the referenced cell is returned, but Excel does not transfer control to that cell.

Passing values to subroutines

You can pass values to command-macro subroutines, exactly as you pass values to function macros. For example, consider the simple command macro (at the top of the following page) and the subroutine it calls.

cmd p	**DoCenterTitle**	
	=PageCenterTitle("Jim's Report") =RETURN()	Pass argument to routine.

cmd subr	**PageCenterTitle**	Adds a centered header.
	=ARGUMENT("title") =PAGE.SETUP("&c"&title) =RETURN()	Get the title. Set the title, centered.

When you press Ctrl-p [Mac—also Option-Command-p], the *DoCenterTitle* macro passes the text value *Jim's Report* to the *PageCenterTitle* subroutine. As with a function macro, the ARGUMENT function assigns this value to the name *title*. Finally, the PAGE.SETUP function centers the contents of the name as the page header in the active document.

Returning values from subroutines

You can also have Excel return a value from a command subroutine. For example, suppose that for some obscure purpose you want to convert a reference found in a cell on the active worksheet to an external reference at the same location on another sheet. Furthermore, you want your macro to use the value found in that sheet. The following two routines accomplish this purpose.

cmd r	**TranslateRefs**	
	...earlier formulas that select a cell	
cellValue	=ProcRef("PROCMAC.XLM")	Pass doc name to routine.
	...later formulas that use the value	
	=RETURN()	

cmd subr	**ProcRef**	Processes ref in active cell.
	=RESULT(8)	
	=ARGUMENT("thisDoc")	Document name.
currRef	=MID(GET.FORMULA(ACTIVE.CELL()),2,999)	Remove equal sign.
newRef	=thisDoc&"!"&currRef	Create new reference.
	=FORMULA("="&newRef)	Enter new formula.
	=RETURN(TEXTREF(newRef))	Return ref as text.

The *TranslateRefs* macro passes the name of the sheet, in this case *PROCMAC.XLM*, to the command macro subroutine *ProcRef*, which assigns the sheet name to the argument *thisDoc*. *ProcRef* gets the formula in the active cell and the MID function removes the preceding equal sign, leaving only the reference itself. The formula in cell *newRef* constructs an external reference to the specified sheet. The FORMULA function in the next cell enters the reference into the active cell, preceding it with an equal sign.

This macro also illustrates the steps you must follow to pass a reference from a subroutine back to the calling formula. To do this, you must include the RESULT(8) function, which specifies that only a reference can be returned. (We discuss the RESULT function in Chapter 3, "Function Macros.") Here the RETURN formula in the *ProcRef* subroutine converts the text form of the reference to a true external reference, and it returns the reference to the cell *cellValue*, which contains the formula that called the subroutine. Excel evaluates this reference to the value stored in the cell referenced. In this case, RESULT isn't really needed; if you deleted the RESULT formula, Excel would evaluate *TEXTREF(newRef)*, produce an external reference that evaluates to the value stored in the referenced cell, and return that value to the calling formula in *TranslateRefs*. However, if you wanted to use the new external reference in another formula, you would want Excel to return the reference of the cell and not the value stored in the cell, requiring the use of the RESULT function.

It might seem surprising at first, but Excel returns the value #N/A to the calling formula if a subroutine uses

```
=RETURN()
```

without passing a value back to the calling formula. This happens because the formula isn't returning anything. Although the RETURN formulas for most subroutines contain no return values, the formula that calls the subroutine expects a return value. As with any function in Excel that is expected to return a value and doesn't, the subroutine returns #N/A.

A command subroutine that returns values acts the same as a function macro, as in these examples:

```
=COLUMN.WIDTH(GetWidth(),GetCol())

=GetTotal()*S5
```

The COLUMN.WIDTH formula sets the width of the columns specified by the *GetCol* macro, using the width calculated by the *GetWidth* macro. The second formula multiplies the results of the *GetTotal* macro by 5.

Although command subroutines perform much the same as function macros, they are different in at least three ways. First, a command subroutine can be called only by a command macro. Second, command subroutines can use the full range of macro commands, not only those limited to function macros. Third, because the *ref()* syntax permits using direct cell references instead of named references, no names need be assigned to command subroutines (although for the sake of clarity we don't recommend you do this).

Function macros can use subroutines as well, of course. But as you would expect, these subroutines can use only the macro functions that function macros themselves can use.

Using HALT in subroutines

Typically, you use the RETURN function to halt the currently running macro. However, sometimes you might like all currently running macros to stop—for example, if a macro has encountered a serious error condition. The HALT function takes the form

HALT(*cancelCloseL*)

where *cancelCloseL* is used only for the rare circumstance when you've put the HALT function inside an Auto_Close macro. If *cancelCloseL* is TRUE, Excel halts the Auto_Close macro but prevents the macro sheet from being closed; if FALSE, Excel still halts the macro but permits closing the macro sheet by hand. If you specify *cancelCloseL* in any macro other than an Auto_Close macro, Excel ignores the argument.

Using CALLER in subroutines

The CALLER function, which takes no argument, returns various types of information about the cell or cells containing the formula that calls either a function macro or an Auto_Open or an Auto_Close macro. The information returned depends on how the macro was called:

- If the custom function (that is, the function that calls a function macro) was entered in a single cell, CALLER returns the reference of the cell.
- If you've entered the custom function as part of an array formula, CALLER returns the reference of the range.
- If you've used CALLER in a subroutine macro called by either an Auto_Open or an Auto_Close macro, CALLER returns the name of the sheet calling the Auto_Open or the Auto_Close macro.
- If you've used CALLER in a macro attached to an object on a worksheet or macro sheet, it returns the identifier of the object.
- Finally, if you've used CALLER in a command macro initiated by the user, it returns the #REF! error value to the macro.

For example, suppose that cell B3 on worksheet TEST.XLS calls the macro function *MyFnc* on macro sheet MACLIB.XLM. The function

```
=REFTEXT(CALLER())
```

returns the reference of the calling cell, or *TEST.XLS!R3C2*. Assuming that cell B3 has been assigned the name *thisCell*, you can find the name of the cell with the following function:

```
=GET.DEF(REFTEXT(CALLER()))
```

Using RESTART in subroutines

The RESTART function provides a means for skipping levels in nested subroutines without requiring you to use the HALT or RETURN function. To see how you might use this function, consider a macro system where one subroutine calls another subroutine, which calls another subroutine, and so on for many levels. Suppose a macro detects an error that requires that it bypass the intervening subroutines in its "return trip" and instead return immediately to the top-level macro. The RESTART function lets you achieve this purpose and takes the form

RESTART(*levelN*)

It bypasses the number of RETURN functions specified by *levelN*. The following example illustrates how this function works:

	MacroA	
	=ALERT("In MacroA")	
	=MacroB()	
	=ALERT("Back to MacroA")	
	=RETURN()	

	MacroB	
	=ALERT("In MacroB")	
	=MacroC()	
	=ALERT("Back to MacroB")	
	=RETURN()	

	MacroC	
	=ALERT("In MacroC")	
	=MacroD()	
	=ALERT("Back to MacroC")	
	=RETURN()	

	MacroD	
	=ALERT("In MacroD")	
	=RESTART(1)	
	=RETURN()	

After Excel encounters the RESTART(1) function in *MacroD*, execution continues normally until it reaches the RETURN function at the end of *MacroD*. Then, instead of returning to *MacroC* as it would if RESTART weren't present, the function returns to the cell containing the formula

=ALERT("Back to MacroB")

Consequently, the second ALERT formula in *MacroC* isn't executed.

If you used a *levelN* argument of 2, the RETURN function in *MacroD* would skip two macro calls and return to the second ALERT function in *MacroA*.

Branching on a decision

To jump, you can use GOTO functions or (preferably) the *ref()* syntax to call macro subroutines. Often, however, you need to choose from two or more alternatives and jump to a corresponding routine. Excel supports several methods for accomplishing this. You can use one of the two forms of the IF function to test for a condition and choose one of two alternatives, depending on whether the condition is met. You can also use the CHOOSE function to choose one alternative from a numbered list of alternatives.

The first form of the IF function

Used alone, GOTO and the *ref()* syntax are unconditional—that is, they redirect program flow to the specified cell under all conditions. But the function

```
=IF(testValue=1000,MacroA(testValue),MacroB(testValue))
```

is conditional: if *testValue* equals 1000, execution continues with *MacroA;* otherwise, execution continues with *MacroB.*

This method of redirecting program flow is called *branching* because the path that the program follows splits into two branches at the IF formula. Form 1 of the IF function can be used on both worksheets and macro sheets and takes the form

IF(testL,*valueIfTrue,valueIfFalse*)

where *testL* is a formula that evaluates to TRUE or FALSE. If *testL* evaluates to TRUE, the function returns *valueIfTrue.* If *testL* evaluates to FALSE, the function returns *valueIfFalse;* if not given, the IF function returns FALSE. For example:

=IF(1=1,"Yes","No")	Returns *Yes* because the expression *1=1* evaluates to TRUE.
=IF(1=1,"Yes")	Also returns *Yes.*
=IF(1=2,"Yes","No")	Returns *No* because the expression *1=2* evaluates to FALSE.
=IF(1=2,"Yes")	Returns FALSE because no second argument is given.

Of course, you can use an expression (such as another function) instead of a constant. In a macro sheet, these expressions can contain macro formulas as well as worksheet formulas. For example, if *testValue* equals 1000, the following functions all execute the expression given as the *valueIfTrue* argument:

```
=IF(testValue=1000,SUM(!$F$3:!$F$88),SUM(!$H$3:!$H$88))

=IF(testValue=1000,SET.VALUE(B45,99),SET.NAME("testValue",99))
```

```
=IF(testValue=1000,RETURN(),GOTO(nextStep))
=IF(testValue=1000,GOTO(B23),GOTO(B30))
```

IF functions can also return references. For example, you can write a slightly shorter version of the last formula by putting the IF function within a GOTO function, like this:

```
=GOTO(IF(testValue=1000,B23,B30))
```

When a macro formula returns FALSE, program execution continues with the next macro function. Therefore, when Excel encounters the formula

```
=IF(testValue=1000,GOTO(B23))
```

it continues macro execution in the next cell when *testValue* is not equal to 1000, but it branches to cell B23 when *testValue* does equal 1000.

Although the *testL* argument for the IF function normally uses a logical test, the IF function can accept any number or any formula that returns a number. If that number is 0, Excel evaluates it as FALSE; otherwise, it evaluates the number as TRUE.

Therefore, Excel returns *Yes* for each of these formulas:

```
=IF(2*3,"Yes","No")
=IF(–99,"Yes","No")
```

And it returns *No* for each of these formulas:

```
=IF(2–2,"Yes","No")
=IF(0,"Yes","No")
```

The IF function, used in this way, offers but two branching alternatives—one for TRUE and one for FALSE. At times, however, you need more than two branches. You can increase the number of branches by "nesting" IF functions, as shown in the following example:

```
=IF(error<0,LessThanZero(error),IF(error=0,EqualsZero(error),
    MoreThanZero(error)))
```

This rather confusing formula continues macro execution with the *LessThanZero* subroutine if *error* is less than 0. Otherwise, Excel executes the second IF function. This function continues macro execution with the *EqualsZero* subroutine if *error* equals 0, or the *MoreThanZero* subroutine if *error* is greater than 0.

The second form of the IF function

The second form of the IF function is available only on macro sheets, and it's very similar to the IF statements used in traditional programming languages such as Basic. When you use it, you must also use the END.IF function. This form of the IF function is

IF(testL)

...formulas to be executed if testL *evaluates to TRUE*

END.IF()

The main benefit of this form of the IF function is that you can have a macro execute more than one formula if *testL* evaluates to TRUE. This programming structure also eliminates one of the main motivations to use the GOTO function.

If you want another set of formulas to be executed if *testL* evaluates to FALSE, you can use the ELSE function, as follows:

=IF(testL)

...formulas to be executed if testL *evaluates to TRUE*

=ELSE()

...formulas to be executed if testL *evaluates to FALSE*

=END.IF()

Finally, if you want to test for and respond to a complex set of conditions, you can use the ELSE.IF function, as follows:

=IF(test1L)

...formulas to be executed if test1L *evaluates to TRUE*

=ELSE.IF(test2L)

...formulas to be executed if test2L *evaluates to TRUE*

=ELSE()

...formulas to be executed if test2L *evaluates to FALSE*

=END.IF()

The group of formulas preceded by the ELSE function in this type of structure constitutes a catchall for conditions not met by the other tests in the chain. For instance, expanding on the nested IF example above, the following formulas call four different macro subroutines, depending on whether *error* is less than 0, 0, between 0 and 10, or greater than 10:

```
=IF(error<0)
=  LessThanZero(error)                Call subroutine.
=ELSE.IF(error=0)
=  EqualsZero(error)                  Call subroutine.
=ELSE.IF(error<=10)
=  LessThanTen(error)                 Call subroutine.
=ELSE()
=  GreaterThanTen(error)              Call subroutine.
=END.IF
```

This example also illustrates another benefit of this type of structure: You can use spaces to indent lines to make the organization of the structure clearer.

The CHOOSE function

Although nested IF functions can branch to multiple locations, the CHOOSE function sometimes provides a more convenient way of accomplishing this when you can assign numbers to the allowable options. This standard worksheet function takes the form

CHOOSE(indexN,value1,*value2*,...)

The *indexN* argument is usually a formula that returns a number indicating the position of one of the values that follow. For example:

```
=CHOOSE(1,10,20,30)
```

returns *10* and

```
=CHOOSE(3,10,20,30)
```

returns *30*. If *indexN* refers to values that don't exist, the function returns an error value. For example, both these functions return *#VALUE!*:

```
=CHOOSE(0,10,20,30)
```

```
=CHOOSE(4,10,20,30)
```

In macros, the CHOOSE function often affords a shorter and clearer way to provide multiple branches than does the nested IF function. If *option* is a number from 1 through 3, for example, the following formula starts one of three subroutines:

```
=CHOOSE(option,PrintRange(ref),RecalcRange(ref),ClearRange(ref))
```

Continuing our error-checking application, you could use the following formula to jump to one of a series of cells, depending on whether *error* is negative, zero, or positive:

```
=GOTO(CHOOSE(SIGN(error)+2,B30,B35,B40))
```

Here the SIGN function returns *–1* if *error* is negative, *0* if it's equal to zero, and *1* if it's positive. Adding 2 to these results returns a value from 1 through 3, which selects one of the three references that follow. (Of course, a formula like this is a good example of the programming principle that the craftiness of a routine is directly proportional to its incomprehensibility six months down the road.)

Using formulas with the *ref()* syntax.

Although you will generally specify a named reference when you use the *ref()* syntax to call a subroutine, you can also assemble a direct cell reference to use as the *ref* portion of the syntax. In fact, you can add a set of parentheses to the end of any in a wide range of expressions, turning an expression that returns an R1C1-text reference into a call to a subroutine. However, this is also a powerful way to turn an otherwise clear set of macros into a plate of spaghetti code.

You could, for example, use the following formula:

```
=CHOOSE(chooseValueN,B30,B35,B40)()
```

Earlier in this chapter, we used this CHOOSE function to specify the cell to which the macro should branch using the GOTO function. But here, by following this CHOOSE function with a set of parentheses, the function now calls one of three subroutines, depending on whether *chooseValueN* is 1, 2, or 3.

The RUN function

Another way to run a command macro is to use the RUN function, which takes the forms

RUN(*reference,stepL*)
RUN?(*reference,stepL*)

This function starts the macro that begins in the top-left cell of *reference*; if *reference* is omitted, Excel begins execution in the active cell. The *stepL* argument, if TRUE, runs the routine in single-step mode; if FALSE or omitted, the routine runs normally.

Generally, *reference* is provided by a named range, as in these examples:

=RUN(PrintReports)

=RUN(MACLIB1.XLM!PrintReports,TRUE)

The first example runs the macro beginning in the top-left cell of the range named *PrintReports*, which does not need to be (but can be) defined as either a function or a command macro. The second example runs the macro of the same name that resides on the macro sheet MACLIB1.XLM.

Additionally, you can run all the Auto_Open or Auto_Close macros on the active macro sheet by setting *reference* to 1 or 2, respectively.

Because the *ref()* syntax provides an easy, clear way to run a macro routine, RUN is seldom used. Its main benefits are in executing Auto_Open and Auto_Close macros collectively, in debugging problem macros, and in debugging routines that start execution at the active cell.

Branching to a macro on an event.

You can have Excel run a macro on what is called an *event*, rather than under direct control. There are several types of events: the passage of time, the occurrence of an error in a macro, sheets being opened or closed, the presentation of data from another application, the pressing of a certain key, and so on. We discuss this type of "branching" in Chapter 12, "Taking Action Through Macros."

Using loops in macros

Using a loop in a macro repeats a process until a certain condition is reached. When the condition is met, the loop stops, and execution continues with the formulas following the loop. Looping lets you multiply the capability of your macros over and over, greatly increasing their power and applicability.

Generally, a macro can use one of two methods to determine when a goal is reached. First, it can loop a certain number of times, having previously determined the number of repetitions that are needed to reach the goal. The FOR-NEXT loop is the most common way to implement this approach.

Second, the macro can continue to loop until a value within it reaches a predetermined condition. Excel provides the WHILE and NEXT functions to use for this approach.

The FOR-NEXT loop

The FOR-NEXT loop is probably the most common loop in programming. It's easy to use, easy to understand, and easy to debug. The FOR function takes the form

FOR(counterT,startN,endN,*stepN*)

...formulas to be executed until counterT *equals* endN

NEXT()

The *counterT* argument must be text or a reference to a name or cell that contains text. When Excel encounters the FOR formula, it defines *counterT* as a name on the macro sheet (listed in the Define Name dialog box after the loop has been executed), and it assigns the number *startN* to the name. Each time the formulas between the FOR and NEXT formulas are executed, *stepN* is added to the value stored in *counterT* until *counterT* exceeds *endN*; if omitted, *stepN* is assumed to be 1.

The following example illustrates how a FOR-NEXT loop works; it begins with the active cell and enters the squares of the first *endN* numbers, moving down one cell with each pass through the loop:

cmd	**TestFOR**	
startN	1	Starting value.
endN	6	Ending value.
stepN	1	Step increment.
	=FOR("count",startN,endN,stepN)	
	= FORMULA(count^2)	
	= SELECT("R[1]C")	
	=NEXT()	
	=RETURN()	

When Excel encounters the FOR formula, Excel defines *count*, setting it to the value stored in *startN*. It then enters the square of *count*, which is 1^2, or 1, and then selects the cell below the active cell. When Excel reaches the NEXT formula, execution returns to the top of the loop, adds *stepN* (that is, 1) to *count*, and begins the loop over again. When the value in *count* is greater than *endN*, execution continues with the cell after the NEXT formula.

The FOR-NEXT loop can be useful when we need to perform a sequential operation in a macro loop using the counter value controlled by the FOR function. For example, as the value assigned to the name *count* increases from 1 through 10 in a FOR-NEXT loop:

```
=SELECT("R"&count&"C1")
```

selects rows 1 through 10 in column A;

```
=MID("Mississippi",count,1)
```

selects characters 1 through 10 in the text *Mississippi;*

```
=INDEX(Database,count,5)
```

returns the value from rows 1 through 10 in the fifth column of *Database;*

```
=OPEN(INDEX(FILES(),count))
```

opens the first through the tenth file (in alphabetic order) in the current directory or folder;

```
=ACTIVATE(INDEX(DOCUMENTS(),count))
```

activates the first through the tenth document (in alphabetic order).

Nested FOR-NEXT loops

Often you'll need to place one FOR-NEXT loop within another, as shown in the following macro, which starts at the active cell and enters the multiplication table, up to 10 times 10, in the cells below and to the right of the active cell:

NestedLoops	
=FOR("count1",1,10)	Start the first loop.
= FOR("count2",1,10)	Start the second loop.
= FORMULA(count1*count2)	Enter the product of the counters.
= SELECT("RC[1]")	Move one cell to the right.
= NEXT()	End the first loop.
= SELECT("R[1]C[-"&count2-1&"]")	Move back to the start of the next row.
=NEXT()	End the second loop.
=RETURN()	

When you run this macro, Excel creates the following table, row by row:

1	2	3	4	5	6	7	8	9	10
2	4	6	8	10	12	14	16	18	20
3	6	9	12	15	18	21	24	27	30
4	8	12	16	20	24	28	32	36	40
5	10	15	20	25	30	35	40	45	50
6	12	18	24	30	36	42	48	54	60
7	14	21	28	35	42	49	56	63	70
8	16	24	32	40	48	56	64	72	80
9	18	27	36	45	54	63	72	81	90
10	20	30	40	50	60	70	80	90	100

Programmers often use the same few names over and over as the names of counters in loops. Traditionally the letters i, j, k, l, m, and n are very common. The benefit of using the same names for counters on macro sheets is that you won't accumulate a range of unneeded names in the Define Name dialog box, but it sometimes helps to use names that reflect the purpose of the counter, such as *thisChar, thisFile,* and so on.

Using the same counter name from macro to macro is probably a reasonable thing to do unless one of these macros calls the other. In that case, a name defined in one loop is used in another loop. Because the same name is being continually redefined, the two macros can behave very strangely indeed. To avoid this problem, change the name of one of the counters.

The WHILE-NEXT loop

The FOR-NEXT loop works well when you know the number of iterations needed beforehand. A WHILE-NEXT loop tests for a condition using a logical test; while the condition is met, the loop continues. If not met, Excel continues execution with the formula following the loop. A WHILE-NEXT loop takes the form

WHILE(testL)

...formulas to be executed until testL *is FALSE*

NEXT()

Here's an example:

	TestWHILE	
lastRow	=GET.DOCUMENT(10)	Number of last row.
	count=0	Initialize loop counter.
	=WHILE(ROW(ACTIVE.CELL())<lastRow)	Start the loop.
	count=count+1	Increment counter.
	= FORMULA(count)	Enter counter in active cell.
	= SELECT("R[1]C")	Move down one cell.
	=NEXT()	End loop.
	=RETURN()	

Cell *lastRow* of this macro contains the row number of the last-used cell in the sheet. As long as the row of the active cell is less than this value, the macro causes the active cell to move down the sheet, row after row. In each iteration of the loop, Excel increments the loop counter and enters the value in the active cell. When the macro ends, the active cell is in the last row of the sheet.

When you use the WHILE function, keep in mind that it tests the logical condition at the beginning of each loop. Therefore, if the breakout condition arises in the middle of the loop, the WHILE function won't discover this fact until the beginning of the next loop.

The following macro has two problems and provides an interesting example. It is supposed to allow the user to put a number into the active cell and move the selection down one row, and then the loop is supposed to begin again. To break out of the loop, the user is supposed to click on Cancel in the Input dialog box or press Esc. This causes the Input dialog box to return FALSE, which causes the WHILE function to break out of the loop.

	TestWHILE2	
	=WHILE(answer<>FALSE)	
answer	= INPUT("Enter the number",7)	
	= FORMULA(answer)	
	= SELECT("R[1]C")	
	=NEXT()	
	=RETURN()	

This macro will never display the Input dialog box because the formula in the cell *answer* returns the value FALSE until the macro executes (recalculates) the formula. However, because the cell does contain FALSE, the WHILE function never lets execution proceed to the cell. Instead, Excel directs execution to the cell after the NEXT formula, which contains the RETURN formula.

To force the WHILE function to execute the initial loop, you could add the following formula as the first line of the macro:

```
=SET.VALUE(answer,TRUE)
```

Even so, this macro would not perform as expected. Yes, it would enter numbers in a column. However, after the user clicks on the Cancel button, the FORMULA function enters FALSE in the active cell before the WHILE function has an opportunity to stop the macro.

The best way to achieve the purpose of this macro is to create a loop that does not use a WHILE function or to use the BREAK function (discussed in a moment) to stop execution of the loop.

The FOR.CELL-NEXT loop

The FOR.CELL-NEXT loop offers an elegant method for applying a procedure to each cell in the selected range, one cell at a time, from left to right, row by row. This function takes the form

FOR.CELL(refNameT,*areaRef,skipblanksL*)

...formulas to be executed for each cell

NEXT()

When Excel encounters a FOR.CELL function, it assigns the reference of the first cell in the range to the name *refNameT*; you can use this name within the FOR.CELL loop. The *areaRef* argument specifies the range to be acted upon; if not supplied, the loop acts upon the current selection. If *skipBlanksL* is TRUE, Excel skips the blank cells in *areaRef*; if FALSE or omitted, the formulas within the loop are applied to every cell in the range. Obviously, skipping blank cells makes the macro run faster.

For example, the following macro solves a common problem in worksheets by combining the contents of two columns containing text into one column.

Jane	Smith
Jane	Austen
Jane	Doe

becomes...

Jane Smith
Jane Austen
Jane Doe

cmd	**TestFOR.CELL**	
	=FOR.CELL("thisCell",,TRUE)	Start loop.
valThisCell	= thisCell	Value of current cell.
valCellRight	= OFFSET(thisCell,0,1)	Value of the cell to right.
newVal	= valThisCell&" "&valCellRight	
	= FORMULA(newVal,thisCell)	Enter concatenated string.
	=NEXT()	End of loop.
	=RETURN()	

To use this macro, select a range on a worksheet—in this case, the three cells that each contain the text *Jane*—and then run the macro. As Excel executes the macro, it assigns the reference of each cell to *thisCell*. Cell *valThisCell* returns the value stored in the cell, and the OFFSET formula in the next cell returns the value in the cell that is one cell to the right of *thisCell*. In cell *newVal* the two values are concatenated with a space inserted between them. Finally, the FORMULA function enters the new value into the cell referenced by *thisCell*. Notice that the FORMULA function does not enter the new value into the active cell, which does not change throughout the execution of the macro. In our example, the three cells that once contained the text *Jane* now contain the text *Jane Smith*, *Jane Austen*, and *Jane Doe*, respectively.

Breaking out of loops

When you use WHILE-NEXT or FOR-NEXT loops, you might occasionally need to break out of them. This requires more than simply jumping to a formula outside the loop. Instead, you must use the BREAK function, which takes the form

BREAK()

Consider this macro, for example:

```
TestBREAK
=FOR("col",1,10)
=  FOR("row",1,10)
=    FORMULA(col&","&row)
=    WAIT(NOW()+"00:00:01")
=    IF(row=5,BREAK())
=  NEXT()
=NEXT()
=RETURN()
```

This macro contains two nested loops, each counting from 1 through 10. When the macro begins, the FORMULA function enters the text *1,1* into the active cell. If the IF function were missing, the macro would count once a second from *1,1* to *1,2* and so on through *1,10*. Then it would count from *2,1* through *2,10*, from *3,1* through *3,10*, and so on through *10,10*.

The IF formula represents a breakout condition, a circumstance in which you want the macro to abort the loop that it's in and continue elsewhere. With this formula in place, the macro counts from *1,1* through *1,5*, from *2,1* through *2,5*, and so on through *10,5*. Notice that because there are two FOR loops, two NEXT functions are necessary—one at the end of each loop.

SECTION THREE

Creating a User Interface

10

Documents, Windows, and Workspaces

The functions described in this chapter provide more information than you ever thought you would want to know about documents, windows (and panes), and workspaces. A *document* is the file that you open: a worksheet, macro sheet, chart, Add-In macro sheet, template, and so on. A *window* is like a lens you can hold up to the document, viewing its formulas or values, for instance. A window can contain one, two, or four *panes*, allowing you to view more than one area in a window simultaneously. Finally, a *workspace* is the environment that Excel provides, in which you work with documents through the contents of their windows.

Excel provides many functions to get information about these elements of the Excel environment and to manipulate them. These functions allow you to change the size of a window, scroll it, eliminate its gridlines, hide it, modify its colors, and so on—all under macro control. Because there are so many of these functions and because each is so easy to use, we'll concentrate on presenting an overview of the range of these functions rather than providing extensive descriptions and examples.

Documents

A document is the file you open or save using the File command. On the Macintosh, the name of a document can take nearly any form. On the PC, document names end in XLS, XLM, XLC, XLA, and so on, depending on the type of document (worksheet, macro sheet, chart, Add-In macro sheet, and so on).

The DOCUMENTS function

The DOCUMENTS function returns a horizontal text array of the names of all open documents, in alphabetic order, and takes the form

DOCUMENTS(*typeN*)

where *typeN* specifies the type of document to include in the list: If 1 or omitted, all open documents except Add-Ins are included; if 2, only open Add-In documents are included; if 3, every open document is included.

For example, to capture the list of every open document except Add-In macro sheets, you can use the following macro:

```
cmd subr    GetDocArray
            =SET.NAME("docArray",DOCUMENTS())
            =RETURN()
```

You can then use the COLUMNS function to return the number of documents returned. For example,

=COLUMNS(docArray)

returns the value 2 when the workspace contains two documents.

You can use the INDEX function to return the document name that's in a specific position in the DOCUMENTS array. For example,

=INDEX(docArray,1)

returns the name of the first document in the list.

The GET.DOCUMENT function

The GET.DOCUMENT information function returns information about a specified document. This function takes the form

GET.DOCUMENT(typeN,*nameT*)

The *nameT* argument specifies the name of an open document; if omitted, Excel assumes the active document. The *typeN* argument determines the type of information returned; it can be a number between 1 and 44 for worksheets and macro

typeN	Data type	Information returned
1	text	Document name.
2	text	Pathname of directory containing document; if document hasn't been saved, or if it isn't open, the function returns #N/A.
3	number	Document type: 1=worksheet, 2=chart, 3=macro sheet, 4=Info window.
4	logical	TRUE if changes were made since document was last saved.
5	logical	TRUE if document is read-only.
6	logical	TRUE if document is protected.
7	logical	TRUE if cells in document are protected.
8	logical	TRUE if document windows are protected.
9	number	First-used row.
10	number	Last-used row.
11	number	First-used column.
12	number	Last-used column.
13	number	Number of windows on document.
14	number	Calculation mode: 1=Auto, 2=Auto Except Tables, 3=Manual.
15	logical	TRUE if iteration is enabled.
16	number	Maximum number of iterations.
17	number	Maximum change between iterations.
18	logical	TRUE if Updating Remote References is enabled.
19	logical	TRUE if Precision As Displayed is enabled.
20	logical	TRUE if document is set to 1904 Date System.
21	4-item horiz. text array	Names of the four default fonts.
22	4-item horiz. numeric array	Sizes of the four default fonts.
23	4-item horiz. logical array	TRUE if one of the four default fonts is bold.
24	4-item horiz. logical array	TRUE if one of the four default fonts is italic.
25	4-item horiz. logical array	TRUE if one of the four default fonts is underlined.
26	4-item horiz. logical array	TRUE if one of the four default fonts is struck through.
27	4-item horiz. numeric array	Color of each font, from 0 (Automatic) through 16.
28	4-item horiz. logical array	TRUE if one of the four default fonts is outlined; always FALSE for Windows and OS/2 versions of Excel.
29	4-item horiz. logical array	TRUE if one of the four default fonts is shadowed; always FALSE for Windows and OS/2 versions of Excel.
30	4-item horiz. text array	Consolidation references for document, #N/A if the list is empty.
31	number	Function used in consolidation, from 1 through 11 (same as specified for CONSOLIDATE function): 1=AVERAGE, 2=COUNT, 3=COUNTA, 4=MAX, 5=MIN, 6=PRODUCT, 7=STDEV, 8=STDEVP, 9=SUM, 10=VAR, and 11=VARP. Returns 9 if not specified.
32	3-item horiz. logical array	TRUE if option is checked in Consolidate dialog box. The three options are: Top Row, Left Column, and Create Links To Source Data.
33	logical	TRUE if Recalculate Before Saving is set.
34	logical	TRUE if Read-Only Recommended is set.
35	logical	TRUE if document is write-reserved, FALSE if not.
36	text	Name of user with current write permission for document (same as owner's name entered when Excel was installed).

(continued)

continued

typeN	Data type	Information returned
37	number	Document file type (same as specified for SAVE.AS function).
38	logical	TRUE if Summary Rows Below Detail is set in Outline dialog box.
39	logical	TRUE if Summary Columns To Right Of Detail is set in Outline dialog box.
40	logical	TRUE if Create Backup File is set in Save As dialog box.
41	number	Number describing display of objects: 1=all are displayed, 2=picture and chart placeholders are used, 3=all objects are hidden.
42	horiz. text array	List of object identifiers.
43	logical	TRUE if Save External Link Values is set in Calculation dialog box.
44	logical	TRUE if objects in document are protected.

sheets. For charts, *typeN* can take the values 1 through 12, 34 through 37, and 40; we'll discuss charts in greater detail in Chapter 13, "Charting with Macros."

Windows Excel uses four fonts, numbered 1 through 4: *typeN* values 21 through 29 return information about these fonts. If a document was created under Windows and then opened on either the Mac or the OS/2 version, these functions continue to return information about the four fonts. If the document was not created under Windows, these functions return information about the Standard Font.

Protecting documents

You can prevent cells in a document from being edited or viewed by the user, through the CELL.PROTECTION function. When you've finished working with a worksheet or macro sheet, you can activate the protection given to cells through the PROTECT.DOCUMENT function. (In Chapter 15, we discuss how to control read and write privileges for a document using the SAVE.AS function.)

The CELL.PROTECTION function is equivalent to setting options in the Cell Protection dialog box and pressing Enter. This function takes the form

CELL.PROTECTION(*lockedL,hiddenL*)

where *lockedL*, if TRUE, locks the currently selected range; if FALSE, unlocks the range. The *hiddenL* argument, if TRUE, hides the range; if FALSE, makes the range become visible. If either argument is omitted, Excel doesn't change the status of the selected range.

To activate the protection of cells in a worksheet, macro sheet (or a chart, even though charts don't contain cells), you must use the PROTECT.DOCUMENT function, which corresponds to the Protect Document and Unprotect Document commands on the Options menu or the Chart menu when a chart is the active document. This function takes the form

PROTECT.DOCUMENT(*contentsL,windowsL,passwordT,objectsL*)
PROTECT.DOCUMENT?(*contentsL,windowsL,passwordT,objectsL*)

where *contentsL*, if TRUE, protects either the cells in a worksheet or macro sheet or an entire chart. The *windowsL* argument, if TRUE, prevents a document's windows from being moved or resized. The *passwordT* argument lets you set a password for the document; if omitted, the user won't need a password to unprotect the document. The *objectsL* argument applies only to worksheets and macro sheets; if TRUE, Excel protects all locked objects on the sheet.

To protect a document, you must set *contentsL*, *windowsL*, and *objectsL* to TRUE; to unprotect the document, set each argument to FALSE.

When you use a password to protect a document through a macro, you should take steps to protect the macro sheet as well so that someone doesn't look in it to discover the password. The measures you take to protect documents and macro sheets with passwords depends on how sensitive the information contained in them is to you and the potential users of your macro applications. The least degree of protection is to protect a document without using a password; this suggests to the user that one should think twice before making changes in the worksheet. At the other end of the scale, you can keep notes on what passwords belong with which documents and macro sheets: Be very careful doing this, because you cannot unprotect a document once its password is lost or forgotten.

Windows

You can view different parts of a document through different windows and in different ways. For example, if you enter the dates in the first window they appear in the second window as well.

Each window can contain one, two, or four panes, as shown in the first window in Figure 10-1 on the following page. The two sets of horizontal panes display information in the same rows, and the two sets of vertical panes show information in the same columns. One of the main uses for panes is for viewing a worksheet's column headings in the two top panes, its row titles in the two left panes, and the remainder of the worksheet data in the bottom-right pane.

The WINDOWS function

The WINDOWS information function returns a horizontal text array of all open windows, displayed in the order in which the documents appear on the screen when they overlap. This function takes the form

WINDOWS(*typeN*)

The *typeN* argument specifies the type of window about which Excel returns information: If 1 or omitted, Excel returns information about every window except those belonging to Add-In documents; if 2, only Add-In documents; if 3, all types of documents.

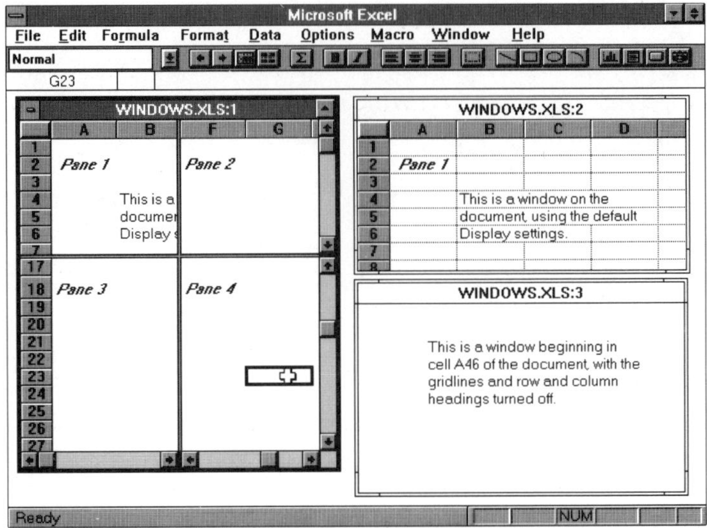

FIGURE 10-1.
This workspace contains three windows on the same document. The first window contains four panes.

For example, suppose you create a macro sheet named MACRO1.XLM in the workspace shown in Figure 10-1 and enter the following macro:

cmd subr	**GetDocWinArray**
	=DEFINE.NAME("docArray",DOCUMENTS())
	=DEFINE.NAME("winArray",WINDOWS())
	=RETURN()

Next, activate in turn windows WINDOWS.XLS:1, WINDOWS.XLS:2, and WINDOWS.XLS:3 on the document, leaving this last window activated. Finally, run the macro. If you then open the Define Name dialog box and select the name *docArray*, you'll see that it is defined as

```
={"MACRO1.XLM","WINDOWS.XLS"}
```

And the name *winArray* is defined as

```
={"WINDOWS.XLS:3","WINDOWS.XLS:2","WINDOWS.XLS:1","MACRO1.XLM"}
```

The *docArray* definition is listed in alphabetic order, but the *winArray* definition lists the active document first, with the document directly beneath it, and so on.

Notice that this macro defines names in the active worksheet, not in the macro sheet; to use either of these arrays in the macro sheet, use the SET.NAME function instead of DEFINE.NAME, as we did when discussing the DOCUMENTS function earlier in this chapter.

The GET.WINDOW function

The GET.WINDOW information function is similar to GET.DOCUMENT, but it returns information about a specified window. This function takes the form

GET.WINDOW(typeN,*windowT*)

The *windowT* argument specifies the name of a window; if omitted, Excel assumes the active window. The *typeN* argument is a value between 1 and 22 specifying the type of information to return, according to the following table. (Note: *typeN* numbers from 8 through 22 apply only to worksheets and macro sheets.)

typeN	Data type	Information returned
1	text	Document name.
2	number	Number of window, with 1 being frontmost window.
3	number	Distance in pixels (screen units) between left edge of window and left edge of workspace (in Windows and OS/2 versions) or screen (in Macintosh version).
4	number	Distance in pixels between top edge of window and top edge of workspace (in Windows and OS/2 versions) or screen (in Macintosh version).
5	number	Width of window, in pixels.
6	number	Height of window, in pixels.
7	logical	TRUE if window is hidden.
8	logical	TRUE if Formulas view is set.
9	logical	TRUE if gridlines are displayed.
10	logical	TRUE if row and column headings are displayed.
11	logical	TRUE if zeros are displayed.
12	number	Color of gridlines and headings, from 0 (automatic) through 16.
13	horiz. numeric array	Leftmost column number of each pane.
14	horiz. numeric array	Top row number of each pane.
15	horiz. numeric array	Number of columns in each pane; fractional numbers indicate that part of a column appears in the pane.
16	horiz. numeric array	Number of rows in each pane; fractional numbers indicate that part of a row appears in the pane.
17	number	Active pane: 1=top, left, or top left; 2=right or top right; 3=bottom or bottom left; 4=bottom right.
18	logical	TRUE if window has vertical split.
19	logical	TRUE if window has horizontal split.
20	logical	TRUE if window is maximized (in Windows or OS/2 versions) or zoomed (in Macintosh version).
21		Reserved.
22	logical	TRUE if outline symbols are displayed.

Values of *typeN* between 13 and 16 return horizontal numeric arrays of information that pertain to the panes in a window. Continuing with the arrangement of windows shown in Figure 10-1, the following macro returns information about the panes in the active window.

cmd subr **GetWinPaneInfo**		Defines names describing active window's panes.
	=SET.NAME("colNArray",GET.WINDOW(13))	={1,6,1,6}
	=SET.NAME("rowNArray",GET.WINDOW(14))	={1,1,17,17}
	=SET.NAME("numColsArray",GET.WINDOW(15))	={1.89,2.1,1.89,2.1}
	=SET.NAME("numRowsArray",GET.WINDOW(16))	={6.625,6.625,10.75,10,75}
	=SET.NAME("activePane",GET.WINDOW(17))	=4
	=RETURN()	

To define each of the first four names as arrays when using GET.WINDOW, enter the first four formulas as arrays. We've entered the values returned by each formula in the third column of the macro listing to show what values would be returned if the top-right pane of the first window in Figure 10-1 were selected. (We've truncated the fractional numbers returned in the arrays for *typeN* values 15 and 16, because Excel returns an array of four numbers of 15 significant digits each.)

Activating windows

Excel offers four functions with which you can activate a window: ACTIVATE, ACTIVATE.NEXT, ACTIVATE.PREV, and FORMULA.GOTO, which we first discussed in Chapter 8. Let's see how to use each of them in macros.

The ACTIVATE and FORMULA.GOTO functions

For most purposes, you'll probably use the ACTIVATE function. This function takes the form

ACTIVATE(*windowT,paneN*)

If you use both arguments, the function activates the window number and pane number that you specify, according to the *typeN* 17 entry of the GET.WINDOW function in the table on page 197. For example, if a worksheet named SALES.XLS contains only two panes set horizontally, the formula

```
=ACTIVATE("SALES.XLS",3)
```

activates the bottom pane. If four panes are set, the formula activates the bottom-right pane. Otherwise, the formula returns a macro error.

If you use only the *windowT* argument, Excel activates the pane in the specified window that had last been active.

If you use only *paneN*, Excel activates that pane in the current window. For example, the formula

```
=ACTIVATE(,4)
```

activates the right pane of the current window when two vertical panes are set or the bottom-right pane when four panes are set.

If the document has more than one window, and *windowT* does not specify a window number, Excel activates the first window containing the document. For example, the formula

=ACTIVATE("BUDGET.XLS")

would activate the window BUDGET.XLS:1.

The FORMULA.GOTO function works much like a combination of the ACTIVATE and SELECT functions. That is, with one formula you can activate the specified window and select the specified area. This function takes the form

FORMULA.GOTO(*referenceR,cornerR*)

where *referenceR* is a reference to a range on the active sheet or an external reference to a range on another open document. The *cornerR* argument specifies the cell in *referenceR* to be made the active cell.

For example, the formula

=FORMULA.GOTO("SALES.XLS!$A$1:$D$5")

activates the worksheet SALES.XLS and selects the range A1:D5, no matter which sheet is active when the formula is executed. You cannot, however, determine which window is activated or which pane is selected if the window contains more than one pane.

The FORMULA.GOTO function can easily activate a sheet and then return to the original sheet without your having to specify the name of either sheet.

For example, the following macro fragment activates the macro sheet containing the fragment, copies a range containing a sample record for a database, reactivates the original sheet, and pastes the record beginning at the cell that was active before Excel encountered this macro:

```
=FORMULA.GOTO(sampleRec)   | Select range on the macro sheet.
=COPY()                    | Copy the range.
=FORMULA.GOTO()            | Return to the original selection.
=PASTE()                   | Paste the range.
```

The second FORMULA.GOTO, which uses no arguments, takes advantage of a useful quirk of the function. Working much like the "last channel viewed" button on the remote control for a television set, this formula reactivates the cell that was active when the FORMULA.GOTO function was last executed.

The ACTIVATE.NEXT and ACTIVATE.PREV functions

In a sense, the ACTIVATE.NEXT and ACTIVATE.PREV functions are like relative references: You can activate the window directly under the active window, or the bottommost window in the workspace, without having to specify (or without even knowing) the name of the window. The ACTIVATE.NEXT function takes the form

ACTIVATE.NEXT()

and is the equivalent of pressing Ctrl-F6 [Mac—also Command-M].

The ACTIVATE.PREV function takes the form

ACTIVATE.PREV()

and is the equivalent of pressing Ctrl-Shift-F6 [Mac—also Command-Shift-M].

These functions might not make much sense at first because using them can activate a window other than the one you might have intended. The key to understanding the functions lies in deciphering what is meant by the terms *next* and *previous.*

To experiment with these commands, set up three worksheets, the third of which is visible in two windows, as shown in Figure 10-2. Be sure that each window overlaps (or lies under) every other window, as shown in the figure. If you activate the next window by pressing Ctrl-F6, two things happen: The topmost window goes to the bottom of the stack, and the second window becomes active, as shown in Figure 10-3.

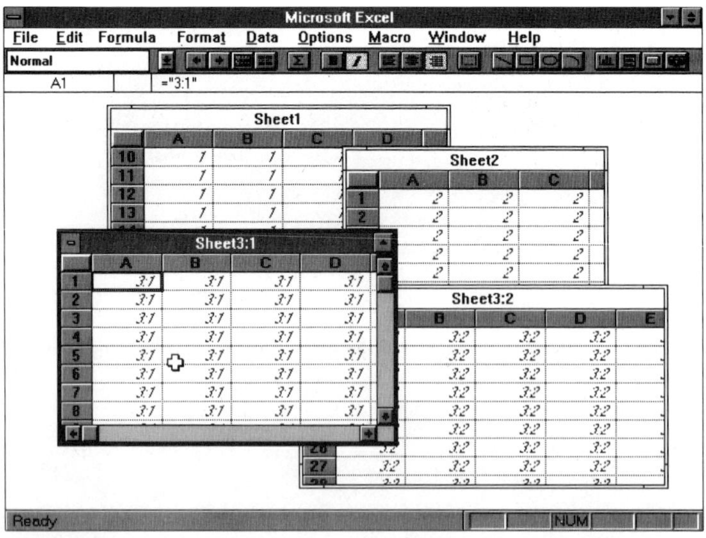

FIGURE 10-2.
Four windows that overlap like this can help you to understand how ACTIVATE.NEXT and ACTIVATE.PREV work.

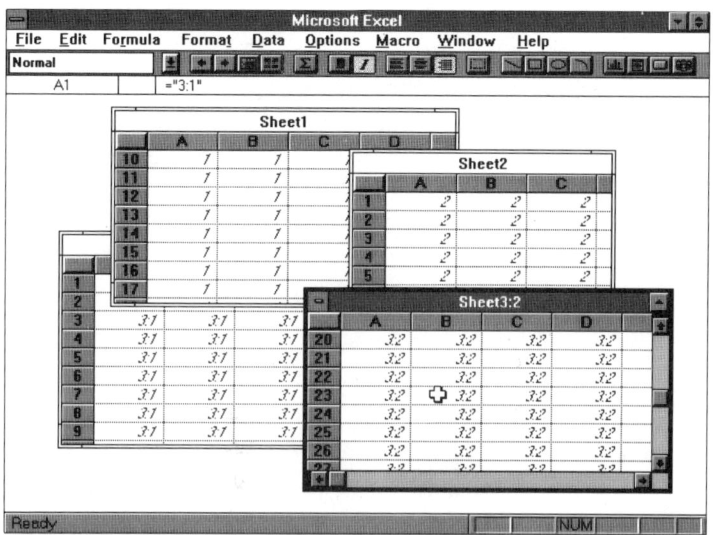

FIGURE 10-3.
When ACTIVATE.NEXT activates the next window in the stack (Sheet3:2), it causes the previous window (Sheet3:1) to become the bottom window in the stack.

I want a macro to switch back and forth between two open windows. What's the easiest way to do this?

If you ensure that only the two windows are open (by hiding the macro sheet, for example), here's an easy approach. First, use the following formula to define the name *other* on the macro sheet:

```
=SET.NAME("other",INDEX(WINDOWS(),2))
```

To activate the other window, simply use the formula

```
=ACTIVATE(other)
```

Here's why this approach works: When you activate a window, the one that was previously active drops into the second position, both on your screen and in the array returned by the WINDOWS function. Therefore, whenever you activate the window whose name is stored in *other*, you always activate that second window.

Be careful, however, if you open a third window. Doing so pushes the other two windows into the second and third positions, changing their order in the array that WINDOWS returns.

When you press Ctrl-Shift-F6, the previous window (Sheet3:1, at the bottom of the stack) becomes active again, and the window that had been active (Sheet3:2) becomes the second window, as shown in Figure 10-2.

When you use the mouse to activate a window, or when you activate it with either the ACTIVATE or FORMULA.GOTO function, the previous window does not go to the bottom but becomes the second window in the stack.

What is the moral of this story? Usually, the lesson is this: Because it's easy to lose track of which window these functions will act upon, don't use these functions unless there's a specific requirement for them. Instead, use ACTIVATE and FORMULA.GOTO to activate the sheets you need.

Changing the appearance of windows

Macros become more interesting when you begin to work with windows. For example, you can remove their gridlines, move them, change their size, hide them, split them into panes, and scroll in them.

Changing the appearance of a single window

The DISPLAY function changes the appearance of a window, and it corresponds to the Options Display command. It takes two forms, the first for windows and the second for controlling the contents of the Info window when displayed (not covered here). The first form has the following syntax:

DISPLAY(*formulasL,gridlinesL,headingsL,zerosL,colorN,reserved, outlineL,pageBreaksL,objectN*), form 1
DISPLAY?(*formulasL,gridlinesL,headingsL,zerosL,colorN,reserved, outlineL,pageBreaksL,objectN*), form 1

The *formulasL* argument, when TRUE, sets a sheet to Formulas view (the default for macro sheets), and when FALSE, sets a sheet to Values view (the default for worksheets). The *gridlinesL* and *headingsL* arguments, when TRUE (the defaults), display gridlines or row and column headings on the sheet.

If you want values of 0 in a sheet to appear as empty cells, set the *zerosL* argument to FALSE (the default is TRUE). The *colorsN* argument determines the color of gridlines and of row and column headings in the window, from 0 (Automatic, the default) through 16, corresponding to the colors available in the Options Display dialog box.

The *outlineL* argument, if TRUE (the default), displays outline symbols in the document. The *pageBreaksL* argument, if TRUE (the default is FALSE), displays automatic page breaks in the window.

Finally, *objectN* determines whether objects in the window are displayed: If 1 or omitted, objects are displayed; if 2, placeholders are substituted for objects (which speeds scrolling in the sheet); and if 3, objects are hidden.

Setting a value for the *formulasL* argument corresponds to using the Ctrl-` key sequence [Mac—also Command-`] to toggle between Values view and Formulas view. You can create a macro that mimics this behavior for other Display options as well, as the following macro demonstrates.

	A	B	C
4	cmd G	**ToggleGridlines**	Toggles display of gridlines.
5		=NOT(B5)	Flip value stored in cell.
6		=DISPLAY(,up1)	Use flipped value to set display.
7		=RETURN()	

Before running this macro, select cell B6, choose the Formula Define Name command, and assign *=B5* to the name *up1*, defining the name as a relative reference to the cell above the active cell. Cell B5 is the cell containing the NOT function; when Excel executes this formula, it takes the value stored in the cell and negates it, changing TRUE to FALSE and vice versa.

Hiding and unhiding documents

The HIDE function, which corresponds to the Window Hide command, hides the active window. Hiding macro sheets keeps them from cluttering your workspace, but you can still use the macros and the values that they contain. This function takes the form

HIDE()

Because the function can only be used to hide the active document, it takes no arguments.

The UNHIDE function, which corresponds to the Window Unhide command, unhides the specified window. This function takes the form

UNHIDE(windowT)

where *windowT* specifies the name of the window you want to unhide.

Moving and sizing windows

Excel provides several functions to help you position windows in the workspace by using macros: MOVE, SIZE, FULL, and ARRANGE.ALL.

The MOVE function moves the top-left corner of a window to the specified position. This function takes the form

MOVE(*xPosN,yPosN,windowT*)
MOVE?(*xPosN,yPosN,windowT*)

The dialog box form of this command is executed only in the Windows and OS/2 versions of Excel, and it corresponds to the Move command on the Microsoft

Windows Control menu at the upper left corner of the screen; on all versions the function is an action equivalent for dragging a window's title bar.

The *windowT* argument specifies the name of the window to be moved: If omitted, Excel moves the active window. The *xPosN* and *yPosN* arguments specify the distance, in pixels, from the left and top edges of the window to the left and top edges of the workspace. Setting both arguments to 0 places the top-left corner of the window at approximately the bottom-left corner of the formula bar, depending on the version of Excel you're using, as shown in Figure 10-4. However, if you've hidden the formula bar and the tool bar (for example), Excel measures distances from the bottom-left corner of the menu bar.

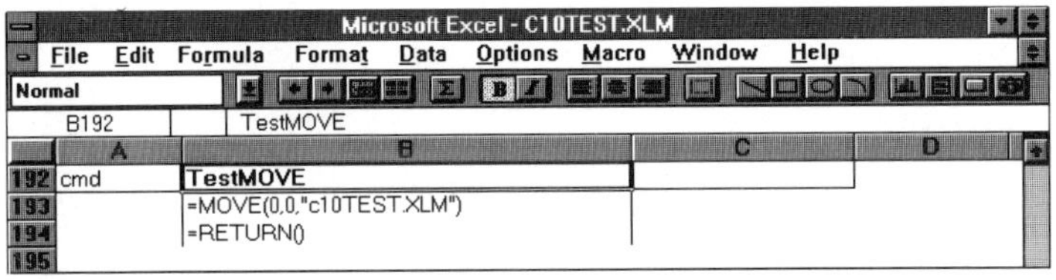

FIGURE 10-4.
Distances for the MOVE function are measured relative to the top-left corner of the workspace.

The SIZE function changes the size of the specified window; it's an action-equivalent function for dragging a window's size box, or in the PC versions of Excel, it's a command-equivalent for the Control menu's Size command. This function takes the form

SIZE(widthN,heightN,*windowT*)

where *windowT* is the name of the window, and *widthN* and *heightN* are the width and the height of the window, in pixels.

The only challenge in using MOVE and SIZE is knowing what numbers to supply for the horizontal and vertical positions or for the height and width. You can find these numbers in two easy ways.

First, you can start the Recorder and manually position or resize the window. Doing so creates a MOVE or SIZE function with all arguments in place. Second, a macro can calculate a new position or size from data supplied by the GET.WINDOW function using *typeN* arguments 3 through 6 or the GET.WORKSPACE function using *typeN* arguments 13 or 14. For example, the macro fragment at the top of the facing page positions the window WIN1.XLS in the top half of the workspace and the window WIN2.XLS in the bottom half.

winWidth	=GET.WORKSPACE(13)	Workspace width.
winHeight	=GET.WORKSPACE(14)/2	Half the workspace height.
	=SIZE(winWidth,winHeight,"WIN1.XLS")	Size WIN1.
	=SIZE(winWidth,winHeight,"WIN2.XLS")	Size WIN2.
	=MOVE(1,1,"WIN1.XLS")	Move WIN1.
	=MOVE(1,winHeight,"WIN2.XLS")	Move WIN2.

The FULL function is an action equivalent for double-clicking a window's title bar or clicking its Maximize button or, on the Macintosh, its Zoom box [PC—Ctrl-F10 and Ctrl-F5]. In the PC versions of Excel, it is also a command-equivalent function for both the Maximize and Restore commands on the Control menu for the window. This function takes the form

FULL(logical)

When *logical* is TRUE, Excel enlarges the window; when FALSE, Excel restores it to its previous size; and when omitted, Excel toggles the size of the window between its original and maximized sizes.

Finally, the ARRANGE.ALL function arranges the open windows in the workspace, performing the same task as the Window Arrange All command. This function takes the form

ARRANGE.ALL()

Splitting windows

The SPLIT function creates, moves, and removes window panes. It is equivalent to dragging the horizontal or vertical split bar for the window, or to the Split command on the Control menu for the document in the PC versions of Excel. This function takes the form

SPLIT(*colSplitN,rowSplitN*)

The *colSplitN* and *rowSplitN* arguments specify where to split the window in the *x* direction and *y* direction, measured in columns and rows, respectively. If an argument is 0, the corresponding split is removed; if omitted, Excel doesn't change the split. For example,

=SPLIT(2,0)

puts a vertical split after the second column displayed in the active window and removes a horizontal split if it exists, and

=SPLIT(,23.6)

sets a horizontal split 60 percent of the way into the 24th row displayed in the active window and has no effect on the vertical split.

After you've created a split, you can freeze the location of the panes with the FREEZE.PANES function, a command that corresponds to both the Options Freeze Panes and Options Unfreeze Panes commands. This function takes the form

FREEZE.PANES(logical)

where *logical*, if TRUE, freezes the panes.

Opening new windows

Use the NEW.WINDOW function to open a new window on the active worksheet or macro sheet; the new window becomes active and the previous window drops into the second position. This function corresponds to choosing New Window from the Window menu and takes the form

NEW.WINDOW()

I saved a document that contains four windows and then closed it. But when I opened the document again, the window extensions had changed. For example, SALES.XLS:1 had become SALES.XLS:3, SALES.XLS:2 had become SALES.XLS:4, and so on. What's happening and what can I do about it?

When Excel opens a document that contains several windows, it assigns the extensions in the order in which windows have been placed in the stack of open windows. (See ACTIVATE.NEXT earlier in this chapter for more on the stack.) Therefore, you need to be sure that the program opens your windows in the order of their extensions.

To do so, you need to know whether you'll open the document directly or whether you'll open it as part of a workspace file.

If you intend to open the document directly, first activate the windows, beginning with the first and ending with the last, to ensure they have been activated in the same order in which they were created. Then, while the last window is active, save the windows using File Save or File Save As.

If you intend to open the document using a workspace, save the file by using the File Save Workspace command. Before you do so, however, activate the windows, beginning with the last and ending with the first. Then, while the first window is active, save the workspace.

When you use NEW.WINDOW, you occasionally need to activate or reference the window that is active when Excel executes this function. Because the previous window is in the second position, you can use the command ACTIVATE.NEXT to activate it. To find the name of the previously active window, use the formula

=INDEX(WINDOWS(),2)

Scrolling in a window

Excel provides six functions for scrolling in a sheet. Three of these allow you to scroll vertically, and three horizontally.

Using VLINE and HLINE lets you scroll the active window by the number of rows or columns specified. Using these functions is equivalent to setting the Scroll Lock key and tapping on a direction key the number of times specified in the function's arguments, or using the scroll bars to move the specified number of rows or columns. These functions take the forms

VLINE(numRowsN)
HLINE(numColsN)

Positive values of *numRowsN* and *numColsN* scroll the window down or to the right, and negative arguments scroll the window up or to the left.

For example, suppose that cell A70 is the active cell and also the top-left cell in the window. The formula

=VLINE(5)

moves the window downward with respect to the sheet until cell A75 is the top-left cell in the window. Cell A70, which is still the active cell, is no longer visible in the window. Similarly, the formula

=HLINE(5)

scrolls the window to the right with respect to the sheet until cell F75 is the top-left cell in the window. Cell A70 remains active, but not visible in the window.

The VPAGE and HPAGE functions work similarly, except you specify the number of window-heights or window-widths you want to page horizontally or vertically, rather than the number of rows or columns. These functions take the forms

VPAGE(numWindowsN)
HPAGE(numWindowsN)

As with VLINE and HLINE, positive numbers scroll the window down or to the right with respect to the sheet and negative numbers scroll the window up or to the left.

Use VSCROLL and HSCROLL to specify the row and column numbers that you want to appear in the top-left cell in a window. These functions take the forms

VSCROLL(positionN,*rowL*)
HSCROLL(positionN,*colL*)

where *positionN* specifies the row or column you want to appear in the top-left corner of the window. You can use as these arguments either the number of the row or column or the percentage representing the distance of that row or column across the document. The *rowL* and *colL* arguments, if TRUE, specify that the *positionN* argument is a number of rows or columns, and if FALSE or omitted, specify that *positionN* is a percentage.

For example, suppose you want to select cell M59, and you want that cell to appear in the top-left cell in the window. To do so, use the following macro fragment.

=SELECT(!$M$59)	Select the cell.
=HSCROLL(COLUMN(ACTIVE.CELL()),TRUE)	Scroll to the column of active cell.
=VSCROLL(ROW(ACTIVE.CELL()),TRUE)	Scroll to the row of active cell.

Or, if you want the active cell to be centered vertically in the window (rather than positioned at the top), you could substitute the following formulas.

	=SELECT(!$M$59)	Select the cell.
	=HSCROLL(COLUMN(ACTIVE.CELL()),TRUE)	Scroll to the column of active cell.
halfDepth	=ROW(ACTIVE.CELL())-INT(GET.WINDOW(16)/2)	Calculate half the depth of window.
	=VSCROLL(MAX(halfDepth,1),TRUE)	Scroll to the row of active cell.

The formula in cell *halfDepth* subtracts from the row of the active cell half the depth of the window, measured in rows. Under normal circumstances, this formula returns the number of the row that must be at the top of the window for the active cell to be vertically centered in the window. If the active cell is in row 1, *halfDepth* is negative. Therefore, the MAX function ensures that VSCROLL uses only positive values.

Other types of windows

Excel offers two commands for opening and closing the Clipboard and Info windows: SHOW.CLIPBOARD and SHOW.INFO.

The SHOW.CLIPBOARD function brings up the Clipboard window, displaying whatever was last cut or copied. The function corresponds to the Window Show Clipboard command in the OS/2 and Macintosh versions of Excel and is an action equivalent for running the Clipboard application in Windows. This function takes the form

SHOW.CLIPBOARD()

Using this function is a little tricky in the Windows environment. If the Clipboard application is already open, you call the function once to display the Clipboard window. If not, you must call the function twice—once to display the icon for the Clipboard application and once to open the Clipboard window.

In any version of Excel, use the CLOSE function (discussed later in this chapter) to close the Clipboard window.

The SHOW.INFO window brings up the Info window for the active cell and corresponds to the Window Show Info command. This function takes the form

SHOW.INFO(logical)

If *logical* is TRUE, Excel opens the Info window for the selected range. If *logical* is FALSE and the Info window is active, Excel activates the window in which the active cell was selected; if the Info window is not active, the function has no effect. To close the Info window, activate it and then use the CLOSE function.

There is no GET.INFO function for returning the contents of the Info window as an array; you can use instead the GET.CELL, GET.NOTE, GET.DEF, GET.NAME, or GET.FORMULA function to acquire information about a selected cell.

To change the contents of what Excel lists in an Info window, use the second form of the DISPLAY function, which corresponds to the commands on the Info menu, visible when an Info window is active. This function takes the form

DISPLAY(*cellL,formulasL,valueL,formatL,protectionL,namesL,* *precedentsN,dependentsN,noteL*)

where the *logical* arguments, if TRUE, present the corresponding information in the Info window. The *precedentsN* and *dependentsN* arguments set the type of precedents or dependents to be listed: If 0, none are listed; if 2, the direct precedents and dependents are listed; if 3, all levels are listed in the Info window. If an argument is omitted, display of that item remains as set previously.

The tricky thing about the DISPLAY function is that whether Excel interprets it as the first or the second form depends on whether the Info window is active: If not, Excel assumes it is the first form (discussed earlier in this chapter) and does the equivalent of setting options in the Options Display dialog box.

Closing windows

You can close windows from a macro in two ways: You can close the active window with the CLOSE function, and you can close all windows with the CLOSE.ALL function. If a document has been changed since the last time it was saved and the window being closed is the only window in the document, Excel presents a dialog box asking whether you want to save the changes before closing the document.

The CLOSE function is the equivalent of double-clicking a window's Control box [Mac—single-clicking the Close box]. This function takes the form

CLOSE(saveL)

where *saveL*, if TRUE, saves the file; if FALSE, does not save the file; and if omitted, presents a dialog box requesting the user to decide whether to save the file.

The CLOSE.ALL function corresponds to holding down the Shift key while choosing the File Close All command. This function takes the form

CLOSE.ALL()

The CLOSE.ALL function is similar to the CLOSE function, except that Excel does not close a document protected with the Options Protect Document command when the Windows protection option is selected.

Workspaces

A workspace is the Excel environment in which you work with open documents. The Options Workspace command lets you modify this environment. In this workspace, you can switch from A1 to R1C1 styles, delete the status bar, change the alternate menu key from / to another key, and so on. Any change you make to the workspace, such as switching to the R1C1 style, affects all open documents.

The WORKSPACE function

It is easy to change the workspace settings by using the WORKSPACE function, although you generally have little occasion to do so in macros. The WORKSPACE function corresponds to the Options Workspace command and takes the form

WORKSPACE(*fixedL,decimalsN,r1c1L,scrollL,statusL,formulaL, menuKeyT,remoteL,enterMoveL,underlinesN,toolsL,notesL,navKeysL, menuKeyActionN*)

where *fixedL* sets a fixed number of decimal places; enter TRUE for the Fixed Decimal setting, and enter FALSE otherwise. The *decimalsN* argument specifies the number of decimal places if *fixedL* is TRUE. The *r1c1L* argument, if TRUE, sets the R1C1 mode. (Note: You can also use A1.R1C1(FALSE) to set the R1C1 mode.)

The *scrollL* argument, if TRUE, displays scroll bars in every worksheet and macro sheet in the workspace. The *statusL* argument, if TRUE, displays the status bar at the bottom of the workspace area. If *formulaL* is TRUE, Excel displays the formula bar.

Settings for the WORKSPACE function.

When you're in doubt about the settings for the WORKSPACE function, start the Recorder, choose the Options Workspace command, specify the settings you want, and then press Enter. When you do, the Recorder creates the WORKSPACE function you need.

The *menuKeyT* argument specifies the alternate menu key, whose default is /. The *remoteL* argument, if TRUE, tells Excel to ignore remote requests from other applications [Mac—has no effect unless you are running System 7.0 or later]. The *enterMoveL* argument, if TRUE, moves the active cell downward when the user presses the Enter key on the PC or presses the Return key on the Mac.

The *underlinesN* argument is valid only for the Macintosh version of Excel: If 1, the argument displays underlines below the commands in the menu; if 2, it turns underlines off; and if 3, it displays underlines only when the alternate navigation key is pressed.

The *toolsL* argument, if TRUE, displays the tool bar. The *notesL* argument, if TRUE, displays a note indicator in those cells having attached notes. The *navKeysL* argument, if TRUE, enables alternate navigation keys in worksheets and macro sheets. (For a list of the alternate navigation keys, see online Help.) Finally, the *menuKeyActionN* argument, if 1 or omitted, tells Excel to activate menu commands after the user presses the key specified by *menuKeyT*; if 2, it tells Excel to bring up Lotus 1-2-3 Help.

The GET.WORKSPACE function

The GET.WORKSPACE function returns information about the workspace. This function takes the form

GET.WORKSPACE(typeN)

where *typeN* specifies the type of information you want returned, according to the table on the following page.

typeN	Data type	Information returned
1	text	Name of environment in which Excel is running, such as *Windows 3.1* or *Macintosh 7.1*.
2	text	Excel's version number.
3	number	Number of decimals if auto-decimals is set; 0 if not.
4	logical	TRUE if in R1C1 mode.
5	logical	TRUE if scroll bars are displayed.
6	logical	TRUE if status bar is displayed.
7	logical	TRUE if formula bar is displayed. (On Macintosh, this type exists for PC compatibility and always returns FALSE.)
8	logical	TRUE if remote DDE requests are enabled.
9	text	Alternate menu key, returns #N/A if no key is set.
10	number	Whether a Data Find (1), Copy (2), or Cut (3) mode is in effect.
11	number	Distance in pixels between left edge of Excel workspace window and left edge of screen. On Macintosh, always returns 0.
12	number	Distance in pixels between top edge of Excel workspace window and top edge of screen. On Macintosh, always returns 0.
13	number	Workspace width, in pixels.
14	number	Workspace height, in pixels.
15	number	Maximized or minimized status of Excel: 1=neither; 2=minimized; 3=maximized. (Always 3 for Macintosh version.)
16	number	Memory free, in kilobytes.
17	number	Total memory available to Excel.
18	logical	TRUE if math coprocessor is present.
19	logical	TRUE if mouse is present.
20	horiz. text array	Names of sheets in a workgroup, if present.
21	logical	TRUE if tool bar is displayed.
22	number?	Error code for DDE applications.
23	text	Full pathname of default startup directory or folder.
24	text	Full pathname of alternate startup directory or folder.
25	logical	TRUE if Excel is set for relative recording.
26	text	Name of user, as entered when Excel was installed.
27	text	Name of user's organization, as entered when Excel was installed.
28	number	1=Excel menus are activated by an alternate menu key, and 2=Lotus 1-2-3 Help is activated.
29	logical	TRUE if alternate navigation keys are activated.

Saving and opening workspace documents

When you use the File Save Workspace command to save the workspace, Excel stores in the workspace file a list of all open documents, the positions of their windows and the options set for their display in the Options Display dialog box, the settings made within the Options Workspace dialog box, the preferred chart type, whether Automatic or Manual recalculation, whether Short or Full menus, and the items displayed in the Info window.

The SAVE.WORKSPACE function is a command-equivalent for the File Save Workspace command. This function takes the form

SAVE.WORKSPACE(*nameT*)

where *nameT* specifies the name of the workspace file, including its full pathname. If you omit the pathname, the file is stored in the same directory or folder as the Excel application itself. If you omit *nameT*, Excel uses the name *Resume*.

To return a workspace to the condition it was in when you saved its state in a workspace file, use the OPEN function (described in greater detail in Chapter 15, "Working with Files"). For example, these simple *Auto_Open* and *Auto_Close* macros return the workspace to the state it was in the last time the user quit Excel.

cmd	**Auto_Open**
	=OPEN("Resume")
	=RETURN()

cmd	**Auto_Close**
	=SAVE.WORKSPACE()
	=RETURN()

If you put the macro sheet containing these macros in Excel's startup directory or folder, each time the user restarts Excel, the workspace is set up as it was left when the user last quit.

Freezing the display

The ECHO function tells Excel not to update the screen while executing a macro, achieving at least two purposes. First, freezing the screen can speed up the execution of macros considerably, because Excel takes a long time to display motion on the screen. Second, freezing the display lets you control the information that users see, while your macros busily zip around behind the scenes preparing charts and worksheets.

The ECHO function takes the form

ECHO(*logical*)

where *logical*, if TRUE, turns on screen updating; if FALSE, it turns off screen updating. If *logical* is omitted, Excel reverses the previous state of screen updating; for example, if screen updating is off, ECHO() turns it on.

Because Excel resumes normal screen updating when a macro ends, most macros that turn off screen updating never need to turn it on again. Consequently, you should insert an ECHO(FALSE) formula in each macro that you want Excel to execute without updating the screen. A convenient way to do this is to define as TRUE (or FALSE) a name that sets (or unsets) screen updating everywhere in a macro sheet at once. For example, if you define a name as *screenUpdate,* you can use the following formula in your macros.

=ECHO(screenUpdate)

Other workspace functions

The SHORT.MENUS function corresponds to the Short Menus command on either the Options or Chart menu, depending on whether a chart is the active document. This function takes the form

SHORT.MENUS(logical)

where *logical,* if TRUE or omitted, sets Excel for Short menus; if FALSE, it sets Full menus.

The INFO function is a standard worksheet function, but it's very useful when you want to create macros that alter their behavior depending on the type of machine running Excel or the amount of memory available. Because you can use this function in worksheets, you can use the FORMULA function to enter the INFO function in a worksheet that you want to adapt to different operating environments, for example. The INFO function takes the form

INFO(typeT)

where *typeT* is a text value that specifies the type of information you want returned. Most of these items of information returned are similar to those returned by the GET.WORKSPACE and GET.DOCUMENT functions, as shown in the following table.

typeT	**Data type**	**Information returned**
directory	text	Pathname of current directory or folder.
memavail	number	Memory available, in bytes; similar to GET.WORKSPACE(16).
numfile	number	Number of open worksheets (not charts and macro sheets), whether hidden or unhidden.
osversion	text	Operating system under which Excel is running; similar to GET.WORKSPACE(1). For example, *DOS Version 3.31* or *Macintosh Version 6.05.*
recalc	text	Recalculation mode, either Automatic or Manual; similar to GET.DOCUMENT(14).
release	text	Version of Excel; similar to GET.WORKSPACE(2).
system	text	Type of operating environment; *mac, pcos2* (OS/2), or *pcdos* (Windows). Similar to GET.WORKSPACE(1).
totmem	number	Total memory available; similar to GET.WORKSPACE(17).
memused	number	Amount of memory used for open documents.

11

Presenting and Requesting Information

You can roughly divide the kinds of interactions between an Excel macro application and a user into two groups: a class of methods for presenting and requesting information (the topic of this chapter) and ways for taking actions in the Excel environment by using custom menus, attaching macros to Excel objects, and responding to certain types of events (topics of the next chapter).

Beyond the presentation of formatted templates and worksheets, Excel offers macro programmers several ways to request information from users.

- You can present simple messages through Alert dialog boxes and by displaying messages in the status bar at the bottom of the workspace.
- You can request information through an Input dialog box, which presents an edit box for a user to enter one item of information.
- You can use the question-mark form of a command-equivalent macro function to present one of Excel's standard dialog boxes in which the user enters information. (However, you can't return the information entered in a standard dialog box to a macro.)

- You can create your own dialog boxes; Excel returns the information a user enters in the dialog box to the macro sheet that brought the dialog box up on the screen.
- You can create help topics, which the user can call up for messages displayed in the status bar, custom dialog boxes, and custom menus and menu commands (discussed in the next chapter). You can use a simple text editor to create files containing the help text you want to add. However, in the current Windows version of Excel, you need to use a special utility, available from Microsoft, to convert these files to the format required by Excel's Help system. (The Macintosh version of Excel doesn't require this utility.)

Issuing messages to the user

Macros often need to issue messages to the user. This need might arise when the user enters incorrect data or performs some action that your macro doesn't understand. At other times, the macro might be performing a long operation, and in such cases the user wants to be informed of its progress. Also, macros need to offer step-by-step instructions to the user. On occasion, macros need to attract the user's attention. Excel provides several ways to send messages to the user, all of which are easy to use.

Using Alert dialog boxes

The ALERT function causes the computer to beep, display one of three Alert dialog boxes, and then suspend operation until the user responds to the message in the box. In other words, the macro won't continue without user involvement.

The ALERT function takes the form

ALERT(*messageT,typeN*)

where *messageT* is the message you want the macro to display to the user, less than Excel's limit of 255 characters per text string.

The *typeN* argument determines the icon Excel displays in the Alert dialog box, and it can take one of three values. Set *typeN* to 1 when you want the user to choose between OK and Cancel. The ALERT function returns TRUE if the user clicks the OK button; it returns FALSE if the user clicks Cancel. You can test this value to alter the behavior of the macro. For example, the formula

```
doDelete     =ALERT("Delete all files in directory?",1)
             =IF(doDelete,DeleteFiles())
```

creates these PC and Mac dialog boxes:

If the user clicks OK, *doDelete* is set to TRUE and Excel executes the *DeleteFiles* macro.

Set *typeN* to 2 when you simply want to present information. In this case, the ALERT function always returns TRUE.

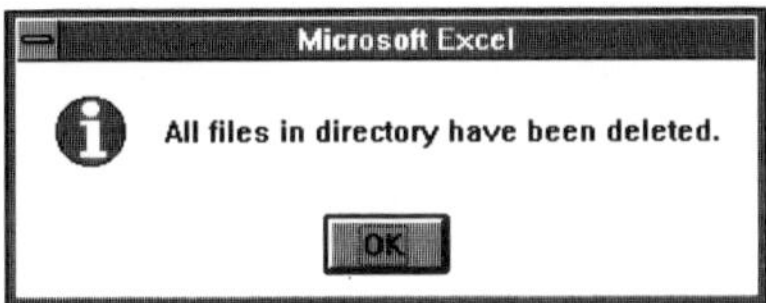

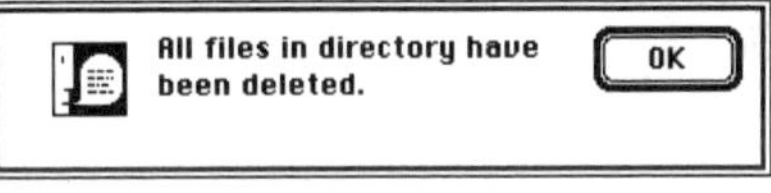

Set *typeN* to 3 when you want to inform the user that an error has occurred but that no choice is available. In this case the ALERT function always returns TRUE.

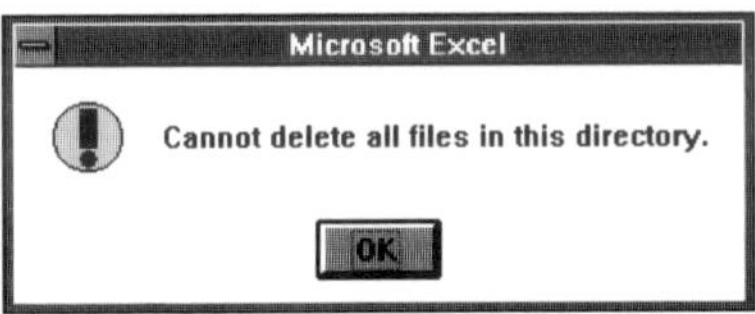

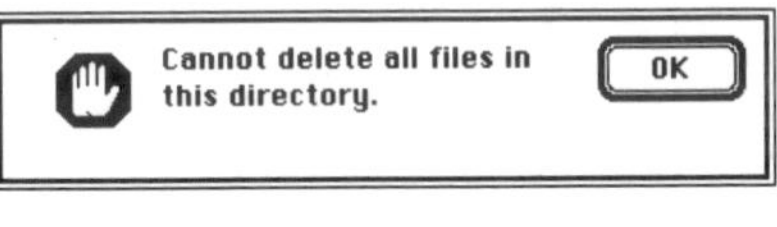

A limited number of formatting options are available to you when using long messages in an Alert dialog box. First, the dialog box lengthens for long messages. Second, you can use internal carriage-return characters (ASCII character 13) or newline characters (ASCII character 10) to cause line breaks in the message. For example, the formula

```
=ALERT("First line..."&CHAR(10)&"Second line..."&CHAR(10)&"Third line..."&
    CHAR(10)&"Fourth line..."&CHAR(10)&"Fifth line..."&
    CHAR(10)&"Sixth line..."&CHAR(10)&"Seventh line...",3)
```

creates the following PC and Mac Alert dialog boxes:

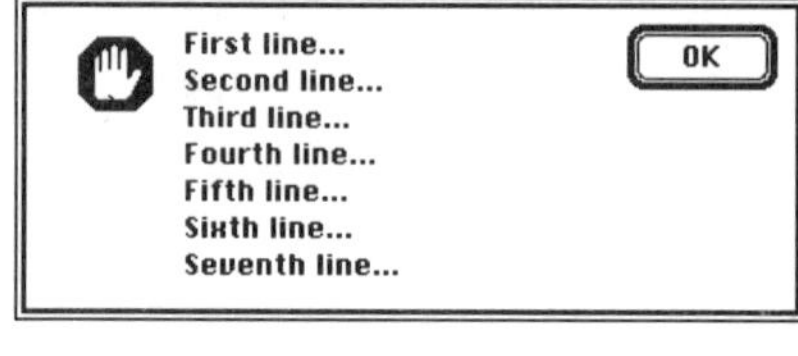

Using the MESSAGE function

The MESSAGE function displays a message in the status bar at the lower left corner of your screen. The more macros you write, the more valuable this simple function becomes, because it provides an easy way to notify users of the progress of a macro, without requiring a response, as is needed with the ALERT function. The MESSAGE function takes the form

MESSAGE(logical,*text*)

If *logical* is TRUE, Excel displays text in the status bar. (The text "" displays a null string, erasing the current message, if any.) If *logical* is FALSE, Excel resets the status bar to the normal display of Excel's messages. (If your workspace doesn't normally display the status bar, choose Options Workspace and select the Status Bar option, or use the WORKSPACE function to display the status bar.)

Because the status bar isn't reset when a macro ends, you need to reset it within your macro if you use this function. Therefore, unless you intend that your macro leave a message displayed when it ends, be sure to include near the end of the macro the formula

```
=MESSAGE(FALSE)
```

to set the messages in the status bar to their normal setting.

People frequently use the MESSAGE function to keep the user informed about the status of long-running macros. Messages such as *Updating July budgets* or *35% Completed* reassure users that the macro is still working, although the display might be frozen. (Changes in the status bar appear on the screen even while ECHO is FALSE.)

For example, the formula

```
=MESSAGE(TRUE,"Modifying each cell")
```

displays the message *Modifying each cell* in the status bar. However, when the task takes a long time, this message offers little comfort to the user. The user wants to know: "Is the macro almost done? Or will it take another hour or two?"

Often you can easily provide the information the user needs. For example, suppose your macro performs an operation, one cell at a time, on every cell in the range A10 through M3010. The following macro fragment displays a message such as *Cell modification nn% completed* to keep the user fully informed about the status of the macro:

colLimit	10	Range width.
rowLimit	3000	Range height.
	=FOR("col",1,colLimit)	For each column.
	= FOR("row",1,rowLimit)	For each row.
	...formulas for processing each cell	
percent	= ((col-1)*rowLimit+row)/(rowLimit*colLimit)	Calc % complete.
percentMsg	= "Cell modification "&TEXT(percent,"#%")&" completed."	Assemble text.
	= MESSAGE(TRUE,percentMsg)	Send message.
	= NEXT()	
	=NEXT()	

The formula in the cell named *percent* calculates the decimal fraction of the total area that has been completed. Cell *percentMsg* assembles the text string, and the formula in the next cell returns the text string as a message.

Also, as we explained in Chapter 6, the MESSAGE function can be a valuable tool for debugging macros. By displaying messages throughout the execution of a macro or by displaying the values returned by certain critical names or cells, you can monitor a macro's operation in ways that aren't otherwise possible.

Using the BEEP function

The BEEP function, as you might suspect, causes your computer to beep. This function takes the form

BEEP(*toneN*)

where *toneN*, which must be a value between 1 and 4, specifies one of four tones. If omitted, *toneN* is assumed to be 1. The tones for each number vary among computers. Some computers, including the IBM PC, the Macintosh, and many 80286 clones, produce the same tones for all four numbers.

When you use the BEEP function in a macro, don't overuse it. Nothing is more irritating than a macro that beeps at every opportunity. In fact, the only time we use BEEP is when a macro runs for such a long time that users leave the computer unattended. Then, when the macro is finished, a beep notifies users that they can return to their computers.

Using the INPUT function

The INPUT function is similar to the ALERT function in that you can use it to present information to the user through a dialog box containing OK and Cancel buttons. However, you can also use an Input dialog box to request information and return it to the cell containing the INPUT function. If the user clicks OK, the information entered in the dialog box is returned to the cell containing the INPUT function; if the user clicks Cancel, the INPUT function returns FALSE to the cell.

The INPUT function takes the form

INPUT(messageT,*typeN,titleT,defaultValue,xPosN,yPosN*)

where *messageT* is the request for information. As in the ALERT function, *messageT* can be up to 255 characters long, and you can use carriage-return and linefeed characters within the message.

The *typeN* argument specifies the data type of the information to be returned to the macro (such as the *typeN* argument used in the RESULT and ARGUMENT functions), according to the following table.

typeN	Returned value's data type
0	Formula, in the form of text. References are converted to R1C1-style references.
1	Number.
2	Text.
4	Logical.
8	Reference. Excel converts references to the absolute form in the A1 style. If you specify the reference of a single cell, Excel returns the value contained in the referenced cell.
16	Error.
64	Array.

As with the RESULT and ARGUMENT functions, you can sum two or more numbers to permit the entry of more than one data type. Unlike these functions, the number 2 (text only) is assumed. Another difference between these functions is that INPUT includes the type number 0 to allow for the entry of formulas. If the user enters data of the wrong type, Excel tries to convert it to, or coerce it into, the specified type; if unsuccessful, Excel displays an error message.

The *titleT* argument specifies the text displayed in the title bar of the Input dialog box; if omitted, Excel uses the text *Input*. You use the *defaultValue* argument to set an initial, expected, value to be presented in the dialog box; this lets the user click OK to return the expected value rather than requiring the user to enter the same value each time the Input dialog box is displayed.

Finally, you can specify (in screen pixels) the initial location of the dialog box with the *xPosN* and *yPosN* arguments. If you omit these arguments or set either to 0, Excel centers the dialog box horizontally or vertically.

For example, the dialog box created by the formula

```
=INPUT("Print how many copies?",1,"Print Reports",10,100,100)
```

looks like this:

A convenient feature of the Input dialog box is that the user can drag it around in the workspace and select a range to enter the reference of the range in the dialog box. As mentioned in the table, the user can enter in the Input dialog box the reference of a single cell, but Excel will return the value contained in the referenced cell. For example, consider this short macro:

cmd	**GetRef1**
thisRef	=REFTEXT(INPUT("Please enter a reference:",8))
	=RETURN()

If you run this macro and click on cell A1 in Sheet1, the formula in cell *thisRef* returns the text *Sheet1!R1C1*. If instead this formula is

```
=INPUT("Please enter a reference:",8)
```

Excel automatically translates the reference to cell A1 into its contents, which are returned to the cell containing the formula.

On the other hand, if you specify a data type of *0* in the macro

cmd	**GetRef2**
thisRef	=INPUT("Please enter a reference:",0)
	=RETURN()

and click on cell A1 in Sheet1, the formula in cell *thisRef* displays *=A1* in the edit box of the Input dialog box. When you press Enter, the function returns to the cell a relative reference in the R1C1-text format, showing the relative position of the selected cell to the active cell. For example, if cell B3 is active when you click on cell A1, INPUT returns the text *=R[–2]C[–1]*. And if you instead enter the formula

=2*$A$1

the INPUT function returns

=2*R1C1

Positioning the Input dialog box

Specifying the *xPosN* and *yPosN* arguments usually requires a little more effort than specifying the other arguments. This is because it can often take a lot of trial and error to determine the numbers you need to use to position the Input dialog box where you want it.

The next macro lets you experiment with the position of the Input dialog box iteratively. To use it, enter a number pair in the dialog box presented, which then becomes the new position of the Input dialog box. To quit the macro, simply click Cancel or press Esc.

	TestInputPosition	Tests INPUT position.
msgT	="Enter INPUT position in the form:"&CHAR(13)&"x,y"	INPUT box message.
titleT	Enter number	INPUT box title.
	coords="0,0"	Initial coordinates.
	=WHILE(NOT(coords=FALSE))	Until coords=FALSE.
commaN	= FIND(",",coords)	Find the comma.
xPosN	= MID(coords,1,commaN-1)	*x*-position value.
yPosN	= MID(coords,commaN+1,999)	*y*-position value.
	coords=INPUT(msgT,2,titleT,coords,xPosN,yPosN)	Display INPUT box.
	= coords	Debug coords.
	=NEXT()	Do it again.
	=RETURN()	

The first two lines of the macro set up the title of the Input dialog box and the message presented within the box. Next, the variable *coords* is set to the text *0,0*; we store the coordinates of the top-left corner of the Input dialog box as text in order to extract each number in the pair, which the macro stores in cells *xPosN* and *yPosN*. If the user presses Esc or clicks Cancel in the Input dialog box, *coords* is set to FALSE instead of storing a new pair of numbers as text, and the WHILE loop ends.

I want to select a cell, start a macro, and have the user enter a number that is added to the value stored in the cell. How do I do it?

Use the following macro formula:

```
=FORMULA(ACTIVE.CELL()+INPUT("Enter amount to add",1))
```

Hiding the Input dialog box

At times, you'll have a problem with the Input dialog box because it's so large. Wherever you drag the box, it seems to obscure important areas of the screen. This problem frequently occurs when you want the user to select an area of a worksheet for your macro to act upon.

One way around this problem is to hide the Input dialog box by positioning it partially or entirely off the screen, using the title area of the Input dialog box to display a prompt message. You can use the *TestInputPosition* macro presented earlier to find the coordinates that place the Input dialog box off the screen, or you can use the following command subroutine macro to position the Input dialog box relative to the bottom of the usable area of the workspace.

	GetRefBottom	
env	=GET.WORKSPACE(1)	Name of environment.
wkSpaceH	=GET.WORKSPACE(14)	Usable workspace height.
statusL	=GET.WORKSPACE(6)	Is status bar displayed?
	=IF(LEFT(env,3)="Mac")	
	yPosn=IF(statusL,wkSpaceH+1,wkSpaceH-17)	Relative to Mac status bar.
	=ELSE()	
	yPosn=IF(statusL,wkSpaceH+10,wkSpaceH-7)	Relative to PC status bar.
	=END.IF()	
getRefTitle	Select range, then press Enter.	Input dialog box title.
getRef	=REFTEXT(INPUT(,8,putTitle,,0,yPosn))	Get ref; convert to text.
	=RETURN(getRef)	Return ref as text.

The GET.WORKSPACE function in the cell labeled *env* returns a text string that describes the environment under which Excel is running. We need to know this because the vertical depth of the workspace (*wkSpaceH*) depends on whether the status bar is displayed (*statusL*), and the height of the status bar varies with the version of Excel that runs the macro.

The IF-ELSE-END.IF group calculates the *y*-coordinate of the Input dialog box, and the formula in the cell *getRef* displays the Input dialog box and converts the range selected in the worksheet to text, which is returned to the calling macro.

The major limitation of this technique is that because the user can't see some or all of the Input dialog box, the user can't review entered data. Therefore, it's often best to use this technique when you want the user to select a range in a worksheet rather than enter data by typing; the marquee that surrounds the selected range provides all the feedback the user needs.

Another way to achieve the same result is by using the MESSAGE function to present the instruction *Select range, then press Enter* and to position the Input dialog box off the screen entirely.

Entering data without using the INPUT function.

Although the INPUT function serves many useful purposes, it does have its limitations, the main one being that a macro can't alter its behavior while values are being entered in the Input dialog box. Chapter 12, "Taking Action Through Macros," contains a macro for using the ON.KEY function to assign actions to keys such as the Enter key and direction keys.

Dialog box functions

At times you want the user to have access to one of Excel's standard dialog boxes before the macro executes a command-equivalent function. The dialog box functions let you accomplish this: Excel provides them for all command-equivalent functions that display dialog boxes. The format of a dialog box function is identical to the format of the comparable macro function except that a question mark follows the function name.

For example, suppose your macro opens a file that contains last year's budget, erases the old data, enters new dates, and then saves the document as this year's budget file. Your macro could use the dialog box form of the SAVE.AS function to suggest the filename, password protection, and so on but it could allow the user to change any of the settings that your macro suggests. The SAVE.AS? function takes the form

=SAVE.AS?(*documentT,typeN,protPwdT,backupL,writeResPwdT,readOnlyRecL*)

The arguments used with a dialog box become the settings that the dialog box suggests. You can usually omit any of the arguments you don't want. If you use a dialog box function without arguments, as in

```
=PRINT?()
```

the macro suggests the same settings that it would if you brought up the same dialog box manually.

Custom dialog boxes

One limitation of Excel's standard dialog box functions is that Excel provides no way for a macro to capture or respond to the changes a user makes in a dialog box. To illustrate, suppose your macro issues the SORT? function, asking a user to specify the sort criteria for a database. It would be nice if the macro could capture these criteria so that it could repeat the sort the next time the user enters more data. Unfortunately, this isn't possible with the standard dialog box functions.

You can get around this problem, however, by creating a custom dialog box that duplicates the Sort dialog box precisely. Custom dialog boxes provide ways to refer easily to each entry in the box and to return the user's entries in the dialog box to the macro sheet.

You can use macros to create custom dialog boxes that have the same look and feel as those generated by standard Excel commands. It's easy to display these dialog boxes, but setting them up takes a little more effort.

An overview of custom dialog boxes

Figure 11-1 shows the PC and Mac versions of a custom dialog box that resembles the Format Number dialog box but contains custom formats that a business might require in its worksheets. Because the descriptions of the number formats listed are stored in the macro sheet rather than on a worksheet, the user can use the

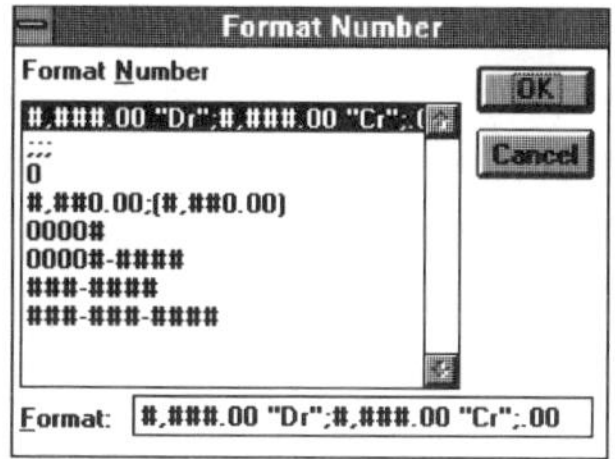

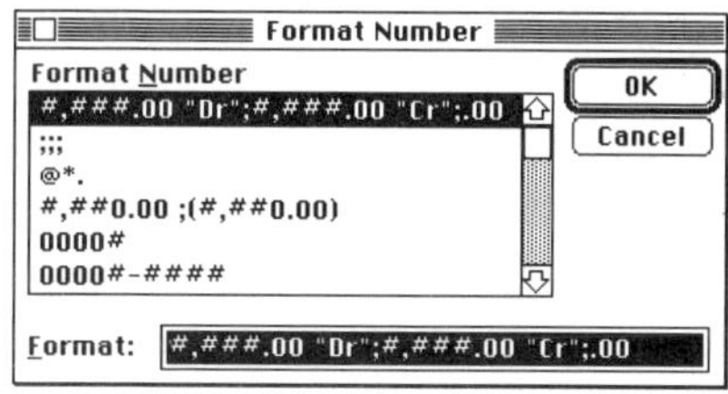

FIGURE 11-1.
The PC and Mac versions of a custom dialog box that resembles the Format Number dialog box.

macro to apply a number format to the active document without having to re-create the format manually. In a sense, this presents a way to support global custom number formats.

The process of creating and presenting this dialog box involves two steps. First, you must create a table, called a *definition table,* that specifies the items in the dialog box. Second, you must write the macro that invokes the dialog box and makes use of the information it returns to the macro sheet.

Entering the definition table

You can create a definition table in two ways. The first method is to manually enter the values contained in the table. The second is to use the Dialog Editor, which lets you arrange the items in the dialog box graphically. When you copy the dialog box in the Dialog Editor and paste it into a macro sheet, Excel converts the graphical image of the dialog box into the definition table. Because you still must deal with a definition table in either case, we'll consider the manual method first and discuss the Dialog Editor a bit later.

To create the definition table that results in the dialog boxes shown in Figure 11-1, do the following.

1. Open a new macro sheet and enter the dialog box definition table shown in Figure 11-2.
2. Format the box as shown. The material that is not in italics (cells F2:L8) is the definition table proper; the italicized entries are labels that will help us name the various rows and columns in the range of the table.

	E	F	G	H	I	J	K	L
1	*dName*	*dItemN*	*dXposn*	*dYposn*	*dWidth*	*dHeight*	*dText*	*dInitResult*
2	***dFormatNumber***		98	62	361	180	Format Number	
3	*dfn.editTextFormat*	6	74	149	279			
4	*dfn.linkedList*	16	6	24	266	124	**dfn.list**	
5	*dfn.textFormat*	5	5	152			&Format:	
6	*dfn.textFormatNumber*	5	6	4			Format &Number	
7	*dfn.defOK*	1	282	8	72		OK	
8	*dfn.nondefCancel*	2	282	35	72		Cancel	

FIGURE 11-2.
The dialog box definition table that generates the dialog boxes shown in Figure 11-1.

3. Select columns E:L by dragging across the column headings, choose the Create Names command, set the Top Row and Left Column options, and press Enter. This assigns the names *dName* through

dInitResult to the columns in the range; *dItemN*, for example, is now defined as

```
=$F$2:$F$16384
```

Similarly, each name in the leftmost column is assigned to the range of its row; *dfn.linkedList*, for example, is defined as

```
=$F$4:$L$4
```

4. Open the Define Name dialog box; you'll see the names you created in step 3. Select the name *dFormatNumber* and then highlight the contents of the Refers To text edit box. Drag the dialog box out of the way so that you can see the range of the definition table, and then select the range F2:L8. Click OK or press Enter. This redefines the first name in the *dName* column, *dFormatNumber*, which is the name assigned to the dialog box itself.

It's a good idea to reserve a consistent range of columns for all the dialog box definition tables you place on a macro sheet; not only will you be able to find the tables more easily, but because the named columns (for example, *dItemN*) extend all the way to the bottom of the macro sheet, you can easily refer to cells in the table by using a row name and a column name, with the intersection operator.

For example, you can enter something in the cell found at the intersection of *dText* and *dfn.editTextFormat* to present a default value for the edit box that this row of the definition table creates in the dialog box. To set the contents of this cell to an initial value for a particular application, you could insert the following formula in a macro:

```
=SET.VALUE((dTEXT dfn.editTextFormat),"my initial value")
```

The next step in setting up the definition table is to enter the list of number formats to be displayed in the list box shown in Figure 11-1. This list isn't strictly part of the definition table, but it's referred to by the cell reference resulting from the expression *dfn.linkedList dText*, which specifies the name of a range containing the list of entries to be displayed in the list box, in this case *dfn.list*. To create this list, do the following.

1. Enter the list of custom formats to be displayed in the list box, shown in Figure 11-3 on the following page. The second column in the table contains comments, and it doesn't affect the creation of the list. As with the definition tables on the macro sheet, it's a good idea to reserve two columns for the lists used by the definition tables. A good place to put these lists is immediately to the right of the definition tables themselves.

	N	O
1	**dfn.list.top**	
2	#,###.00 "Dr";#,###.00 "Cr";.00	Debits and Credits.
3	;;;	Hide Numbers and Text.
4	="@*."	Text Plus Dotted Line.
5	#,##0.00 ;(#,##0.00)	Standard Currency.
6	0000#	Zip Code.
7	0000#-####	Zip Code +4.
8	###-####	Local Phone Number.
9	###-###-####	Long Distance Phone Number.
10	**dfn.list.bottom**	

FIGURE 11-3.
A list of custom formats to be displayed in the Format Number dialog box.

2. Select the cell containing the text *dfn.list.top,* choose the Define Name command, and press Enter. Do the same for the cell containing the text *dfn.list.bottom.*
3. Call up the Define Name dialog box again, enter the text *dfn.list,* and assign it the value

   =OFFSET(dfn.list.top,1,0):OFFSET(dfn.list.bottom,-1,0)

   This defines the name *dfn.list* in terms of the location of *dfn.list.top* and *dfn.list.bottom;* doing this lets you or a macro insert new rows in the range for new number formats without requiring you to redefine the range each time you do. (This capability will come in handy later in this chapter, when we add Insert and Delete buttons to the dialog box.)

Creating the macro that calls up the dialog box

To display the dialog box and make use of the user's responses in it, enter the macro shown in Figure 11-4.

cmd N	**MyFormatNumber**	Global number formats.
mfn.dialogN	=DIALOG.BOX(dFormatNumber)	Number of item chosen.
	=IF(mfn.dialogN=FALSE,RETURN())	If Cancel, quit macro.
mfn.dItemT	=OFFSET(dFormatNumber,mfn.dialogN,-1,1,1)	Name of item chosen.
	=IF(mfn.dItemT="dfn.defOK")	If OK, format the range.
	=FORMAT.NUMBER(dfn.editTextFormat dInitResult)	
	=END.IF()	
	=RETURN()	

FIGURE 11-4.
This macro presents the dialog box and responds to the changes the user makes in it.

The first formula in the macro shown in Figure 11-4 uses the DIALOG.BOX function. This function takes the form

DIALOG.BOX(dialogRef)

where *dialogRef* refers to the range containing the definition table of the dialog box you want to display. In the case of our macro, this range is named *dFormatNumber.*

At this point in the execution of the macro, Excel presents the dialog box and waits for the user to take some action. This can take three forms:

- The user can select a number format presented in the list box or enter a new format in the text edit box.
- The user can click OK or press Enter, dismissing the dialog box.
- The user can click Cancel or press Esc, dismissing the dialog box.

After the user clicks the OK or Cancel button, Excel returns control to the macro. If the user clicked Cancel or pressed Esc, the DIALOG.BOX function returns FALSE. The second line of the macro tests for this condition; if it exists, the macro ends.

On the other hand, if the user clicks OK, the DIALOG.BOX function does two things. First, it returns the number of the item chosen, in the order in which it is listed in the definition table. For example, in our macro, if the user clicks OK or presses Enter, *mfn.dialogN* becomes *5*; the formula in cell *mfn.dItemT* takes this number and uses it to determine the name of the item chosen, according to what we've entered in the *dName* column in the definition table. If the user clicked the OK button, this name is *dfn.defOK.*

Second, the DIALOG.BOX function enters in the *dInitResult* column the results of options selected or entries made in text edit boxes, as you can see when you run the macro and then activate the sheet containing the definition table. In our example, the text displayed in the text edit box is transferred to the cell at the intersection of column *dInitResult* and row *dfn.editTextFormat*. Similarly, Excel enters the number of the list entry, selected at the time the user clicked the OK button, in the cell at the intersection of *dfn.linkedList* and *dInitResult*. If the user selects the sixth entry in the list, Excel puts the number *6* at this position in the definition table, as well as the corresponding number format (as text). (See Figure 11-5.)

dName	dItemN	dXposn	dYposn	dWidth	dHeight	dText	dInitResult
dFormatNumber		98	62	361	180	Format Number	
dfn.editTextFormat	6	74	149	279			0000#-####
dfn.linkedList	16	6	24	266	124	**dfn.list**	6
dfn.textFormat	5	5	152			&Format:	
dfn.textFormatNumber	5	6	4			Format &Number	
dfn.defOK	1	282	8	72		OK	
dfn.nondefCancel	2	282	35	72		Cancel	

FIGURE 11-5.
The definition table after selecting the sixth entry in the list box.

Our macro uses this information in the FORMAT.NUMBER formula inside the IF-END.IF structure. If the name of the item chosen is *dfn.defOK*, then the FORMAT.NUMBER function applies the format defined by the text returned to the definition table to the selected text. A side effect of this is that the format is also added to the active sheet's list of number formats: If you choose the Format Number command and scroll to the bottom of the list, you'll see the new number format.

Now let's go over the structure of the definition table in detail and then discuss the range of items you can use in your custom dialog boxes.

The definition table

Properly, the definition table we used in the previous example consists of only the range F2:L8, as shown in Figure 11-2 on page 230. The column headings in row 1 and the names in column E are not strictly necessary, but they are so useful for finding your way around a definition table that we recommend you incorporate them into the dialog box definition tables you create.

These headings follow a terminology that is a little different from that of the Excel documentation, the main reason for this being that we use each heading to name the column in which the heading resides.

It's a good idea to put all the dialog boxes you create in the same range of columns so that the column widths will remain the same and because the column names let you use the intersection operator to reference cells in the definition table. To define the row names for any definition table beyond the first, simply select the cell containing the name of the dialog box through the bottom-right corner of the definition table, and use the Create Names command. For example, if the table shown in Figure 11-2 were actually the second definition table you were creating, you would select the range E2:L8, choose the Format Create Names command, set only the Left Column option, and click OK. Because the names of the columns were assigned when you set up the first definition table, you need only define the row names for the second table.

When discussing dialog boxes, the term *item* refers to any object that you put in a dialog box. For example, Figure 11-1 on page 229 contains six items: two buttons, two text labels, a list box, and a text edit box.

The first column of our table, *dName*, contains the labels used to name the rows in the table. We've used what is called a *structured* naming convention for these labels, which both documents the item being specified in the table and greatly reduces the probability that these names would be used elsewhere on the macro sheet. Of course, you don't have to use the same naming convention, or even name the columns and rows of the definition table at all.

The first column of the body of the table, column *dItemN*, contains the type number of each item in the dialog box. A type number specifies whether an item is an OK button, block of text, check box, and so on. For example, type *6* specifies an edit box, such as that displayed at the bottom of Figure 11-1, that contains the text describing the format to be applied; type *16* specifies the list box in the figure that contains the list of formats; and type *5* specifies that an item is text. We'll cover the range of items you can add to dialog boxes in the next section.

The second and third columns of the table, columns *dXposn* and *dYposn*, specify in pixels the coordinates of the top-left corner of the item relative to the top-left corner of the dialog box. The exception is the first row of the table, which describes the dialog box as a whole and is relative to the top-left corner of the available workspace.

The fourth and fifth columns of the table, columns *dWidth* and *dHeight*, specify in pixels the width and height of the item. You can often omit these values, and Excel will calculate the dimensions of the item automatically.

The sixth column of the table, column *dText*, contains text that determines what is displayed in the dialog box; the type of item determines how this text is used. In the range *dFormatNumber*, for example, the text *Format Number* becomes the title displayed at the top of the dialog box. If you do specify text for the dialog box as a whole, Excel adds a title bar and puts the specified text in the title bar, enabling the user to drag the box around on the screen.

The *dText* column also specifies the text displayed within buttons and text labels; for certain items, it specifies the name of a range that determines what is displayed in the dialog box. For example, the list box described by *dfn.linkedList* above refers to *dfn.list*, which contains the list of number formats to be placed in the dialog box.

You can use the ampersand character (&) to tell Excel to use the character following the ampersand character as the accelerator key for the item. These accelerator keys are underlined when the dialog box is displayed. Use Alt plus the underlined letter to activate the corresponding item by using the keyboard [Mac—use Command plus the underlined letter].

The sixth column of the table, column *dInitResult*, contains the initial values for the dialog box and also its results. If you don't want previous results to appear as initial values in a dialog box, have your macro set the initial values you do want before you bring up the dialog box.

For example, the next time the *MyFormatNumber* macro is run, the last values returned in the *dInitResult* column become proposed values in the dialog box. This can be either a bug or a feature, depending on the behavior you want. If you want to clear the dialog box before displaying it again, insert the following formula before the DIALOG.BOX formula in *MyFormatNumber*:

```
=FORMULA.FILL("",(dFormatNumber dInitResult))
```

To preset the proposed values in the text edit box and the selected entry in the list, use the following formula instead:

=FORMULA(5,(dfn.linkedList dInitResult))

Although this formula does not, in this case, change the contents of the cell *dInit-Result dfn.editTextFormat*, because the text edit box is linked to the linked list box, presetting the selected entry in the list also predetermines the contents of the text edit box. We'll cover the relationship between the items in a dialog box in greater depth in the next section.

Items in a dialog box

The *dItemN* column in the definition table determines the type of object created in the dialog box. The order in which objects are defined is sometimes important, and the meaning attached to the entries in the *dText* and *dInitResult* columns often varies with the object being created.

OK buttons (item numbers 1 and 3)

When you click an OK button in a custom dialog box, two things happen. First, Excel transfers the values for the items in the dialog box to the *dInitResult* column of the definition table. Second, the DIALOG.BOX function returns the line number in the definition table that contains the definition for that OK button.

Figure 11-6 shows the PC and Mac versions of a dialog box containing the OK and Cancel buttons, and the definition table that generates them.

dName	dItemN	dXposn	dYposn	dWidth	dHeight	dText	dInitResult
dOKCancel		150	72	92	100		
doc.defOK	1	8	12	64		OK	
doc.nondefCancel	2	8	39	64		Cancel	
doc.nondefOK	3	8	66	72		Delete	

FIGURE 11-6.
PC and Mac dialog boxes containing the OK and Cancel buttons, and the definition table that generates them.

In a row specifying an OK button within a definition table:

- The *dItemN* cell for the OK button contains *1* when the OK button is the default button or *3* otherwise. (Note: A default button is the button chosen if the user presses Enter.)
- The *dText* cell contains the text presented in the OK button. When you title an OK button, you can use any text in place of *OK*. For example, you could create an OK button that contains the text *Delete*.
- The *dInitResult* cell is ignored for type numbers 1 and 3.

Cancel buttons (item numbers 2 and 4)

When you click on Cancel in a custom dialog box, Excel closes the box, returns FALSE to the DIALOG.BOX function, and does not update the *dInitResult* column of the definition table. Figure 11-6 also shows a Cancel button.

In a row specifying a Cancel button within a definition table:

- The *dItemN* cell contains *2* for a standard Cancel button, or *4* when you want the Cancel button to be the default button, which is chosen if the user presses Enter.
- The *dText* cell contains the text appearing in the Cancel button. (Note: As with OK buttons, Cancel buttons can contain text other than Cancel.)
- The *dInitResult* cell is ignored for Cancel buttons.

Dialog boxes that do not include OK or Cancel buttons.

Even if a dialog box doesn't contain an OK or a Cancel button, you can still press Enter instead of clicking OK, or you can press Esc instead of clicking Cancel. However, eliminating these buttons from your dialog boxes is not a good idea because it's in your best interest to provide as consistent and clear a user interface as possible.

Text (item number 5)

The text item lets you display text in the dialog box: the titles of text edit boxes, brief instructions, and so on. (Figure 11-9 on page 240 illustrates the use of text in a definition table.)

In a row specifying a text item in a definition table:

- The *dText* cell generally contains the text to be displayed. (However, see the section "Linked file/directory boxes" later in this chapter for an exception.)
- The *dInitResult* cell is ignored.

Edit boxes (item numbers 6 through 10)

Users use edit boxes to enter data into dialog boxes. To ensure that the correct data is entered, specify one of the five types of edit boxes. Figure 11-7 illustrates the five types of edit boxes.

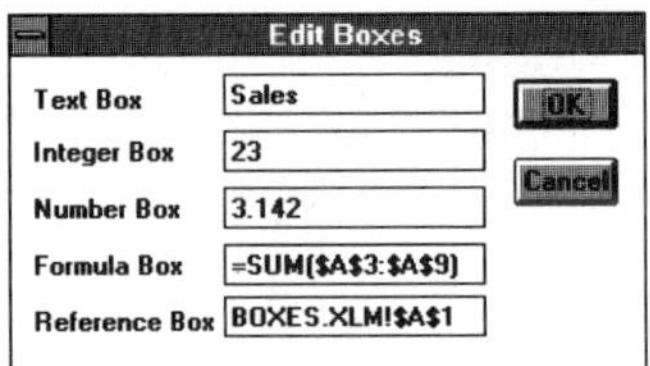

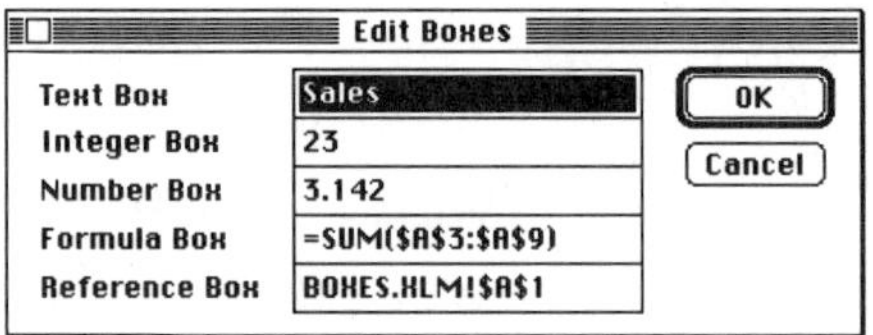

dName	*dItemN*	*dXposn*	*dYposn*	*dWidth*	*dHeight*	*dText*	*dInitResult*
dEdit		10	68	390	137	Edit Boxes	
de.textText	5	14	12			Text Box	
de.textInteger	5	14	35			Integer Box	
de.textNumber	5	14	59			Number Box	
de.textFormula	5	14	82			Formula Box	
de.textRef	5	14	106			Reference Box	
de.textEditText	6	131	8	160			Sales
de.textEditInt	7	131	32	160			23
de.textEditNum	8	131	55	160			3.142
de.textEditForm	9	131	79	160			=SUM(R3C1:R9C1)
de.textEditRef	10	131	102	160			BOXES.XLM!R1C1
de.defOK	1	310	11	64		OK	
de.nondefCancel	2	310	44	64		Cancel	

FIGURE 11-7.
PC and Mac dialog boxes containing edit boxes, and the definition table that generates them.

In a row specifying an edit box in a definition table:

- The *dItemN* cell contains a number from 6 through 10, according to the table at the top of the facing page.
- The *dText* cell is ignored. (To label a text edit box, use a text item of type number 5.)
- The *dInitResult* cell can be blank; if it contains a value, that value is presented when the dialog box is displayed.

dItemN	Edit box type	Accepts	Returns
6	Text	Any entry	Text.
7	Integer	Integers from -32765 to 32767	Integers from -32765 through 32767.
8	Number	Any number	Any number.
9	Formula	Any entry	Formulas as text in R1C1 style.
10	Reference	References	References as text in R1C1 style. (See Note.)

Note: When the user enters simple references (A1 or the name of a range, for example), Excel assumes the user is referring to the macro sheet that presents the dialog box, and it returns an external reference to that area. Also, the user can enter data into a formula or reference edit box by selecting cells on any open sheet. On the Mac, multiple selections are separated by plus (+) signs. To separate them with a comma, hold down the Command key while you select an area.

Option buttons (item numbers 11 and 12)

Option buttons appear in groups in a dialog box because they represent a series of options, only one of which can be selected; selecting one of the options deselects the others in the group. To specify that a series of option buttons belong in a group, you precede the series with an option button group item (item 11). Figure 11-8 illustrates three option buttons surrounded by an option group box.

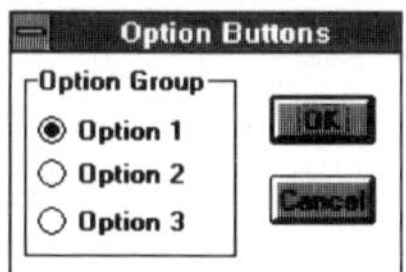

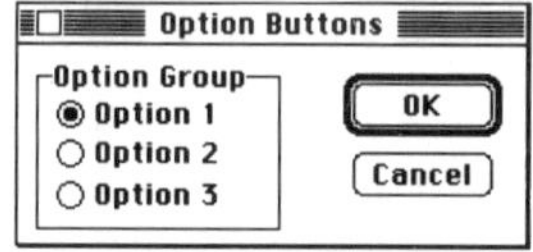

dName	*dItemN*	*dXposn*	*dYposn*	*dWidth*	*dHeight*	*dText*	*dInitResult*
dOptionButtons		187	212	234	97	Option Buttons	
dob.optGroup	11					Option Group	1
dob.opt1	12	16	25		18	Option 1	
dob.opt2	12	16	44		18	Option 2	
dob.opt3	12	16	64		18	Option 3	
dob.defOK	1	155	18	64		OK	
dob.nondefCancel	2	155	52	64		Cancel	

FIGURE 11-8.
PC and Mac dialog boxes containing option buttons, and the definition table that generates them.

In a row that defines an option button or option button group within a definition table:

- The *dItemN* cell contains the number *11* to define a group and the number *12* to define each option button.
- If you enter text in the *dText* cell for a group (item 11), the text becomes the title of the option group and a border is drawn around the group of option buttons. Otherwise, the text entered in the *dText* cell of an option button becomes the text displayed next to the button.
- The *dInitResult* cell for an option group (item 11) contains the button number to be selected when the dialog box is opened. The first button in the group is 1, the next is 2, and so on. When the dialog box is closed, the number of the button the user selected is stored in this cell. If the *dInitResult* cell initially contains #N/A, no buttons are selected when the dialog box is opened; if empty, the first button is selected. The *dInitResult* cell is ignored for option buttons (item 12).

In Excel's standard dialog boxes, double-clicking an option button both selects an option and dismisses the dialog box. Custom dialog boxes behave in the same way.

Check box buttons (item number 13)

Check boxes, a form of button, let the user select options. Unlike option buttons, however, the user can select more than one check box at a time. Check boxes can have either two states or three. Two-state check boxes can be either checked or unchecked. Three-state check boxes can be checked, unchecked, or grayed. A grayed check box usually indicates that an option is "partially" set, as in Excel's standard Borders dialog box, where it means that not all the selected cells have the indicated border. Figure 11-9 illustrates the PC and Mac versions of a dialog box with three check boxes.

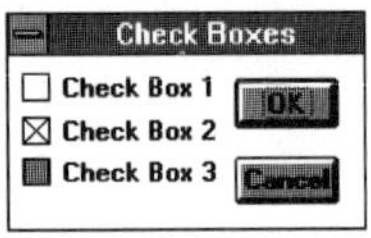

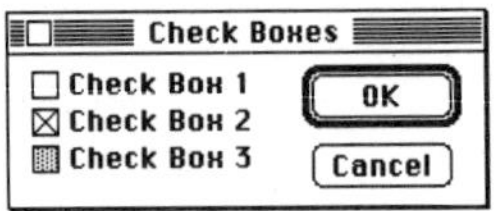

dName	dItemN	dXposn	dYposn	dWidth	dHeight	dText	dInitResult
dCheckButtons		10	68	219	74	Check Boxes	
dcb.check1	13	8	6			Check Box 1	FALSE
dcb.check2	13	8	24			Check Box 2	TRUE
dcb.check3	13	8	42			Check Box 3	#N/A
dcb.defOK	1	140	10	64		OK	
dcb.nondefCancel	2	140	44	64		Cancel	

FIGURE 11-9.
PC and Mac dialog boxes containing check boxes, and the definition table that generates them.

You can group check boxes visually by using a group box (item 14), although using a group box isn't required, as is the option group item for a series of option buttons.

In a row specifying a check box in a definition table:

- The *dItemN* cell contains the number *13*.
- The *dText* cell contains the label associated with the check box.
- If the *dInitResult* cell is empty or contains FALSE, the check box is unchecked when the dialog box opens. If the cell contains TRUE, the check box is checked. In these instances, the check box cycles between two states. If the *dInitResult* cell contains #N/A when the dialog box is displayed, the check box is grayed. When this happens, the check box cycles among three states: grayed, unchecked, and checked.

Therefore, if you want a check box to preserve its state from one display of the dialog box to the next, you must preset the value stored in the *dInitResult* column, as described in our example above.

Group box (item number 14)

A group box consists of a border and a text label that you can use to visually group items within a dialog box. Group boxes are very much like the boxes created when you specify a title for an option group, but they are not required by any item created in a dialog box. Figure 11-10 shows the same dialog boxes as in Figure 11-9 but with an additional group box.

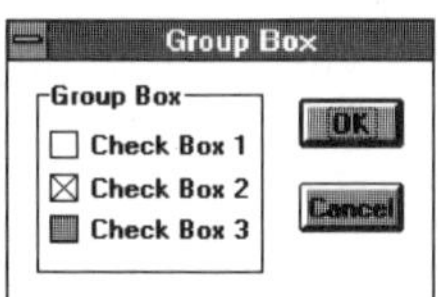

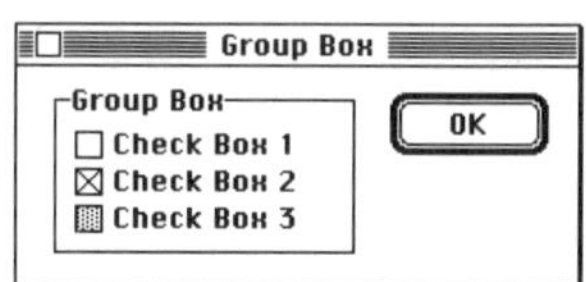

dName	dItemN	dXposn	dYposn	dWidth	dHeight	dText	dInitResult
dGroupBox		150	250	257	107	Group Box	
dgb.groupBox	14	17	9	138	82	Group Box	
dgb.check1	13	25	29			Check Box 1	FALSE
dgb.check2	13	25	47			Check Box 2	TRUE
dgb.check3	13	25	65			Check Box 3	#N/A
dgb.defOK	1	175	17	64		OK	
dgb.nondefCancel	2	175	52	64		Cancel	

FIGURE 11-10.
PC and Mac dialog boxes containing check boxes and a group box, and the definition table that generates them.

In a row specifying a group box in a definition table:

- The *dItemN* cell contains the number *14.*
- The *dText* cell contains the text that appears at the top of the group box. If this cell is blank, the box is displayed as a rectangle and without a title.
- The *dInitResult* cell is ignored.

Standard list box (item number 15)

A standard list box displays a list of entries that the user can scroll in, leaving an entry selected; the Formula Paste Name command uses this type of list box. Figure 11-11 illustrates a standard list box.

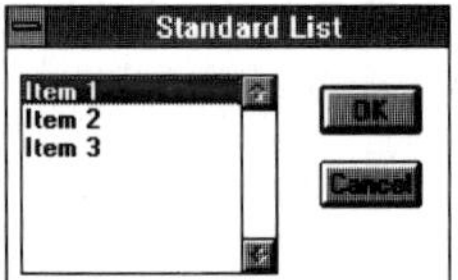

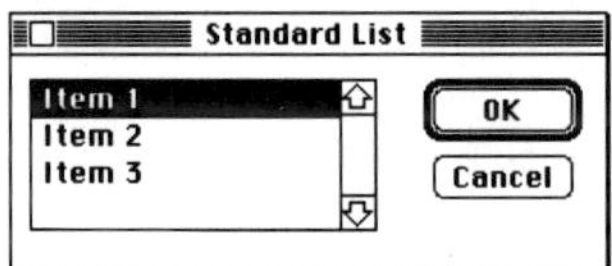

dName	*dItemN*	*dXposn*	*dYposn*	*dWidth*	*dHeight*	*dText*	*dInitResult*
dStandardList		20	68	273	106	Standard List	
dsl.listBox	15	8	12	160	84	**dsl.list**	1
dsl.defOK	1	194	16	64		OK	
dsl.nondefCancel	2	194	48	64		Cancel	

FIGURE 11-11.
PC and Mac dialog boxes containing a standard list box, and the definition table that generates them.

In a row specifying a standard list box within a definition table:

- The *dItemN* cell contains the number *15.*
- The *dText* cell contains a reference, either as a name or in the R1C1-text format, to a range of cells containing the list. You can use a simple reference to a range on the macro sheet or an external reference to a separate sheet. In Figure 11-11, for example, the cell *dText dsl.listBox* contains the name *dsl.list,* which refers to a range containing the list *Item 1, Item 2,* and *Item 3* in a column of three cells and was defined in the same manner as was the list in Figure 11-3 on page 232.
- The *dInitResult* cell for the list box item contains the number of the item selected within the list box. For example, in the figure the cell contains *1* to select the first entry in the list. If the cell is blank, the

first entry is selected by default. If the cell contains #N/A, no entries are selected. After the user selects an entry in the list, the number of its position in the list is returned to this cell.

A few of Excel's list boxes permit selecting more than one entry in a list. This type of list box is called a *multiple-selection list box*. In the list box of the Formula Apply Names dialog box, for example, you can hold the Shift key down to select more than one entry. (In the Macintosh version, you can select a continuous range of entries by holding down the Shift key while clicking on the entries, and you can select a discontinuous collection of entries by holding down the Command key while clicking the entries.)

You can achieve the same effect in a custom dialog box by putting in the *dInitResult* cell of the linked list item a name to which Excel assigns a horizontal array of the numbers of the selected items. For example, if you put the name *dsl.resultArray* into the cell *dInitResult dsl.listBox* of Figure 11-11, and the user selected entries *Item 1* and *Item 3*, Excel would define *dsl.resultArray* as *={1,3}*.

Linked list box (item number 16)

A linked list box, also called a *combination* (or *combo*) box, links a list box to an edit box. When the user selects an entry in the list box, the entry appears in the edit box. However, the user can also use the edit box to enter items that don't appear in the list box or to edit a selected entry. The Format Number command uses a linked list box, as does the example we presented in Figure 11-2 earlier in this chapter. Figure 11-12 illustrates a linked list box.

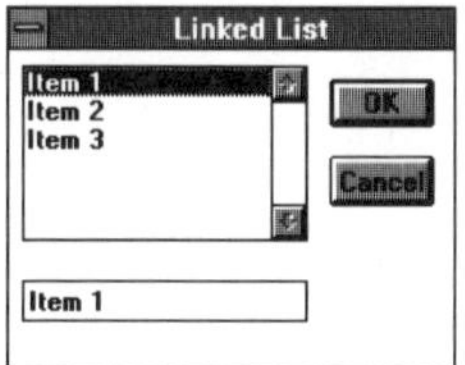

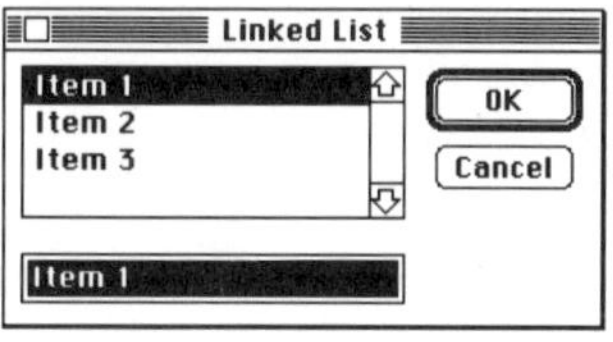

dName	*dItemN*	*dXposn*	*dYposn*	*dWidth*	*dHeight*	*dText*	*dInitResult*
dLinkedList		20	68	274	133	Linked List	
dll.textEdit	6	7	98	176			Item 1
dll.linkedList	16	7	8	176	83	**dll.list**	1
dll.defOK	1	197	12	64		OK	
dll.nondefCancel	2	197	45	64		Cancel	

FIGURE 11-12.
PC and Mac dialog boxes containing a linked list box, and the definition table that generates them.

As the figure shows, the text edit box to which the list is linked precedes the linked list item. In a row specifying a linked list box within a definition table:

- The *dItemN* cell contains the number *16* for a linked list box and *6* for the preceding text edit box.
- The *dText* cell of the linked list item contains a reference, either as a name or in the R1C1-text format, to a range of cells containing the list. The *dText* cell for the text edit box is the same as for a normal text edit box.
- The *dInitResult* cell for the list box is the same as for the standard list box. The *dInitResult* cell for the text edit box is the same as for a normal text edit box. These two cells can contain different results when the user clicks OK. If the user simply selects an entry in the list, the number of that entry's position in the list is returned in the *dInitResult* cell for the linked list item. If the user edits an entry in the text edit box or enters completely new text, the text is returned in the *dInitResult* cell for the text edit box, and Excel puts #N/A in the *dInitResult* cell for the linked list item.

Icons (item number 17)

The icons presented by an icon item in a custom dialog box are the same as those displayed by the ALERT function, described earlier in this chapter. Figure 11-13 presents the PC and Mac versions of a dialog box containing three icons.

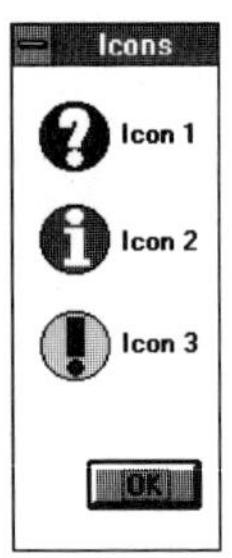

dName	dItemN	dXposn	dYposn	dWidth	dHeight	dText	dInitResult
dIcons		246	150	126	204	Icons	
di.text1	5	65	23			Icon 1	
di.text2	5	65	67			Icon 2	
di.text3	5	65	111			Icon 3	
di.icon1	17	16	15			1	
di.icon2	17	16	59			2	
di.icon3	17	16	103			3	
di.defOK	1	44	167			OK	

FIGURE 11-13.
PC and Mac dialog boxes containing icons, and the definition table that generates them.

In a row specifying an icon in a definition table:

- The *dItemN* cell for the icon contains the number *17.*
- The *dText* cell contains a number from 1 through 3, exactly as in the ALERT function: *1* for signifying a choice, *2* for presenting information, and *3* for notifying the user of an error.
- The *dInitResult* cell is ignored.

Linked file/directory boxes (item numbers 18 through 20)

Dialog box items numbered 18 through 20, available only in the PC versions of Excel, let you create dialog boxes that are similar to Excel's File Open dialog box, in which you can change drives and directories and select a file from the list box presented. The file selected is then returned to the *dInitResult* column of the dialog box definition table. Figure 11-14 illustrates linked file/directory boxes.

To create this kind of dialog box, you need to set up a definition table containing the items whose *dItemN* numbers are shown in boldface type in the figure, in the same order listed. You could put the text labels (*dItemN* 5) either before this sequence or after it, however.

The row named *dlf.editLinkedFile* specifies an edit box that is linked to the file list box specified in the next row, *dlf.linkedFileList*. The *dInitResult* cell contains the

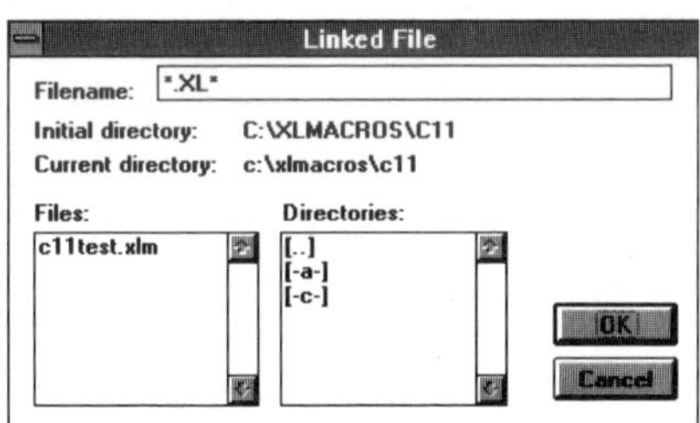

dName	dItemN	dXposn	dYposn	dWidth	dHeight	dText	dInitResult
dLinkedFile		69	69	486	183	Linked File	
dlf.editLinkedFile	**6**	106	5	362			*.XL*
dlf.linkedFileList	**18**	18	87	160	84		
dlf.linkedDir	**19**	191	87	160	84		
dlf.textCurrDir	**5**	165	45	300	17		
dlf.dirText	20	165	29	300	17		
dlf.textFiles	5	18	70			Files:	
dlf.textDirectories	5	193	71			Directories:	
dlf.textInitDirLabel	5	18	30			Initial directory:	
dlf.textCurrDirLabel	5	18	47			Current directory:	
dlf.textFilename	5	18	10			Filename:	
dlf.defOK	1	384	122	88		OK	
dlf.nondefCancel	2	384	149	88		Cancel	

FIGURE 11-14.
PC dialog box containing linked file/directory boxes, and the definition table that generates it.

text *.XL*, which describes the type of file listed in the file list box. When the user selects a file and clicks OK, Excel returns the name of the file to this cell. Because the prior contents of the *dInitResult* cell are replaced by the filename returned, usually you need to initialize this *dInitResult* cell before calling up the dialog box—with the following formulas. For example:

```
=FORMULA("*.XL*",(dlf.editLinkedFile dInitResult))
=DIALOG(dLinkedFile)
```

The row named *dlf.linkedDir* contains a *dItemN* number of *19* and specifies a list box in which the user can change the current directory; the file list box then updates to reflect the files matching the pattern displayed in the *deditLinkedFile* edit box. The text label specified by the next row, *dlf.textCurrDir*, is linked with the directory list box; when the user changes directories, the pathname of that directory is displayed in this label. For this reason, Excel ignores the *dText* cell of the text label in the row after that specifying the directory list box.

Curiously, when the user clicks OK, the current pathname is not returned to the *dInitResult* cell of either row *dlf.linkedDir* or row *dlf.textCurrDir*, but the current directory actually changes to what is displayed in *dlf.textCurrDir*. Extending the last macro fragment, you would have to use the INFO function to return the pathname of the current directory, as follows:

```
              =FORMULA("*.XL*",(dlf.editLinkedFile dInitResult))
              =DIALOG(dLinkedFile)
thisFile      =dlf.editLinkedFile dInitResult
currDirectory =INFO("directory")
```

The final item you might want to put in a dialog box such as the one we've described is represented by row *dlf.dirText* of Figure 11-14, which contains the *dItemN* number *20*. This item displays the pathname of the initial directory—the directory that was current at the moment the dialog box was displayed—and doesn't update as the user changes directories in the directory list box. The main use for this item is to limit the user's file choices to a specific directory when the user isn't using a directory list box at all. We've included it in this example so that you can compare the behavior of this item with the behavior of linked items 19 and 5.

Drop-down list box (item number 21)

A drop-down list box is similar to a standard list box, but it displays the list in a menu format when the user clicks anywhere in the drop-down box. Figure 11-15 illustrates this type of list box.

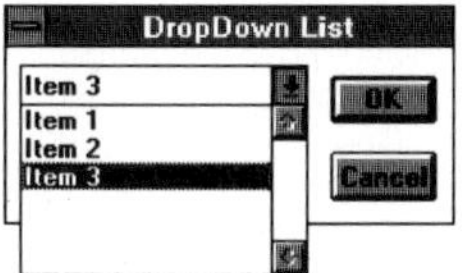

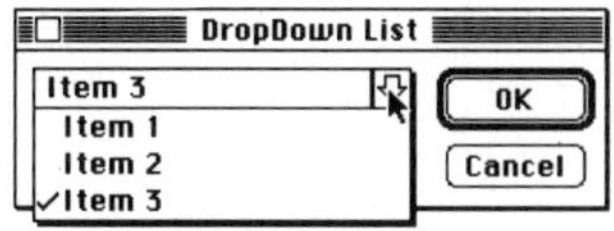

dName	*dItemN*	*dXposn*	*dYposn*	*dWidth*	*dHeight*	*dText*	*dInitResult*
dDropDownList		122	170	270	75	DropDown List	
dddl.dropDown	21	7	8	176	83	dddl.list	3
dddl.defOK	1	197	12	64		OK	
dddl.nondefCancel	2	197	45	64		Cancel	

FIGURE 11-15.
PC and Mac dialog boxes containing a drop-down list box, and the definition table that generates them.

In a row specifying a drop-down list box in a definition table:

- The *dItemN* cell contains the number *21.*
- The *dHeight* cell describes the height of the list when the user clicks in the box; if needed, you can make the list extend below the bottom of the dialog box.
- The *dText* cell contains an R1C1-text format reference to a range containing the list to be displayed, a name associated with that range, or the name of an array stored in the sheet containing the definition table. (A good approach is to define this list by using the techniques described immediately after Figure 11-2 earlier in this chapter.)
- The *dInitResult* cell contains the number of the item to be selected when the dialog box is first called up. If the user selects another item in the list and clicks OK, Excel returns the number of that item in the list to this cell.

A major difference between a drop-down list box and a standard list box is that only in the latter can you hold down the Ctrl key [Mac—also Command] to select more than one item in the list.

Drop-down combination edit/list box (item number 22)

In the same way that a drop-down list box is similar to a standard list box, a drop-down combination edit/list box (*combo box,* for short) is similar to a linked list box. The user can edit or replace the proposed entry in the edit box or pull down the list to enter any of several alternatives. Figure 11-16 on the following page illustrates this type of list box.

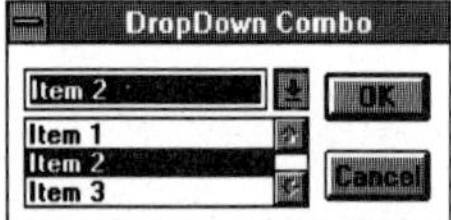

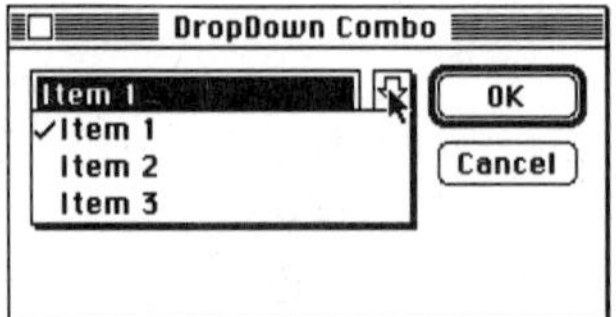

dName	*dItemN*	*dXposn*	*dYposn*	*dWidth*	*dHeight*	*dText*	*dInitResult*
dDropDownCombo		20	68	274	133	DropDown Combo	
dddc.editText	**6**	10	10	178	27		Item 1
dddc.combo	**22**	10	37	178	45	**dddc.list**	1
dddc.defOK	1	197	12	64		OK	
dddc.nondefCancel	2	197	45	64		Cancel	

FIGURE 11-16.
PC and Mac dialog boxes containing a drop-down combination edit/list box, and the definition table that generates them.

Note: The Mac version of the combo box appears different from the PC version. The functionality, however, is the same.

You specify a combo box by pairing a text edit box (*dItemN* 6) and a combo box (*dItemN* 22); the text edit box must precede the row defining the combo box item.

In a row specifying a combo box in a definition table:

- The *dItemN* cell contains the number 22.
- The *dHeight* cell describes the height of the list when the user clicks in the box; if needed, you can make the list extend below the bottom of the dialog box.
- The *dText* cell contains an R1C1-text format reference to a range containing the list to be displayed, a name associated with that range, or the name of an array stored in the sheet containing the definition table. (A good approach is to define this list by using the techniques described immediately after Figure 11-2 earlier in this chapter.)
- The *dInitResult* cell contains the number of the item to be selected when the dialog box is first called up. If the user selects another item in the list and clicks OK, Excel returns the number of that item in the list to this cell, and it returns the text of the list entry to the *dInitResult* cell of the text edit box. If the user edits the text, creating an entry not found on the list, Excel returns the text to the *dInitResult* cell of the row defining the text edit box, and it returns #N/A to the *dInitResult* cell of the row defining the combo box.

Using the Dialog Editor

The Dialog Editor lets you create dialog boxes without having to build a dialog box definition table from scratch or lets you adjust the arrangement of items in a dialog box without having to edit the numbers in the definition table. To run the Dialog Editor on the PC, choose Excel's Control Run command, select Dialog Editor, and press Enter or click OK. On the Macintosh, launch the Dialog Editor from the Finder. When the Dialog Editor workspace appears, you'll see only an empty dialog box, waiting for the items you'll place within it.

To use the Dialog Editor to create a dialog box from scratch, use the commands on the Item menu to add each item: Choosing any but the Text and Group Box commands brings up a dialog box in which you can select the type of item you want. When you choose an item, it appears in the dialog box; use the mouse or the direction keys to place it where you want.

Choosing some commands results in the addition of more than one item in the dialog box. For example, if you choose the Item List Box command and select the Combination option, the Dialog Editor adds two items: an edit box (*dItemN* 6) and a standard list box (*dItemN* 15).

When you add an item, the Dialog Editor places each new item below the previous one; if you add an item and then move it, the next item you add will be positioned below the item you just moved.

If you select an item and press Enter, the Dialog Editor often adds another of the same item, just below the selected item. For example, to add a series of check boxes, you can use the Item Button command to add a check box, use the keyboard to enter the name of the check box, and then press Enter to add another check box.

If you press Enter after entering an OK button, however, the Dialog Editor adds a Cancel button. Similarly, pressing Enter after adding a group box automatically adds an option button within the group box.

To change the dimensions of an item, place the mouse pointer over any of its edges or corners: When you do so, the shape of the pointer changes to indicate the directions in which you can move the edge. To constrain movement, hold down the Shift key before dragging.

You can also change the characteristics of an item by selecting it and choosing Edit Info or by double-clicking the item. When you do so, the dialog box at the top of the following page appears (assuming that you're working with a text label, for example).

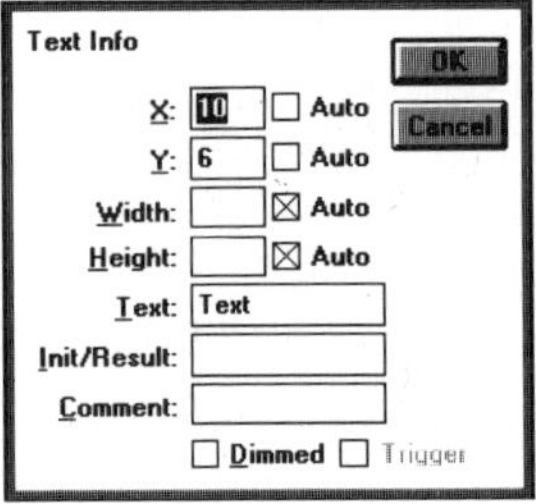

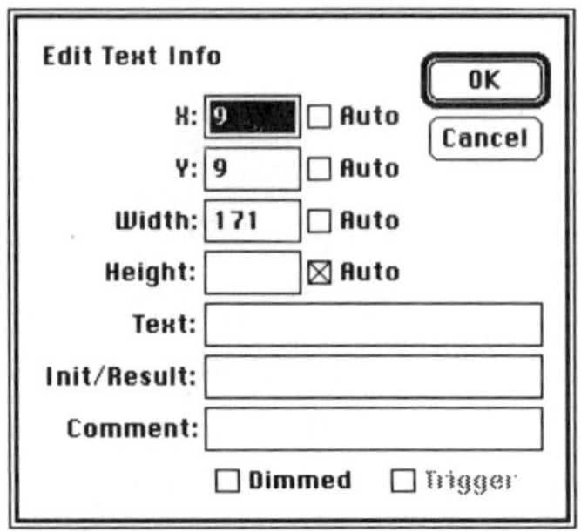

The fields in the Info dialog box correspond to each cell in the row of a definition table describing the resulting item. If an Auto check box is set for the *x* or *y* component of the item's position, the Dialog Editor positions the object relative to the item that was created last. If an Auto check box is set for the width or height of the object, the Dialog Editor adjusts the size of the item automatically.

One of the main uses of the Info dialog box is to precisely align the edges of items in a dialog box. For example, to align the left edges of two items, double-click on the first item to find its *y*-position and then double-click on the next item and enter the same *y*-position.

The Info dialog box is useful for several other purposes as well. You can enter text corresponding to the *dText* cell for the item in the Text field, and you can specify an initial value to appear in edit boxes using the Init/Result field.

You can enter text into the Comment field to document the item; this text doesn't appear in the dialog box but appears in the column immediately to the right of the definition table when you transfer the dialog box back to Excel. If you want to follow the naming convention we've used in this chapter, you can use the Comment field to enter the name to be assigned to that row of the definition table and then to move the column containing the names to the left side of the definition table.

Finally, you can make the item appear dimmed in the dialog box or make the item a trigger. (We'll discuss these options in the section entitled "Dynamic dialog boxes" a little later in this chapter.)

When you've completed the dialog box, you can transfer it to your macro sheet by doing the following.

1. Choose Select Dialog Box from the Edit menu and then choose Edit Copy. When you do this, the Dialog Editor converts the dialog box as it appears on-screen into the definition table, which is then copied to the Clipboard.
2. Switch back to Excel, activate the macro sheet on which you want to place the definition table, and select the cell where you want the

top-left cell of the table to go. If you're following the convention we've presented in this chapter for the arrangement of definition tables in your macro sheets, this would be a cell in column F.

3. Choose Edit Paste. Excel inserts the table and leaves the table selected.
4. With the definition table still selected, choose Formula Define Name and enter the name that you want for the dialog box. Alternatively, you can use the method described earlier in this chapter to add row and column labels to make it easier to navigate in the table.
5. Use some formatting scheme to make the dialog box stand out from the other material on the macro sheet, such as what we've done with the definition tables in this chapter.

To use the Dialog Editor to refine a dialog box you've already created, copy the definition table (the Formula Goto command is useful for selecting an entire table), switch to the Dialog Editor, and choose the Dialog Editor's Edit Paste command. When you do so, the Dialog Editor converts the definition table to an image of the dialog box on the screen.

Making dialog boxes respond to changing circumstances

You can make a dialog box respond to changing circumstances in three ways. First, you can have a macro establish the contents of the dialog box, but you can adjust the characteristics of the items in it to fit a particular circumstance before the dialog box is displayed. Second, you can have a macro respond to changes made in a dialog box while the dialog box is still being displayed. Third, you can add help messages to a custom dialog box by using the methods covered in the next chapter.

Recalculating a dialog box

Often you need to present slightly different variations of the items in a dialog box. For example, if you want to develop an Excel application that will run under the PC versions of Excel as well as under the Macintosh version, you could use GET.WORKSPACE(1) in a macro to determine which operating system is being used and to refine the appearance of the worksheets and dialog boxes used by the application.

There are three main ways to modify or recalculate the contents of a dialog box definition table before displaying the dialog box. In the first, you set up a macro that replaces the contents of one or more cells in a definition table, by using the FORMULA and FORMULA.FILL functions. This is very convenient if you combine this with a row-naming and column-naming convention, as described earlier in this chapter.

For example, you could display the current date in a dialog box by creating a text label item for the dialog box and inserting before the DIALOG.BOX function the following line (assuming that *dateTextItem* names the row defining the text item and *dText* names the column defining the text used in the dialog box):

```
=FORMULA((dateTextItem dText),TEXT(NOW(),"d mmm yyyy"))
=DIALOG.BOX(MyDialogBox)
```

The second method, most useful when many items within a given column must change with varying circumstances, is to insert a formula in one or more cells in a column of the definition table, enter a RETURN function after the last row of the definition table, and "call" the column as a macro.

For example, to enter the current date in a dialog box, you could use the following structure in the definition table. The row defining a text item that reflects the current date is in the last row.

dName	*dItemN*	*dXposn*	*dYposn*	*dWidth*	*dHeight*	*dText*	*dInitResult*
dDateFormats		164	103	349	155	Date Formats	
ddnf.listBox	15	8	9	248	109	**ddnf.list**	2
ddnf.OK	1	271	13	64		OK	
ddnf.Cancel	2	271	46	64		Cancel	
ddnf.textLabel	5	8	126			Sample:	
ddnf.textSample	5	76	126	208		=TEXT(NOW(),"yy.mm.dd")	
						=RETURN()	

To recalculate whichever formulas exist in the *dText* column of the definition table, use the following formulas in the macro that brings up the dialog box.

```
=RUN(dDateFormats dText)
=DIALOG.BOX(dDateFormats)
```

The first line in this fragment transfers execution to the first *dText* cell in the macro, which is the intersection of the range containing the definition table and the *dText* column. The second formula, of course, calls up the modified definition table.

Finally, you can put the definition table on a worksheet instead of a macro sheet. To do this, simply use an external reference in the DIALOG.BOX function instead of a reference to a range on the macro sheet containing the macro. This flexibility offers you a choice: Where's the best place to put your dialog box definition tables?

Most people put each definition table on the macro sheet that calls up the dialog box, as we've done in this chapter. This approach uses slightly less memory, causes dialog boxes to run slightly faster, and keeps everything together.

However, when you want to create a recalculating or dynamic dialog box, it can be convenient to put its definition table on a worksheet instead of on a macro sheet, because the formulas in it recalculate automatically. On a macro sheet, of course, you must run a macro to recalculate the formulas in the definition table.

Dynamic dialog boxes

If you want a dialog box to change when the user takes actions within it, you can create what is called a *dynamic dialog box.* Excel's Data Series dialog box provides one example of this: When you select the Date option in the Data Series dialog box, the Date Unit group becomes undimmed and available.

To create such a dialog box, you designate in the definition table for the dialog box that one or more items are *triggers* for an action to occur. You designate an item as a trigger by adding 100 to its *dItemN* number. Similarly, to dim an item, you add 200 to its *dItemN* number.

When the user clicks on a trigger, Excel returns the selections made in the dialog box to the *dInitResult* column of the definition table and returns the number of the selection made to the cell containing the DIALOG.BOX function that brought up the dialog box, but Excel does not remove the dialog box from the screen. Your macro can then respond to the changes made in the dialog box by altering and then redisplaying the dialog box, if wanted.

Let's consider an example. Suppose you want to create a variation of the custom number format dialog box presented earlier in this chapter, but for dates instead. For this dialog box, however, you want the current date and time displayed in the date format selected so that the user can see a sample before clicking OK to apply the format. Figure 11-17 on the following page shows the PC and Mac versions of the dialog box, its definition table, the list of formats displayed in the dialog box, and the macro that brings it up on the screen.

The definition table creates the dialog box shown, depending on which version of Excel you're using. It contains the name of a list, shown in the macro below the definition table; we've used a method for defining the name of the list relative to the cells above the top and below the bottom of the list so that you can easily insert new date formats without having to redefine *ddnf.list*. Notice that we've added 100 to the *dItemN* number for the list box (normally item 15), making it a trigger.

The *MyDateFormats* macro calls up the dialog box. If the user selects one of the items in the list box, Excel returns the number of the selected item in *ddnf.listBox dInitResult* (using the intersection operator) and the number of the item chosen in *dnf.dialogN*. If the user clicks the Cancel button, the DIALOG.BOX function returns FALSE, and the formula in the next cell stops the execution of the macro.

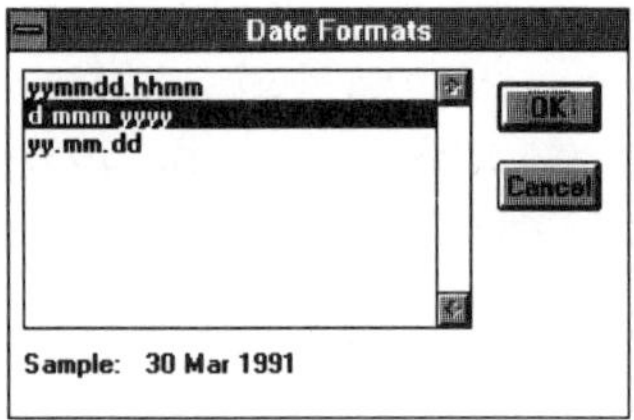

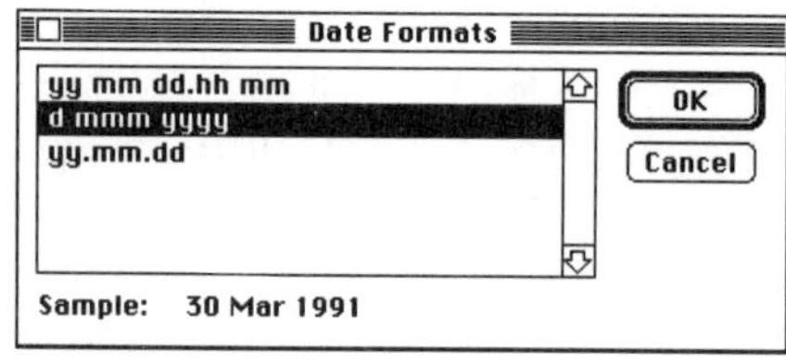

dName	*dItemN*	*dXposn*	*dYposn*	*dWidth*	*dHeight*	*dText*	*dInitResult*
dDateFormats		138	179	379	155	Date Formats	
ddnf.listBox	115	8	9	276	109	**ddnf.list**	2
ddnf.textLabel	5	8	126			Sample:	
ddnf.textSample	5	76	126	208		**30 Mar 1991**	
ddnf.OK	1	300	13	64		OK	
ddnf.Cancel	2	300	46	64		Cancel	

ddnf.list.top
yy mm dd.hh mm
d mmm yyyy
yy.mm.dd
ddnf.list.bottom

Define *ddnf.list* as
=OFFSET(ddnf.list.top,1,0):OFFSET(ddnf.list.bottom,-1,0)

cmd d	**MyDateFormats**	Global date formats.
dnf.dialogN	=DIALOG.BOX(dDateFormats)	Number of item chosen.
	=IF(dnf.dialogN=FALSE,RETURN())	If Cancel, quit macro.
dnf.dItemT	=OFFSET(dDateFormats,dnf.dialogN,-1,1,1)	Name of item chosen.
dnf.thisFormat	=INDEX(ddnf.list,ddnf.listBox dInitResult)	Get the format selected.
	=IF(dnf.dItemT="ddnf.listBox")	If the list box...
dnf.newNow	= " "&TEXT(NOW(),dnf.thisFormat)	Put NOW in this format.
	= FORMULA(dnf.newNow,(ddnf.textSample dText))	Update the date sample.
	= GOTO(dnf.dialogN)	Redisplay dialog.
	=END.IF()	
	=IF(dnf.dItemT="ddnf.OK")	If the OK button...
	= FORMAT.NUMBER(dnf.thisFormat)	format the range
	= RETURN()	and quit.
	=END.IF()	
	=RETURN()	

FIGURE 11-17.
Creating a dynamic dialog box that contains the current time and date, displayed in the selected format.

The OFFSET formula in *dnf.dItemT* finds the name of the item chosen, which is found in the first column of the definition table as presented in Figure 11-17. (Again, this column is not strictly required, but it's very useful for naming the items in the definition table.)

The INDEX formula in *dnf.thisFormat* gets the format that the user selected, as text, from the list defined as the range *ddnf.list*, using the index returned in the *dInitResult* cell of item *ddnf.listBox*.

At this point, the user could actually have clicked either the OK button or on one of the items in the list box. The two IF-END.IF clauses test for both these conditions by testing for the name of the item chosen, and they change the behavior of the macro accordingly.

If the name of the item selected is *ddnf.listBox,* the user clicked on an item in the list box, which has been made a trigger. The formula in *dnf.newNow* puts the current date and time into the format specified by that selection, which is stored in cell *dnf.thisFormat.* Notice that we've preceded the text with a space character; we'll explain why we did this in a moment.

The FORMULA function in the next cell puts this text into the *dText* cell of item *ddnf.textSample,* making it the next sample. Interestingly, if the space character didn't precede the text used as a date sample, Excel would coerce the text into a date format and add the format for the date to the list of number formats contained in the macro sheet. Subsequent uses of the dialog box would use the date format as it's displayed in the cell, not in the format into which the macro might have put the text. Preceding the text with a space character defeats the coercion of the date back into a serial date number, so next time the macro brings up the dialog box, the user will see the correct date format.

Next, the GOTO formula directs execution of the macro back to the DIALOG.BOX formula in cell *dnf.dialogN,* which redisplays the dialog box, but this time with the current date and time expressed in the new date format. When the user clicks OK, the second of the IF-END.IF clauses takes the number format and applies it to the range that was selected when the macro was run. This action also adds the date format to the worksheet containing the selected range.

Finally, because this macro does not preset the contents of the *dText* or *dInitResult* columns in the definition table, the next time the user runs the macro, the last item selected becomes the selection proposed in the dialog box.

In this example we made a list box a trigger. Some of the other items in a dialog box can also be made triggers.

- OK and Cancel buttons. The Format Styles dialog box provides an example of this. When you click the Define button, the dialog box expands to reveal options for defining the style.

  You can create a similar effect in your custom dialog boxes. Suppose you create a dialog box that is 400 pixels high; the items you want always displayed are in the upper 200 pixels of the dialog box, and the optional items are in the lower 200 pixels. You can make a button (call it *Options*) a trigger, and you can put it in the upper half of the dialog box, by giving it the *dItemN* number 101. If your macro initializes the dialog box with the *dHeight* value 200, Excel will display only the upper half of the dialog box. If the user clicks the trigger button, your macro changes the *dHeight* value to 400 and redisplays the dialog box.

- Option buttons and option button groups (that is, when an option button group has a title entry in the *dText* field, which draws a border around the group and adds the title). If the user selects an option button in an option group that is also a trigger, the option button has priority over the option group. You can make an option group a trigger, for example, to reset the options in the group to a default selection.

  When the user clicks an option button in an option button group, Excel returns the position of the option button in the group to the DIALOG.BOX function that called up the dialog box.
- Check boxes (but not the group boxes that you use to draw a border around a group of check boxes). The Data Series dialog box, mentioned at the beginning of this section, provides an example of using a check box as a trigger.
- Linked list boxes and drop-down list boxes.
- All the file and directory items except the directory text item (*dItemN* 20).

12

Taking Action Through Macros

In this chapter, we'll discuss some of the ways you can assign actions to elements in the Excel environment. We've already used the method of assigning a key sequence to a command macro through the Define Name dialog box, and we've also discussed the use of triggers in a dynamic dialog box, discussed in the previous chapter. In these two cases, an action taken by the user—pressing a key sequence or clicking on an object in a dialog box—tells Excel to run the associated macro. You can assign actions to other elements in the Excel environment as well.

- New menu commands, which you can add to existing Excel menus, to new menus, and to new menu bars. The associated macro runs when the user chooses the new menu command.
- Objects, such as buttons or text boxes. The associated macro runs when the user clicks on the object.
- Events, such as the opening or closing of a macro sheet, the activation of a window, the pressing of a certain key sequence, and the passage of a certain period of time. The associated macro runs when the event occurs.

Creating new commands, menus, and menu bars

You can create new menu commands in any of three ways, with each being a little more complicated than the last: by adding commands to existing menus, by adding a new menu of commands to an existing menu bar, or by creating an entirely new menu bar.

A menu bar consists of the string of menus arranged along the top of the screen: The Excel environment contains six default menu bars, each named by an identification (ID) number.

Bar number	Menu bar
1	Full menus; worksheets and macro sheets.
2	Full menus; charts.
3	Menu bar displayed when no Excel documents are open.
4	Menu bar displayed when the Info window is open.
5	Short menus; worksheets and macro sheets.
6	Short menus; charts.

To get information about menu bars, you can use the GET.BAR macro function, which can take two forms:

GET.BAR()
GET.BAR(barN,menuNT,commandNT)

The first form takes no arguments, and it returns the number of the current menu bar. For example, if a worksheet is the currently active document and Excel is set to Full menus, GET.BAR() returns *1*.

Use the second form of the GET.BAR function to get information about an existing command or menu. The *barN* argument specifies the number of an existing menu bar. The *menuNT* argument can be either the number of a menu on the menu bar (the number 1 corresponding to the leftmost menu) or the name of the menu, as text. Similarly, the *commandNT* argument can be either the number of the command on the specified menu or the name of the command.

If you want to find the name of a command appearing on a menu given its numeric position on the menu, use its position number as the *commandNT* argument: GET.BAR then returns the name of the command, as text. If you want to find the position of a command given its name, supply the name as the *commandNT* argument: GET.BAR then returns a number representing the command's position on the menu, 1 being the topmost position. If *commandNT* is 0, GET.BAR returns the name of the menu or its position, depending on whether *menuNT* is the name of the menu or its position number.

One handy use for the GET.BAR function is to determine whether a given command exists on a given menu; if it doesn't, GET.BAR returns #N/A. For example, the following macro inserts a list of the commands on the current File menu.

cmd P	**PasteFileCommands**	Enters list of current File commands.
	n=1	Set counter to 1.
pfc.barN	=GET.BAR()	Number of current menu bar.
	=WHILE(NOT(ISNA(GET.BAR(pfc.barN,"File",n))))	If there is a command...
	= FORMULA(GET.BAR(pfc.barN,"File",n))	insert its name,
	= SELECT("R[1]C")	move down one cell,
	n=n+1	increment counter.
	=NEXT()	Do it again.
	=RETURN()	

This macro gets the ID number of the current menu bar and uses it, through the GET.BAR function, to get the name of each command on the menu. In every pass through the WHILE-NEXT loop, *n* is incremented by 1, and the name of the corresponding command is entered into the active cell. When *n* corresponds to the position beyond the last command on the menu, the GET.BAR function returns *#N/A*, and the loop ends.

To test this macro, select a cell in a new worksheet and run the macro. When you do so, Excel enters a list similar to that in the second column, which was copied from the Macintosh version of Excel:

n	**Menu name returned**
1	&New...
2	&Open...
3	&Close
4	&Links...
5	-
6	&Save
7	Save &As...
8	Save &Workspace...
9	&Delete...
10	-
11	Print Pre&view
12	Page Se&tup...
13	&Print...
14	-
15	&1 :c12 docs:c12test.xlm
16	&2 XLM data2.1
17	&3 Moon:Worksheet1
18	&4 Moon:Macro1
19	-
20	&Quit

Notice that an ampersand (&) precedes the access key in each command name returned by the GET.BAR function. (In the Macintosh version, you can see these access keys by choosing Options Workspace and setting the Command Underline option.) Also, the dotted lines that separate groups of commands from each other are named by a single hyphen, or minus sign.

Custom menu commands

Excel provides five macro functions for working with custom commands. You can add a command to a menu, place or remove a check mark from before the command, enable or disable (dim) the command, rename it, and delete it.

Adding a command to a menu

To add a new command to an existing menu, use the ADD.COMMAND function. This function takes the form

ADD.COMMAND(barN,menuNT,commandRef,*positionNT*)

The *barN* argument specifies the menu bar ID number. As before, the *menuNT* argument can be either the number of the menu or its name; generally, it's better to specify menus and commands by name rather than by number because your macros can easily change the positions of the menus and commands.

The *commandRef* argument specifies a horizontal range containing information that defines the command to be added. This definition range, similar to the dialog box definition table discussed in the previous chapter, consists of between two and five columns and contains the following information:

1. The name of the command to be added. Place an ampersand before the letter you want to become the access key for the command.
2. The name of the macro that you want to run when the user chooses the command. This can be a reference to an area on the macro sheet.
3. *Macintosh version only:* The command key, if any, associated with the command (optional).
4. The text to appear in the status bar when the user drags across the command on the specified menu (optional).
5. The help topic associated with the command (optional).

Let's consider an example. Suppose you want to add a command to the Options menu that initiates a macro that displays or removes the status bar at the bottom of the Excel workspace. The following macros add and service the new menu command.

cmd A	**AddCmdToggleStatus**	Adds ToggleStatus cmd.
acts.test	=ISNA(GET.BAR(1,"Options",acts.cmdDef))	Does command not exist?
	=IF(acts.test)	If command is absent,
	= ADD.COMMAND(1,"Options",acts.cmdDef)	add the command;
	=ELSE()	else,
	= ALERT("The command already exists!")	alert the user.
	=END.IF()	
	=RETURN()	

	Command name	*Macro to run*
acts.cmdDef	Toggle &Status	ToggleStatus

cmd subr	**ToggleStatus**	Toggles status bar.
ts.status	=NOT(GET.WORKSPACE(6))	Alternate between T & F.
	=WORKSPACE(,,,,ts.status)	Set status to this value.
	=RETURN()	

The *acts.cmdDef* range between the two macros defines the command to be added. To define this range name, select the label and the two cells within the border, choose the Create Names command, verify that the First Column option alone is set, and then click OK. The first cell in the bordered area determines the name of the command; the ampersand before the *S* in *Status* establishes the access key for the command. The second cell in the bordered area specifies the macro to run when the user chooses the new command. To run the *ToggleStatus* macro, the user would choose the new Options Toggle Status command or press /OS [PC—also Alt-OS].

Before the *AddCmdToggleStatus* macro adds the command, it needs to test whether the command already exists on the Options menu. This test is important because Excel lets you add to a menu as many commands having the same name as you want—something you must guard against.

The ADD.COMMAND formula has three arguments. The first specifies the ID number of the menu bar, and the second specifies the name of the menu to which the command will be added. The third argument is a reference to the area that defines the command. This area can be on the current macro sheet, on another macro sheet, or on a worksheet; in this case the area is the range *acts.cmdDef* on the macro sheet.

When the user chooses the new Options Toggle Status command, the *ToggleStatus* macro determines whether the status bar is being displayed and sets the status bar to the opposite state.

Enabling and disabling a command

Use the ENABLE.COMMAND function to enable or disable a menu command that you've added. When a command is dimmed, it cannot be chosen, and pressing its access key (or, in the Macintosh version, its command-key shortcut) has no effect. This function takes the form

ENABLE.COMMAND(barN,menuNT,commandNT,enableL)

where the first three arguments are as described previously. (However, you can disable an entire custom menu if *commandNT* is 0.) If *enableL* is FALSE, the function disables (dims) the specified command. If *enableL* is TRUE, the function enables the command.

For example, if you wanted to disable the Toggle Status command added by the *AddCmdToggleStatus* macro above, you could use the formula

=ENABLE.COMMAND(1,"Options",acts.cmdDef,FALSE)

To enable the command, simply change FALSE to TRUE. As with the other functions for handling menu commands, the macro that enables or disables the command should check whether the command exists by using the GET.BAR function.

Adding or removing a check mark before a command

You can also have a macro add or remove a check mark before a given menu command. Unlike enabling or disabling a command, adding or removing a check mark has no effect on the ability to choose the command and simply serves as a visual reminder of a current condition. The CHECK.COMMAND function takes the form

CHECK.COMMAND(barN,menuNT,commandNT,checkL)

If *checkL* is TRUE, the function adds a check mark before the specified command. If *checkL* is FALSE, the function removes the check mark.

For example, the *ToggleStatus* macros could be rewritten so that the command reads *Status Bar* instead and displays a check mark if the status bar is visible, as in the following macros:

cmd	**AddCmdStatusBar**	Adds Status Bar command.
acsb.test	=ISNA(GET.BAR(1,"Options",acsb.cmdDef))	Does command not exist?
	=IF(acsb.test)	If command is absent,
	= ADD.COMMAND(1,"Options",acsb.cmdDef)	add the command;
	=ELSE()	else,
	= ALERT("The command already exists!")	alert the user.
	=END.IF()	
	=RETURN()	

	Command name	*Macro to run*
acsb.cmdDef	&Status Bar	CheckStatusBar

cmd subr	**CheckStatusBar**	Toggles status bar.
csb.status	=NOT(GET.WORKSPACE(6))	Reverse state.
	=WORKSPACE(,,,,csb.status)	Set status to state.
	=CHECK.COMMAND(1,"Options",acsb.cmdDef,csb.status)	Add/remove check.
	=RETURN()	

The only real difference between these two macros and the *ToggleStatus* versions is that *CheckStatusBar* contains a CHECK.COMMAND function to mirror the state of the status bar by placing a check mark before its command on the Options menu.

Renaming a command

Occasionally you'll need to change the name of a command. To do this, use the RENAME.COMMAND function. This function takes the form

RENAME.COMMAND(barN,menuNT,commandNT,nameT)

The only new argument here is *nameT*, which is the new name of the command. If *commandNT* is 0, this function renames the entire menu. As when defining new menu commands, you can use the ampersand character to indicate the access key for the menu.

For instance, continuing the example of displaying or removing the status bar, you could create one command called Show Status Bar and another called Hide Status Bar. Using this technique requires a little more care, however; when your macro alters or removes a command, the command's name might have changed. Therefore, you should always use the GET.BAR function to check for the existence of the command before enabling it or deleting it, as shown in the following macros.

cmd	**AddCmdShowStatus**	Adds Status Bar command.
acss.test1	=ISNA(GET.BAR(1,"Options",acss.cmd1))	Does Show command not exist?
acss.test2	=ISNA(GET.BAR(1,"Options",acss.cmd2))	Does Hide command not exist?
	=IF(AND(acss.test1,acss.test2))	If neither command present,
acss.status	= GET.WORKSPACE(6)	is status bar displayed?
	= IF(acss.status)	If so,
	= ADD.COMMAND(1,"Options",acss.cmd2)	Add Hide command ;
	= ELSE()	else,
	= ADD.COMMAND(1,"Options",acss.cmd1)	Add Show command.
	= END.IF()	
	=END.IF()	
	=RETURN()	

	Command name	*Macro to run*
acss.cmd1	Show &Status Bar	RenameShowStatus
acss.cmd2	Hide &Status Bar	RenameShowStatus

cmd subr	**RenameShowStatus**	Renames Status bar command.
rss.status	=NOT(GET.WORKSPACE(6))	Reverse state.
	=WORKSPACE(,,,,rss.status)	Set status to this state.
	=IF(rss.status)	If status bar present,
	= RENAME.COMMAND(1,"Options",acss.cmd1,acss.cmd2)	change name to Hide;
	=ELSE()	else,
	= RENAME.COMMAND(1,"Options",acss.cmd2,acss.cmd1)	change name to Show.
	=END.IF()	
	=RETURN()	

As you can see, the logic for handling commands having more than one name is more complicated than for handling commands having only one name.

Deleting a menu command

When you no longer need a menu command, you can delete it by using the DELETE.COMMAND function. This function takes the form

DELETE.COMMAND(barN,menuNT,commandNT)

where *barN*, *menu*, and *commandNT* specify a menu command as described earlier. If the command to be deleted is a dash used to produce a horizontal line in the menu, *commandNT* must be a position number rather than a name.

Continuing the last example, the following macro deletes either the Show Status Bar command or the Hide Status Bar command, depending on which is the current name.

cmd	**DelCmdShowStatus**	Deletes Status Bar command.
dcss.test1	=NOT(ISNA(GET.BAR(1,"Options",acss.cmd1)))	Does Show command exist?
dcss.test2	=NOT(ISNA(GET.BAR(1,"Options",acss.cmd2)))	Does Hide command exist?
	=IF(dcss.test1,DELETE.COMMAND(1,"Options",acss.cmd1))	If Show command present.
	=IF(dcss.test2,DELETE.COMMAND(1,"Options",acss.cmd2))	If Hide command present.
	=RETURN()	

This macro tests for the existence of both commands and then deletes one or the other—or both, if through some error in programming both commands have been added to the Options menu.

Custom menus

Adding an entire menu of commands to an existing menu bar is a little more complicated than adding single commands, if only because you must add the name of the menu to a range that defines the menu and the commands on it.

Excel provides only two functions for working with entire menus, ADD.MENU and DELETE.MENU. To work with the individual commands on a custom menu, you can use the functions described in the previous section.

Adding a custom menu

To add a menu to an existing menu bar, use the ADD.MENU command. This command takes the form

ADD.MENU(barN,menuRef,*positionNT*)

The *barN* argument specifies an existing menu bar, as described previously. The *menuRef* argument specifies a range on a macro sheet or worksheet that defines the menu and the commands on it. The *positionNT* argument is either the menu's new position number or the name of the menu to the left of which the new menu is to be placed; if omitted, Excel adds the menu to the right of the rightmost menu.

Let's say that you want to add a custom menu called *New* to the right of the Window menu in the Full Menus worksheet menu bar (whose ID number is 1). On the New menu are three new commands: Worksheet, Chart, and Macro Sheet, which create or open template documents containing the styles, headings, and formats you find most useful. The following macro adds the New menu.

cmd	**AddMenuNew**	Adds menu to existing bar.
amn.test	=ISNA(GET.BAR(1,"&New",0))	Does menu not exist?
	=IF(amn.test)	If so,
	= ADD.MENU(1,amn.menu)	add New menu;
	=ELSE()	else,
	= ALERT("Menu already exists!")	alert the user.
	=END.IF()	
	=RETURN()	

amn.menu	&New	
	&Worksheet	NewWorkDoc
	&Chart	NewChartDoc
	&Macro Sheet	NewMacroDoc

cmd subr	**NewWorkDoc**	Creates a new worksheet.
	=ECHO(FALSE)	No screen updating.
	=NEW(1)	New worksheet.
	=DEFINE.STYLE("Normal",0,1,0,0,0,0)	Set Normal style.
	=DEFINE.STYLE("Normal",3,"Times",9,0,0,0,0,0,0,0)	
	=DISPLAY(0,0,1,1,0,,1,0,1)	No gridlines.
	=RETURN()	

cmd subr	**NewChartDoc**	Creates a new chart.
	=NEW(2,3)	New scatter chart.
	...set styles, formats, and so on in new chart.	
	=RETURN()	

cmd subr	**NewMacroDoc**	Creates a new macro sheet.
	=NEW(3)	New macro sheet.
	...set styles, formats, and so on in new macro sheet.	
	=RETURN()	

The bordered area labeled *amn.menu* contains the definition table for the New menu; as before, ampersands determine the access keys for the menu and its commands. The first row sets the name of the menu, and the remaining rows specify each command on the menu. To separate groups of commands, enter a single hyphen.

We've inserted the menu definition table after the macro that creates the menu. As with dialog box definition tables (discussed in Chapter 11), however, it's often a good idea to put all the menu definition tables you use in a range of columns to the right of the area containing your macros so that they're easier to format and maintain.

To define the range, select the area marked by the border, choose the Define Name command, enter *amn.menu*, and click OK. We've specified only the first two columns of the possible five columns of a full menu definition table; in the third column you could add command keys (for the Macintosh version only); in the fourth column you could add text that would appear in the status bar when the user drags the cursor across the command; and in the fifth the name of a custom help topic.

Removing a custom menu

To remove a menu after it's been added, use the DELETE.MENU function. This function takes the form

DELETE.MENU(barN,menuNT)

where *barN* is the number of the bar to which you've added the menu, and *menuNT* is the name or number of the menu.

For example, the following macro deletes the New menu created in the previous example.

cmd	**DelMenuNewDoc**	Deletes New menu.
dmnd.test	=NOT(ISNA(GET.BAR(1,"&New",0)))	Does menu exist?
	=IF(dmnd.test)	If so,
	= DELETE.MENU(1,"&New")	delete menu.
	=END.IF()	
	=RETURN()	

As mentioned before, a macro that changes or removes a menu or command should use the GET.BAR function to check for the existence of a menu or command beforehand, either by specifying a name explicitly or by entering the reference of the top-left cell in the menu definition table.

Custom menu bars

Excel provides four macro functions for use with custom menu bars: ADD.BAR adds a menu bar and returns its ID number, DELETE.BAR removes the menu bar, SHOW.BAR displays an existing menu bar, and GET.BAR (discussed earlier) returns information about commands, menus, and menu bars.

Excel can support a total of 21 menu bars at any one time. Because the first 6 ID numbers are used by the built-in menu bars, the 15 custom menu bars that you create can have ID numbers between 7 and 21.

The first step in creating a custom menu bar is to tell Excel that you want a new menu bar and its ID number. To do this, use the ADD.BAR function, which takes the form

ADD.BAR(*barN*)

where *barN* is the number of a menu bar. The use of this argument in creating a custom menu bar is unusual, however, because you should not supply a number for the *barN* argument. When you don't supply *barN*, the function returns the next available ID number for the new menu bar; you can then use the ID number to add menus and commands as described earlier in this chapter.

After you've told Excel to create a new menu bar, you use the SHOW.BAR function to display the menu bar. This function takes the form

SHOW.BAR(*barN*)

where *barN* is the number returned by the ADD.BAR function; if omitted, Excel displays the default menu bar that is appropriate for the active document. For example, if you've set Full menus and the active document is a chart, Excel displays the default chart menu, whose ID number is 2.

Also, Excel lets you display only the default menu bar that applies to the currently active document, returning an error and stopping the macro otherwise. For example, if you use SHOW.BAR(2) when the active document is a worksheet, the function returns an error value and Excel stops the macro.

Note: There is no macro command for hiding the current menu bar; to "hide" a bar, you must show another bar.

To delete a menu bar, you use the DELETE.BAR function. This function takes the form

DELETE.BAR(barN)

Excel does not let you delete any of the default menu bars.

An example

The set of macros at the top of the following page creates for a mythical application a menu bar and two menus. The File menu contains commands that open either of two databases, close the active database, and quit the application. The Edit Record menu contains various commands for finding and editing records in the two databases.

In an application intended for users who aren't familiar with the Excel environment or those you don't want getting inside your macro application, it's common to create a menu bar, switch to it, and provide no way to switch to any other

cmd	**AddAppBar**	Adds app menu bar.
aab.barN	=ADD.BAR()	Add the bar, get its number.
	=ADD.MENU(aab.barN,aab.menu1)	Add File menu.
	=ADD.MENU(aab.barN,aab.menu2)	Add Edit Record menu.
	=SHOW.BAR(aab.barN)	Show the menu bar.
	=RETURN()	

aab.menu1	&File	
	Open &Client Database	OpenClient
	Open &Inventory Database	OpenInventory
	C&lose	CloseDB
	&Quit	QuitApp

aab.menu2	&Edit Record	
	&Find	FindRec
	&New	NewRec
	&Cut	CutRec
	C&opy	CopyRec
	&Paste	PasteRec
	C&lear	ClearRec

cmd	**ShowAppBar**	Switches to app menu bar.
sab.test	=NOT(ISNA(GET.BAR(aab.barN,"&File",0)))	Is File menu defined?
	=IF(sab.test,SHOW.BAR(aab.barN))	If so, show bar.
	=RETURN()	(If not, menu bar deleted.)

cmd X	**DelAppBar**	Deletes app menu bar.
	=SHOW.BAR(1)	Switch to default menu bar.
	=DELETE.BAR(aab.barN)	Delete app bar.
	=RETURN()	

menu. The *AddAppBar* macro defines its custom menu bar and then switches to it. (The macro names defined in the two menu definition tables aren't listed above, but they would support the various actions taken in the environment of the application.)

If for some reason you'd like to switch from this menu bar to the standard menu bar for working with the internals of the application, all your macro need do is use the formula

```
=SHOW.BAR(1)
```

as shown in the tip on the facing page. The *ShowAppBar* macro returns the user to the custom menu bar, and the *DelAppBar* macro deletes the menu bar if necessary. Depending on the degree of isolation you'd like to provide between the user of an Excel application and the standard Excel environment, choosing the Quit command from the File menu could either call *DelAppBar* or close every open document and quit the Excel application without permitting the user to gain access to the data structures and macros that support the application. (Later in this chapter we'll discuss how you can start up a custom Excel application automatically, one in which the first menu the user sees is the one presented by the application.)

The *HomeBar* macro.

The following macro is perhaps the most important one you can write when you're experimenting with custom menu bars. This two-line macro displays menu bar 1, the standard menu bar.

cmd H	**HomeBar**	Displays menu bar 1.
	=SHOW.BAR(1)	
	=RETURN()	

To understand why this macro is so important, enter and then save it. (Be sure to define the shortcut key as shown for this macro.) Then enter and run the following macro.

cmd	**NewNullBar**	Creates menu without commands.
nnb.barN	=ADD.BAR()	Define new menu bar.
	=SHOW.BAR(nnb.barN)	Add bar without commands.
	=RETURN()	

When you run *NewNullBar*, a new menu bar containing no menus replaces the standard menu bar. With this new menu bar in place, you are denied use of every menu command in Excel. Without the *HomeBar* macro, you have only one way to return to the standard menu bar: pressing Ctrl-F4 [Mac—also Command-W] until you've closed every open sheet. Doing so displays the standard Excel null menu bar, which lets you open documents and proceed normally.

Consequently, the *HomeBar* macro is important because it offers a way to return to normal operation without closing every sheet in the workspace.

Assigning macros to objects

Assigning a macro to the action of typing a key sequence or choosing a menu command are the two most common ways to operate a custom Excel application, but they aren't the most fun. New in the current version of Excel is the capability of assigning macros to various objects: When the user clicks on the object, Excel runs the associated macro. In this way, you can create a graphical user interface that can give your Excel application much of the feel of a modern, professional application.

You can assign macros to the following objects.

- *Buttons:* To create a button, click the Button tool in the tool bar and drag to create a button object in a worksheet or macro sheet. When you release the mouse button, Excel presents the Assign To Object dialog box, in which you can select a macro that runs whenever a user clicks the object.
- *Lines, ovals, rectangles, and arcs:* When you select the corresponding tool and drag to create an object in a worksheet or macro sheet, Excel doesn't automatically bring up the Assign To Object dialog box. Instead, you must select the object and choose the Macro Assign To Object command.
- *Text boxes:* Text boxes are normally used for placing formatted text in a worksheet without regard for the need to distribute text among the cells of a worksheet. To edit the text in a text box, you simply click in the box where you want to insert text or change existing text. You can also assign a macro to the text box, but when you do so you can no longer edit the text without first using the Selection tool to select the text box or holding down the Control key [Mac—also Command] while clicking on the object.
- *Embedded charts:* To create an embedded chart in a worksheet, you select the range of data for which you want to create the chart, click the Chart tool in the tool bar, and drag to create the chart object in the worksheet or macro sheet and establish its location and size. Next, select the chart and choose the Assign To Object command. Assigning macros to charts is a handy way to perform complex updating procedures when simple recalculation isn't enough. Unfortunately, you can't assign a macro to the action of clicking on objects in a standard chart window.

- *Graphical images that you've pasted into a worksheet or macro sheet:* You can in this way create graphical "buttons" containing custom icons that you've prepared in a graphics application and transferred to an Excel worksheet or macro sheet.

The appendixes list the macro functions you can use to alter, format, and rearrange objects attached to a worksheet or macro sheet. Let's consider an example of using macros with objects you've added to a sheet.

The *ButtonOpenDoc* macro is assigned to a button placed to the left of a cell containing the name of a document you might want to open. When the user clicks the button, the macro looks at the cell immediately to the right of the cell over which the button has been placed. (Shown here are Macintosh filenames.)

	A	B	C
3			
4	Open	c12test.xlm	
5	Open	KEY_CHAR.XLS (codes)	
6	Open	WorldCorp Database	
7			

cmd subr	**ButtonOpenDoc**	Button-activated macro.
bod.objID	=CALLER()	Get object ID.
bod.ref	=GET.OBJECT(4,bod.objID)	Get reference of underlying cell.
bod.docT	=OFFSET(TEXTREF("!"&bod.ref,FALSE),0,1)	Document name one cell to right.
	bod.posn=1	
	=WHILE(ISNUMBER(SEARCH(":",bod.docT,bod.posn)))	If full pathname,
	bod.posn=SEARCH(":",bod.docT,bod.posn)+1	find position of last colon.
	=NEXT()	
bod.docT2	=MID(bod.docT,bod.posn,99)	Extract document name.
	=IF(ISNUMBER(GET.DOCUMENT(3,bod.docT2)))	If document already open...
	= ALERT(bod.docT2&" is already open.")	alert user and quit;
	=ELSE()	else,
	= OPEN(bod.docT)	open document.
	=END.IF()	
	=RETURN()	

The CALLER formula starts the macro by finding the ID of the object that called this macro. (Note: The ID of an object is the text that Excel displays at the left side of the formula bar, which normally shows the reference of the currently selected range.) For objects to which you can assign macros, this ID number is in the form *object n*, where *n* is the number of the object in the sheet, in the order created, and *object* is the object's type, according to the table on the following page.

Object name	Code	Description
Line	1	Line, created with the Line tool.
Rectangle	2	Rectangle, created with the Rectangle tool.
Oval	3	Oval, created with the Oval tool.
Arc	4	Arc, created with the Arc tool.
Chart	5	Embedded chart, created either with the Chart tool or by selecting a chart, copying it, and pasting it into a sheet.
Text	6	Text box, created with the Text Box tool.
Button	7	Button, created with the Button tool.
Picture	8	Graphical image, created either with the Camera tool or by pasting a graphical image into the sheet.

For example, if the first button in the graphic above were actually the second button you've created on the worksheet, its object ID would be *Button 2*. If you delete an object having a lower ID number than the others on the sheet, the remaining objects are not renumbered. You can also name an object by selecting it, choosing the Define Name command, and entering a name in the Refers To field.

The next line in the macro uses the GET.OBJECT function to find the reference of the cell lying under the top-left corner of the button. The GET.OBJECT function returns a wide range of information about an object. This function takes the form

GET.OBJECT(typeN,*objectID,startN,countN*)

where *typeN* specifies the type of information you want to get about the object. (See your Microsoft Excel Function Reference for a lengthy list of these type numbers.) Here *typeN* is 4. The *objectID* argument specifies the ID of the object about which you want to get the information; if omitted, Excel returns information about the currently selected object. The *startN* and *countN* arguments apply only when the object is a text box or button; these arguments are for getting information about the text or formats belonging to the text inside the text box or button.

Because the document name entered into the cell to the right of the button might include the path to the document, we need to extract the name of the document from the full pathname. The macro does this by searching for colons. (If you want to use this macro on the PC, change : to \ in both SEARCH functions.) The last colon in the full pathname separates the path from the document. The MID formula extracts the document name based on the position of the last colon in the string. Finally, we use GET.DOCUMENT(3) to determine whether the document has already been opened, displaying an Alert dialog box if so, and opening the document if not.

Assigning actions to events

When you start a command macro, you generally start it with a shortcut key or, at times, with the Macro Run command. However, there are other ways to start a macro. Excel can start a macro when you open or close a sheet or when you press any specified key on your keyboard. It can start a macro at a specific time or when you activate a particular sheet or window.

You'll find these ways to start macros quite useful. For example, this chapter explains how to use macros to maintain a clock in the status bar and to expand or contract a window automatically when the user activates it.

Opening a specified sheet on startup

When you start Excel, you can have any worksheet, macro sheet, chart, or workspace open automatically. While this capability doesn't relate directly to macros, it's a feature that lets macros run automatically on startup.

People commonly establish a startup file for several reasons. For example, you might prefer to begin each session with a worksheet that contains specific display modes or print settings. To do so, you set these preferences in an empty sheet, and then you make the sheet a startup file.

If you develop a library of macros that you use often, you can make the library a startup file. To do so, simply place the file or workspace in the Excel startup directory or folder on your hard disk. That's it. In the Windows version of Excel, this directory is called *xlstart*, and it's usually in the same directory as the Excel application. In the Macintosh version of Excel, this folder is called *Excel Startup Folder*, and it's either in the System Folder (in System 6.x) or in the Preferences folder inside the System Folder (System 7.x). When Excel launches, it searches for a folder of the appropriate name; if found, Excel opens every document in the folder.

Running a macro when a sheet opens

It's often convenient to run certain macros when a macro sheet opens. For example, you might want to add custom menus, start a clock, or initialize an entire Excel application. To do this, make a macro on the macro sheet an Auto_Open macro by beginning its name with the text *Auto_Open*. You can define more than one Auto_Open macro on a given sheet: When Excel loads the macro sheet, every macro that begins with *Auto_Open* runs, in alphabetic order. (For example, *Auto_Open* would run before *Auto_Open_Dialogs*, which would run before *Auto_Open_Menus*.)

The following macro is an Auto_Open macro that we commonly use. It defines global values such as the name of the current operating environment (very useful if you're developing macro systems that work well across platforms), the delimiter for pathnames, and the name of the macro sheet and its current pathname. Finding the latter two values is very useful because many macro functions use the name of their own macro sheet in their arguments, and you'd like to be able to use this name and path elsewhere on the sheet without having to hunt down every instance to edit them if necessary.

cmd subr	**Auto_Open**	Defines globals.
ao.env	=GET.WORKSPACE(1)	Name of this operating environment.
ao.pathDelim	=IF(LEFT(ao.env,3)="Mac",":","\")	If Mac, then ":", else "\".
ao.myName	=GET.CELL(32,thisCell)	Name of this macro sheet.
ao.myPath	=GET.DOCUMENT(2,ao.myName)&ao.pathDelim	Path to this macro sheet.
ao.m1	="Auto_Open Macro."&CHAR(13)	Alert dialog box message,
ao.m2	="My full pathname is..."&CHAR(13)&CHAR(13)	listing name of this macro
ao.m3	=ao.myPath&ao.myName	and its path.
	=ALERT(ao.m1&ao.m2&ao.m3)	
	=RETURN()	

The only tricky thing about this macro is the use of the GET.CELL formula, which makes a reference to *thisCell,* defined as a relative reference to the cell containing the GET.CELL formula itself. This formula returns the name of the macro sheet on which it resides.

When a macro sheet containing this macro opens, Excel displays a dialog box such as this:

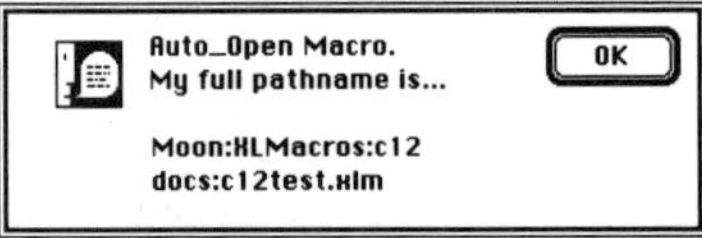

Of course, having this kind of dialog box appear every time an Auto_Open macro sheet opened might be useful when you're experimenting with many different macro sheets—and annoying otherwise.

You might wonder whether you could use the GET.DOCUMENT(1) function in the Auto_Open macro instead. Because the document is obviously active when first opened, this function should return the name of the macro sheet. However, the macro sheet isn't activated when it's opened as a hidden document; in this case, GET.DOCUMENT(1) returns the name of the document that is active when the hidden macro sheet is opened. If the workspace is empty when the hidden macro sheet is opened, GET.DOCUMENT(1) returns *#N/A.*

Attaching an Auto_Open macro to a worksheet

The process of specifying a macro that runs whenever the user opens a worksheet is very similar to setting up an Auto_Open macro in a macro sheet. To see how this works, open a new worksheet and a new macro sheet, and then do the following:

1. In the macro sheet, enter the macro you want to run when the worksheet opens, and name it anything you want. (It doesn't have to start with *Auto_Open*.)
2. In the worksheet, open the Define Name dialog box and define the name *Auto_Open* as an external reference to the macro you want to run. If the name of the macro sheet were MACLIB1.XLM, for example, you would enter the definition

   ```
   =MACLIB1.XLM!MyMacro
   ```

3. Save the worksheet using any name, and then close both the macro sheet and the worksheet.

When you open the worksheet, Excel opens the macro sheet referred to in the *Auto_Open* name definition and then runs the specified macro. In the example, after you load the worksheet, the macro sheet MACLIB1.XLM opens and runs the *MyMacro* macro.

If the macro sheet also contains an Auto_Open macro, Excel will not run the macro. Therefore, if you want Excel to run the Auto_Open macro as well, you must call it from within the macro specified by your worksheet.

Finally, to open the worksheet without running the macro, choose File Open, select the document, and then hold down Shift while either pressing Enter or choosing Open. If any other dialog boxes appear afterward, hold down the Shift key while clicking OK in these dialog boxes as well.

Running a macro when a sheet closes

When you close the macro sheets that support the features you've added through an Auto_Open macro, you generally need to return the workspace to its prior condition. To do so, use an Auto_Close macro.

Creating an Auto_Close macro is much like creating an Auto_Open macro: Simply begin the macro's name with the text *Auto_Close*. For example, you could use a macro named *Auto_Close_ResetStatus* to reset the status bar after displaying a special message in the status bar.

You can call an Auto_Close macro from a worksheet in the same way you can call an Auto_Open macro. However, for the Auto_Close macro to run, the macro sheet that contains it must be open when the worksheet is closed. Unlike Auto_Open macros, Auto_Close macros won't open a macro sheet to run a macro.

Auto_Close macros are designed to work only when you close the macro sheet manually, either one file at a time or by using the File Close All command. However, if you close the macro sheet by using another macro, Excel does not execute these macros.

Running a macro at a certain time

The ON.TIME function runs a specified macro at a specified time, but only if Excel is in the READY, COPY, CUT, or FIND mode. This function takes the form

ON.TIME(time,macroT,*toleranceN,insertL*)

The *time* argument is a serial date value that specifies when to run the macro named by the *macroT* argument. If *time* is less than 1 (that is, you specify a time of day but not a date), Excel runs the macro every day at the time specified. If *time* is greater than 1, Excel runs the macro once, on the date and at the time specified.

The *macroT* argument is the name of the macro you want to run at the specified time. The text can be an external reference to a macro on a macro sheet other than the one containing the ON.TIME formula.

The optional *toleranceN* argument is a date/time serial number that specifies the time beyond which Excel will give up trying to run the macro. If this argument is omitted, it is assumed to be infinite. If Excel doesn't return to the Ready, Copy, Cut, or Find mode before the tolerance time specified, the request is canceled.

If two or more ON.TIME requests are issued for the same time, and if the *insertL* argument is TRUE or omitted, Excel executes the requests in the reverse order they were posted. To illustrate, consider the following macros.

```
cmd            SimultaneousMacro                               Tests simultaneous ON.TIME reqs.
sm.trigger     =NOW()+"00:00:10"                               10 seconds from now...
sm.tolerance   =sm.now+"00:00:10"                              Tolerance point 10 seconds beyond
                                                               that.
               =ON.TIME(sm.trigger,"Sim1",sm.tolerance)        Run three macros.
               =ON.TIME(sm.trigger,"Sim2",sm.tolerance)
               =ON.TIME(sm.trigger,"Sim3",sm.tolerance)
               =RETURN()
```

```
cmd subr       Sim1                                            The first macro.
               =ALERT("This is the Sim1 macro.")
               =RETURN()
```

```
cmd subr       Sim2                                            The second macro.
               =ALERT("This is the Sim2 macro.")
               =RETURN()
```

```
cmd subr       Sim3                                            The third macro.
               =ALERT("This is the Sim3 macro.")
               =RETURN()
```

The cell labeled *sm.trigger* sets the time when all three macros are to be executed, and *sm.tolerance* sets the time beyond which pending requests are ignored. Because Excel is so handy with the coercion of data from one type into another, you can specify a date or time or both by entering a text string, which Excel coerces into the serial number required.

If you run *SimultaneousMacro* and wait 10 seconds, you'll see the Alert dialog boxes appear in reverse order. If you don't click OK in the *Sim3* and *Sim2* Alert dialog boxes within 10 seconds of seeing the *Sim3* Alert dialog box, Excel will not display the *Sim1* dialog box.

Use an *insertL* value of FALSE to cancel an ON.TIME request. You must also specify the time and macro name that you want to cancel; Excel returns an error and stops the macro if the time that you specify doesn't have a corresponding request. To illustrate, let's say that to the previous four macros you add the following:

cmd Y	**StopSim1**	Stops request for Sim1 macro.
	=ON.TIME(sm.trigger,"Sim1",,FALSE)	
	=RETURN()	

Immediately after starting *SimultaneousMacro*, run *StopSim1*. Ten seconds later, you'll see *Sim3* and *Sim2* dialog boxes—but not the *Sim1* dialog box. If, however, you run *StopSim1* after all three dialog boxes have appeared, Excel displays an error dialog box and stops the *StopSim1* macro because the pending request for the *Sim1* macro at the time specified has already been fulfilled.

Let's consider another example. The following macro demonstrates a method for generating repeating ON.TIME requests at any specified interval. The *StatusTime* macro displays the current time and the amount of free memory in the status bar, at the specified interval.

cmd	**StatusTime**	Puts date, free memory in status.
st.dT	="00:00:10"	Time interval.
st.nextTime	=NOW()+st.dT	Time for next update.
	=ON.TIME(st.nextTime,"StatusTime")	Run this macro again next time.
st.nowT	=TEXT(NOW(),"mmm d, yyyy, h:mm:ss am/pm")	Current date and time.
st.memT	="...free memory: "&GET.WORKSPACE(16)&"K"	Amount of free memory.
	=MESSAGE(TRUE,st.nowT&st.memT)	Display date and memory.
	=RETURN()	

Cell *st.dT* contains the interval between updates of the status bar. In cell *st.nextTime* this value is added (through data coercion) to the current time. The ON.TIME formula in the next cell generates a request to run the *StatusTime* macro again: Every time Excel services the ON.TIME request, the macro runs itself again. The remaining formulas get the current time and the amount of free memory and put them in the status bar.

Notice that the TEXT formula displays the time in seconds. When you run the macro, you'll see the time update every 10 seconds, in effect adding *10* to the value you see in the status bar. For example, if you had started the macro at 1:30:32, the successive values to appear in the status bar would be

1:30:42
1:30:52
1:31:02

and so on. If you wanted to update the time every minute and also synchronize the time to whole-minute intervals, you could replace the first two formulas in the macro with the following:

st.dT	="00:01"	Time interval.
st.nextTime	=INT(NOW()*24*60)/(24*60)+st.dT	Time for next update.

Here the formula in *st.nextTime* does the equivalent of rounding the current time to the nearest whole minute, and then it adds an increment of 1 minute.

The following *StopTime* macro stops the chain of repeated ON.TIME requests by canceling the next pending event.

cmd S	**StopTime**	Stops status bar info.
	=ON.TIME(st.nextTime,"StatusTime",,FALSE)	Cancel pending request.
	=MESSAGE(FALSE)	Reset status bar.
	=RETURN()	

The *StopTime* macro first cancels the next ON.TIME instruction, referencing the same time value that *StatusTime* used to post the request. Next, the macro resets the status bar to normal.

Running a macro when a certain key is pressed

The ON.KEY function tells Excel to run the specified macro whenever the user presses the specified key sequence. This function takes the form

ON.KEY(keyT,*macroT*)

where *keyT* is a code for the key to be associated with the macro specified by *macroT*, according to the following table.

Key code	Meaning
{BACKSPACE} or {BS}	Backspace
{BREAK}	Break
{CAPSLOCK}	Caps Lock
{CLEAR}	Clear
{DELETE} or {DEL}	Delete or Del
{DOWN}	Down direction key
{END}	End
{ENTER} [PC—also ~ (tilde)]	Enter
{ESCAPE} or {ESC}	Esc (Escape)
{HELP}	Help
{HOME}	Home
{INSERT}	Insert
{LEFT}	Left direction key
{NUMLOCK}	Num Lock
{PGDN}	Page Down
{PGUP}	Page Up
{PRTSC}	Print Screen
{RIGHT}	Right direction key
{RETURN} [Mac—also ~ (tilde)]	Return
{SCROLLLOCK}	Scroll Lock
{TAB}	Tab
{UP}	Up direction key
{F1} through {F15}	Function keys F1 through F15

You can define a key command in either uppercase or lowercase characters. You can also combine keys with the following "modifier keys."

Code	Meaning
+ (plus sign)	Shift
^ (caret)	Ctrl
% (percent)	Alt or Option
* (asterisk)	Command [Mac only]

(Note: As of this writing, the Microsoft Excel Function Reference incorrectly states that you can assign repeated key sequences to a macro.)

PCs and Macintoshes differ in the way their keyboards are labeled. The PC and Macintosh versions of Excel also differ in how they respond to the {ENTER} and

{RETURN} key codes. The PC keyboard has two Enter keys, one near the alphanumeric keys and one near the numeric keypad. Both are labeled *Enter*. If you use the key code {ENTER} in an ON.KEY function in the PC versions of Excel, both Enter keys work equally well. If, however, you use the {RETURN} key code in a PC Excel macro, only the Enter key near the alphanumeric keys will be used as the macro's trigger key. Pressing the numeric keypad's Enter key will have no effect.

A Macintosh keyboard, on the other hand, has an Enter key *and* a Return key. The Return key is the one near the alphanumeric keys. In the Macintosh version of Excel, the {ENTER} key code applies only to the Enter key (near the numeric keypad), whereas the {RETURN} code applies only to the Return key (near the alphanumeric keys).

As in the ON.TIME function, *macroT* can be an external reference to a macro on a macro sheet other than the one containing the ON.KEY formula. If *macroT* is "" (null text), nothing happens when you press the specified key, effectively disabling the key. If you omit *macroT*, the specified key reverts to its normal meaning.

To experiment with this function, enter the following macros.

cmd	**SetKey**	Sets handler for key.
sk.key	/	The key to redefine.
	=ON.KEY(sk.key,"KeyHandler")	
	=RETURN()	

cmd subr	**KeyHandler**	Handles the key.
	=ALERT("This macro handles the "&sk.key&" key.")	
	=RETURN()	

cmd	**ResetKey**	Resets key assignment.
	=ON.KEY(sk.key)	
	=RETURN()	

If you enter and run the *SetKey* macro, you might notice that pressing the Slash key doesn't bring up the Alert dialog box displayed by the *KeyHandler* macro, but it activates the access key menuing system instead. If this happens, it's because the alternate key set in the Workspace dialog box is the Slash key itself, which demonstrates that whatever key is set in the dialog box takes precedence over the ON.KEY function.

When the alternate menuing key is not the Slash key, the *KeyHandler* macro presents an Alert dialog box that tells you the key that activated the macro.

To disable the assignment of the macro to the Slash key (or any other key code you've entered in cell *sk.key*), run the *ResetKey* macro; when the *macroT* argument of the ON.KEY function is omitted, the key returns to its default action.

Entering data without using the INPUT function

Although the INPUT function serves many useful purposes, it does have its limitations. Several of these become apparent when you want to create a macro that helps a user enter columns of data in a worksheet. For example, consider this simple macro system.

cmd	**DataEntryINPUT**	Data entry using INPUT.
dei.maxCol	=INPUT("Data in how many columns?",1)	Number of columns.
	=IF(NOT(ISNUMBER(des.maxCol)),RETURN())	Quit if not a number.
dei.loop	=FOR("n",1,dei.maxCol)	For each column,
	= FORMULA(DataEntryGetData())	enter new data,
	= SELECT("RC[1]")	move right one cell.
	=NEXT()	
	=SELECT("R[1]C["&-dei.maxCol&"]")	Move to next row.
	=GOTO(dei.loop)	Repeat again.
	=RETURN()	

cmd subr	**DataEntryGetData**	Gets next data item.
degd.inpData	=INPUT("Enter data",7)	Get the data.
	=IF(NOT(degd.inpData),HALT())	If Esc, halt.
	=RETURN(degd.inpData)	

These macros display an Input dialog box that asks you to enter data. If you select Cancel or press Esc, the system stops. Otherwise, the FORMULA formula enters the data in the active cell, the selection moves to the right one cell, and the FOR-NEXT loop starts the process again.

Although these macros work as described, they're inconvenient to use, for two reasons. First, the Input dialog box takes up room on the screen. You can't cure this problem by hiding the Input dialog box off screen because you need to be able to view the data in the Edit box before pressing Enter. Second, if you do happen to enter incorrect data in a cell, you must stop the macros to correct it.

The following macros work a little better for automating the task of data entry. To use this set of macros, you select the first cell in the first column into which you want to enter data. When you start the *DataEntrySetup* macro, an Input dialog box requests the number of columns into which you're entering data. Then the macro redefines the Enter and Esc keys so that pressing Enter runs a macro that manages the movement of the active cell, and Esc resets the key assignments. (Remember that the Enter keys on the PC and on the Macintosh differ in the way they respond to the {ENTER} key codes.)

cmd E	**DataEntrySetup**	Sets up data entry keys.
des.maxCol	=INPUT("Data in how many columns?",1)	Number of columns.
	=IF(NOT(ISNUMBER(des.maxCol)),RETURN())	Quit if not a number.
des.startCol	=COLUMN(ACTIVE.CELL())	
	=ON.KEY("{ENTER}","DataEntryMove")	Move macro.
	=ON.KEY("{ESC}","DataEntryReset")	Reset key assignments.
des.msgT	="Enter data: press Enter to move, Esc to end."	Status bar message.
	=MESSAGE(TRUE,des.msgT)	Display message.
	=RETURN()	

cmd subr	**DataEntryMove**	Moves selection after Enter.
dem.thisCol	=COLUMN(ACTIVE.CELL())	Current column number.
	=IF(dem.thisCol-des.startCol+1=des.maxCol)	If thisCol = maxCol,
	= SELECT("R[1]C"&des.startCol)	go to start of next row;
	=ELSE()	else,
	= SELECT("RC[1]")	go right one cell.
	=END.IF()	
	=RETURN()	

cmd subr	**DataEntryReset**	Resets data entry keys.
	=ON.KEY("{ENTER}")	Reset Enter key.
	=ON.KEY("{ESC}")	Reset Esc key.
	=MESSAGE(FALSE)	Reset status bar.
	=ALERT("Data entry mode terminated.")	
	=RETURN()	

If you want to correct an error, save the sheet, or format the data entered, you need take no special action. You simply make the correction, save the worksheet, format the range, or whatever: When you're ready to continue with data entry, select the next cell that requires data, and continue.

Running a macro when a window is activated

The ON.WINDOW function runs when the user manually activates a window. It won't run when a macro causes it to be activated; otherwise, you might have two macros trying to run at the same time. This function takes the form

ON.WINDOW(*windowT,macroT*)

The *windowT* argument is the name of the window in the form of text. If you omit this argument, the macro specified by *macroT* runs whenever you activate any window except those named in other ON.WINDOW formulas. If *macroT* is omitted, Excel stops running the macro when the window is activated.

To see how this function works, first open a new macro sheet, save it under any name, and then create second and third windows on the sheet by choosing Window New Window twice. Next, enter the following macros.

cmd subr	**StartWindow**	Starts ON.WINDOW routines.
sw.thisDoc	=GET.DOCUMENT(1)	Get name of this document.
	=ON.WINDOW(sw.thisDoc&":1","Win2")	Run Win1 if first window.
	=ON.WINDOW(sw.thisDoc&":2","Win1")	Run Win2 if second window.
	=ON.WINDOW(,"Win1")	Run Win1 if any other window.
	=RETURN()	

cmd subr	**Win1**	Window 1 handler.
	=ACTIVATE(sw.thisDoc&":1")	Activate window 2.
	=RETURN()	

cmd subr	**Win2**	Window 2 handler.
	=ACTIVATE(sw.thisDoc&":2")	Activate window 1.
	=RETURN()	

cmd	**StopWindow**	Stops ON.WINDOW routines.
	=ON.WINDOW()	
	=ON.WINDOW(sw.thisDoc&":1")	
	=ON.WINDOW(sw.thisDoc&":2")	
	=RETURN()	

After you've defined these macros, run *StartWindow* and then experiment with trying to activate various windows in your workspace. Eventually, you'll be able to work only with the first window, because activating any other window takes you right back to window 1. When you've gotten frustrated enough, you can turn off the assignment of macros to these windows by running *StopWindow*.

Here's a more useful application. Suppose you use several worksheets for a task, each of which requires a different set of macros to be used effectively. For example, one of these might contain a database, another might contain a report that extracts data from the database, and still another might contain an analysis of the report. Using the ON.WINDOW function, you can assign custom menus to each worksheet. When you activate a sheet, the ON.WINDOW function displays the custom menu for that sheet.

Running a macro when a worksheet is recalculated

The ON.RECALC function has a similar structure to that of the ON.WINDOW function; with it you can run a macro when the specified window is recalculated. The exception to this is when the worksheet is recalculated by the actions of another macro, such as when CALCULATE.NOW or CALCULATE.DOCUMENT is executed. The ON.RECALC function takes the form

ON.RECALC(*sheetT,macroT*)

where *sheetT* is the name of a document, and *macroT* is the macro to run when the document is recalculated. If *sheetT* is omitted, the macro is run whenever any sheet is recalculated, except for documents specified in other ON.RECALC formulas that have already been executed. To turn off the assignment of a macro to the recalculation, specify *sheetT* but omit *macroT*.

Running a macro when an error occurs

The ERROR function lets you redirect execution to a specified macro when Excel would otherwise generate an error dialog box. This function takes the form

ERROR(enableL,*macroRef*)

The *enableL* argument, if FALSE or 0, turns off all error checking; if Excel encounters an error condition, execution continues without notifying the user. If *enableL* is TRUE or 1 and you don't specify the *macroRef* argument, Excel displays its normal error dialog boxes. If you do specify *macroRef*, Excel doesn't display error dialog boxes, but it runs the routine specified by *macroRef* instead. If *enableL* is 2 and you don't specify *macroRef*, Excel presents an error dialog box when an error is encountered; if the user clicks Cancel in the dialog box, the ERROR function returns FALSE and Excel continues executing the macro. Finally, if *enableL* is 2 and you do specify *macroRef*, Excel runs the specified routine.

This redirection of error handling continues until the end of the macro that contains the ERROR formula is encountered or until the formula ERROR(TRUE) is encountered.

The system of macros on the facing page uses the ERROR function twice—once when activating a document given the document's name and once in *CheckActivateError*, which handles an error in attempting to open the document.

The *CheckActivate* macro accepts the name of a document to activate and then calls *Globals*, which defines several key values as well as finding the pathnames to various commonly used directories. Cell *g.myName* contains a GET.CELL formula that uses the name *thisCell*, which you need to define as a relative reference to the cell containing the GET.CELL formula itself. Also, the range *g.dirList* refers to the range marked by italics in the macro, and *g.dirListN* determines the number of rows in this list.

The *CheckActivate* macro then establishes the *CheckActivateError* macro as the handler for any errors that occur until the macro executes the RETURN formula at the end of *CheckActivate*.

If next the ACTIVATE formula is unable to activate the specified document, instead of displaying an error dialog box, Excel transfers control to *CheckActivate-Error*. The first line of this macro turns off error checking. (We'll get to the reason for this in a moment.) Next, for each pathname specified in *g.dirList*, the macro tries to open a document in the directory specified by the pathname. If the OPEN formula is unsuccessful, it returns the #VALUE! error value—however, instead of stopping the macro, Excel continues execution with the IF formula in the next cell.

cmd	**CheckActivateTest**	Tests error handling.
	=CheckActivate("xxx.XLS")	
	=RETURN()	

cmd subr	**CheckActivate**	Activates or opens document.
	=ARGUMENT("ca.thisDoc")	Name of document to activate.
	=Globals()	Define current globals.
	=ERROR(1,CheckActivateError)	Redirect errors.
	=ACTIVATE(ca.thisDoc)	Try to activate document.
	=RETURN()	

cmd subr	**CheckActivateError**	Handles document-not-found error.
	=ERROR(FALSE)	
	=FOR("n",1,g.dirListN)	For each directory in list,
cae.pathname	= INDEX(g.dirList,n,1)&ca.thisDoc	find full pathname,
	= MESSAGE(TRUE,"Searching for: "&cae.pathname)	send message,
cae.openL	= OPEN(cae.pathname)	try to open document.
	= IF(NOT(ISERROR(cae.openL)))	If successful,
	= MESSAGE(FALSE)	turn off messaging,
	= HALT()	halt.
	= END.IF()	
	= WAIT(NOW()+"00:00:01")	Wait for time to see message.
	=NEXT()	Next directory.
	=ERROR(TRUE)	
	=MESSAGE(FALSE)	Turn off messaging.
	=ALERT("Document not found.")	
	=RETURN()	

cmd	**Globals**	Returns global values.
g.env	=GET.WORKSPACE(1)	Name of this operating system.
g.delim	=IF(LEFT(ao.env,3)="Mac",":","\")	If Mac, then ":", else "\".
g.myName	=GET.CELL(32,thisCell)	Name of this macro sheet.
	g.dirList	
g.macPath	*=GET.DOCUMENT(2,g.myName)&g.delim*	Path to this macro sheet.
g.startPath	*=GET.WORKSPACE(23)&g.delim*	Path to startup directory.
g.curPath	*=DIRECTORY()&g.delim*	Path to current directory.
g.macRoot	*=LEFT(g.macPath,SEARCH(g.delim,g.macPath))*	Root of this macro sheet.
g.startRoot	*=LEFT(g.startPath,SEARCH(g.delim,g.startPath))*	Root of startup directory.
g.curRoot	*=LEFT(g.curPath,SEARCH(g.delim,g.curPath))*	Root of current directory.
g.dirListN	=ROWS(g.dirList)	List of common directories.
	=RETURN()	

This is why we set ERROR(FALSE) at the beginning of *CheckActivateError;* if we hadn't, the error condition generated by the OPEN formula would have caused Excel to continue execution back at the beginning of *CheckActivateError* because the ERROR formula in *CheckActivate* was still in effect.

The FOR-NEXT loop continues trying to open the specified document given each pathname in *g.dirList* until either the OPEN formula is successful (halting the macro) or the macro determines that the document isn't in any of the listed directories (turning error checking back on so that the subsequent Alert dialog box would be displayed).

SECTION FOUR

Special Topics

13

Charting with Macros

When people begin learning about Excel macros, they often pass by the chart macro functions, for two reasons. First, there is so much to learn about charting with macros that most people decide to study other areas first. Second, people don't usually perceive a real need to develop macros for manipulating charts.

When you start to experiment with the macro functions devoted to charts, you'll discover that they're easy to write and also useful. Charting macros are easy to write because nearly all the functions that they contain are command-equivalent functions, so they're very easy to generate with the Recorder.

Several practical reasons exist for using macros with charts.

- You can more accurately position text within a chart than you can with the mouse.
- You can automatically generate dozens of different management reports with chart macros.
- You can quickly produce charts that are difficult to produce manually.
- And finally, you can create an Apply Names macro that saves significant time whenever you create a chart manually.

Using the chart macro functions

Appendixes A and B list the chart macro functions provided by Excel. Almost all these are command-equivalent functions, which are easy to generate with the Recorder. Because a few of the functions present special challenges, let's take a closer look at them.

The GET.DOCUMENT function

The GET.DOCUMENT function provides information not only about worksheets and macro sheets, but also about charts. To reiterate, this function takes the form

GET.DOCUMENT(typeN,*nameT*)

where *typeN* specifies the type of information you want, and *nameT* is the name of an open document. For charts, *typeN* can take the values 1 through 12, 34 through 37, and 40, as discussed in Chapter 10. However, *typeN* arguments from 9 through 12 have one meaning when *nameT* refers to a chart and another meaning for macro sheets and worksheets, according to the following table:

typeN	Data type	Information returned
9	number	The type of the main chart: 1=2-D area, 2=2-D bar, 3=2-D column, 4=2-D line, 5=2-D pie, 6=2-D scatter (*xy*) plot, 7=3-D area, 8=3-D column, 9=3-D line, 10=3-D pie.
10	number	The type of the overlay chart, as for *typeN* 9. Returns #N/A if there is no overlay chart.
11	number	Number of series in the main chart.
12	number	Number of series in the overlay chart.

To illustrate, suppose you want a macro to select and modify every SERIES formula in a chart. To do so, you could use a FOR-NEXT loop structured like the following macro fragment.

```
mainN        =GET.DOCUMENT(11)                    Number of main series.
overlayN1    =GET.DOCUMENT(12)                    Number of overlay series.
overlayN2    =IF(ISNA(overlayN1),0,overlayN1)     Convert #N/A to 0.
             =FOR("n",1,mainN+overlayN2)          For each series.
             =   ProcessSeries(n)                 Process the series.
             =NEXT()
```

The formula in *mainN* returns the number of series in the main chart. The formula in *overlayN1* returns the number of series in the overlay chart, but if there is no overlay chart, GET.DOCUMENT returns #N/A. If so, *overlayN2* is set to 0.

Finally the FOR-NEXT loop runs a subroutine called *ProcessSeries* once for each series in the chart, whether in the main chart or the overlay chart.

Using SELECT with charts

As discussed in Chapter 8, the SELECT function takes three forms. When used with charts, this function takes the form

SELECT(itemT,*singlePointL*), form 3

The *itemT* argument specifies the item within a chart that you want to select, according to the following table.

Use this text	To select
Chart	Entire chart.
Plot	Plot area.
Legend	Legend.
Axis 1	Main chart value axis.
Axis 2	Main chart category axis.
Axis 3	Overlay chart value axis or 3-D series axis.
Axis 4	Overlay chart category axis.
Title	Chart title.
Text Axis 1	Label for the main chart value axis.
Text Axis 2	Label for the main chart category axis.
Text *n*	*n*th floating text item.
Arrow *n*	*n*th arrow.
Gridline 1	Major gridlines of value axis.
Gridline 2	Minor gridlines of value axis.
Gridline 3	Major gridlines of category axis.
Gridline 4	Minor gridlines of category axis.
Gridline 5	Major gridlines of series axis.
Gridline 6	Minor gridlines of series axis.
Dropline 1	Main chart droplines.
Dropline 2	Overlay chart droplines.
Hiloline 1	Main chart hi-lo lines.
Hiloline 2	Overlay chart hi-lo lines.
S*n*	Entire series.
S*n*P*m*	Data associated with point *m* in series *n*, if *singlePointL* is TRUE.
Text S*n*P*m*	Text attached to point *m* of series *n*.
Text S*n*P*m*	Text attached to point *m* of series *n*.
Text S*n*	Series title text of series *n* of an area chart.
Floor	Base of a 3-D chart.
Walls	Back of a 3-D chart.

As mentioned in the table, the *singlePointL* argument is available only when *itemT* is in the form S*n*P*m*. If TRUE, Excel selects only a single point. If FALSE or omitted, Excel selects a single point only if the chart contains one series. If the chart contains more than one series, Excel selects the entire series.

Let's consider a few examples. If you want to select the first point in the second series, you could use this formula:

```
=SELECT("S2P1")
```

If you wanted to select the first point in a series referred to by the name *thisSeries* defined on the macro sheet, you could use this formula:

```
=SELECT("S"&thisSeries&"P1")
```

To deselect the currently selected chart item, you could use this formula:

```
=SELECT("")
```

The GET.CHART.ITEM function

The GET.CHART.ITEM function returns the horizontal or vertical position of a point on a chart item. This function takes the form

GET.CHART.ITEM(xyIndexN,*pointIndexN,itemT*)

where *xyIndexN* is either 1 to return the horizontal position (*x*-coordinate) or 2 to return the vertical position (*y*-coordinate). The *itemT* argument specifies the item you want to select, according to the table given in the section on the SELECT function in this chapter. If *itemT* is omitted, Excel assumes the currently selected item.

The *pointIndexN* argument specifies the point about which you want the information; if omitted, the argument is assumed to be 1. The range and assignment of values to this argument depends on the type of item specified, according to the following table.

Item	*pointIndexN*	Assignment of position to *pointIndexN*
Point	1	(*pointIndexN* must be 1.) *Example:* =GET.CHART.ITEM(1,1,"S2P1") Returns the *x*-coordinate of point 1 of series 2.
Any line other than a data line	1 2	Lower or left. Upper or right. *Example:* =GET.CHART.ITEM(1,2,"Axis 2") Returns the *x*-coordinate of the right end of the *x*-axis. (To get the position of a data line, you must find the coordinates of each endpoint.)

(continued)

continued

Item	*pointIndexN*	Assignment of position to *pointIndexN*
Rectangle, or an area in an area chart	1	Upper left.
	2	Upper middle.
	3	Upper right.
	4	Right middle.
	5	Lower right.
	6	Lower middle.
	7	Lower left.
	8	Left middle.
		Example:
		=GET.CHART.ITEM (1,2,"Axis 2")
		Returns the *x*-coordinate of the right end of the horizontal axis.
Arrow	1	Shaft of arrow.
	2	Head of arrow.
		Example:
		=GET.CHART.ITEM(2,1,"Arrow 1")
		Returns the *y*-coordinate of the tail of an arrow.
Pie slice	1	Outermost counterclockwise point.
	2	Outer center point.
	3	Outermost clockwise point.
	4	Midpoint of the most clockwise radius.
	5	Center point.
	6	Midpoint of the most counterclockwise radius.
		Example:
		=GET.CHART.ITEM(2,5,"S1P1")
		Returns the *y*-coordinate of the center point of a pie chart.

Let's consider an example. Suppose you use a detached text box to comment on some aspect of a chart, as follows:

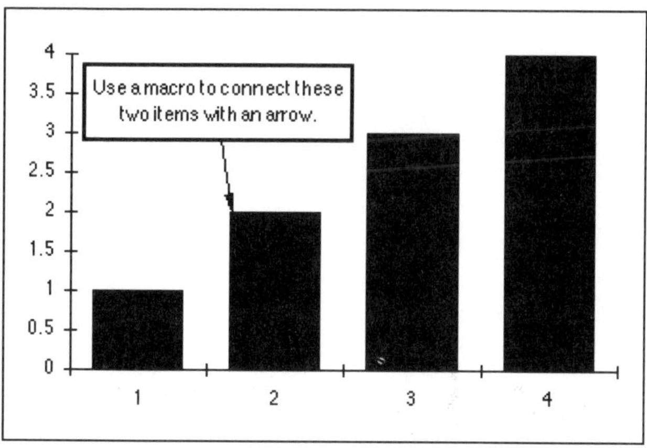

To position an existing arrow so that it points as shown from the text block to the second data point, you can use a macro fragment such as the one shown at the top of the following page.

cmd subr	Comment	Adjusts text box arrow.
xS1P2	=GET.CHART.ITEM(1,1,"S1P2")	Upper left of column.
yS1P2	=GET.CHART.ITEM(2,1,"S1P2")	Upper left of column.
xText1	=GET.CHART.ITEM(1,6,"Text 1")	Lower middle of text box.
yText1	=GET.CHART.ITEM(2,6,"Text 1")	Lower middle of text box.
	=SELECT("Arrow 1")	
	=FORMAT.MOVE(xText1,yText1)	Move the arrow's base.
	=FORMAT.SIZE(xS1P2-xText1,yS1P2-yText1)	Size arrow so that it points to top-left corner of S1P2.
	=RETURN()	

The formulas in cells *xS1P2* and *yS1P2* return the *x*- and *y*-coordinates of the top-left corner of item 2 in the bar graph. The formulas in cells *xText1* and *yText1* return the bottom-center point for the text box. After the formula in the next cell selects the arrow, the FORMAT.MOVE formula moves the arrow's base to the bottom center of the text box. Finally, the FORMAT.SIZE formula moves the head of the arrow by calculating the horizontal and vertical distance from the base to the top-left corner of the bar graph for point 2.

The GET.FORMULA function

The GET.FORMULA function, when used with a chart, returns as text the SERIES formula that generates a data point. It also returns the text in specified text blocks. This function takes the form

GET.FORMULA(*reference*)

When used with a chart, use as the *reference* argument the name of the item about which you want information, as given in the section on the SELECT function earlier in this chapter.

For example, the formula

=GET.FORMULA("S1P1")

returns the SERIES formula for the first series in the active chart. Similarly, the formula

=GET.FORMULA("Title")

returns the title of the chart.

The FORMULA function

The GET.FORMULA and the FORMULA functions are mirror images of each other: Use GET.FORMULA to return the SERIES formulas and text from a chart, and use FORMULA to create or modify these items. This lets you design a macro that can modify the contents of a chart without knowing ahead of time what data it contains.

The FORMULA function takes the form

FORMULA(formulaT,*reference*)

In a chart, the *formulaT* argument specifies the formula or text you want to add to the chart. You can often use the *reference* argument to specify the item you want to change; if omitted, Excel assumes the currently selected chart item. Therefore, if you don't specify the *reference* argument, you must use the SELECT function before using the FORMULA function.

For example, the following fragment replaces the title of a chart with a new title:

```
=SELECT("Title")
=FORMULA("Sales History")
```

To create a new item with the FORMULA function, use a SELECT function that doesn't specify a chart item. For example, to create a new text block, use a macro fragment such as

```
=SELECT("")
=FORMULA("Notice our improvement in only one year!")
```

After Excel executes these two formulas, the chart's title remains selected. You can then use the SIZE function to change the size of the text block, the MOVE function to move it within the chart, and so on.

The SELECT formula deselects the current selection, if any, and the FORMULA formula enters the text as an unattached text block. If the SELECT formula didn't exist, the specified text would replace whatever text was associated with the current selection. For example, if the FORMULA formula were placed after the last line in the previous example, it would have replaced the title with the new text, because the title was still selected from the previous example.

When you use the FORMULA function, you must take care to handle quotation marks correctly. For example, suppose you want to enter the following formula in the chart:

```
=SERIES("Test Data","A","B","C",1,2,3)
```

To do so, use this macro formula:

```
=FORMULA("=SERIES(""Test Data"",""A"",""B"",""C"",1,2,3)")
```

Here the first and last quotation marks in the FORMULA formula define the SERIES formula as text. Each paired set of quotation marks within the SERIES function tells Excel to return a single set of quotation marks as text.

A macro for editing chart items.

The following macro automates the process of editing any chart item that contains text or a formula:

cmd E	**EditChartItem**	Edits chart items.
eci.item	=INPUT("Enter item name to edit",2,"Edit Item")	Get item name.
	=IF(NOT(eci.item),RETURN())	If Cancel or Esc, quit.
	=SELECT(DEREF(eci.item))	Select the item.
eci.formula	=GET.FORMULA(DEREF(eci.item))	Get the associated text.
eci.isFormula	=LEFT(eci.formula)="="	Is it a formula?
eci.remEqual	=IF(eci.isFormula,MID(eci.formula,2,999),eci.formula)	If so, remove "=".
eci.newItem	=INPUT("Enter the new text.",2,"New Text",eci.remEqual)	Enter the new text.
	=IF(NOT(eci.newItem),RETURN())	If Cancel or Esc, quit.
	=FORMULA(IF(eci.isFormula,"=","")&eci.newItem)	Assign text to item.
	=SELECT("")	Deselect item.
	=RETURN()	

To use this macro, first enter the item name from the table provided in the section on the SELECT function earlier in this chapter. For example, to edit the title, you enter *Title,* or to edit the SERIES formula for series number 2, you enter *S2P1.*

When you press Enter, the macro displays a second Input dialog box that displays as a default value the current contents of the item you selected. After you edit the contents and press Enter, the macro updates the item and then quits.

The SERIES function

The SERIES function, which applies only to charts, specifies the information Excel uses to plot data. This function takes the form

SERIES(*nameRef,categoriesRef,*valuesRef,plotOrderN)

where *nameRef* specifies the name of the data series that the chart's legend displays; the name can be text, an external reference to a single cell, or an external reference to a name applied to a single cell. The *categoriesRef* argument specifies the category values, and the *valuesRef* argument specifies the values to be plotted; either can be an external reference to the cells on a worksheet, a name applied to a range, or an array constant. Finally, the *plotOrderN* argument specifies the order in which a data series is plotted, and it must be a positive integer.

As with other Excel functions, the SERIES function does not update external cell references when you move the data in those cells. Therefore, it's always a good idea to assign range names to the data and then replace the cell references in the SERIES formula with the appropriate range names.

The SERIES function is more limited than worksheet or macro functions. It cannot contain other functions such as INDEX, VLOOKUP, or IF, nor can it be entered as an array.

Let's consider some examples, beginning with the formula

```
=SERIES("Sales",,SALES.XLS!$A$1:$A$3,1)
```

This SERIES formula assigns the name *Sales,* which appears when the chart's legend is displayed. Because the formula contains no category data, the categories are labeled with the values *1, 2, 3,* and so on. The chart displays the values contained in the range A1:A3 in SALES.XLS.

The formula

```
=SERIES(BUDGET.XLS!title,BUDGET.XLS!dates,BUDGET.XLS!sales,1)
```

draws its data from the worksheet BUDGET.XLS. It displays the *sales* data for the specified *dates,* and it titles the data series using the label contained in the cell named *title.*

The formula

```
=SERIES("Temp",{"A","B","C"},{1,2,3},1)
```

does not reference any other sheet; it displays the data *1, 2,* and *3,* assigning the category titles *A, B,* and *C* respectively, and names the data series *Temp.*

To return the SERIES formula for the first data series in a chart, use the following formula:

```
=GET.FORMULA("S1")
```

You could also use as an item identifier the text *s1pN,* where *N* is the number of a point in the series. But because this format returns an error value if *N* refers to a point in the series that doesn't exist, it's safer to refer to point 1 or to not specify the point number at all.

To enter a new SERIES formula, you can use a pair of formulas, as shown in this example:

```
=SELECT("")
=FORMULA("=SERIES(""Customers"",SALES.XLS!R10C1:R50C1,
    SALES.XLS!cust,1)")
```

The SELECT formula deselects any element in the chart that might be selected. Then the FORMULA function enters the SERIES formula shown. Notice that cell references must be entered in R1C1 style and that pairs of quotation marks are used to represent each quotation mark that is to be entered as such. (Because the SERIES formula specifies plot order 1, the SERIES formula that had been in the number 1 position drops to the number 2 position, number 2 drops to number 3, and so on.)

To replace a SERIES formula with a new formula, you can use a pair of macro formulas, as shown in this example:

```
=SELECT("S3")
=FORMULA("=SERIES(""Customers"",,SALES.XLS!cust,3)")
```

The SELECT formula selects the data series you want to modify. The FORMULA formula replaces the formula for that series.

To delete a SERIES formula, use a pair of formulas, as in this example:

```
=SELECT("S3")
=FORMULA("")
```

Here the FORMULA formula erases the series selected. If the SELECT formula had selected the chart title, for example, the FORMULA formula would have erased the title instead.

The EDIT.SERIES function

The EDIT.SERIES function replaces most of the functionality of a SELECT/FORMULA pair when you're working with a series in a chart. It corresponds to the Chart Edit Series command and takes the form

EDIT.SERIES(*seriesN,nameRef,xRef,yRef,zRef,plotOrderN*)
EDIT.SERIES?(*seriesN,nameRef,xRef,yRef,zRef,plotOrderN*)

where *seriesN* specifies the number of the series you want to edit; if 0 or omitted, Excel creates a new series. The *nameRef* argument specifies the name of the series, which can be an external reference to a cell, the name of a cell containing the name, or a constant.

The *xRef*, *yRef*, and *zRef* arguments specify the ranges associated with the category, *y*-axis, and *z*-axis values in the series; *zRef* applies only to 3-D charts. Finally, *plotOrderN* is a number from 1 through 255 that specifies the plot order of the series: If you assign a plot-order number to a series when another series has the same plot-order number, Excel adds 1 to the plot-order number of that other series and any other series having a higher plot-order number; if you omit *plotOrderN*, Excel plots the series last.

Charting macro case studies

Here's a selection of macros that illustrate some real-world applications for charting macros: automating presentations, generating multiple reports containing charts, charting stock prices, and a macro that simulates the Formula Apply Names command but for Excel's charting environment.

Automating presentations

One of the more enjoyable applications for charting macros is in automating presentations; you can develop a set of macros that emulate the behavior of a slide projector or presentation graphics system, "playing" one chart after another, altering the contents of a given chart under macro control, or interspersing charts and tables.

Figure 13-1 presents a simple example of this type of macro application. When the presentation begins, the audience sees the first chart, containing three series that describe past sales for a company whose sales follow a yearly cyclical pattern.

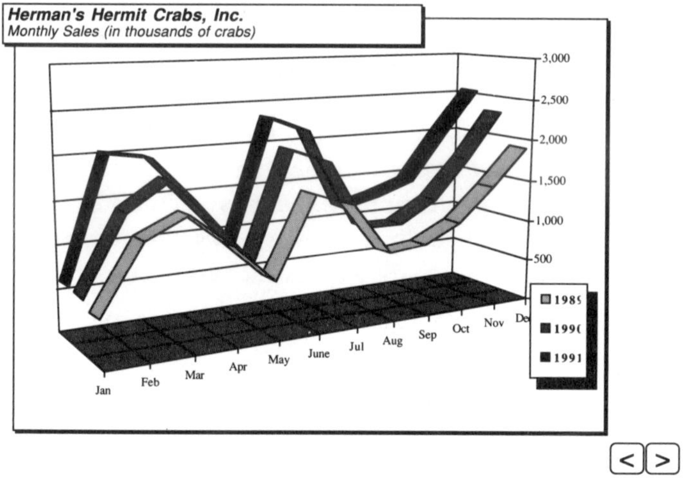

FIGURE 13-1.
The first chart in the presentation.

When the speaker clicks the > button in the lower right corner, the chart changes to the next "slide," shown in Figure 13-2 on the following page, which contains a fourth series of sales data for the next year.

Figure 13-3 shows the three short macros that manage the presentation up to this point and also the source data for the charts. To create the charts, open a new

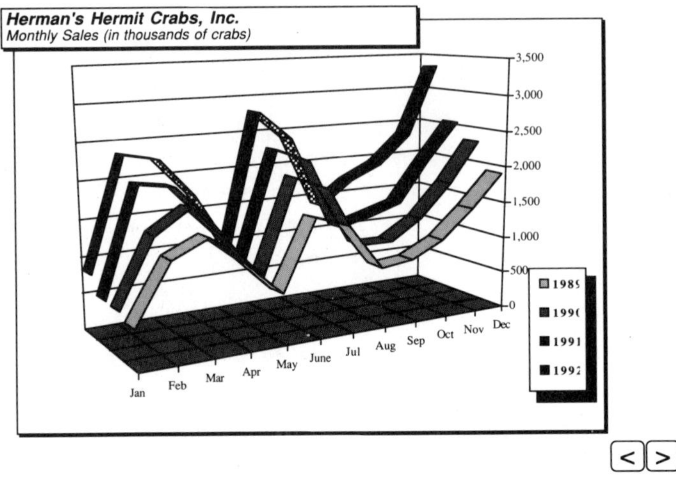

FIGURE 13-2.
The second chart, showing the fourth series.

worksheet, enter the data shown in the figure, and then name the worksheet PRESENT.XLS. Select the range A6:E18, click the embedded Chart icon in the toolbar, and drag out a rectangle from approximately H6 through P32. (The exact cell references aren't important, as long as the chart can be displayed in a full window without displaying any part of the table on screen.)

To minimize confusion, we've embedded the chart in the worksheet that contains the data. If a presentation contains many charts, you could embed the series of charts vertically in one worksheet, instead of storing them in separate chart files, and use the VSCROLL function to display each chart in succession.

	A	B	C	D	E
6		1989	1990	1991	1992
7	Jan	511	599	616	837
8	Feb	1271	1472	2029	2344
9	Mar	1488	1775	1960	2243
10	Apr	1104	1273	1449	1719
11	May	653	763	885	939
12	Jun	1571	2014	2327	2788
13	Jul	1412	1833	2140	2392
14	Aug	796	1010	1160	1392
15	Sep	842	998	1273	1707
16	Oct	1051	1261	1420	1915
17	Nov	1446	1727	2001	2319
18	Dec	1894	2295	2532	3320

FIGURE 13-3. *(continued)*
The data and macros used to create the two charts. The FORMULA formula wraps to a second line in this table.

FIGURE 13-3. *continued*

cmd S	**StartPresentation**	Starts the presentation.
	=ECHO(FALSE)	Turn off screen updating.
	=WORKSPACE(f,,f,f,f,f,"/",f,t,3,f,f,f,t)	Set up workspace.
	=OPEN("PRESENT.XLS")	Open presentation sheet.
	=FULL(TRUE)	Full-screen.
	=DISPLAY(f,f,f)	No formulas, gridlines, headings.
	=SELECT(!$A$1)	Move selection off-screen.
	=HSCROLL(7,TRUE)	Scroll to first chart.
	=VSCROLL(1,TRUE)	
	=RETURN()	

cmd C	**PresentChart2**	Second "slide", button-activated.
	=ECHO(FALSE)	Turn off screen updating.
	=ACTIVATE("PRESENT.XLS Chart 1")	Activate embedded chart.
	=FORMULA("=SERIES(PRESENT.XLS!ser1992, PRESENT.XLS!titles,PRESENT.XLS!dat1992,4)")	Add fourth series.
	=ACTIVATE("PRESENT.XLS")	Move selection off-screen.
	=SELECT("R1C1")	Deselect chart.
	=HSCROLL(7,TRUE)	Scroll to first chart.
	=VSCROLL(1,TRUE)	
	=RETURN()	

cmd X	**UndoPresentChart2**	Reverses PresentChart2.
	=ECHO(FALSE)	Turn off screen updating.
	=ACTIVATE("PRESENT.XLS Chart 1")	Activate embedded chart.
	=SELECT("s4")	Select series 4.
	=FORMULA("")	Delete series 4.
	=ACTIVATE("PRESENT.XLS")	Move selection off-screen.
	=SELECT("R1C1")	Deselect chart.
	=HSCROLL(7,TRUE)	Scroll to first chart.
	=VSCROLL(1,TRUE)	
	=RETURN()	

You can format the chart in any way you want. We've added a text box containing the title of the chart, and formatted the chart as a 3-D line graph. The two buttons just beyond the lower right corner of the chart should be added after you've entered the macros shown in Figure 13-3.

The *StartPresentation* macro sets up the workspace by suppressing the display of the toolbar, the formula bar, the status bar, and the scroll bars. (We've shortened the formula by using the names *t* and *f* for TRUE and FALSE.) The macro then opens the worksheet containing the data and the embedded chart, expands the window to full-screen, and sets the display of the worksheet to Values view, with no gridlines or row-and-column headings. The SELECT function ensures that the screen containing the chart won't have anything selected in it, and it scrolls the worksheet so that the chart is centered in the window.

After you've entered and defined the *PresentChart2* and *UndoPresentChart2* macros, go back to the worksheet, and add the two buttons displayed in the lower right corner of the figure. To the right button, attach the *PresentChart2* macro; and to the left button, attach the *UndoPresentChart2* macro.

The *PresentChart2* macro activates the "window" belonging to the embedded chart. (This is the equivalent of selecting the chart.) The FORMULA formula adds a SERIES formula that defines the fourth series; it uses names that you need to define on the worksheet, as follows:

ser1992	=$E$6
titles	=$A$7:$A$18
dat1992	=$E$7:$E$18

The remaining formulas in the macro deselect the embedded chart, move the selection back to cell A1, and scroll the window back so that the chart is centered in the window again.

The *UndoPresentChart2* macro reverses the effects of *PresentChart2*, in effect returning the screen to the first "slide." It has the same structure as *PresentChart2*, but it deletes series 4 instead of creating it.

We've developed this example to demonstrate the use of charting macros to manipulate embedded charts in a worksheet. If you were going to assemble a larger collection of charts and tables for a presentation, however, it would probably be a better idea to create each chart separately, rather than develop a macro that manipulated the items in a single chart to create each slide. You can then use the VSCROLL function alone to move between slides, increasing the speed and smoothness of the presentation and lessening confusion on your part as well.

Charting stock prices

Figure 13-4 presents a variation of a "candlestick" chart showing the trading range of a stock and its opening and closing values. This chart is similar to one that an online service makes available to subscribers.

Formulas view

	A	B	C
3	Code	Helvetica	Zapf Dingbats
4	161	=CHAR(A4)	=B4
5	=A4+1	=CHAR(A5)	=B5
6	=A5+1	=CHAR(A6)	=B6
7	=A6+1	=CHAR(A7)	=B7
8	=A7+1	=CHAR(A8)	=B8
9	=A8+1	=CHAR(A9)	=B9
10	=A9+1	=CHAR(A10)	=B10
11	=A10+1	=CHAR(A11)	=B11
12	=A11+1	=CHAR(A12)	=B12
13	=A12+1	=CHAR(A13)	=B13
14	=A13+1	=CHAR(A14)	=B14
15	=A14+1	=CHAR(A15)	=B15
16	=A15+1	=CHAR(A16)	=B16
17	=A16+1	=CHAR(A17)	=B17
18	=A17+1	=CHAR(A18)	=B18

Values view

	A	B	C
3	Code	Helvetica	Zapf Dingbats
4	161	°	❡
5	162	¢	❢
6	163	£	❣
7	164	§	❤
8	165	•	❥
9	166	¶	❦
10	167	ß	❧
11	168	®	♣
12	169	©	♦
13	170	™	♥
14	171	´	♠
15	172	¨	①
16	173	≠	②
17	174	Æ	③
18	175	Ø	④

FIGURE 13-4.
Invisible bar graphs and a hi-lo overlay produce this variation of a "candlestick" chart.

Using special characters in charts.

Special symbols can be used to make a chart more interesting. One way is to construct shapes from formatted arrows; you can use the Format Patterns command to eliminate the arrowhead, letting you "draw" patterns by positioning the headless arrows where you want.

Another way is to embed the chart in a worksheet and then use the object tools in the toolbar to construct shapes from lines, rectangles, ovals, and arcs. The shapes you create belong to the worksheet, not the embedded chart, and you can place the shapes over the embedded chart.

A third way is to use the symbols that certain fonts provide. To see what's available, you can create a font table, an excerpt of which is shown in Figure 13-5, in both Formulas view and Value view.

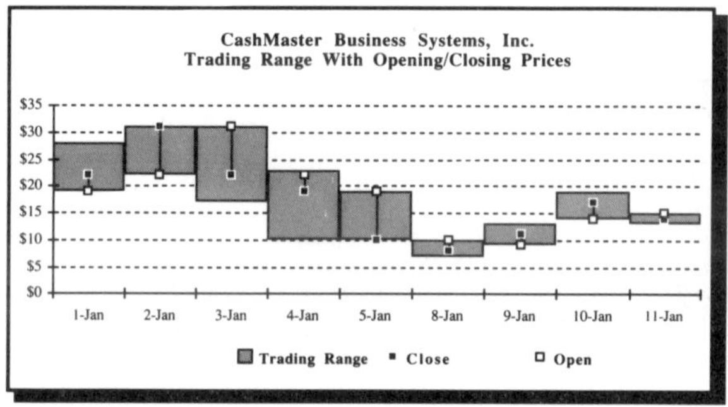

FIGURE 13-5.
A worksheet for creating a font table.

After entering the formulas in columns A through C, format the cells under the heading in the third column in whatever font you want to view. (In this example, we've used Zapf Dingbats.) To start the table at any desired code number, enter the number in cell A4. To use a given symbol in a chart, copy the cell containing the character, press Tab to move the active cell one cell to the right, choose Edit Paste Special, and select the Values option. Then, click in the formula bar, select and copy the character, switch to the chart, click in the formula bar again, and choose Edit Paste. Finally, format the text in the desired font.

Unlike the original chart, this one uses hi-lo symbols to present the opening and closing values for the stock. By doing so, we can see how the opening and closing values of the stock relate to its trading range during a day. One interesting feature of this chart is that the bar graphs of the trading range appear to be suspended in air. In truth, this chart uses a stacked-bar graph in which the series that creates the bottom bar is formatted in white, making it invisible.

Figure 13-6 presents the data used to create the chart. To create this worksheet, enter it as shown and then define the name *data* to refer to the range A4:E14.

	A	B	C	D	E
3	Date	High	Low	Open	Close
4					
5	1-Jan	28	19	19	22
6	2-Jan	31	22	22	31
7	3-Jan	31	17	31	22
8	4-Jan	23	10	22	19
9	5-Jan	19	10	19	10
10	8-Jan	10	7	10	8
11	9-Jan	13	9	9	11
12	10-Jan	19	14	14	17
13	11-Jan	15	13	15	14
14					

FIGURE 13-6.
This is the data plotted in the preceding figure.

The macro system shown in Figure 13-7 creates the chart shown in Figure 13-4. The *Stock* macro first sets the variable *s.debug*, which is used with the ECHO function in every macro in the system to freeze the screen. Setting *s.debug* to FALSE lets you watch as the chart is created. Later, after you've debugged the macro, you can speed up its operation by setting *s.debug* to TRUE.

cmd C	**Stock**	"Candlestick" stock-price chart.
s.debug	FALSE	Freeze screen updating, if not debugging.
	=ECHO(s.debug)	
	=StockSetData()	Prepare chart data.
	=StockChart()	Create chart.
	=StockHiLow()	Format as candlestick chart.
	=StockFormats()	Format text in chart.
	=RETURN()	Quit (updating on).

FIGURE 13-7. *(continued)*
The longest macro system in this chapter. This system creates a candlestick chart.

FIGURE 13-7. *continued*

cmd subr	**StockSetData**	Prepares data for chart.
	=ECHO(s.debug)	Freeze screen?
	=IF(ISERROR(GET.NAME("!data")))	If no Data range...
ssd.msg	= "The name ""data"" hasn't been defined."	
	= ALERT(ssd.msg,3)	ALERT and
	= HALT()	quit.
	=END.IF()	
	=SELECT(!data)	Select and
	=COPY()	Copy data.
	=NEW(1)	New worksheet.
	=PASTE()	Paste data.
	=FORMULA("Trading Range","R1C3")	Enter names to appear in
	=FORMULA("Open","R1C4")	legend box.
	=FORMULA("Close","R1C5")	
	=DEFINE.NAME("top","=R1C1")	Name cell A1 Top.
ssd.rowsN	=ROWS(SELECTION())	Find number of rows in data.
	=FOR("n",1,ssd.rowsN-2)	Modify data in columns
ssd.min	= MIN(OFFSET(!top,n,1),OFFSET(!top,n,2))	B and C:
ssd.abs	= ABS(OFFSET(!top,n,1)-OFFSET(!top,n,2))	
	= FORMULA(ssd.min,OFFSET(!top,n,1))	Col B = low price,
	= FORMULA(ssd.abs,OFFSET(!top,n,2))	Col C = trading range.
	=NEXT()	
	=SELECT(OFFSET(SELECTION(),0,1))	Select the numeric data.
	=FORMAT.NUMBER("$#,##0")	Format it with $ signs.
	=RETURN()	

cmd subr	**StockChart**	Creates chart of new data.
	=ECHO(s.debug)	Freeze screen?
	=SELECT("R1C1:R"&ssd.rowsN-1&"C5")	Select cell A1 thru last data.
	=COPY()	Copy data.
	=NEW(2)	New chart.
	=SIZE(500,300)	
	=PASTE.SPECIAL(2,t,t,f)	Paste into chart.
	=ADD.OVERLAY()	Add overlay chart.
	=RETURN()	

cmd subr	**StockHiLow**	Modifies to show range, open, close.
	=ECHO(s.debug)	Freeze screen?
	=MAIN.CHART(3,t,f,f,t,f,f,100,3,0)	Overlapped stacked chart.
	=SELECT("S1")	Select Series 1, bottom stack.
	=PATTERNS(2,,,,f,2,,,,f,f)	Make this series invisible.
shl.text	=GET.FORMULA("S4P1")	This section switches 3rd and 4th
shl.newText	=MID(shl.text,1,LEN(shl.text)-2)&"3)"	series numbers, causing legend
	=SELECT("S4")	(when created) to display "Open"
	=FORMULA(shl.newText)	before "Close".
	=SELECT("S2")	Select 2nd series, range.
	=PATTERNS(1,,,,f,0,4,1,2,f,f)	Gray pattern for B&W printing.
	=SELECT("S3")	Select 3rd series, closing price.
	=PATTERNS(2,,,,1,,,,f)	Eliminate connecting lines.
	=SELECT("S4")	Select 4th series, opening price.
	=PATTERNS(2,,,,1,,,,f)	Eliminate connecting lines.
	=OVERLAY(4,f,f,f,f,f,t,0,50,0,3,t)	Hi-lo line from 3rd to 4th series.
	=GRIDLINES(f,f,t,f)	Produce horizontal gridlines.
	=SELECT("Gridline 1")	Select first gridline.
	=PATTERNS(0,3,3,1)	Dashed red gridline.
	=RETURN()	

(continued)

FIGURE 13-7. ***continued***

cmd subr	**StockFormats**	Formats chart.
	=ECHO(s.debug)	Freeze screen?
	=SELECT("Chart")	Select chart.
	=PATTERNS(0,1,1,3,t,1,,,,f)	Draw a shadow border around it.
	=LEGEND(t)	Create legend.
	=SELECT("Legend")	Select it.
	=FORMAT.LEGEND(1)	Move legend to bottom.
	=PATTERNS(2,1,1,1,f,1,1,2,1,f)	Remove its border.
	=FORMAT.FONT(0,1,f,"Times",10,t,f,f,f,f,f)	
	=ATTACH.TEXT(1)	Attach text shown as title for chart.
sf.msg1	="CashMaster Business Systems, Inc."	CHAR(13) is a carriage return,
sf.msg2	="Trading Range With Opening/Closing Prices"	causing following text to appear
sf.msg3	="="""&sf.msg1&CHAR(13)&sf.msg2&""""	on next line in title.
	=FORMULA(sf.msg3)	
	=FORMAT.FONT(0,1,f,"Times",12,t,f,f,f)	Format title's font.
	=SELECT("Axis 2")	Select horizontal axis.
	=FORMAT.FONT(0,1,f,"Times",10,f,f,f,f)	Format its font.
	=SELECT("Axis 1")	Select vertical axis.
	=FORMAT.FONT(0,1,f,"Times",10,f,f,f,f)	Format its font.
	=SELECT("")	Deselect current selection.
	=RETURN()	

The *StockSetData* routine prepares the data for charting. To do so, the routine first copies the data and moves it to a new worksheet and then modifies it slightly. We could have had the macro enter the modified data in the columns to the right of column D, but this method preserves the original worksheet.

The macro also enters the labels *Trading Range, Open,* and *Close* as shown in row 1 of Figure 13-8. By entering these labels in the positions shown, the chart automatically assigns them as titles when we create the chart. The macro then uses a series of formulas containing the OFFSET function to enter the low value for each day in column B and the trading range in column C.

	A	B	C	D	E
1			Trading Range	Open	Close
2	1-Jan	$19	$9	$19	$22
3	2-Jan	$22	$9	$22	$31
4	3-Jan	$17	$14	$31	$22
5	4-Jan	$10	$13	$22	$19
6	5-Jan	$10	$9	$19	$10
7	8-Jan	$7	$3	$10	$8
8	9-Jan	$9	$4	$9	$11
9	10-Jan	$14	$5	$14	$17
10	11-Jan	$13	$2	$15	$14
11					

FIGURE 13-8.
To create the candlestick chart shown in Figure 13-4, the preceding macro first creates this temporary spreadsheet.

After the data is prepared for charting, the *StockChart* macro creates the chart, first selecting the range of data, then opening a new chart document, sizing it, and pasting the data into the chart. We've defined the names *t* and *f* to refer to the values TRUE and FALSE, in order to shorten the length of formulas in the figure. This improves readability but slows the macro a bit; you could use the values 1 and 0 instead. This initial chart bears little resemblance to the chart shown in Figure 13-6 on page 304. The *StockHiLow* routine continues the formatting of the chart. The MAIN.CHART formula creates the stacked-bar graph; the subsequent formulas make the bottom graph invisible and create and format a hi-lo graph.

Finally, the *StockFormats* routine formats the chart as a whole, adding a border, legend, and title and formatting the text in the chart to Times. (Of course, you could substitute any other available font.)

Using Apply Names with charts

When you create a new chart, the SERIES formulas in the chart reference worksheet data by direct cell addresses rather than by range names. Because charts don't change these addresses as the worksheet changes, you must manually replace these references or replace the direct cell addresses with range names. In Excel's worksheet and macro sheet environments, the Formula Apply Names command performs this operation automatically, but in the charting environment this command is missing.

The macro shown in Figure 13-9 is by far the most complex macro in this chapter, and perhaps the most useful because it brings the Formula Apply Names command to Excel's charting environment.

cmd A	**ChartApplyNames**	Replaces cell refs in chart with names.
	=IF(GET.DOCUMENT(3)<>2,HALT())	Quit if active doc isn't a chart.
	rtn=CHAR(13)	Carriage return.
can.mainSeriesN	=GET.DOCUMENT(11)	Number of series in main chart.
can.overSeriesN	=GET.DOCUMENT(12)	Number of series in overlay.
can.overSeriesN2	=IF(ISNA(can.overSeriesN),0,can.overSeriesN)	Convert #N/A to 0.
can.totSeriesN	=can.mainSeriesN+can.overSeriesN2	Total number of series.
can.chartName	=GET.DOCUMENT(1)	Chart name.
	can.graf=0	Initialize can.graf counter.
	=FOR("seriesN",1,can.totSeriesN)	Begin Series loop.
can.oldSeries	= GET.FORMULA("s"&seriesN)	Get first SERIES formula.
	can.newSeries=can.oldSeries	Start out with new=old.
	= ProcessSeries()	Process series.
	= ACTIVATE(can.chartName)	Activate chart.
	= SELECT("s"&seriesN)	Select current SERIES formula.
	= FORMULA(can.newSeries)	Enter new SERIES formula.
	=NEXT()	Loop back for next SERIES formula.
	=SELECT("")	Deselect current chart selection.
	=RETURN()	

FIGURE 13-9. *(continued)*
This macro brings the Formula Apply Names command to Excel's charting environment.

FIGURE 13-9. *continued*

cmd subr	**ProcessSeries**	ChartApplyNames routine.
	ps.startPos=8	Set left position marker to 8.
	=FOR("args",1,3)	Begin args loop.
ps.delim	= IF(args=1,"(",",")	Find text bounded on left by "(" for first
ps.findText	= SEARCH(ps.delim&"*!",can.oldSeries,ps.startPos)+1	arg or by "," for other args, and on
	= IF(ISERROR(ps.findText),GOTO(ps.next))	right by "!". Also, look for commas.
ps.findExclam	= FIND("!",can.oldSeries,ps.findText)	Commas exist if FINDing "," returns
ps.findComma	= FIND(",",can.oldSeries,ps.findText)	lower value than FINDing "!".
	= IF(ps.findExclam<ps.findComma,GOTO(ps.linkDoc))	Continue if text does not contain ",";
	ps.startPos=ps.findComma	otherwise, update startPos to begin
	= GOTO(ps.next)	with next arg, and then go to NEXT.
ps.linkDoc	= MID(can.oldSeries,ps.findText,ps.findExclam-ps.findText)	Return doc name linked to this
	= ACTIVATE(ps.linkDoc)	formula, and then activate doc.
ps.endComma	= FIND(",",can.oldSeries,ps.findExclam)	Find position of current ending comma.
	ps.startPos=ps.endComma	Set starting position for next arg.
ps.oldRef	= MID(can.oldSeries,ps.findExclam+1,ps.endComma-ps.findExclam-1)	Capture quoted ref of current arg.
ps.isName	= GET.NAME("!"&ps.oldRef)	Find whether ref is already a name.
	= IF(NOT(ISERROR(ps.isName)),GOTO(ps.next))	If ref is a name, go to NEXT.
ps.nameDef	= GET.DEF(ps.oldRef,ps.linkDoc)	Find name assigned to quoted ref.
	ps.newName=ps.nameDef	Capture name in ps.newName cell.
	= IF(NOT(ISERROR(ps.nameDef)),GOTO(ps.substitute))	If name exists, branch to cell shown.
	= SET.VALUE(ps.grafN,0)	Set counter to 0.
ps.grafN	= ps.grafN+1	Increment counter for graf name.
ps.grafT	= "_graf"&ps.grafN	Return new name to suggest.
	= IF(NOT(ISERROR(GET.NAME("!"&ps.grafT))), GOTO(ps.grafN))	If name already defined, increment grafN.
ps.selNoName	= SELECT(DEREF(ps.oldRef))	Select unnamed area.
ps.msgA1	= "No recognizable name is assigned to this area."&rtn	Text of INPUT prompt.
ps.msgA2	= "What name do you want to assign?"	More text for INPUT prompt.
ps.msgA	= ps.msgA1&ps.msgA2	
ps.nameIn	= INPUT(ps.msgA,2,"Assign Name",ps.grafT)	INPUT new name.
	= IF(NOT(ps.nameIn),HALT())	Stop if Cancel chosen.
ps.noName	= ISERROR(GET.NAME("!"&ps.nameIn))	Return TRUE if name does not exist.
	= IF(ps.noName,GOTO(ps.defNewName))	If name doesn't exist, define it.
	= ERROR(TRUE,ps.msgB1)	Branch to 2nd INPUT if SELECT fails.
ps.selectRef	= SELECT(DEREF(ps.nameIn))	Select name.
	= ERROR(TRUE)	Resume normal error checking.
ps.selText	= REFTEXT(SELECTION())	If selection equals old ref,
ps.testRef	= MID(ps.selText,FIND("!",ps.selText)+1,999)	name doesn't need to be defined.
ps.isOldRef	= ps.testRef=ps.oldRef	Branch so that name
	= IF(ps.isOldRef,GOTO(ps.assignName))	will be used.
ps.msgB1	= """"&ps.nameIn&"""" defines other data. Enter:"&rtn	Generate error statement
ps.msgB2	= "1--to use another name"&rtn	for INPUT prompt,
ps.msgB3	= "2--to redefine the name"&rtn	and then ask for instructions.
ps.msgB4	= "3--to use the name's old definition."	
ps.msgB	= ps.msgB1&ps.msgB2&ps.msgB3&ps.msgB4	
ps.input	= INPUT(ps.msgB,1)	
	= IF(NOT(ps.input),HALT())	Halt if Cancel chosen.
ps.choose	= GOTO(CHOOSE(ps.input,ps.selNoName,ps.defNewName, ps.assignName))	Perform action specified by INPUT.
	= GOTO(ps.input)	INPUT again if another number entered.
ps.defNewName	= DEFINE.NAME(ps.nameIn,"="&ps.oldRef)	Define new name using original ref.
ps.assignName	ps.newName=ps.nameIn	Assign name to ps.newName cell.
ps.substitute	can.newSeries=SUBSTITUTE(can.newSeries,ps.oldRef, ps.newName)	Substitute new ref for old in newSer.
ps.next	=NEXT()	Loop back for next arg.
	=RETURN()	

An overview of the macro

One by one, the *ChartApplyNames* macro collects the SERIES formulas in the chart, assigns them to the variables *can.oldSeries* and *can.newSeries*, and calls the *ProcessSeries* macro. *ProcessSeries* looks at every argument in a SERIES formula; every time an argument contains an external reference, the macro activates the referenced worksheet. If the reference uses a range name, the macro loops to the next argument in the SERIES formula. Otherwise, the macro searches for a name that matches the cell address that the SERIES formula uses. When the macro finds such a name, it substitutes that name for the cell address in the SERIES formula.

When the macro can't match a cell address with any of the range names, it selects the range on the worksheet that needs to be defined and displays the following Input dialog box:

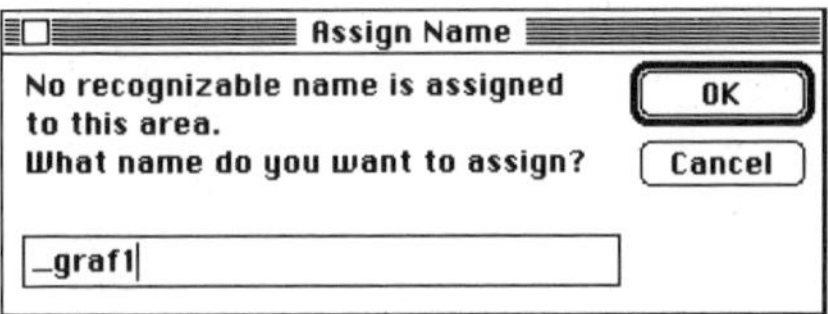

You enter a name or you press Enter if you want to use the name that the Input dialog box suggests. If you enter another name, the macro checks to see whether that name exists. If the name does not exist, the macro assigns the name and continues to the next argument. If the name does exist, the macro selects the range that the name defines (if possible) and displays this Input dialog box:

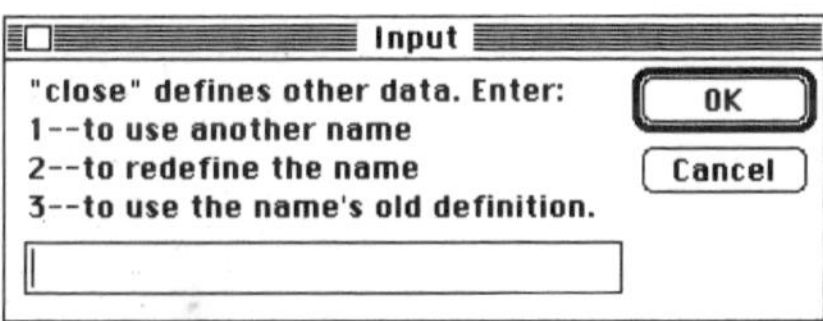

If you enter *1* in this box, the macro displays the previous Input dialog box so that you can enter a new name. If you enter *2*, the macro redefines the name, assigning the new definition. If you enter *3*, the macro uses the old definition, but it updates the SERIES formula with the name you assigned.

The details of the macro

This macro system uses the equivalent of two nested FOR-NEXT loops. The loop in the *ChartApplyNames* macro cycles through the macro once for each SERIES formula in the chart; the GET.FORMULA function in cell *can.oldSeries* returns each SERIES formula, one at a time. The loop in *ProcessSeries* cycles through each of the SERIES formulas three times, once for each argument that might contain external references.

The SEARCH and FIND formulas at the beginning of *ProcessSeries* find the left and right positions in the SERIES formula that contain the name of the document to which the next argument is linked. To do so, they find the first position of the text that is bounded on the left by *(* for the first SERIES argument or by *,* for the other arguments, and bounded on the right by *!*. If commas are contained within these left and right boundaries, we must shift the left boundary to the right until the commas are not included.

When no commas are between these two boundaries, we know that only the document name remains. Therefore, the function in cell *ps.linkDoc* returns the name of that document, and the next cell activates it.

The function in cell *ps.oldRef* finds the reference that follows the name of the document. Cell *ps.isName* checks whether this reference is already a defined name. If so, the macro branches to the NEXT formula at the end of the loop so that the next argument can be checked. Cell *ps.nameDef* checks whether the reference is one for which a name can be found. If a name can be found, the macro substitutes the reference in the new SERIES formula and goes on to the next argument.

If a name can't be found for this reference, the macro creates a name to suggest, selects the range to be named, and displays the Input dialog box that asks for a new name. If the new name does not exist, the macro branches to the cell *ps.defNewName*, where the name is defined. If the name does exist, the macro attempts to select it in cell *ps.selectRef*. If the new selection matches the old selection, the macro uses the new name as is. Otherwise, the macro displays the second Input dialog box, which asks how you want to proceed.

The GOTO formula in cell *ps.choose* branches to the cell that corresponds to the entry in the Input dialog box. That is, the formula lets you either enter another name, redefine the existing name, or use the existing name and its existing definition.

After the FOR-NEXT loop has cycled through the SERIES formula three times, the text of the SERIES formula in *can.newSeries* contains range names rather than the cell references. The ACTIVATE, SELECT, and FORMULA formulas in the *ChartApplyNames* macro activate the chart, select the SERIES formula that needs updating, and replace the formula.

Finally, after *ChartApplyNames* has cycled through each SERIES formula, the macro deselects the current selection in the chart and quits.

14

Creating Print Macros

Printing is one of the most common uses for macros, and the reason for this is obvious: Simple print macros are easy to create and can save a great deal of time. After all, a simple print macro can print dozens of reports while you sleep. Without the macro, printing the same reports could keep you and your computer tied up for hours.

This chapter presents a series of print macros, beginning with a very simple one that prints a single worksheet and ending with a sophisticated one that prints reports based on a report-distribution list.

Creating print macros using macro functions

Excel offers a number of macro functions to control printers and printing. We'll discuss them briefly and then describe how you can use them to manage the printing process.

Setting up the page and the printer

Two functions—PAGE.SETUP and PRINTER.SETUP—are useful for setting up the printer. (The latter function is available only in the PC versions of Excel.)

The PAGE.SETUP function corresponds to the File Page Setup command, and it can take one of two forms. If the active document is a worksheet or macro sheet, the function takes the form

> **PAGE.SETUP(*headT,footT,leftN,rightN,topN,botN,headingL,gridL, hCenterL,vCenterL,orientationN,paperSizeN,scalingN*), form 1**
> **PAGE.SETUP?(*headT,footT,leftN,rightN,topN,botN,headingL,gridL, hCenterL,vCenterL,orientationN,paperSizeN,scalingN*), form 1**

The *leftN, rightN, topN,* and *botN* arguments set the corresponding margin, in inches. Margin settings do not affect the placement of headers and footers; headers and footers are always printed 0.5 inch from the top and bottom of the page and 0.75 inch from the side of the page. Therefore, top and bottom margins must be large enough to allow space for them; if not, Excel will print the body of the document over the header or footer.

If you want row and column headings to be printed, set *headingL* to TRUE. If *gridL* is TRUE, Excel prints gridlines. If the *hCenterL* and *vCenterL* arguments are TRUE, the printed area of the sheet is centered horizontally or vertically on the page. If *orientationN* is 1, the top of the document is printed along the shorter edge of the page (known as *portrait* orientation); if 2, Excel prints the top of the document along the longer edge of the page (known as *landscape* orientation).

The *paperSizeN* argument is a number from 1 through 26 that sets the size of the paper on which the document is to be printed; not every number has a meaning for every printer. The sizes are as follows:

paperSizeN	Meaning	Size
1	Letter	8.5 by 11 inches
2	Letter (small)	8.5 by 11 inches
3	Tabloid	11 by 17 inches
4	Ledger	17 by 11 inches
5	Legal	8.5 by 14 inches
6	Statement	5.5 by 8.5 inches
7	Executive	7.25 by 10.5 inches
8	A3	297 by 420 millimeters
9	A4	210 by 297 millimeters
10	A4 (small)	210 by 297 millimeters

(continued)

continued

paperSizeN	Meaning	Size
11	A5	148 by 210 millimeters
12	B4	250 by 354 millimeters
13	B5	182 by 257 millimeters
14	Folio	8.5 by 13 inches
15	Quarto	215 by 275 millimeters
16	10x14	8.5 by 14 inches
17	11x17	8.5 by 14 inches
18	Note	8.5 by 11 inches
19	ENV9	3.875 by 8.875 inches
20	ENV10	4.125 by 9.5 inches
21	ENV11	4.5 by 10.375 inches
22	ENV12	4.75 by 11 inches
23	ENV14	5 by 11.5 inches
24	C Sheet	8.5 by 11 inches
25	D Sheet	8.5 by 11 inches
26	E Sheet	8.5 by 11 inches

The *scalingN* argument sets the percentage to reduce or enlarge the document; however, if *scalingN* is TRUE, the argument corresponds to the Fit To Page option in the File Page Setup dialog box in the PC versions of Excel, and it fits the document within the page margins.

If the active document is a chart, the PAGE.SETUP function takes the form

PAGE.SETUP(*headT,footT,leftN,rightN,topN,botN,sizeN,hCenterL, vCenterL,orientationN,paperSizeN,scalingN*), form 2
PAGE.SETUP?(*headT,footT,leftN,rightN,topN,botN,sizeN,hCenterL, vCenterL,orientationN,paperSizeN,scalingN*), form 2

The arguments for the chart form are the same as for the worksheet form, except that there are no *headingL* and *gridL* arguments. Also, there is an additional *sizeN* argument, which determines how a chart is mapped onto the page: If 1, the chart is printed as it appears on-screen; if 2, the chart is printed in the same aspect ratio as the chart that appears on-screen, but it's enlarged to fit just within the margins; if 3, the chart is enlarged to the limits of the top and side margins without preserving the chart's aspect ratio.

The *headT* and *footT* arguments control the contents of the header and footer; within a text string specifying a header or footer, you can use any of the formatting codes listed in the table on the following page.

Code	Meaning
Alignment	
&l	Left-align the following text.
&c	Center the following text.
&r	Right-align the following text.
Font Style	
&b	Print the following text in bold.
&i	Print the following text in italic.
&s	Print the following text in strikeout style.
&u	Print the following text in underline style.
&o	Print the following text in outline style.
&h	Print the following text in shadow style.
&"fontname"	Print the following text in the specified font. This style is not available through Windows version 2.10. Instead, headers and footers are formatted using the number 1 font for the spreadsheet.
&*nn*	Print the following text in the font size specified by *nn*, in points. For example, to use 9-point text, use the code *&09.*
Information	
&d	Print the current date.
&t	Print the current time.
&f	Print the name of the document.
&p	Print the page number.
&p+*n*, &p-*n*	Add *n* to or subtract *n* from the page number and print the result.
&n	Print the total number of pages in the document. For example, *Page &p of &n* would print *Page 1 of 10* on the first page.
&&	Print a single ampersand. (For example, to print "Smith & Jones" use "Smith && Jones".)

You can combine any of these codes in a header or footer with other text. For example, the first page generated by the text

&l&d &t&cSales Report&rPage &p+2

would generate a header or footer that looks something like this:

8/31/92 11:33 AM Sales Report Page 3

You can specify codes in either uppercase or lowercase in your macros; we prefer using lowercase codes for two reasons. First, header text such as *&cCosts* is easier to read than is *&CCosts*, even though both arguments center the heading *Costs*. Second, because Excel generally uses proportional fonts, lowercase codes take less horizontal space in a cell than do uppercase codes, making macro formulas a little shorter.

In PC versions of Excel, you can also specify that the document be printed on a particular printer. The PRINTER.SETUP function corresponds to the File Printer Setup command. This function takes the form

PRINTER.SETUP(printerT)
PRINTER.SETUP?(*printerT*)

where *printerT* is the name of the printer you want to use; this name should match exactly the name shown in the File Printer Setup dialog box.

Printing a range of pages

To print one or more pages from within a macro, use the PRINT function, which corresponds to the File Print command. This function takes the form

PRINT(*rangeN,fromN,toN,copiesN,draftL,previewL,printWhatN, colorL,feedN*)
PRINT?(*rangeN,fromN,toN,copiesN,draftL,previewL,printWhatN, colorL,feedN*)

where *rangeN* is 1 to print the entire document or 2 to print only a selected range. If *rangeN* is 2, the *fromN* and *toN* numbers, which specify the beginning and ending page numbers, are required. The *copiesN* argument specifies the number of pages to print.

The *draftL* argument, if TRUE, prints the document in draft quality, and if FALSE, prints the document at the normal level of quality. (This argument is ignored in the Macintosh version of Excel.) The *previewL* argument, if TRUE, brings up the Print Preview window instead of printing the document.

The *printWhatN* argument applies only if the active document is a worksheet or macro sheet, and it specifies which parts of the document to print: If 1, only the document is printed; if 2, only the document's cell notes are printed; and if 3, first the document and then the notes are printed.

The *colorL* argument applies only to the Macintosh version of Excel; if TRUE, Excel prints the colors established for the elements in a document or converts the colors to appropriate gray levels if the document is being printed to a gray-scale printer.

The *feedN* argument determines the feeding mechanism being used by the printer and applies only to the Macintosh version of Excel: If 1, the paper is continuous (either fan-fold or in a cassette); if 2, each sheet is loaded manually.

Setting the print area

Excel offers several ways to determine which areas in a worksheet or macro sheet are printed. The first is the SET.PRINT.AREA function, which corresponds to the Options Print Area command. This function takes the form

=SET.PRINT.AREA()

This function takes no arguments, and it defines the current selection as the print area. If you look in the Define Name dialog box, you'll see that Excel has defined the name *Print_Area* and assigned to it the range that was selected when this function was executed. To change the area to be printed back to the entire sheet, you can use the DELETE.NAME function

=DELETE.NAME("Print_Area")

You could also select another range and use the SET.PRINT.AREA function again.

To define the current selection as a print title, use the SET.PRINT.TITLES function, which corresponds to the Options Set Print Titles command. This function takes the form

=SET.PRINT.TITLES()

Remember that you must select entire rows and/or columns for your print titles and that you must not overlap print titles with your print area. As with SET.PRINT.AREA, this function defines the name *Print_Titles* in the active worksheet; to remove the name, you can use the DELETE.NAME function.

To set a page break, you can select a cell and use the SET.PAGE.BREAK function, which corresponds to the Options Set Page Break function. This function takes the form

=SET.PAGE.BREAK()

and creates forced page breaks at the top and left edges of the active cell. To remove a forced page break, select the cell again and use the REMOVE.PAGE.BREAK function, which takes the form

=REMOVE.PAGE.BREAK()

Unfortunately, you can't find these page breaks because (unlike SET.PRINT.AREA and SET.PRINT.TITLES) no name is defined that specifies the location of the page breaks you've created. The best alternative (if the entire document is selected) is REMOVE.PAGE.BREAK, which removes the forced page breaks from the entire document. You can then reapply the page breaks you want.

Printing a simple report

Using the Recorder is the easiest way to create a simple print macro. Let's consider an example. Open a new macro sheet, select cell B3, choose the Macro Set Recorder command [/MT], and start the Recorder by choosing Macro Start Recorder [/MS].

To set up the sheet for printing, choose File Page Setup [/FT] and then set the headers, margins, and other elements that you want. To print the sheet, choose File Print [/FP] and press Enter; then stop the Recorder by choosing Macro Stop Recorder [/MC].

When you've finished, your macro looks like this if you accepted the default settings for page setup and printing:

	A	B
3		=PAGE.SETUP("&f","Page &p",0.75,0.75,1,1,FALSE,TRUE,FALSE,FALSE)
4		=PRINT(1,,,1,FALSE,FALSE,1,FALSE,1)
5		=RETURN()

When used with any worksheet, this macro sets up the page for printing and then prints the entire worksheet.

The earlier discussion of the PAGE.SETUP function describes the codes you can use to create your own headers and footers; with this information, you can easily modify the previous macro to print using only the settings you want.

For example, the *&d* and *&t* codes generate a date and time in one format only. However, you can easily get around this problem by using the TEXT and NOW functions to format text in the way you want and then passing on the text to a PAGE.SETUP function. The following macro creates a header containing a date in the form *January 3, 1991*, centered on the page. To save space in the table, we've defined the names *t* and *f* for the values TRUE and FALSE, respectively.

cmd H	**MyDateHeader**	
headerT	="&c"&TEXT(NOW(),"mmmm d, yyyy")	Header text.
	=PAGE.SETUP(headerT,"Page &p",0.75,0.75,1,1,f,t,f,f)	
	=PRINT(1,,,1,f,f,1,f,1)	
	=RETURN()	

Printing a named range

With a print macro, you can print a named range within a worksheet at the push of a macro shortcut key. To do this, use the FORMULA.GOTO function to select the area, and use the SET.PRINT.AREA function to define the name *Print_Area* as the selection, as in the macro on the following page.

cmd R	**PrintBudgetRange**	
	=FORMULA.GOTO("budget")	Select budget range.
	=SET.PRINT.AREA()	Set *Print_Area*.
	=PAGE.SETUP("&f","",0.75,0.75,1,1,FALSE,FALSE)	
	=PRINT(1,,,1,,TRUE,1)	Print the range.
	=DELETE.NAME("Print_Area")	Delete *Print_Area*.
	=FORMULA.GOTO()	Return to orig selection.
	=RETURN()	

One interesting feature of this macro is that you can test your printing macros very economically by setting the *previewL* argument of the PRINT function to TRUE. When you run this macro, instead of printing the *budget* range to paper, you'll first see the document in Print Preview mode on-screen.

Another way to print a specific named range, without the overhead of actually selecting the range, is to find the definition of the range you want to print and assign it to *Print_Area*, as shown in Figure 14-1.

cmd R	**PrintBudgetRange2**	
	=DEFINE.NAME("Print_Area",!budget)	Transfer def of *!budget*.
	=PAGE.SETUP("&f","",0.75,0.75,1,1,FALSE,FALSE)	
	=PRINT(1,,,1,,TRUE,1)	Print the range.
	=DELETE.NAME("Print_Area")	Delete *Print_Area*.
	=RETURN()	

FIGURE 14-1.
A macro for printing a specific range on a worksheet.

Also, notice that this version of the macro doesn't need FORMULA.GOTO() at the end to return the selection to its original position, because the selection is never moved.

Printing one of several named areas

To quickly specify one of several ranges that you want to print in a worksheet, you can use a dynamic name instead of a lengthy macro. For example, suppose you must frequently print one of twenty different areas on a sheet and that these areas are named *Print1* through *Print20*. To select one of these areas to print, you enter a number from 1 through 20 in a cell of the sheet, and then you choose File Print to print the area.

To do so, first assign any name to the cell that contains the number of the print range that you want to choose. Then, assuming that you name this cell *choice*, define the name *myPrintArea* as

```
=INDIRECT("Print"&choice):INDIRECT("Print"&choice)
```

Finally, define the name *Print_Area* as *=myPrintArea*. Now, to choose many of the 20 print ranges, enter the number of your choice in the *choice* cell, and then print.

If you want to print an area that doesn't have a print range assigned to it, specify the print area as you normally do. Then, when the printing is completed, redefine *Print_Area* as *=myPrintArea*.

Printing several areas

When you start to print several areas, print macros really start to save you time. The reason for this is that when a macro prints several areas, you can let the computer and printer do their jobs while you do something more interesting.

Suppose you have a worksheet containing three ranges to print, which are labeled *sales1*, *sales2*, and *sales3*. You can use two general methods to print these areas. First, you can define *Print_Area* to be the union of all three areas. Second, you can let a macro select and print each area.

Using the union operator to print multiple areas

To manually define the three areas as *Print_Area*, select all three ranges as a discontinuous selection by holding down the Ctrl key [Mac—also Command] and dragging across all three ranges. Then, to set the print area to this multiple selection, choose Options Set Print Area. To set the same print area in a macro, you could use the union operator in two formulas, as is done in this macro fragment:

```
=SELECT("sales1,sales2,sales3")
=SET.PRINT.AREA()
```

The major advantage to this approach is that it doesn't require special programming. However, it does have several disadvantages.

First, when you print the selection, each area prints using the same page setup. Second, page numbers count successively as all areas are printed. In our example, the printout for *sales3* would be on page 3. And third, all areas that are referenced by a *Print_Area* range must be on the same worksheet. If they aren't, Excel ignores *Print_Area* and prints the entire active worksheet.

Using a macro to print multiple areas

Another way to print multiple areas is to reference each area with a macro and then print each in turn. Perhaps the most straightforward way to do this is to define a generalized printing routine that accepts the name of a range and prints the range, as shown in Figure 14-2 on the following page.

cmd subr	**PrintRange**	Prints specified range.
	=ARGUMENT("pr.ref",8)	Get range ref.
	=DEFINE.NAME("Print_Area",pr.ref)	Transfer def of ref.
	=PRINT(1,,,1,,TRUE,1)	Print the range.
	=DELETE.NAME("Print_Area")	Delete *Print_Area*.
	=RETURN()	

cmd P	**PrintSalesRanges**	
	=PAGE.SETUP("&r&b&i&f","",0.75,0.75,1,1,f,f)	
	=PrintRange(!sales1)	
	=PAGE.SETUP("&r&b&iPage &p","",2,1,1,1,f,f)	
	=PrintRange(!sales2)	
	=PrintRange(!sales3)	
	=RETURN()	

FIGURE 14-2.
A command subroutine that prints a named range, and another routine that calls it with three different ranges.

Printing two separate areas on a worksheet on the same page.

No general-purpose way exists to do this. However, several workarounds are available.

- You can copy and paste one area so that it adjoins the other, or you can copy both areas to a new worksheet. (You might need to use the Paste Special command to paste values rather than formulas.) Then you print the new, combined, area.
- Set the column widths or row heights that separate these two areas to 0, making the two areas appear to be joined, and then print the sheet.
- Set one area as a Print Titles selection, and set the other as a Print Area selection.
- Print one area at the top of the page, and then put the same sheet of paper back in the printer and print the other area at the bottom. Although this technique sounds primitive, several companies known for their sophisticated reporting techniques often use it to combine text and graphics on the same printout.

The *PrintRange* routine is a variant of the one shown in Figure 14-1 on page 318, but we've added an ARGUMENT function and removed the PAGE.SETUP function. The *PrintSalesRanges* routine sets up each page, and then it calls *PrintRange* with the range to be printed.

If you wanted to make *PrintRange* even more general, you could add another argument called *pr.previewL* (for example) and change the PRINT formula to

```
=PRINT(1,,,1,,pr.previewL,1)
```

If *pr.previewL* is TRUE, the user sees a preview of the report instead of receiving the printed copy.

Printing from multiple sheets

So far, the examples have printed from only one sheet. We also can easily print from two or more sheets. The most direct way to do this is to develop a series of macros, similar to those shown in Figure 14-2, that activate each worksheet and then print a range on it. Often, however, you might simply want to prepare a list of documents and the printing parameters needed and to have one general-purpose macro print each of them in turn.

Figure 14-3 on the following page presents such a general-purpose macro, which uses a list of the macros containing the printing jobs to be run, in the format of the list shown in Figure 14-4 on the following page. This list describes the path, filename, and area to print, as well as the number of copies needed and the header and footer for the printed report. When you create this worksheet, define the name *data* as the range A3:F8.

The *PrintBatch* macro assumes that the active worksheet contains a range of data (named *data*) that describes each print job. The macro begins with the first line in the list, and it uses a series of INDEX functions to move information about each print job to the macro. Interestingly, the IF formulas in *pb.pageHeader* and *pb.pageFooter* are needed because without them, if the Header or Footer column of the batch-list table were blank, the INDEX formulas would return 0 rather than "" (empty text) to the macro sheet, and the printed report would contain 0 at the top or bottom of that report.

The formula in cell *pb.isOpen* checks whether the document in question is open: If open, the IF-ELSE-END.IF clause activates the document; if closed, the clause opens the document.

cmd B	**PrintBatch**	Prints areas from batch list.
pb.previewL	1	1 to preview, 0 to print.
pb.batchFile	=GET.DOCUMENT(1)	Active doc assumed batch list.
	=SET.NAME("pb.dataRef",TEXTREF(pb.batchFile&"!data"))	Get data range.
pb.dataRows	=ROWS(pb.dataRef)-1	Number of rows in data, less 1.
	=FOR("n",2,pb.dataRows)	Begin printing loop.
pb.filePath	= INDEX(pb.dataRef,n,1)	Path to file.
pb.fileName	= INDEX(pb.dataRef,n,2)	Filename.
pb.range	= INDEX(pb.dataRef,n,3)	Range in file to print.
pb.copies	= INDEX(pb.dataRef,n,4)	Number of copies.
pb.pageHeader	= IF(INDEX(pb.dataRef,n,5)<>0,INDEX(pb.dataRef,n,5),"")	Page Setup params.
pb.pageFooter	= IF(INDEX(pb.dataRef,n,6)<>0,INDEX(pb.dataRef,n,6),"")	
pb.isOpen	= ISNUMBER(MATCH(pb.fileName,DOCUMENTS(),0))	Is file already open?
	= IF(pb.isOpen)	If so,
	= ACTIVATE(pb.fileName)	activate it;
	= ELSE()	else,
	= OPEN(pb.filePath&pb.fileName)	open it.
	= END.IF()	
pb.extRef	= pb.fileName&"!"&pb.range	External ref of print range.
	= FORMULA.GOTO(INDIRECT(pb.extRef))	Select print range.
	= SET.PRINT.AREA()	Set the print area.
	= PAGE.SETUP(pb.pageHeader,pb.pageFooter)	
	= PRINT(1,,,pb.copies,FALSE,pb.previewL,1)	Print the file.
	= IF(NOT(pb.isOpen),CLOSE(FALSE))	Close file if not open at start.
	=NEXT()	
	=RETURN()	Quit.

FIGURE 14-3.
When used in combination with the database shown in Figure 14-4, this macro could print hundreds of documents without human intervention.

	A	B	C	D	E	F
1	*Print File Data*				*Page Setup parameters*	
2	**Path**	**File**	**Print Area**	**copies**	**header**	**footer**
3						
4	HardDisk:SalesReports:	FileA.xls	data1	1	&f	Page &p
5	HardDisk:SalesReports:	FileB.xls	A1:B4	1	Page &p	
6	HardDisk:InventoryReports:	FileC.xls	data2	10		&rPage &p
7	HardDisk:InventoryReports:	FileD.xls	data3	1		&rPage &p
8						

FIGURE 14-4.
The worksheet containing the batch list of printing jobs to be run. (This example is from the Macintosh environment.)

PrintBatch then selects the range in the document that is to be printed, and it uses the SET.PRINT.AREA function to define the name *Print_Area*. Next the PAGE.SETUP and PRINT formulas use the data returned from the batch list to set up and print the batch job. If *pb.previewL* was set to 1 at the beginning of the macro, the user sees a preview of each document instead. Finally, if the document was not already open when the macro was run, the document is closed without saving the changes made in it (that is, without saving the redefinition of *Print_Area* and the change in its Page Setup options).

This process continues until every report in the list is printed. If you need to maintain several batches of reports to print—to process a series of reports for a distribution list, for example—you can create a number of batch-list worksheets, and you can develop a macro that opens each batch list and then calls *PrintBatch,* once for each list.

We've tried to keep this macro fairly simple so that you can improve it in many ways. Here are a few ideas.

- *PrintBatch* doesn't determine whether the active document is a legal batch list that conforms to its requirements before beginning to extract data from it for printing. Instead of using the name *data* to define the range containing the batch list, you could use instead a less common name, such as *printBatchData,* check for its existence in the active document, and abort the macro if the name isn't defined.
- You could replace the contents of cell *pb.previewL* with an ALERT function that asks whether the user wants to preview or print each document, instead of requiring the user to enter the appropriate number in the cell.
- When the formula in cell *pb.isOpen* checks whether the specified document is already open, it's possible that another document with the same filename is open but that it's from a different directory. If this happened, *PrintBatch* would still print the document. You could use a formula containing GET.DOCUMENT(2) to check the path-name of the document as well as its filename.
- If no printing range were specified in the table, the macro should print the entire document or use the *Print_Area* that already exists in that document. However, the macro halts at the FORMULA.GOTO formula because the *pb.range* returned from the batch list is *0.* Instead, you could test for this condition and print the document without trying to select a range in it.

The print spooler on the PC can contain a maximum of 20 reports. Therefore, if you plan to print more than 20 reports in a batch, you must take special measures.

The safest approach is to disable the print spooler in the WIN.INI file. To do so, change the formula *spooler=yes* to *spooler=no* in the first few lines of the file.

Alternatively, insert a WAIT formula that suspends the macro for a while and gives the spooler a chance to empty. For example, suppose you want to print 30 reports and you know that it takes about an hour to print the first 15 of them. You could insert a formula such as this somewhere in the macro:

```
=IF(docCount=15,WAIT(NOW()+55/(24*60)))
```

This formula causes Excel to wait about 55 minutes after the fifteenth report is sent to the spooler. Doing so lets the spooler nearly empty before allowing the print macro to send it the next 15 reports.

15

Working with Files

Excel provides two groups of macro functions for working with files. The first group of functions are for opening, closing, and saving *normal files*—worksheets, macros, and charts. The second group of functions are for working with *text files;* these functions are easy to recognize because they all begin with the letter F: FOPEN, FCLOSE, FREAD, and so on.

In addition, two functions are available that apply to both classes of files; they help you navigate the drives and directories attached to your computer.

Getting around your disk drive

Excel provides two functions that help you get around your disk drive: FILES and DIRECTORY. Both serve as information functions, but you can also use DIRECTORY as an action-equivalent function.

The FILES function

The FILES function returns a horizontal text array of the names of up to 255 files in a specified directory. This function takes the form

FILES(*directoryT*)

where *directoryT* is the full pathname of a directory; if omitted, Excel returns the names of the files in the current directory.

It's often very helpful to use the TRANSPOSE function to convert the horizontal array returned by FILES to a vertical array, as in the following macro, which pastes into a macro sheet a list of the files contained in the current directory, starting at the active cell.

cmd f	**PasteFileList**	Pastes files in curr. directory.
pfl.filesN	=ROWS(TRANSPOSE(FILES()))	Number of files in directory.
	=SELECT("RC:R["&pfl.filesN-1&"]C")	Select a range to paste into.
	=FORMULA.ARRAY("=transpose(files())")	Enter the array formula.
	=COPY()	Copy it,
	=PASTE.SPECIAL(3)	and paste only the names.
	=RETURN()	

The ROWS function finds the number of files in the list, which is used in the SELECT formula to select a vertical range of cells. Next, *PasteFileList* enters an array formula that puts the list of files into the selected range. Finally, the macro copies the list and pastes only the values in it back into the same range.

You can also use in the argument to the FILES function the wildcard characters * (asterisk) and ? (question mark) to search for certain types of files. For example, in the PC versions of Excel you can use *.XLM to return a list of the macro sheets in the current directory. Unfortunately, because filenames in the Macintosh environment do not use file extension codes such as XLM and XLS, no comparable way exists to search for file types with the Macintosh version of the FILES function.

These wildcard characters work somewhat differently on the PC and Macintosh, as shown in the following examples.

On the Mac,

```
=FILES("*Chart")
```

returns an array of all files in the current directory that end in *Chart*, while

```
=FILES("*Chart*")
```

returns an array of all sheets that contain *Chart* anywhere in their name.

On the PC,

```
=FILES("*Chart*.*")
```

returns an array of all files in the current directory, whether or not they contain *Chart* in their names. This occurs because the beginning asterisk tells Excel to return every filename. As a result, you cannot use wildcard characters to look for embedded characters in a filename—unless you know the exact position of these characters, as in the following examples.

On the PC,

```
=FILES("???S*.XLM")
```

returns the names of all macro sheets in the current directory in which *S* is the fourth character in the filename.

On the Mac,

=FILES("???S*")

returns the names of all files in the current directory in which *S* is the fourth character in the filename.

On the PC,

=FILES("C:\BUDGETS\WEST*.XLS")

returns the names of all worksheets in the path shown that begin with the characters *WEST*.

On the Mac,

=FILES("Hard Disk:Budgets:West*")

returns the names of all files in the path shown that begin with *WEST*.

The DIRECTORY function

The DIRECTORY function changes the current drive and directory and returns the full pathname of what becomes the new current directory. This function takes the form

DIRECTORY(*pathT*)

where *pathT* specifies the directory; if omitted, Excel returns the full pathname of the current drive and directory.

On the PC, for example, the following macro fragment captures the full pathname of the current directory, changes the path to the root directory of drive C, stores an array of all files in that directory in the name *fileList*, and then returns to the original directory stored in the cell *currDirec*.

```
currDirec     =DIRECTORY()
              =DIRECTORY("C:\")
              =SET.NAME("fileList",FILES())
              =DIRECTORY(currDirec)
```

The DIRECTORY function works in the same way on the Macintosh when you provide *pathT* in the correct format. For example, the formula in the cell *currDirec* should read

```
currDirec     =DIRECTORY("Hard Disk:")
```

Other ways to get information about files and pathnames.

You can also use the DOCUMENTS function to get a list of the documents that are open in the Excel environment, and you can use

```
=GET.DOCUMENT(2,docNameT)
```

to get the full pathname of the active document where *docNameT* is the name of the document you want information about; if *docNameT* is omitted, Excel returns the full pathname of the active document.

Also, you can use the CELL standard worksheet function to find the full pathname of a document referred to by a reference. For example, the formula

```
=CELL("filename",BUDGET.XLS!data)
```

returns the full pathname of the BUDGET.XLS sheet.

To find the name of Excel's startup directory and the directory in which the Excel application is located, you can create a macro sheet containing an Auto_Open macro in Excel's startup directory and include the following macro:

cmd subr	**Auto_Open**	Startup auto-open macro.
ao.env	=GET.WORKSPACE(1)	
ao.pathDelim	=IF(LEFT(ao.env,3)="Mac",":","\")	If Mac, then ":", else "\".
ao.startupPath	=GET.WORKSPACE(23)&ao.pathDelim	Pathname of startup dir.
ao.excelPath	=DIRECTORY()&ao.pathDelim	Pathname of Excel's dir. at startup.
	=RETURN()	

When Excel starts, this Auto_Open macro is run before the environment becomes available to the user; the DIRECTORY function in it then returns the current directory, which is the same as the directory containing Excel. You can then use *ao.excelPath*, for example, to open any file that you know is stored in the same directory as Excel, regardless of which directory is the current directory.

Working with normal files

Excel's macro functions for handling normal files cover the tasks of finding your way around the floppy-disk and hard-disk drives attached to your system, opening documents, saving them, and deleting them.

Opening files

Excel provides two functions—NEW and OPEN—that open normal files and that behave as you might expect.

The NEW function

The NEW function corresponds to the File New command. This function opens a new worksheet, chart, or macro sheet, and it takes the form

NEW(*typeN,xySeriesN*)
NEW?(*typeN,xySeriesN*)

where *typeN* is the type of file to create, according to the following table.

typeN	Document
1	Worksheet.
2	Chart.
3	Macro sheet.
4	International macro sheet.
Quoted text	Template.
Omitted	The active sheet type.

If *typeN* is omitted, the same type of document as the currently active document is created. If you specify the name of a document instead of a number, Excel opens a template document from its startup directory having that name.

The *xySeriesN* argument applies only if *typeN* is 2, or the template document you're opening is a chart, and specifies the arrangement of data in the new chart from the currently selected range, according to the following table.

xySeriesN	Action
0	If the selection can be interpreted in more than one way, Excel displays a dialog box.
1 or omitted	First row or column contains the first data series.
3	First row or column contains the *x*-axis labels.
4	First row or column contains the *x*-values in an *xy* plot (scatter diagram).

The OPEN function

The OPEN function opens an existing file or workspace and corresponds to the File Open command. This function takes the form

**OPEN(fileT,*updateLinksN,readOnlyL,formatN,protPwdT,*
writeResPwdT,ignoreRORecL,fileOriginN)**
**OPEN?(*fileT,updateLinksN,readOnlyL,formatN,protPwdT,*
writeResPwdT,ignoreRORecL,fileOriginN)**

where *fileT* is the name of the file to open; the function can include a full pathname. You might want to specify the full pathname when you want to open a file without changing the current directory or when two files have the same name and you want to be sure you're opening the correct file.

In the dialog box form of the function you can use in *fileT* the same wildcard characters as in the FILES function described earlier in this chapter. On the PC, if the extension of the filename isn't specified, Excel looks for a worksheet having the name *fileT*.

The *updateLinksN* argument controls the updating of external and remote references, according to the following table.

updateLinksN	Action
0	Update neither external references (other sheets) nor remote references (other applications).
1	Update external references only.
2	Update remote references only.
3 or omitted	Update both.

The *readOnlyL* argument corresponds to the Read Only check box in the File Open dialog box: If TRUE, Excel opens the file as a read-only file; if FALSE or omitted, Excel opens the file normally.

If your macro is opening a text file, the *formatN* argument specifies whether the values to be placed in the cells of the new worksheet or macro sheet are delimited by tabs or commas: If 1 or omitted, tabs are used; if 2, commas are used.

If the file is password protected, the *protPwdT* argument must specify that password; if omitted, Excel displays a dialog box instructing the user to enter the password. Similarly, the *writeResPwdT* argument specifies the password needed in order for the user to make changes in a read-only file.

If the file is read-only recommended, the *ignoreRORecL* argument determines whether Excel displays its Read-Only Recommended dialog box; a value of TRUE suppresses display of the dialog box.

Finally, the *fileOriginN* argument describes the environment used to create the file, according to the following table.

fileOriginN	**Source environment**
1	Macintosh.
2	Windows (ANSI).
3	DOS or OS/2.
Omitted	Whichever is the current operating environment.

Macros can use various techniques to specify the name of a file to open. The following examples illustrate some common methods.

Inputting part of the filename

If the current directory contains files named BUDGET1, BUDGET2, BUDGET3, and so on, the following macro lets the user specify which file to open.

inputN	=INPUT("Enter number of budget file to open: 1, 2, or 3",1)
	=OPEN("BUDGET"&inputN,0)

Because the OPEN formula doesn't specify a filename extension, on the PC this formula would look for a worksheet having the specified name.

Looking up the filename

If the range *data* contains a code number in column A and a corresponding filename in column B, the following formula opens the file, assuming that *serialNum* is a valid code number:

```
=OPEN(VLOOKUP(data,serialNum,2),1)
```

This formula instructs Excel to update external references when the file is opened.

Opening a filename entered in the active cell

The following macro opens the file whose filename is entered in the active cell; it works well with the *PasteFileList* macro presented earlier in this chapter.

cmd o	**OpenSelected**	Opens filename in active cell.
os.actRef	=ACTIVE.CELL()	Text in active cell.
	=IF(ISNUMBER(GET.DOCUMENT(3,os.actRef)))	If doc is already open...
	= ALERT(os.actRef&" is already open.")	alert,
	= RETURN()	and quit.
	=END.IF()	
	=OPEN(myPath&os.actRef)	Otherwise, open the file.
	=RETURN()	

The ACTIVE.CELL formula returns the value in the currently selected cell to the macro sheet. The GET.DOCUMENT(3) function finds the type of the file: If the function evaluates to a number, a document having that name is already open, in which case the macro displays a dialog box to that effect and quits; if the file isn't already open, the OPEN formula opens it, using the file's pathname, which is stored in *myPath*.

Saving files

Excel provides three macro functions that are equivalent to the three methods for saving normal files: SAVE, SAVE.AS, and SAVE.WORKSPACE.

The SAVE function corresponds to the File Save command and takes no arguments. It saves the active document.

The SAVE.AS function corresponds to the File Save As command. This function takes the form

SAVE.AS(*documentT,typeN,protPwdT,backupL, writeResPwdT,readOnlyRecL*)

The *documentT* argument specifies the name of the document, which can include the full pathname if you want to save it in a directory other than the current directory; if omitted, Excel saves the active document.

The *typeN* argument sets the file type of the document to be saved, according to the table on the facing page.

The *protPwdT* argument specifies a password of 15 characters or less. The *writeResPwdT* argument sets a password that lets a user write to a file if it has been saved as a read-only file. The *readOnlyRecL* argument specifies whether to save the document as read-only recommended.

Finally, enter a *backupL* value of TRUE to create a backup document. Otherwise, enter FALSE or omit this argument.

For example,

```
=SAVE.AS(,5)
```

saves the current document as a WK1 file.

```
=SAVE.AS("Foo.TXT",3)
```

saves the document as text and names it *Foo.TXT.*

```
=SAVE.AS("Trash.XLS",1,"MyFile")
```

saves the document as a normal file, assigns the name *Trash.XLS*, and assigns the password *MyFile*.

typeN	Applies to...			File Type	Description
	work	macro	chart		
1	√	√	√	Normal	Normal format for worksheets, macro sheets, and charts.
2	√	√		SYLK	Coded text format for transfer to another worksheet or to another environment.
3	√	√		Text	Tab-delimited values as text.
4	√			WKS	Lotus 1-2-3 version 1A or Symphony.
5	√			WK1	Lotus 1-2-3 version 2 or Symphony.
6	√	√		CSV	Comma-separated values as text. On PCs, Excel adds the extension CSV.
7	√			DBF2	Transfer of range *Database* to dBASE II.
8	√			DBF3	Transfer of range *Database* to dBASE III.
9	√	√		DIF	Data-interchange format, for exchange of values with other spreadsheet programs, such as VisiCalc.
10				(reserved)	
11	√			DBF4	Transfer of range *Database* to dBASE IV.
12				(reserved)	
13				(reserved)	
14				(reserved)	
15	√			WK3	Lotus 1-2-3 version 3.
16	√	√	√	Excel 2.x	Excel 2.1 or 2.2 format.
17	√	√	√	Template	Normal templates; on PCs, Excel adds the extension XLT.
18		√		Add-In macro	Add-In macro sheet format. On PCs, Excel adds the extension XLA.
19	√	√		Text	Transfer of values to Macintosh.
20	√	√		Text	Transfer of values to Windows.
21	√	√		Text	Transfer of values to DOS or OS/2.
22	√	√		CSV	Comma-separated values for transfer to Macintosh.
23	√	√		CSV	Comma-separated values for transfer to Windows.
24	√	√		CSV	Comma-separated values for transfer to DOS or OS/2.
25		√		International macro	Add-In macro sheet format. On PCs, Excel adds the extension XLM.
26		√		International Add-In macro	International Add-In macro sheet format. On PCs, Excel adds the extension XLA.

The SAVE.WORKSPACE function

The SAVE.WORKSPACE function corresponds to the File Save Workspace command. This function takes the form

SAVE.WORKSPACE(*nameT*)
SAVE.WORKSPACE?(*nameT*)

The *nameT* argument can include the full pathname, such as *C:\SALES\JANSALES.XLS* on the PC or *Hard Disk:Sales:Jan Sales* on the Mac. If you omit the argument, Excel uses the name of the last-used workspace document, if there is one; otherwise, the program uses *RESUME.XLW* on the PC or *Resume* on the Mac. (If you use a startup workspace file, as described in the previous chapter, this will be the last-used workspace document.)

Saving hidden files

It's often convenient for macro sheets to be saved as hidden files. This allows you to run the sheets' macros and access their values without having those documents clutter the workspace.

To hide a document, activate it and choose Window Hide. To unhide the document, choose Window Unhide, select the document from the list, and press Enter.

You have three ways to save a document as a hidden file. First, you can hide the document and save your workspace. Then, when you open the workspace, the document opens as a hidden file.

Second, you can manually save a single file as a hidden file. To do so, first make any change to the document so that Excel knows to save the file. A quick way to do this is to press the Edit key [PC—F2; Mac—Command-V] or click on the formula bar and then press Enter. Then hide the file. Finally, hold down the Shift key and choose File Close All (or choose File Exit on the PC or File Quit on the Mac). When asked whether you want to save changes to the hidden document, answer yes. After you do so, the worksheet is saved as hidden.

Third, you can write a short macro to save the document after you have hidden it. For example, if the hidden document is named TEST.XLS, the following macro saves it:

```
=ACTIVATE("TEST.XLS")
=SAVE()
=RETURN()
```

Closing files

Excel provides three functions for closing files, but two of these are virtually identical.

The FILE.CLOSE function corresponds to the File Close command. This function takes the form

FILE.CLOSE(*saveL*)

If *saveL* is TRUE, Excel saves the file before closing it; if FALSE, Excel doesn't save the file; if omitted, Excel displays a dialog box asking whether the user wants to save the file.

The CLOSE function corresponds to the File Close command and closes the active window. This function takes the form

CLOSE(*saveL*)

If *saveL* is TRUE, the document is saved before it's closed; if FALSE, the document isn't saved. If *saveL* is omitted, and if your document has been changed since it was last saved, Excel displays a dialog box asking whether the user wants to save the document. If the active document has more than one active window, the CLOSE function closes the active window only.

The CLOSE.ALL function corresponds to the File Close All command. This function takes the form

CLOSE.ALL()

It closes all unprotected windows and all hidden windows; if the user has made changes in any of the open documents, Excel displays a dialog box asking whether the user wants to save the changes.

When you compare the performance of CLOSE with that of FILE.CLOSE, you see that these functions perform a similar task. To see the difference between them, first open a new worksheet, choose Window New Window to open another window on the same worksheet, and then choose Window New Window again to open a third window.

On the PC, close one of the windows by clicking on the control bar in the top-left corner of the active window and choosing Close. On the Mac, close the active window by clicking its Close box. The CLOSE function corresponds to these actions—it closes the active window.

Then, on either machine, choose File Close. When you do so, Excel closes the entire document, closing both of the remaining windows.

Excel provides no function that lets you close a document that isn't active. Nor does it provide a function that lets you close all windows without saving them; however, the following macro fragment lets you do so.

```
=FOR("n",1,COLUMNS(WINDOWS()))
=  ACTIVATE(INDEX(WINDOWS(),n))
=  CLOSE(FALSE)
=NEXT()
```

Alternatively, if you wanted to close all documents except macro sheets, you could use the DOCUMENTS function to step through each open document and use GET.DOCUMENT(3) to find the type of the document. If the type number returned isn't 3, the document is not a macro sheet, in which case you can use FILE.CLOSE to close the document.

I have a macro that opens a series of files from a list and continues until it can't find a file, and then performs other operations and quits. But when the macro tries to open a missing file, Excel displays an error message telling me that it can't find the file. When I select OK, it then gives me a macro error message. How can I make it do what I want?

You can use the ERROR function to control error checking. For example, the formula

```
=ERROR(FALSE)
```

turns off error checking entirely. The formula

```
=ERROR(TRUE,ref)
```

tells Excel where to resume operation when an error is encountered. The formula

```
=ERROR(TRUE)
```

resets error checking to normal operation.

To open a series of files, quitting when Excel encounters an error condition, use a series of formulas similar to the following:

```
loop        =ERROR(TRUE,fileError)
            =OPEN("your filename list ref")
            =ERROR(TRUE)
            :
            ...other macro formulas
            :
            =GOTO(loop)
fileError   =ERROR(TRUE)
            ...remaining macro formulas
```

Notice that *ERROR(TRUE)* appears not only where we handle the file error but also immediately after the OPEN function. When you modify error checking, reset it to normal operation as quickly as possible so that only the error you're expecting is trapped by the macro.

Deleting files

To delete a specified file, even if the file wasn't created by Excel, you can use the FILE.DELETE function, which corresponds to the File Delete command. This function takes the form

FILE.DELETE(fileT)
FILE.DELETE?(*fileT*)

The *fileT* argument, of course, is the name of the document to delete, which can include the file's complete pathname.

If Excel can't find the file, the program issues a macro error dialog box. To trap this error, you can use formulas such as

```
=ERROR(TRUE,NoFile())
=FILE.DELETE(thisFile)
=ERROR(TRUE)
```

Here, if the file stored in the name *thisFile* can't be found in the current directory, Excel branches to the *NoFile* routine, where the problem can be handled.

Working with text files

When the subject is text files, many users of Excel first ask, "Why should we use them?" rather than, "How should we use them?" Here, then, are five practical uses for text files.

- Each week, you download data from an information service as text and then open it in Excel. The problem, however, is that the file has grown too large to open as one worksheet. By using text-file functions, you can begin with a file of any size that your hard disk can hold, and you can create as many worksheets as necessary to contain the data.
- Occasionally, you might need to open a document created by a word processing program that you don't own. These files contain text and many word processing characters. You can use the text-file functions to read the document into a worksheet, use the CLEAN function to strip away the word processing characters, use the text-file functions again to create a new document without these characters, and then open the document using any word processing program you want.

- Many word processing programs do an excellent job of mail merging but a terrible job of managing mailing lists. You can keep mailing lists in Excel, use macros to select the names you want to send mail to, and then use text-file functions to create a mail-merge file for your word processor.
- Printing continuous mailing labels on the PC can be difficult. This is because Windows and the Program Manager don't allow you to suppress the formfeed that these programs provide at the end of each 11-inch page. However, you can print mailing labels using the text-file functions. You do so by fooling your computer into thinking that your printer is a text file. After you do so, you merely write to your printer exactly as you would write to a file.
- At times, macros need to store values for future reference. For example, a macro that generates invoices needs to store the last-used invoice number. Rather than saving the number on the macro sheet itself, it's much faster and easier for the macro to save the number as text in a separate small file.

First, we'll review the range of functions you can use to access text files, and then we'll present some applications for their use.

Functions for working with text files

Similar to the macro functions for working with normal files, the functions for working with text files offer a similar range of purposes: You can open files, read from them, and write to them. None of these functions are command-equivalents or action-equivalents, however.

You can use many of the macro functions for working with normal files with the text-file functions as well. For example, you can use the DIRECTORY function to change the current directory, the FILES function to get a list of the files in a directory, and the FILE.DELETE function to delete a temporary file after a macro has finished processing it.

Opening a text file

To open a text file, you use the FOPEN function. This function takes the form

FOPEN(fileT,*accessN*)

where *fileT* is the name of the file from which you want to read, including the drive and pathname if desired. The *accessN* argument specifies the type of access that should be given to the file, according to the following table.

accessN	Type of access
1 or omitted	Can both read the file and write to it.
2	Can only read the file.
3	Creates a new file with read/write permission.

In general, you should use an access number that will cause the least harm if you make a mistake. Because access number 2 provides read-only access to a file, use this number whenever you expect to only read a file. Access number 1 provides both read and write access; use this number when you plan to write to an existing file.

Access number 3 serves two purposes. If you open a text file that doesn't exist, this access number creates the file for you and then opens it. However, if the file already exists, access number 3 erases the file when it is opened.

If Excel can't open the file, because it expects a preexisting file that doesn't exist, or because the file is already open in another application, for example, it returns #N/A to the cell containing the FOPEN function.

If Excel successfully opens the file, it returns to the cell a number that uniquely identifies the file. In a sense, this number becomes the file's "name" in any other operation done on the file. For example, to write data to the file, you must specify not the name of the file but its file number. For this reason, you should generally use FOPEN in a construction such as the following:

```
fileNumber      =FOPEN("MyFile")
```

Any subsequent formula that uses the file would then refer to it by the number stored in the name *fileNumber*.

Reading from a text file

Two functions are available for reading text from a file: FREAD and FREADLN. The FREAD function reads a specified number of characters from a file. This function takes the form

FREAD(fileN,numChars)

where *fileN* is the number of the file you want to read from (returned by the FOPEN function), and *numChars* is the number of characters you want to read, starting at the current position in the file. When first opened, this position is the first character in the file; as characters are read from the file, the current position in the file is incremented by the number of characters read.

If Excel can't read the file, it returns #N/A to the formula containing the FREAD function. Typically, this happens because the current file position is at the end of the file: When the total number of characters read is equal to the length of the file, the current file position is at the end of the file, and there are no more characters to read.

If Excel reads the file successfully, it returns the text (up to 255 characters) to the formula containing the FREAD function.

The FREADLN function is very similar to FREAD, but it reads entire lines of text from the source file, starting at the current file position. This function takes the form

FREADLN(fileN)

where *fileN* is the number of the file returned by a previously executed FOPEN function. Generally, you'll use this function more often than FREAD because the main use for the file functions is to read records having a fixed length, such as those exported from a database.

What constitutes the end of a line of text varies with the operating environment and application used to create the text file. In the PC versions of Excel, this is typically a carriage-return character (ASCII 13) and a linefeed character (ASCII 10). In the Macintosh version of Excel, the line's end is typically marked by a carriage-return character only.

Writing to a text file

Two functions are available for writing to a file: FWRITE and FWRITELN. The FWRITE function writes a specified number of characters to a file. This function takes the form

FWRITE(fileN,text)

where *fileN* is the file number of the file you want to write to, and *text* is the text you want to write. The text is written starting at the current file position. If successful, Excel returns the number of characters written to the formula containing the function.

The FWRITELN function operates in the same way that FWRITE does. This function takes the form

FWRITELN(fileN,text)

The only difference between FWRITE and FWRITELN is that the latter adds a carriage return (and, in the PC versions of Excel, a linefeed).

Finding the size of a text file

You can use the FSIZE function in a macro to find the size of a file. This function takes the form

FSIZE(*fileN*)

where *fileN* is the file's number. When Excel encounters this function, it returns the size of the open file, in characters, to the formula containing the function.

For example, the following subroutine macro returns the size of a file, given the file's name.

cmd subr	**GetFileSize**	Returns size of a file.
	=ARGUMENT("gfs.filename")	Get filename.
gfs.fileN	=FOPEN(gfs.filename,2)	Open it.
gfs.fileSize	=FSIZE(gfs.fileN)	Get its size.
	=FCLOSE(gfs.fileN)	Close it.
	=RETURN(gfs.fileSize)	

cmd subr	**TestGetFileSize**	Tests the subroutine.
	=GetFileSize("Worksheet1")	
	=RETURN()	

This size corresponds to the size shown on the PC when you enter *dir* at the DOS prompt or on the Macintosh when you view the files by size in the Finder.

Setting the current file position

As mentioned earlier, many of Excel's file operations are made relative to the current file position, which marks the next position after the last character either written to or read from a file. When a function writes to or reads from a file, it begins at the new position. You can think of the file position as a bookmark: With a book, you start at the beginning and then insert a bookmark when you must stop temporarily; when you resume, you do so at the position of the bookmark.

The FPOS function takes the form

FPOS(fileN,*positionN*)

where *fileN* is the number of the file returned by the FOPEN function. The *positionN* argument is the new position in the file; a value of 1 would set the current file position to the beginning of the file, and the number returned by FSIZE would be the end of the file. However, if you omit *positionN*, the function returns the current file position.

Closing a text file

To close an open text file, use the FCLOSE function, which takes the form

FCLOSE(fileN)

where *fileN* is a file number. This function and FILE.CLOSE are not interchangeable; the latter is for closing an active document, not an open text file.

After my macro opened a text file, it encountered an error that stopped the macro. Therefore, the macro never closed the file. Is this a problem?

It could be. Text files don't close when a macro stops because of an error. Depending on what you're doing with the file, failing to close it can reduce the total number of files that you can open during a session, consume extra memory, or even destroy data in the file. Failing to close a file can also prevent a macro from being able to open the file again—because the file is still open. To handle this problem, you can use the following macro to close the file.

cmd subr	**CloseFileNum**	Closes a file, given its number.
	=ARGUMENT("cfn.fileN")	
	=FCLOSE(cfn.fileN)	
	=RETURN()	

You could create an error-handling routine that calls this macro, passing it the number of the file you want to close. If the file closes successfully, nothing appears to happen. However, if you try to close a file that isn't open, you'll get a macro error dialog box. If this is a problem for your application, you can insert an ERROR(FALSE) formula before the FCLOSE function and an ERROR(TRUE) after it—as in the following macro, which closes all open files up through the tenth file.

cmd C	**CloseAllFiles**	Closes all open files, up to #10.
	=ERROR(FALSE)	
	=FOR("n",0,10)	
	= FCLOSE(n)	Close file # n.
	=NEXT()	
	=ERROR(TRUE)	
	=RETURN()	

Reading and writing lines of text

When you read from and write to a text file, you'll usually work with lines of text rather than with individual characters. You'll therefore use the functions FREADLN and FWRITELN. To see how these functions work, let's begin by creating a text file. Any text will do, but we'll assume you're using the text shown in Figure 15-1. Enter it into a worksheet as shown, and save it first as a worksheet (named POEM.XLS) and then as a text file (named POEM.TXT).

	A
1	Hear the voice of the Bard!
2	Who Present, Past, & Future sees
3	Whose ears have heard,
4	The Holy Word,
5	That walk'd among the ancient trees.
6	...William Blake, The Songs of Experience

FIGURE 15-1.
Sample text for experimenting with text files.

Although it isn't necessary, you can close the file at this point. Doing so helps to emphasize that text-file functions work directly with data on your disk, not with a copy of the file in memory.

Using the FREADLN function

To read the POEM.TXT file, let's create a macro that reads the text file, entering one line into each cell of a vertical range, beginning with the active cell, as follows:

cmd F	**InsertTextFile**	Inserts text file at active cell.
itf.fileN	=FOPEN("POEM.TXT")	Open text file.
itf.fSize	=FSIZE(itf.fileN)	
	=WHILE(FPOS(itf.fileN)<itf.fSize)	Until end of file...
itf.lineT	= FREADLN(itf.fileN)	read a line,
	= FORMULA(itf.lineT)	enter it into active cell,
	= SELECT("R[1]C")	move one cell down.
	=NEXT()	
	=FCLOSE(itf.fileN)	Close file.
	=RETURN()	

If you then open a new worksheet, select cell B6, and run the *InsertTextFile* macro, you'll see the following text appear in the worksheet.

	B
6	Hear the voice of the Bard!
7	"Who Present, Past, & Future sees"
8	"Whose ears have heard,"
9	"The Holy Word,"
10	That walk'd among the ancient trees.
11	"...William Blake, The Songs of Experience"

The formula in the cell *fileN* opens the file POEM.TXT for access. If this is the first file you've opened and you switch to Values view, you'll see that Excel has assigned the number 0 to this file. The next file to be opened would be assigned 1, the next 2, and so on.

The cell *itf.fSize* contains the size of the file, in characters, that is used in the WHILE formula to control the number of lines read. If the current file position is before the end of the file, the FREADLN formula gets a line of text and enters it into the active cell. The SELECT formula then moves the active cell down one cell, and the WHILE loop gets another line of text. Finally, the macro closes the file.

Note that some of the lines retrieved from the file are surrounded by double quotation marks, an artifact of saving the file in Excel's Text format: Every line containing a comma is surrounded by quotes. To avoid this, use a word processor to open the file, remove the quotes, and save the file in the ASCII file format.

One of the problems with this macro is a result of Excel allowing no more than 255 characters in a cell: If a line contains more than 255 characters, such as in a long paragraph of a word processing text file, the excess characters will disappear when the text is transferred to the worksheet. To get around this problem, you would have to use the FREAD function to retrieve fixed-length blocks of text and develop a macro to search for period characters (for example) and to reassemble the text in sentences instead of lines.

Using the FWRITELN function

The FWRITELN function writes a line of text to a text file. Using this function provides more power and flexibility than merely saving a file as a text file. For example, you can use FWRITELN to save selected cells from a worksheet, rather than saving the whole file as a text file; you can save text that contains commas without having to put quotes around the text; and you can save single values to a file.

To illustrate FWRITELN, suppose a macro system prints your company's invoices. The following macro fragment uses FREADLN to get the last-used invoice number from the text file INVNUM.TXT. The macro then increases the invoice number by 1 and stores it in the name *invNum*.

cmd subr	**GetNextInvNum**	Gets next invoice number.
gni.fileN	=FOPEN("INVNUM.TXT",2)	Open record file.
	invNum=FREADLN(gni.fileN)+1	Increment number.
	=FCLOSE(gni.fileN)	Close file.
	=RETURN()	

After another macro generates the invoice, the following macro fragment uses FWRITELN to save the last-used invoice number back to INVNUM.TXT.

cmd subr	**SaveInvNum**	Records current inv. number.
sin.fileN	=FOPEN("INVNUM.TXT",3)	Open file.
	=FWRITELN(sin.fileN,invNum)	Replace invoice number.
	=FCLOSE(sin.fileN)	Close file.
	=RETURN()	

Working with number formats and FWRITELN

When FWRITELN writes a numeric value to a text file, it writes the unformatted value: dates as their date serial numbers, percentages as decimal numbers, and currency values without dollar signs or commas. However, this is usually an easy problem to solve. You simply need to convert numbers to text before writing them to the text file.

Suppose, for example, that you want to write the formatted number in the active cell to a text file. The following formulas write the unformatted number.

```
fileN          =FOPEN("MYFILE.TXT",1)
               =FWRITELN(fileN,ACTIVE.CELL())
```

The following fragment, however, preserves the number's format.

```
fileN          =FOPEN("MYFILE.TXT",1)
thisFormat     =GET.CELL(7,ACTIVE.CELL())
thisText       =TEXT(ACTIVE.CELL(),thisFormat)
               =FWRITELN(fileN,thisText)
```

The cell *thisFormat* returns the number format of the active cell as text. The cell *thisText* uses this information to return the contents of the active cell in properly formatted text, and the FWRITELN formula writes this text to the file.

When you use this technique, however, you must test for two conditions. First, test whether the active cell contains a number. If it does not contain a number, write the cell contents using the unformatted approach. The reason for this is that blanks are written as zeros if you use the formatted approach, unless you specifically create a number format that does not diplay zeros.

Second, because the TEXT function cannot use the General or repeating number formats, you must test for each of these formats and then use the unformatted approach when you encounter them. Because doing so can often make these numbers look different than they do in the worksheet, it's a good idea to alert the user when these formats are found.

Reading and writing blocks of characters

The functions FREAD and FWRITE offer more power for use with text files than their line-oriented counterparts because they're more general. The *ReadFileChars* macro below contains the FREAD function, analogous to FREADLN except that you control the number of characters read.

cmd subr	**ReadFileChars**	Reads sample file by chars.
rfc.fileN	=FOPEN("POEM.TXT")	Open file.
rfc.fSize	=FSIZE(rfc.fileN)	Size of file.
	=FORMULA(FREAD(rfc.fileN,rfc.fSize))	Put entire file into active cell.
	=FCLOSE(rfc.fileN)	Close file.
	=RETURN()	

If you select cell B6 in a worksheet and run the macro, you'll see the following text appear, assuming you've given the cell Wrapped Text alignment.

	B
6	Hear the voice of the Bard! "Who Present, Past, & Future sees" "Whose ears have heard," "The Holy Word," That walk'd among the ancient trees. "...William Blake, The Songs of Experience"

This macro first opens the POEM.TXT file. The FSIZE function returns the size of the file. The formula in the next cell reads the entire file and enters the text into the active cell. Finally, the macro closes the file and quits.

This macro illustrates the major difference between FREADLN and FREAD. FREADLN reads only to the end of a line, whereas FREAD can read as many characters as you specify (up to 255 characters), including the characters that mark the end of each line. Text files generated in PC applications typically end lines with a carriage-return character (ASCII 13) and a linefeed character (ASCII 10); text files generated in Macintosh applications typically end lines with only the carriage return.

Cleaning word processing characters from a file

The following macro reads a stream of characters from a file, removes any unprintable characters that it finds (such as carriage returns, linefeeds, and word processing codes), and then writes the characters to a new file. The macro also breaks word processing text into a series of sentences, one to a line; this represents one way to deal with FREADLN's inability to read lines of more than 255 characters.

cmd subr	**CleanFile**	Cleans up imported text file.
	=ARGUMENT("cf.oldFile")	Get name of old file.
	=ARGUMENT("cf.newFile")	Get name of new file.
	=ECHO(FALSE)	
cf.isPC	=NOT(LEFT(GET.WORKSPACE(1),3)="Mac")	Running a PC version?
cf.endSent	!?.	Chars that end sentence.
cf.endLine	=CHAR(13)&IF(cf.isPC,CHAR(11),"")	CR + LF (if PC).
cf.oldFileN	=FOPEN(cf.oldFile,2)	Open old file.
cf.newFileN	=FOPEN(cf.newFile,3)	Open new file.
cf.oldSize	=FSIZE(cf.oldFileN)	Size of old file.
	=FOR("n",1,cf.oldSize)	For each char in old file...
	= MESSAGE(TRUE,"Reading char "&n&" of "&cf.oldSize)	Display msg (delete after debug).
	cf.oldText=FREAD(cf.oldFileN,1)	Read one char.
	= IF(CODE("cf.oldText")=13)	If it's a CR,
	= FWRITE(cf.newFileN," ")	write a space.
	= ELSE()	else,
	= FWRITE(cf.newFileN,CLEAN(cf.oldText))	write the cleaned char.
	= END.IF()	
	= IF(ISNUMBER(SEARCH(cf.oldText,cf.endSent)))	If we want to break line,
	= FWRITE(cf.newFileN,cf.endLine)	write end-of-line codes.
	= END.IF()	
	=NEXT()	Next char.
	=FCLOSE(cf.oldFileN)	Close old file.
	=FCLOSE(cf.newFileN)	Close new file.
	=MESSAGE(FALSE)	Restore status bar.
	=RETURN()	Return.

cmd X	**TestCleanFile**	Tests CleanFile.
	=CleanFile("POEM.TXT","POEM2.TXT")	
	=RETURN()	

The *CleanFile* macro takes the names of the old file and a new file passed to it through the ARGUMENT functions. The formula in the cell *cf.isPC* determines whether we're running the PC version (as opposed to the Mac version) of Excel; if we are, we want to end lines with a linefeed as well as a carriage return.

The cell *cf.endSent* contains a text string that sets the characters constituting an end of a sentence; you could make this variable an argument to the macro, to break a file into lines based on any other set of characters passed to the routine. Next, the macro opens the source file with read-only access and creates a new file given the name passed to the routine.

The core of the macro is the FOR-NEXT loop, which reads each character in the file. The first IF-ELSE-END.IF clause tests whether the character is a carriage return. If so, the macro writes a space character to the file; if not, it writes the cleaned version of the character, removing nonprinting characters. The subsequent IF-END.IF clause tests whether the character is one of the characters at which we want to end a line, by searching for the character in *cf.sent*; if so, the macro writes to the file the appropriate characters for ending a line as defined by *cf.endLine*. Finally, the macro closes both files.

Adding data to the end of a file

All the preceding examples wrote to the beginning of a text file. Often, however, you'll want to append data to an existing text file. To do this, simply set the file position to the next character after the end of the file. This position is 1 plus the size of the file, as shown in the following macro fragment, where SAMPLE.TXT is the file to which you want to append data.

```
fileN     =FOPEN("SAMPLE.TXT",1)
          =FPOS(fileN,FSIZE(fileN)+1)
          =FWRITELN(fileN,"New text for the file")
```

Erasing a text file intentionally

At times, you want to erase an existing file before you write to it. For example, if you use a text file to record the last date on which payroll checks were printed, you might want to replace the date *February 15, 1992* with *March 1, 1992*. However, if you fail to erase the file before you write the new date to it, you'll get unexpected results, as the following series of formulas demonstrates.

```
fileN=FOPEN("SAMPLE.TXT",3)
=FWRITELN(fileN,"February 15, 1992")
=FCLOSE(fileN)
```

This section of the macro opens the file, writes the beginning date to the file, and then closes it. No problem so far.

```
fileN=FOPEN("SAMPLE.TXT",1)
=FWRITELN(fileN,"March 1, 1990")
=FCLOSE(fileN)
```

The cell *fileN* opens the file for read/write access. The FWRITELN formula writes the new date on top of the old date, and then we close the file again. To see the results of this activity, let's continue.

```
fileN=FOPEN("SAMPLE.TXT",2)
=FREAD(fileN,FSIZE(fileN))
=FCLOSE(fileN)
=RETURN()
```

Because we don't plan to write to the file at this point, we use an access number of 2. The next formula reads the entire file, and then we close it. To see the results in the cell containing the FREAD formula, switch to Values view. If you're running Excel on a PC, you'll see

March 1, 1990(CR)(LF)90(CR)(LF)

If you're running Excel on the Mac, you'll see

March 1, 1990(CR)990(CR)

Here *(CR)* stands for the carriage-return character and *(LF)* stands for the linefeed character.

In other words, when the FWRITELN function writes to an area of a text file that already exists, it replaces only the characters that it must, and it leaves undisturbed other characters in the file. Here it replaced most of the characters in a long date with a shorter date, leaving the last few characters of the long date undisturbed.

Therefore, in this instance, you need to change the access number from *1* to *3*. Doing so erases the data from the existing file so that the shorter date can take up exclusive residence in the file.

Creating a file only when it doesn't already exist

At times, you'll want a macro to create a text file only if it doesn't already exist. The following macro illustrates a simple method for testing for the existence of a specified file.

cmd subr	**FileExists**	Returns TRUE if file exists.
	=ARGUMENT("fe.fileT")	Name of file.
	=ERROR(FALSE)	Turn off error checking.
fe.fileN	=FOPEN(fe.fileT)	Open file.
	=FCLOSE(fe.fileN)	Close file.
	=ERROR(TRUE)	Turn on error checking.
	=RETURN(NOT(ISERROR(fe.fileN)))	If no file, return FALSE.

cmd subr	**TestFileExists**	
tfe.fileT	POEM3.TXT	Name of file.
	=IF(FileExists(tfe.fileT))	If it exists,
	= ALERT("File already exists!",3)	alert;
	=ELSE()	else,
tfe.fileN	= FOPEN(tfe.fileT,3)	open file,
	= FWRITELN(tfe.fileN,"Sample text.")	write sample text,
	= FCLOSE(tfe.fileN)	close file.
	=END.IF()	
	=RETURN()	

If the file passed to the *FileExists* macro doesn't exist, Excel does not return an error dialog box, but *fe.fileN* evaluates to #N/A, and the macro returns TRUE. If the file does exist, the macro opens it, closes it, and returns FALSE.

My printer has a paper sorter attached to it. When I use other software, I can send all output to a particular bin by sending special codes to the printer. Can I do the same thing in Excel?

You can send setup codes to a given printer from a PC but not from a Macintosh. On the PC, you can use the text-file functions to send setup codes and data directly to a printer. For example, you could use the following macro fragment to send the setup code for a particular sorter bin.

fileN	=FOPEN("LPT1",1)	Open file.
	=FWRITE(fileN,setupCodeText)	Write codes.
	=FCLOSE(fileN)	Close file.

16

Speeding Up Your Macros

Your new macro is working perfectly. A job that used to take 2 hours to do manually now takes 10 minutes to do with your macro. Everyone's thrilled for about a day and a half, and then someone says, "Can't this thing run any faster?"

Yes, your macro probably can run faster. This chapter discusses the many steps you can take to optimize your macros for speed. Most of these tips are "free," in the sense that you sacrifice nothing to use them, other than the time you take to implement them. However, a number of these tips are not free because they force you to choose between speed and readability.

Think three times before you choose speed over readability, for two important reasons. First, macros that are easy to read tend to have fewer errors than those that are difficult to decipher. Second, you and your successors can maintain readable macros much more easily over the long haul than those that are optimized for speed at the expense of clarity. Thus, well structured, well documented, readable macros have their own kind of speed—ease of development and support.

Benchmarking macros

As you write macros, alternative methods will often occur to you, and you'll wonder whether one method is significantly faster than another. You can experiment to determine which method is faster. The concept is simple: You time the two methods, and the one that takes the least amount of time is the faster. The benchmarking macro shown in Figure 16-1 embodies this procedure for measuring macro performance.

cmd X	**Benchmark**	Time to execute N iterations.
b1.iterations	500	
	=ECHO(FALSE)	
b1.start1	=NOW()	***Test #1***
	=FOR("n",1,b1.iterations,1)	Testing loop 1.
	:	
	...first routine you want to test	
	:	
	=NEXT()	
b.end1	=NOW()	
b.time1	=(b.end1-b.start1)*24*60*60	
	=FORMULA(b.time1)	Enter time1.
	=SELECT("R[1]C")	Move down one cell.
b.start2	=NOW()	***Test #2***
	=FOR("n",1,b.iterations,1)	Testing loop 2.
	:	
	...second routine you want to test	
	:	
	=NEXT()	
b.end2	=NOW()	
b.time2	=(b.end2-b.start2)*24*60*60	
	=FORMULA(b.time2)	
	=RETURN()	

FIGURE 16-1.
Use this macro to compare the execution speeds of different routines.

As you can see, this macro contains two FOR-NEXT loops, each of which is preceded and followed by a NOW formula. When Excel executes each of these formulas, the effect is that of taking a snapshot at the moment of execution. The FORMULA formula after the first loop enters the difference between the starting time and the ending time in the active cell, and the SELECT formula moves the active cell down one cell. The FORMULA formula after the second loop also enters the time needed to execute its FOR-NEXT loop, and it enters the result in the cell below the first measurement.

Let's experiment with *Benchmark* by determining whether blank lines significantly slow the execution of a macro. First, prepare the macro by deleting the rows between the first FOR and the first NEXT in the macro shown in Figure 16-1, leaving an empty FOR-NEXT loop. Also, delete two of the three lines in the second FOR-NEXT loop, and delete the contents of the single cell remaining in the loop.

Next, prepare a worksheet similar to the one shown in Figure 16-2 for receiving the data.

	A	B	C	D
1			trial 1	
2	Empty FOR-NEXT loop	time1		
3	FOR-NEXT loop with one blank line	time2		
4		time2-time1		
5		% difference		
6		sec/cycle		

FIGURE 16-2.
Worksheet table for calculating the differences in time between two routines.

In cells C4:C6, enter the formulas as shown here.

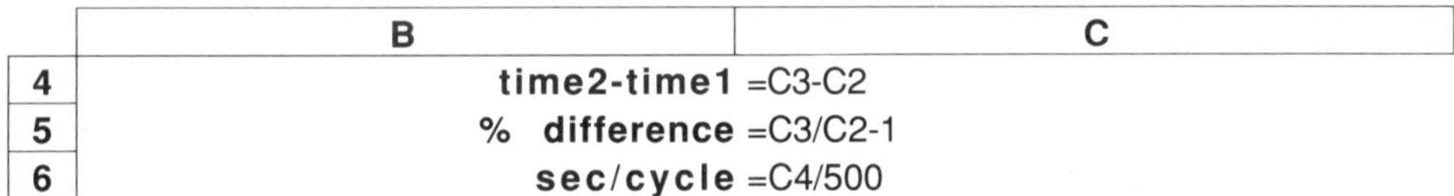

	B	C
4	time2-time1	=C3-C2
5	% difference	=C3/C2-1
6	sec/cycle	=C4/500

The formula in cell C4 measures the difference, in seconds, between the two routines. The formula in cell C5 expresses this difference as a percentage. The formula in cell C6 is perhaps the most important of the three because it divides the time difference by the number of iterations (in this case, 500), resulting in a measurement of how much more time it takes to perform the second loop over the first, in seconds.

If you then select cell C2 and press (in this case) Ctrl-X [Mac—also Command-Option-X], the *Benchmark* macro enters the first time in cell C2 and the second time in cell C3. You can copy the formulas in cells C4:C6 several cells to the right and run the test repeatedly. Running the above test five times generates the following statistics (for a Macintosh IIsi):

	trial 1	trial 2	trial 3	trial 4	trial 5
time1	4	4	5	5	4
time2	6	6	6	6	7
time2-time1	2	2	1	1	3
% difference	50%	50%	20%	20%	75%
sec/cycle	0.004	0.004	0.002	0.002	0.006

One of the first things to notice is the intrinsic inaccuracy in the way the macro reports the execution times. This happens because the NOW function is accurate only to increments of a second, plus or minus a minor variation due to the fact that it stores numbers accurate to 15 significant digits. Consequently, you should be sure that the number of iterations you use to test a routine is large enough to make an increment of one second small by comparison.

Alternatively, you could use the ON.TIME function to develop a macro that runs for a fixed period of time and count the number of iterations executed in that period of time. For example, if Excel were able to execute a loop 452 times in a 5-second period, this would result in a time of 0.0111 second per cycle.

In any case, Excel seems to take about four-thousandths of a second (0.004 sec) to process an empty cell in a macro. Is this a significant amount of time? Not usually: If you inserted an empty cell inside a loop that processes the contents of 1000 cells, you would slow the macro by roughly 4 seconds. If you inserted an empty cell outside the loop in the same macro, no one would notice the difference.

The moral is: Rather than spending time to shave another fraction of a second off a macro, you should usually spend it to document the macro more carefully. This documentation could save users many hours of work and frustration when they try to use the macro, and it could save you many hours of study when you need to modify the macro months after you wrote it.

Tips for speeding up macros

This section provides a number of tips for making your macros run faster. Some of these tips are obvious, and some are not.

Minimize file operations

Most macro formulas take but a fraction of a second to execute. However, Excel might take several seconds to close a file and nearly a minute to open a file. Large, complicated worksheets can take many minutes to recalculate and save because worksheets recalculate before they're saved.

Therefore, to speed up macros, try to minimize file operations. Also, if your macro must frequently save data to a file, you can often write the data to a text file rather than to a normal file, as described in the previous chapter. Doing so takes much less time than does saving a normal file.

Minimize screen motion

Because any motion on your screen slows a macro significantly, avoid screen motion wherever possible. For example, minimizing screen motion can take the forms of eliminating or reducing unnecessary activation of documents and of eliminating screen updating after every editing operation completed.

Use references instead of ACTIVATE or SELECT

Excel takes a long time to activate and update the contents of a window and a relatively long time to select a new cell in the same window. Therefore, whenever possible, use references instead of using ACTIVATE or SELECT.

For example, suppose you want to enter the value *99* into cell B2 of Sheet1. You might be tempted to use a macro fragment such as the following:

	A	B
1		=ACTIVATE("Sheet1")
2		=SELECT("R2C2")
3		=FORMULA(99)

If you simply insert these three lines of code in the previous *Benchmark* macro, Excel activates the same sheet over and over. It also inserts the execution time of the second loop on Sheet1. If the specified document window is already activated, Excel doesn't need to update the screen, and the code runs in about 0.8 second.

However, you can force Excel to reveal a document window in each activation by using the following code in a slightly modified *Benchmark* macro.

cmd X	**Benchmark**	Benchmarking for short processes.
b1.iterations	=ACTIVE.CELL()	Get num. of iterations from BENCH.XLS.
b1.start1	=NOW()	***Test #1***
	=FOR("n",1,b1.iterations,1)	Reference loop.
	=NEXT()	
b1.end1	=NOW()	
b1.time1	=(b1.end1-b1.start1)*24*60*60	Calc time between NOWs.
b1.start2	=NOW()	***Test #2***
	=FOR("n",1,b1.iterations,1)	Testing loop.
	=ACTIVATE("Sheet1")	Activate first sheet.
	=SELECT("R2C2")	
	=FORMULA(99)	Enter a number.
	=ACTIVATE("Sheet2")	
	=SELECT("R2C2")	
	=FORMULA(99)	
	=NEXT()	
b1.end2	=NOW()	
b1.time2	=(b1.end2-b1.start2)*24*60*60	Calc time between NOWs.
	=ACTIVATE("BENCH.XLS")	Activate benchmark result sheet.
	=SELECT("R[1]C")	Move down one cell.
	=FORMULA(b1.time1)	Enter time1.
	=SELECT("R[1]C")	Move down one cell.
	=FORMULA(b1.time2)	Enter time2.
	=RETURN()	

In this case, the macro updates Sheet1 and then Sheet2 in every loop, forcing Excel to update each window. (You can also experiment with overlapping the windows to change the region of the screen updated.)

We've also inserted an ACTIVE.CELL formula to take the number of iterations from a worksheet named BENCH.XLS, and we've moved to the end of the macro the formulas for entering the execution times in the following table into the worksheet.

	B	C	D	E	F	G	H
25		trial 1					
26	iterations	100	<< Enter the number of iterations to test.				
27	time1: empty loop	1	<< The macro enters the first loop time here,				
28	time2: test loop	124	<< and the second loop time here.				
29	time2-time1	123	<< Formula: =C28-C27				
30	sec/cycle	1.23	<< Formula: =C29/C26				

To use the macro with this table (for example), enter the number of iterations to run in cell C26, and run the macro: It executes both loops and enters the execution times into the two cells below. As shown in the table, running this code on a Mac IIcx results in a cycle time of about 1.23 seconds, but because there are two screen updates per loop, we should divide this number by 2 to get the time required for updating one sheet, or about 0.61 second.

On the other hand, you can use an external reference in a FORMULA function to enter the data on a sheet without having to activate the sheet beforehand, as shown here:

	A	B
1		=FORMULA(99,"Sheet1!R2C2")

The following tables compare the three methods.

Testing value entry using one activation.

```
=ACTIVATE("Sheet1")
=SELECT("R2C2")
=FORMULA(99)
```

iterations	500
time1: empty loop	7
time2: test loop	70
time2-time1	63
sec/cycle	0.126

Testing value entry using two activations.

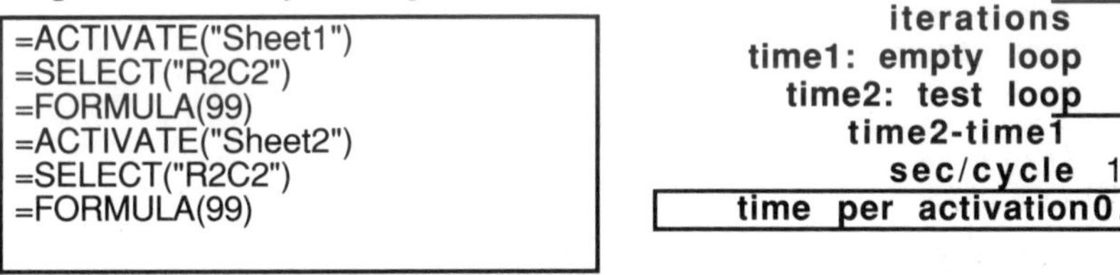

```
=ACTIVATE("Sheet1")
=SELECT("R2C2")
=FORMULA(99)
=ACTIVATE("Sheet2")
=SELECT("R2C2")
=FORMULA(99)
```

iterations	500
time1: empty loop	7
time2: test loop	732
time2-time1	725
sec/cycle	1.450
time per activation	0.725

Testing value entry using FORMULA.

```
=FORMULA(99,"Sheet1!R2C2")
```

iterations	500
time1: empty loop	7
time2: test loop	49
time2-time1	42
sec/cycle	0.084

As you can see, there's almost a 10-to-1 difference in speed between the slowest and the fastest methods. If you're transferring many values from one sheet to another, the fastest can amount to a substantial savings in time.

Use ECHO(FALSE)

Because Excel takes a long time to update your screen, setting ECHO to FALSE to freeze the screen can speed up macro execution by a factor of 10 or more, depending on the computer you're using and the number and complexity of the windows in the Excel workspace.

Use HIDE

At times, you might want to see what's happening on a worksheet while a macro acts on other sheets that you don't need to see. You can use the HIDE function to hide such sheets. When your macro moves frequently from one sheet to another, hiding those sheets can speed up macro execution almost as much as does setting ECHO to FALSE.

When you use HIDE, however, remember that you still need to activate the hidden sheets that your macro needs; otherwise, the macro won't perform as expected. For example, if a macro hides a window, Excel deactivates it: If the macro needs to operate on the hidden window, it must therefore activate it again. Also, when you open a hidden document, Excel doesn't activate it automatically, as it does with unhidden windows.

Use fast forms of reference

To review, Excel offers several methods for assigning values to cells, including named cells and defined names, either on a macro sheet or on a worksheet. Which of these is the most efficient in terms of speed, as opposed to clarity? Let's use the *Benchmark* macro to grade each of the following methods.

1. You can use direct cell references in a macro to retrieve the results of formulas for use in other formulas, as in the following:

	A	B
1		
2		BUDGET
3		=B2&".XLS"

2. You can name the cells that contain these values and use the name instead of the corresponding direct cell reference; this is the course we've adopted for this book because a named cell documents the purpose of the formula in that cell, and macros that use named references are much easier to understand than those that use direct cell references. For example:

	A	B
1		
2	fileT	BUDGET
3	newFileT	=fileT&".XLS"

3. You can use SET.VALUE to insert the result of a formula into a cell on the macro sheet, as in the following:

	A	B
1		
2		=SET.VALUE(B3,"BUDGET"&".XLS")
3		

4. You can use SET.NAME to assign a value to a name on the macro sheet. This operation can take either of two forms. In the first, you use the SET.NAME function explicitly, as in the following:

	A	B
1		
2		=SET.NAME("fileT","BUDGET")
3		=fileT&".XLS"

In the second, you can use an equal sign as a name-assignment operator, as in the following:

	A	B
1		
2		fileT="BUDGET"
3		=fileT&".XLS"

5. You can use DEFINE.NAME to assign a value to a name. You can do this on the worksheet or on the macro sheet if it's active, with the following macro:

	A	B
1		
2		=DEFINE.NAME("fileT","BUDGET")
3		=fileT&".XLS"

Alternatively, you can define a name on a worksheet that is external to the macro sheet by activating it and using *!fileT* instead of *fileT* in cell B3 of the macro fragment.

To make the test as fair as possible, we've made each fragment two lines long and attempted to make each fragment accomplish the same task, that of assigning a value to a name or a cell and then using the value in an expression. The following table (which uses the last form of the *Benchmark* macro) shows the results when the fragments are run through the benchmarking macro on a Macintosh IIsi:

Method		Avg. time/cycle	Factor
1:	Direct cell references	0.013	1.00
2:	Named cell references	0.013	1.00
3:	SET.VALUE	0.018	1.38
4a:	Explicit SET.NAME	0.019	1.46
4b:	Implied SET.NAME	0.017	1.31
5a:	DEFINE.NAME...same sheet	0.043	3.31
5b:	DEFINE.NAME...external sheet	0.064	4.92

As you can see, there isn't any significant difference between using direct cell references and named references in a macro—the two fastest ways to access stored values. Obviously, named references are far superior to direct references for writing clear, self-documenting macro code and cost you nothing in terms of execution speed.

At the other end of the scale, Excel takes roughly three times as long to define a name on the macro sheet as to access a named cell reference and over twice as long to define a name as to use either the explicit or the implied form of the SET.NAME function.

Finally, the SET.VALUE function takes about the same time to execute as does SET.NAME, but because overuse of SET.VALUE can make macros more difficult to read, we favor the implied form of SET.NAME.

Optimize cell editing

CUT, COPY, PASTE, and CLEAR take a long time to operate within a macro, for two reasons. First, the functions themselves take a relatively long time to perform. Second, to use these functions you must move the selection, which takes a long time as well.

Therefore, if you're copying, cutting, or clearing a few cells (say, two to five), it's usually faster to use the FORMULA function with its reference argument. For example, the following formula copies the value in cell B3 of the active sheet to cell B3 on Sheet2.

```
=FORMULA(!B3,"Sheet2!R3C2")
```

The next formula copies the formula in cell B3 of the active sheet to cell B3 on Sheet2.

```
=FORMULA(GET.FORMULA(!B3),"Sheet2!R3C2")
```

The following formula enters a blank in cell B3 on Sheet2.

```
=FORMULA("","Sheet2!B3C2")
```

This formula is equivalent to selecting cell B3 and using the CLEAR() or CLEAR(3) macro function.

Make loops more efficient

Because loops perform the same action many times, they can magnify small differences in speed between two techniques. A macro that searches a 100-by-100 range of cells in a worksheet for a particular number format could process 10,000 cells or more, and a 0.01-second inefficiency would result in a delay of 100 seconds over the course of the macro.

As a general rule, therefore, you need to be more careful of speed issues within loops...but not always. A print macro, for example, can run for hours; but using a slow looping method for this application probably wouldn't affect the macro's execution time by more than a second or two.

The best advice for speeding up loops, other than to analyze the execution speed of every formula in the loop, is to put outside the loop every formula and calculation that doesn't truly need to be there. For example, consider the formula

```
=FOR("n",1,ROWS(SELECTION()))
```

Here the FOR formula recalculates the number of rows in the selection at the beginning of each loop. Not only does this recalculation take extra time, but it is also dangerous. If the selection is moved within the loop, *n* is aiming at a moving target.

Instead, use a macro fragment such as this:

```
rowsN      =ROWS(SELECTION())
           =FOR("n",1,rowsN)
```

Here *n* counts up from 1 through a specific number of rows. These two formulas take less time to execute than the single formula run many times, and they're safer to use.

Optimize custom dialog boxes and menus

Excel takes a long time to create custom dialog boxes and to execute custom menus. The longer they are, the more time it takes to execute them. To speed up your macros, avoid custom dialog boxes and menus; or if you do use them, use short ones.

The best way to shorten the response time of a dialog box is to reduce its complexity, which also might reduce its usefulness. When other people use your macros, they might not notice that your custom dialog boxes are "slow" to respond. However, they *will* notice if a dialog box is unclear or inconvenient, or if a macro doesn't perform as advertised.

Instead of using one large dialog box, you could try using several smaller ones, dividing a large set of options into more than one group. If necessary, you can provide buttons in each box that let the user bring up related boxes.

Making macros seem *to run faster*

There's an online information service that takes 2 or 3 seconds to respond each time you press the Page Down key when reading a document. As soon as you press this key, the service immediately updates the bottom 25 percent of the screen with a paid advertisement. These ads achieve two worthwhile goals for the information service. First, of course, the ads represent a major source of revenue. And second, when users read the ads, they don't tend to notice the slow response time.

It probably isn't feasible to include paid advertisements with your macros, but you can use various tricks to make your macros seem to run more quickly than they actually do.

Use MESSAGE

When you freeze the screen and provide the user with no information about the progress of the macro, the macro seems to take forever to run. Worse, when nothing happens on the screen, users start wondering whether something is wrong with your macro. That's when they start pushing keys at random—perhaps even rebooting their machine, believing that the system has crashed.

The MESSAGE function cures both these conditions. This function, which is not affected by ECHO(FALSE), provides information in the status bar about the current status of the macro. The information might include messages such as *34% Done* or *Searching Account Number 7893* or *Roughly 89 minutes remaining.*

When you use the MESSAGE function, use detailed messages. For example, if a macro processes three different files, each of which takes 20 minutes to run, it doesn't help the user much if the MESSAGE function merely updates the name of the file every 20 minutes. Instead, provide additional information such as *Updating SALES.XLS for Sep 9.*

Use status screens

At times, you want to provide more information than you can easily condense into the status bar. Also, you might want to provide a friendlier message than a terse one such as *Processing the BUDGET.XLS file.*

At such times, you can call up a special worksheet that contains a message, such as the one shown in Figure 16-3.

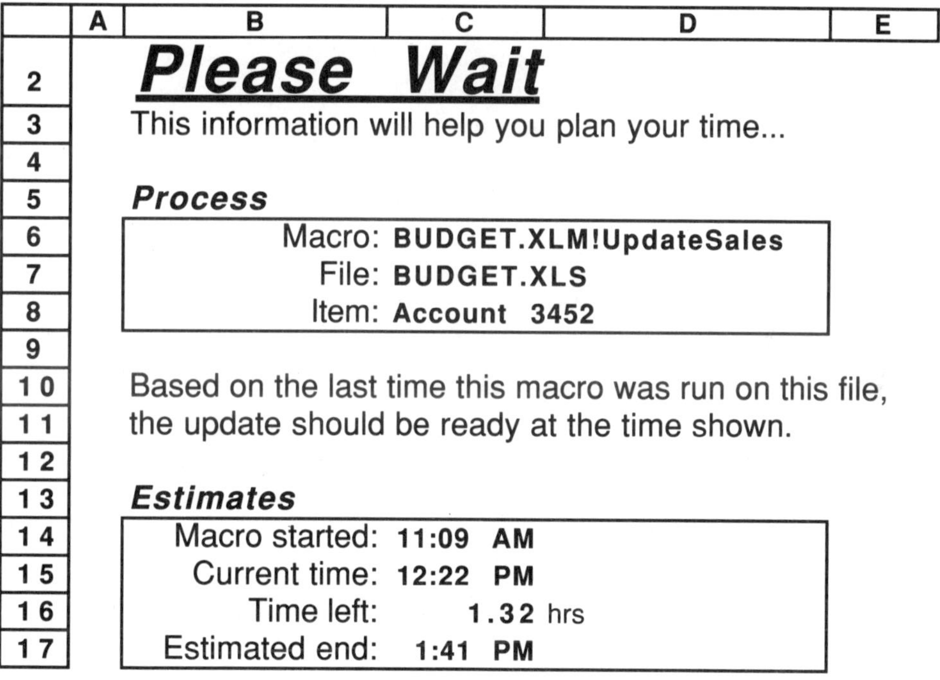

FIGURE 16-3.
This worksheet keeps users informed about the status of a macro that takes a long time to run.

To update the values for the ending and remaining times at convenient intervals (say, every minute), use the ON.TIME function as described in Chapter 12. So that users can see the updated information in a status sheet, set ECHO to TRUE within the macro routine that updates the status window.

Process during user inactivity

Even if macro formulas could execute instantly, many macros perform tasks that would still cause the user to wait—for example, during a print job or while the user is reading instructions on the screen, studying a chart, or selecting a menu item. Therefore, another way to make a macro seem to execute faster is to defer processing to times of inactivity.

Spread the wait

Suppose a macro asks the user to enter information by using three Input dialog boxes, and suppose it takes about a second to process each response. You could write the macro so that it asks for one input and then processes, asks for more input and then processes, and so on. Or you could ask for input for all three items and then have the macro process for three seconds. Which will seem faster?

Many programmers spread the wait. That is, they sandwich the processing times between each input. This technique works well if the wait isn't too long and if users can utilize the time to think about the next response to enter.

However, if your macro will be used over and over again by the same people, they'll soon become expert at providing the data that your macro requires—in which case, the macro will begin to seem very slow as users become used to the small delay after each Input dialog box while your macro processes the data. In this instance, it usually makes more sense for the user to enter all the responses quickly and for the macro to process the responses while the user pauses to do something else.

Function macros

Most of the preceding tips for speeding up macros also apply to function macros. However, there are additional ways to speed up function macros.

Use a formula instead

Because normal formulas calculate much more quickly than do function macros, try to find solutions that do not use function macros. This isn't always possible, of course, but if it is, the time savings can be tremendous. The rule to apply is simple: If you can express the procedure used in a function macro within one cell, you're usually better off creating a formula on the worksheet rather than on a macro sheet. If you need to use the formula in more than one worksheet, you can create a macro that contains the DEFINE.NAME function to assign the formula to a name in each worksheet.

Call function macros with an IF formula

When you use function macros, you often don't need them to recalculate continuously. Instead, you might need them to calculate only when it's time to analyze or print results. To print at such times, enter a formula such as the following in the worksheet:

```
=IF(switch=1,MyFunction(value),defaultValue)
```

To turn off the function macro, define *switch* on the worksheet as the value *0*. When you do so, the formula returns the default value rather than calling the macro. To turn the function macro back on, define *switch* as *1*. Another way to achieve the same result, without having to edit every formula that calls the function macro, is to assign the above formula to a name, such as *MyFunctionSwitch*, in the worksheet.

SECTION FIVE

Platform-Specific Topics

17

Translating Lotus 1-2-3 Macros

Years ago, Spiro Agnew complained in jest that the foreign press kept reporting what he said, not what he meant to say. In that respect, the Macro Translation Assistant (MTA) is much like the foreign press: It translates into an Excel macro what it thinks your Lotus 1-2-3 macro says, not necessarily what you want it to say.

The MTA is a separate program included in your Windows Excel 3 package. If you're an experienced Lotus 1-2-3 macro writer, the MTA can quickly introduce you to the more powerful Excel macro language. When run in the Verbose mode, the MTA interleaves the old Lotus 1-2-3 macro commands with the equivalent Excel functions, letting you compare the Lotus 1-2-3 and Excel macros line by line.

Just as the foreign press might report exact translations of Mr. Agnew's comments, the MTA records the exact operation of the 1-2-3 macro. It does so even though a more appropriate way might exist to achieve the same purpose in Excel. As you gain familiarity with Excel, you can rewrite the macro so that it's more efficient.

Also, the MTA doesn't optimize the resulting code. Instead, it tends to generate code for worst-case macros in an attempt to get as much of the macro to function as possible. Therefore, you can often improve the performance of translated macros significantly by eliminating extraneous commands.

This chapter summarizes the incompatibilities between Excel and Lotus 1-2-3 macros that you need to keep in mind when you use the MTA, and it discusses what to do about the problems that develop.

Getting along without the MTA

The MTA generates lots of macro code; and, in a manner similar to macros created with the macro recorder, it strings this macro code across your macro sheet like laundry on a clothesline.

Therefore, after the MTA translates your macro, you'll need to rearrange the code on the macro sheet and document it. As you do so, you should simplify the macro where you can. After you document an MTA macro several times, you might decide to skip the MTA entirely and write your macro directly from the 1-2-3 macro. If you decide to do so, first document your 1-2-3 macro using the same format shown in this book for documenting Excel macros. Open your 1-2-3 spreadsheet in Excel, and then open a new macro sheet. Copy the macros from the 1-2-3 spreadsheet to the macro sheet. Then, using the explanations for the 1-2-3 macros to guide you, replace the 1-2-3 macro formulas in the macro sheet with formulas for Excel. Where you run into problems, use the MTA to translate short sections of the 1-2-3 macro.

If you use Excel on the Macintosh, or if you want to translate macros from Symphony or some other spreadsheet, you won't be able to use the MTA. In such instances, use the same approach to manually translate your macros to Excel, or translate the macro on a PC, and then use Excel to save the resulting macro in a form that the Macintosh version of Excel can read.

Translation considerations before running the MTA

While most Lotus 1-2-3 functions translate to Excel functions without difficulty, you must change some functions in the Lotus 1-2-3 macro prior to translation. To do so, you don't need to reboot 1-2-3. Simply change the macro on the 1-2-3 spreadsheet opened in Excel.

Macros and the Ready mode

The MTA assumes that most macros begin and end in the Ready mode. But a macro that edits a formula or changes a graph will start in some other mode. Macros that don't start in the Ready mode won't translate to any meaningful function. To properly translate this type of Lotus 1-2-3 macro, you must first modify it so that it can be run in Lotus 1-2-3 from the Ready mode. For example, if the macro expects to start from the main Graph menu, you should type */G* at the beginning of the macro before translating it.

Also, macros that don't end in the Ready mode might not run properly. For example, the following macro activates Lotus 1-2-3's formula bar, enters some text, and then positions the cursor at the beginning of the formula bar, leaving it active so you can insert text.

```
A1: "TOTAL SALES{EDIT}{HOME}"'
```

Because an Excel macro can't end with the formula bar active, and because no formula was actually entered by it, the MTA will issue a warning message and generate no code.

Incomplete commands

The MTA can only translate complete commands. A one-cell macro such as *'Name:*, which begins a label entry but doesn't complete it, would not translate. Similarly, */WGFF* wouldn't translate, because the command begins a Worksheet Global Format command but doesn't complete it. In Lotus 1-2-3, these macros might be used as shortcuts for oft-performed tasks.

The MTA does, however, handle the Pause {?} command, which allows the kind of interactive input for which these macros are used. (See "The Pause {?} command," later in this chapter.) Therefore, *'Name:{?}~* would translate correctly, as would */WFGG?~*.

Self-modified code

The MTA supports most cases of self-modified code, where one instruction in a Lotus 1-2-3 macro changes the contents of another cell that is part of the same macro. It does so where you enter commands into a cell of the macro by using the {LET}, {GETNUMBER}, {/XN}, {GETLABEL}, or {/XL} function.

However, more involved self-modified code might not be translatable.

- One Lotus 1-2-3 command can't be substituted for another. For example, *{read}* can't be changed to *{readLn}*, nor can *{/WIC}* be changed to *{/WIR}*.
- Branch locations can't be changed. For example, *{branch e3}* can't be changed to *{branch f3}*, nor can */XCsub1~* (a subroutine call) be changed to */XCsub2~*.

The reason for these limitations is that when these self-modifications occur the MTA doesn't know what the modified code will be and therefore has no way to translate it. For example, the following macro is not translatable.

```
A10:    /F
A11:    {GETLABEL "Enter filename, preceded by S to save or R to load,
        and with ~", A12}
```

The following example shows another self-modified macro that is a problem. Here the macro opens the file with the filename specified by the contents of cell A1.

```
A10:    +"/FR"&A1&"~"
```

However, the MTA doesn't know that a formula is in the cell. Therefore, it assumes that the formula is a text constant. The resulting translated macro is a macro to open the file whose name is equal to the value of cell A1 at translation time. No warning message is given for this condition. The fix is to change

```
A10:    {getlabel "File to open:",A1}
A11:    +"/FR"&A1&"~"
```

to

```
A10:    {getlabel "File to open:",A12}
A11:    /FR
A12:
A13:    ~
```

File commands

Lotus 1-2-3 has several file commands that do different things depending on different runtime conditions. The MTA makes certain assumptions in each of these commands, and if the assumptions aren't correct, you'll have to alter the Excel macro manually. The MTA issues a warning message when it makes any of these assumptions.

Passwords

If a Lotus 1-2-3 macro opens a password-protected file, it must provide the password. If the file is unprotected, however, the password isn't needed. A string following the name of the file is interpreted as a password if the file is protected but will otherwise be interpreted as a label entry.

There is no way of knowing at translation time whether a file will be password protected. The MTA assumes that an alphanumeric string is a password if it ends with a ~ (tilde) and is in the same cell as the filename.

Macros with the {?} command immediately after a filename are assumed to be pausing for entry of the file password. In this case, the MTA generates code to prompt you for a password to be entered in the FILE.OPEN formula. Anything else is assumed to be a separate command.

If a label entry on the same line as the name of a file to be opened is falsely interpreted to be a password, you can insert an extra ~ between the filename and the label, and it will be properly interpreted.

A password in the cell below the one containing the filename will be incorrectly interpreted as a label entry. However, you can move the password into the same cell as the filename, and it will be correctly interpreted.

Even if a password is read, it won't be used, because Excel's OPEN() function does not take a password. Interactive passwords (using the Pause {?} command), however, will cause the FILE.OPEN function to become interactive, and you can supply the password in the File Open dialog box.

The Cancel/Replace menu

When it saves a file, Lotus 1-2-3 brings up a Cancel/Replace menu if that file already exists, but it does not bring up the menu if the file does not exist. The MTA interprets a {?} after the Save command as an interactive Cancel/Replace, prompting you for *C* or *R*.

If a macro has a *C* or an *R* following a filename in a Save command, the MTA assumes that the character was meant for this command. If no such characters appear after this command, the MTA assumes that the menu won't come up.

As with passwords, the *C*, *R*, or *{?}* must be in the same cell as the end of the filename, or it will be interpreted as a label entry.

If the MTA makes the wrong assumption, several commands could be translated incorrectly. Correct translation resumes when the macro returns to the Ready mode.

At the top of the following page is a portion of a macro that does not translate because of MTA's incorrect assumption.

```
A1:     {GETLABEL "Save file as:",A4}
A2:     {GOTO b1}{blank b1}
A3:     /FS
A4:
A5:     ~C~
A6:     {IF b1="C"}{BRANCH a13}
A7:     {GETLABEL "Enter Y to overwrite file"&A4,B1}
A8:     {IF b1<>"Y"}{BRANCH a13}
A9:     {LET a11,a4}
A10:    /FS
A11:
A12:    ~R
A13:    (Macro continues here)
```

Cell A3 issues the File Save command. If the Cancel/Replace menu comes up, cell A5 cancels the command. If the menu does not come up, cell A5 enters C into cell B1. The macro then tests cell B1. If cell B1 does not contain C, it knows that the Cancel/Replace menu came up, and it prompts for whether to overwrite the file. If cell B1 contains C, the macro knows the File Save command worked properly, and it proceeds.

This macro won't translate correctly because the MTA always assumes that the C in cell A5 is intended for the Cancel/Replace menu. Therefore, the instance in which B1 contains C never occurs.

To work around this problem, translate this section of the macro with the SAVE.AS?() command instead of trying to emulate the 1-2-3 macro exactly.

The {DISPATCH} command

The Lotus 1-2-3 {DISPATCH} command allows the macro to perform an indirect GOTO. For example, *{dispatch A1}* means look at the value in cell A1, assume that it's a reference, and branch to that reference. Because the MTA can't know what values will be assumed by A1 at runtime, it displays an error message for this command.

To implement this command in Excel, manually enter the following macro formula.

```
=GOTO(TEXTREF(A1,TRUE))
```

Other indirect branching

Indirect branching—when a macro branches to a name that is defined by other parts of the macro—is common within Lotus 1-2-3 macros. The MTA does not check for indirect branching, but if it does encounter a branch to a name, it assumes that the name will stay defined to its current value. If the branch is to an undefined name, the MTA issues an error message. Indirect branching situations must be corrected in the same manner as described for the Dispatch instruction.

Translation considerations after running the MTA

The following considerations involve corrections that must be made in the Excel macro after you translate a 1-2-3 macro.

Formula- or string-too-long error messages

In some cases, translation of a long 1-2-3 formula can cause an even longer Excel formula. When this occurs, the formula might be too long for Excel, in which case, you need to break up the formula and translate it manually. This situation is rare, however, because the limits on formula lengths for Lotus 1-2-3 and Excel are about the same.

Default formats

Excel has no equivalent (other than redefining the Normal style) to Lotus 1-2-3's Worksheet Global Format command, which assigns the default format to cells not assigned a specific format. In Excel, the translated */WGF* command reformats all cells to the new default setting and deletes existing formats for individual cells. As a result, macros that first set the default format and then proceed to format specific cells and ranges operate correctly. However, macros that first format specific cells and ranges and then set the defaults don't work correctly.

Default column widths and alignment

The MTA translates the Worksheet Global Column Widths and Column Alignment commands to reset the widths and alignments of all the columns. In Excel, this deletes the width settings for all columns that have been sized previously. As with number formats, macros that first set the defaults and then set individual columns translate correctly. But those that first set individual columns and then set the defaults don't translate correctly.

International formats

Some of 1-2-3's date and time formats have an additional level of indirection that allows them to be changed by altering the configuration settings. The MTA does not support this feature, and an appropriate error message is generated when this condition is encountered. You must change these commands manually on the target macro sheet, substituting the format you want in an appropriate FORMAT.NUMBER function.

Recalculation order

Excel can recalculate only those cells that change, greatly reducing calculation times during program operation. Although Lotus 1-2-3 does not have this capability, it does have three options for recalculation: Row, Column, and Natural. Row recalculation operates on cells starting at A1 and moving across the row. Column recalculation starts at A1 and moves down the column. Natural recalculation determines dependencies as recalculation takes place and recalculates the source data in the same manner. Excel recalculates in worksheets only according to dependencies.

Printing

When you translate Lotus 1-2-3 printing commands, the MTA attempts to set such things as margins and page size, which might not be correct for some printer drivers. Some Lotus 1-2-3 print commands have no translation because they set print parameters that, under Windows, are controlled by the printer driver. Generally, translating macros that do printing might not be worth the time you spend, because much of the work these macros do isn't necessary in Excel.

Selective formula display

In Lotus 1-2-3, the display formula mode is part of the cell format rather than a display option as it is in Excel. Having the {DISPLAY} option coded as part of the cell format allows Lotus 1-2-3 users to specify a section of their worksheet to display formulas while the rest of the sheet displays values. Excel has no equivalent feature, so the MTA translates these commands by changing the {DISPLAY} option to be set appropriately and by generating a warning message.

Names

Names in Lotus 1-2-3 are quite different from names in Excel. In Excel, a name in a formula becomes part of the formula. In Lotus 1-2-3, a name in a formula isn't really part of the formula; it's simply an alias for a cell address. If you delete a name in Lotus 1-2-3, none of the formulas change in value, and they depend on exactly the same cells they depended on before the name was deleted. The formulas simply refer to the cell address rather than to the name. Therefore, Lotus 1-2-3 macros that delete or change the definitions of names don't translate correctly because Excel's formulas do change with the name.

By the same token, 1-2-3's Range Name Reset command deletes all the names on the sheet but leaves the formulas intact. Because this command does not exist in Excel, the MTA generates an appropriate warning.

You should also pay attention to the use of certain characters in the name string. Lotus 1-2-3 can use parentheses, commas, operators, and so on in names, but Excel can't. Therefore, names such as *this(item* and *this,item* look the same to Excel. The MTA converts one of the names to *this_item* and drops the other. However, formulas that had referred to either name before translation all refer to *this_item* after translation. Therefore, many of the formulas will be incorrect. No warning message can be issued for this case.

Names in extracted ranges

When you extract a range to a separate worksheet in Lotus 1-2-3, the top-left corner of the extracted range becomes cell A1 on the new worksheet. Names within the extracted range are updated to reflect their new location in the shifted range. For example, if the range C3:E5 is extracted, that range becomes A1:C3 in the new Lotus 1-2-3 worksheet. If cell D4 within the original range was named *PROFIT,* then *PROFIT* becomes cell B2.

If Excel reads such a worksheet created by a translated Lotus 1-2-3 macro, any names assigned to cells are not modified. As a result, the name PROFIT in this example would still refer to cell D4 and not cell B2. Macros that use such names can have unpredictable results. However, normal cut, copy, and paste operations work well.

The Pause {?} command

Lotus 1-2-3 has a mode that causes a macro to pause so that you can do whatever you want until you press Return, at which point the macro resumes. Because there is no way of knowing at translation time what mode Lotus 1-2-3 will be in when you've finished, a full translation of this command is impossible. Instead, the MTA offers a limited pause command providing for its most common uses.

If the Pause {?} command shows up in non-Ready mode, the MTA assumes that the macro expects you to supply an argument to a command, such as a filename. The MTA might translate the {?} as FILE.OPEN? or with an Input dialog box.

Lotus 1-2-3 macros often use a pause in the arguments to a command to allow you to enter one of the arguments, creating an interactive version of the command. The MTA assumes this is the purpose of the pause and displays an Input dialog box that allows you to enter an argument.

A Pause command in the Ready mode is usually used to allow you to enter or edit data in one or more cells. A translated macro simulates this with a special dialog box that lets you move between cells and edit them. A similar special dialog box handles a pause in the Data Find command.

Range input

Lotus 1-2-3 has a Range Input command that only permits alteration of the contents of a specified range of cells. When you press Enter, the macro continues. The MTA translates this command with the same library macro used to translate the Pause {?} command, and thus it does not restrict movement to only the selected range.

File extraction

Lotus 1-2-3 allows a section of a worksheet to be saved, along with any names and global settings. The MTA translates this by creating a new worksheet, copying the part of the worksheet to be extracted, and saving the copy. In this copy operation, the names and global settings associated with the extracted part of the worksheet are lost, and any formulas that refer to the names are no longer valid.

The File List command

The Lotus 1-2-3 File List command lists filenames on a separate screen. Excel has no equivalent command. However, Excel's FILES macro function provides similar information.

Print to a file

Lotus 1-2-3 can redirect the printer output to a file. Excel does not provide this function.

Charting

Charting differs greatly between Lotus 1-2-3 and Excel. Lotus keeps its graphs with the worksheet; Excel maintains charts as independent files unless you embed the chart. When Excel loads a Lotus 1-2-3 spreadsheet, the program asks whether you want to convert the spreadsheet's charts to Excel charts. If the spreadsheet's translated macros are to act on the charts, you must generate the charts, and they must be in the current directory when you run the translated macros.

At the end of a session, you need to save changes that the translated macro has made to the Excel charts. (Note: The charts won't be saved automatically with the sheet, even if the macro issues a Save command.)

Display of graphs

Because Excel charting commands act on an activated graph, the graph is displayed as long as it's being acted upon. This is in contrast to Lotus 1-2-3, which displays graphs only during an explicitly issued Graph View command.

Order of graph series

Lotus 1-2-3 preserves the order of its graph ranges (for example, A through F) even if these ranges are not entered in order. Excel, however, assigns numbers to its graph series in the order in which they are entered. Thus, even if an Excel series is assigned the number 4, it becomes the second series if only one series is already defined for the current chart. This means that Lotus 1-2-3 series might become scrambled if they're not defined in order initially.

Formula editing

Macros that edit formulas can't be translated correctly. For example, a macro to replace *@SUM(A1..A5)* with *@AVG(A1..A5)* might be implemented as

```
{EDIT}{HOME}{RIGHT}{DEL 3}AVG~
```

This macro fails in Excel because the @ character is omitted from the AVG formula name. Similarly, editing macros that use periods instead of colons to define ranges also might not work.

In some cases, the translation of macros that enter formulas results in errors because the Excel FORMULA function needs text in R1C1-style format, and Lotus 1-2-3 takes A1-style references only. This can cause problems in those cases in which macros enter formulas and then copy them.

Values of cells containing strings

In Lotus 1-2-3 versions 1A and 2.1, cells containing strings evaluate to 0. Excel does not support this, but it does ignore cells containing strings in functions such as SUM that return numbers. However, macros that test for strings by looking for cells that contain zeros won't translate correctly.

The {LET} and {PUT} commands

Lotus 1-2-3's {LET} and {PUT} commands enter into a cell an expression that can be either a label or a value. If no type is assigned to this expression (for example, *:label* or *:value*), the MTA must guess the type. Lotus 1-2-3 decides the type on the basis of whether the expression is a valid Lotus 1-2-3 formula. The MTA can't always make the correct choice, and so it might assume that the expression is a formula. In this case, the MTA generates a warning message.

If the expression was intended to be a label, you can append the *:label* suffix to the original Lotus 1-2-3 macro and then translate the macro again.

The {RECALC} and {RECALCCOL} commands

These commands recalculate only part of a Lotus 1-2-3 worksheet. Because Excel does not have a similar command, the MTA translates these commands into CALCULATE.NOW.

Direction key selection of filenames and defined names

Lotus 1-2-3 macros can select filenames and defined names using direction keys. For example, it can choose the second file listed or the third name defined. The MTA does not translate this (seldom-used) type of command because it doesn't know what names and files will exist when the macro is run.

Subroutine names and predefined macro commands

If you write a subroutine macro called *Blank* in Lotus 1-2-3 and then execute a {BLANK A1} command, 1-2-3 calls the subroutine rather than the predefined macro function, *Blank*. The MTA scans the list of predefined macro commands first, and then it assumes that the function is a subroutine call if it doesn't find a match in the list. Therefore, if a match is found, the MTA generates code as if it were the {BLANK} command rather than the subroutine call.

Optimization

The primary function of the MTA is to produce code that as nearly as possible emulates what the original Lotus 1-2-3 macro did. By attempting to fully handle all cases, the MTA often generates inefficient macros. You can often improve macro performance by reviewing and optimizing the macro "by hand."

Special names

Lotus 1-2-3 maintains a number of internal ranges and values. For example, whenever you perform a Data Fill command, Lotus 1-2-3 remembers the *Data Fill* range so that the next time a Data Fill command is given Lotus 1-2-3 defaults to this range. The MTA maintains these special ranges and values as worksheet names, and it redefines them as they are changed by the translated macro. If your macro doesn't need this range name information, eliminate the DEFINE.NAME code that defines these names.

Filenames

To handle all cases, the translation of macros that open files is often more complicated than it needs to be, and often it can be easily optimized. For example,

```
A10:        ="test"&IF(ISERR(FIND(".","test")),"*"&".PRN","")
A11:        =OPEN?(A10)
```

could be

```
A10:        =OPEN?("test*.PRN")
```

Temporary names

The MTA often defines temporary names such as *Arg1, Arg2, String1,* and so forth. These names might occur in editing macros or in macros that branch in the middle of arguments to functions. In many instances, code using these names can be simplified.

Entry formatting

Often Lotus 1-2-3 macros go to great lengths to simplify user input. For example, you can remove code that lets the user enter a date in the *mm/dd/yy* format and then converts the date to a number so that the date value can be entered into a cell. Excel does this automatically.

Error, warning, and translation messages

Following are lists of some of the error, warning, inexact translation, and other messages that might be reported when you translate a 1-2-3 macro.

Error messages while translating

The MTA sometimes displays a dialog box during translation containing one of the following messages. Before the translation can continue, you must choose an option from the dialog box.

Message	**Meaning**
Document *no longer open*	Open document, and restart translation.
Document *not translatable*	Only worksheets containing Lotus 1-2-3 macros can be translated.
Can't communicate with Microsoft Excel	Excel is no longer running, or MTA can't open target macro sheet.
Can't find Excel	Excel is no longer running, or Ignore Remote Requests has been set in Workspace dialog box.
Disk operation failed	Problem occurred while reading or writing a file.
Formula in source cell *too long*	Formula is too long; break it into smaller expressions.
Out of columns on target macro sheet	MTA enters pieces of translated macro code into separate columns; if MTA runs out of columns, break macro into segments and translate them separately.
Translation still in progress	User is trying to quit from Windows before translation is finished.

Error messages on translated sheet

Message	**Meaning**
BRANCH or subroutine call to undefined name	Name is not defined on the source spreadsheet.
Branch through undefined menu name	The /XM, {MENUBRANCH}, or {MENUCALL} function refers to an undefined location.
Expected reference *to be a reference*	Illegal reference was found.
Expected type *to be an argument type*	*Type* is not a value or label.
Formula is too long to translate	Resulting formula is longer than 255 characters and is truncated.
Return in multiple states	Edit the routine so that all returns occur in Ready mode.
String too long	Text string that is part of a formula is too long.

Warning messages

Message	Meaning
Assuming char *is cancel/replace character*	In a command that writes to a file, specified character can signify Cancel or Replace. If it doesn't, add ~ (tilde) before it in source macro, and retranslate.
Assuming interactive cancel/replace	In a command that writes to a file, a {?} command can signify a request to let user specify whether to replace file or cancel.
Assuming interactive password	In a cell that opens a file, {?} can signify a pause to let user enter a password: MTA translates command to OPEN?
Assuming no cancel/replace character	In a command that writes to a file, MTA did not find a *C*, *R*, or {?} command.
Assuming no password	In source Lotus 1-2-3 macro, put password in same cell as filename, and end it with ~ (tilde).
Assuming password *to be password*	MTA assumes that an alphanumeric string that is in same cell as filename, terminated by a ~ (tilde), is a password.
Assuming self-modified cell begins label	Self-modified cell can evaluate to either a label or a formula: MTA assumes it will be a label.
Axis scaling not applied to empty charts	Edit the source macro so that a series is defined before its axes are formatted.
Axis title not attached to pie charts	If chart is a pie chart, axis titles are not translated.
Edited formula may be incorrect	Formula in source macro is being edited by macro; same operations done on Excel version of formula might make it become incorrect.
Edited name may be incorrect	Name in source macro is being modified through ? command or by macro, and name cannot be guaranteed to be correct.
Edited range may be incorrect	Named range in source macro is being modified through ? command or by macro, and name cannot be guaranteed to be correct.
Gridlines not applied to pie charts or empty charts	Edit the source macro so that a series is defined before its gridlines are formatted. Also, gridlines don't apply to pie charts.
Line formatting not applied to empty charts	Edit the source macro so that a series is defined before its lines are formatted.
Line formatting only applied if series exists	Edit the source macro so that a series is defined before its lines are formatted.
Line formatting only applied to line and scatter charts	Line formats apply only to line and scatter charts; /GOF is not translated.
No type given; assumed to be a formula	MTA treats an expression entered into a cell as a formula, because {LET} or {PUT} command did not specify whether expression was a value or a label.

(continued)

continued

Message	Meaning
Selection depends on window size	The {BIGLEFT}, {BIGRIGHT}, {PGUP}, and {PGDN} commands scroll by window; however, size of window might be different in Excel environment.
Shading, coloring, and exploded wedges not translated	Second graph series formats in 1-2-3 have no equivalents in Excel; instead, use PATTERNS to set shading and coloring, and use FORMAT.MOVE to move pie wedges.
Title not attached to empty charts	Edit the source macro so that a series is defined before titles are added.
X axis scaling only applied to scatter charts	*X*-axis scaling applies only if chart is an *xy* (scatter) chart.

Function-not-translated messages

Message	Meaning
+/- format not available	/WGF+ and /RF+ are not translated, but you can duplicate these formats with the formula =IF(ref=0,".",REPT(IF(ref>0),"+","-"),ABS(ref))) where *ref* is reference of a cell.
All printing is formatted	/PPOOU, /PFOOU, /PPOOF, and /PFOOF enable and disable headers, footers, and page breaks; instead, use functions PAGE.SETUP and SET.PAGE.BREAK.
All recalculation is natural	Excel always recalculates by dependency rather than by rows or columns.
Can't translate ABS key	MTA doesn't support ABS key; instead, you'd have to create a macro for changing style of reference.
Can't translate complex self-modified macros	MTA can translate only certain types of self-modifying macros.
Charts are separate files	MTA does not support translation of source charts into embedded charts.
Configuration file not available	Only equivalent to configuration files in Lotus 1-2-3 are workspace files and templates.
Default status not available	/WGDS isn't translated; instead, use DIRECTORY, GET.WORKSPACE, and so on to determine analogous settings.
DISPATCH destination could change	MTA can't determine where a {DISPATCH} command will continue execution; instead, to translate the Lotus 1-2-3 command {DISPATCH location} use the Excel formula =GOTO(TEXTREF(location,TRUE)).

(continued)

continued

Message	Meaning
File listing not available	Excel doesn't list files in the way that Lotus 1-2-3 does; instead, use the FILES function.
Formatting scale numbers not available	Excel doesn't support formatting of axis value labels; instead, format values in supporting worksheet.
Intercept is always computed	Excel always calculates the intercept in a linear regression.
International currency format not available	To change currency format, create custom number format or use the TEXT or FORMAT.NUMBER function.
International date format not available	To change date format, create custom number format or use TEXT or FORMAT.NUMBER.
International punctuation format not available	To change number format, create custom number format or use TEXT or FORMAT.NUMBER.
International time format not available	To change time format, create custom number format or use TEXT or FORMAT.NUMBER.
LOOK not available	LOOK has no equivalent in Excel; instead, create replacement macro that uses ON.KEY.
Lotus 1-2-3 clock not available	Excel does not support an on-screen clock.
Lotus 1-2-3 help type not available	Help screens in Excel remain open until closed.
Lotus 1-2-3 worksheet status not available	Instead, use the GET.CELL, GET.DOCUMENT, GET.WINDOW, and GET.WORKSPACE functions.
Microsoft Excel handles file replacement	Command in source macro writes to a file but doesn't specify whether to cancel the save or replace the file.
Printer connections are not numbered	Instead, use the PRINTER.SETUP function.
Printer driver handles auto-linefeed	The printer driver sends linefeeds after carriage returns.
Printer driver handles page length selection	Instead, use PRINTER.SETUP? and SEND.KEYS functions.
Printer driver handles print wait	Printer driver handles single-sheet printing; instead, use PRINTER.SETUP? and SEND.KEYS.
Printer driver handles printer alignment	Printer driver handles printer alignment.
Printer driver handles printer movement	Instead, use SET.PAGE.BREAK to start a new page.
Printer driver handles printer setup	Printer setup is handled by the printer driver. You can also use the text-file handling functions described in Chapter 15.
Printer names are not numbered	Instead, use PRINTER.SETUP.
Range reset not available	Instead, create a macro that contains the DELETE.NAME function to delete every name in a sheet.

(continued)

continued

Message	Meaning
Skipping data points not available	Instead, create macro to move desired points to another range, and chart that range.
Split windows are always synchronized	Instead, use NEW.WINDOW function.
System call not available	Instead, use DLL techniques to access operating system.

Inexact-translation messages

Message	Meaning
Aligns all labels	Destination macro changes alignment of all cells in worksheet.
Always translated into data find	MTA always translates {QUERY} into DATA.FIND(TRUE).
Displays formulas on entire document	Instead, use DISPLAY to display formulas or values for entire document, or open another window.
Formats whole document	Instead, redefine the Normal style, or create new styles.
International data format not available	To change date format, create custom number format or use the TEXT or FORMAT.NUMBER function.
International time format not available	To change time format, create custom number format or use TEXT or FORMAT.NUMBER.
Movement not limited to input range	Excel does not support limiting the movement of the selection, unless in protected worksheet.
Names and global settings not saved	Instead, create macro that copies names and settings you want to transfer.
Password ignored	Instead, use the OPEN? function so that user can enter a password.
Recalculates the whole document	Excel calculates entire document, with exception of tables. Instead, create macro that replaces equal signs with equal signs, as discussed in Chapter 3.
Sets all column widths	Translated formulas change all column widths.
Unhidden columns given default width	MTA sets unhidden columns to 8 characters.

18

Using SEND.KEYS

The two versions of Excel for the PC contain a very useful function that the current version for the Macintosh lacks: SEND.KEYS. This macro function lets you create keystroke macros using Excel. With keystroke macros, you can control other applications, duplicate certain Lotus 1-2-3 macro functions that are otherwise impossible to duplicate, and perform other tasks that the normal Excel macro functions don't permit.

An introduction to SEND.KEYS

The SEND.KEYS function sends the specified text to the active application, exactly as if it were typed from the keyboard. This function takes the form

SEND.KEYS(keyT,*waitL*)

The *keyT* argument consists of combinations of the standard character keys with the same key codes that you can use with the ON.KEY function (discussed in Chapter 12, "Taking Action Through Macros"), according to the table at the top of the following page.

Key code	Meaning
{BACKSPACE} or {BS}	Backspace
{BREAK}	Break
{CAPSLOCK}	Caps Lock
{CLEAR}	Clear
{DELETE} or {DEL}	Delete or Del
{DOWN}	Down direction key
{END}	End
{ENTER} or ~ (tilde)	Enter
{ESCAPE} or {ESC}	Esc (Escape)
{HELP}	Help
{HOME}	Home
{INSERT}	Insert
{LEFT}	Left direction key
{NUMLOCK}	Num Lock
{PGDN}	Page Down
{PGUP}	Page Up
{PRTSC}	Print Screen
{RIGHT}	Right direction key
{SCROLLLOCK}	Scroll Lock
{TAB}	Tab
{UP}	Up direction key
{F1} through {F15}	Function keys F1 through F15

You can put a key command in either uppercase or lowercase characters. To repeat a key, use the key, a space, and the number of times you want to repeat the character, and enclose the sequence in curly braces. For example, to enter 25 asterisks, you could use the following formula:

```
=SEND.KEYS("{* 25}")
```

You can also combine keys with the following "modifier" keys.

Code	Meaning
+ (plus sign)	Shift
^ (caret)	Ctrl
% (Alt)	Alt

For example, to issue the key sequence to copy a selected range, you might use the following formula:

```
=SEND.KEYS("^{insert}")
```

The meaning of the *waitL* argument depends on whether Excel is the active application: If *waitL* is TRUE, Excel waits for the keys to be processed in the application before returning control to the macro. If *waitL* is FALSE or omitted, Excel returns control to the macro without waiting for the keys to be processed in the other application. If Excel is already active when SEND.KEYS is executed, *waitL* is always considered to be FALSE, even if set to TRUE, because Excel doesn't process keystrokes while a macro is running.

One benefit of SEND.KEYS is that it allows you to "extend" the set of features belonging to the standard macro functions. For example, the FORMAT.FONTS function doesn't have an argument that corresponds to the Printer Fonts option in the Fonts dialog box, but you can easily add this feature with SEND.KEYS. To do so in the Windows version of Excel, use the following formula:

```
=SEND.KEYS("%(TFR)~")
```

The formula first issues the keystrokes Alt-t (Format), Alt-f (Font), and Alt-r (toggling the Printer Fonts check box on or off) and then issues the Enter keystroke to dismiss the Fonts dialog box. Here % designates the Alt key. Because the letters that follow the Alt-key code are in parentheses, the Alt key is treated as if it were being held down while each key is "pressed."

Using SEND.KEYS within the Excel application

When Excel executes a SEND.KEYS function while Excel is the active application, it does not enter the keys in the exact order in which they are encountered in the macro; instead, it places the keystrokes in a queue, to be entered when the macro finishes execution.

Consider the following macro: Will cell B1 contain the letter *X* or the letter *Y* after Excel has finished executing the following fragment?

	A	B
2		=SELECT(B1)
3		=SEND.KEYS("X~")
4		=FORMULA("Y")
5		=RETURN()

An answer of *Y* seems logical. After all, SEND.KEYS enters *X* in the cell, and then FORMULA enters *Y* in the same cell. This answer is logical—but incorrect.

Here's why. When Excel executes the SEND.KEYS formula, it doesn't send the characters to the sheet immediately; it places the keys in a *message queue*, a section of computer memory that stores messages from Excel and other applications. Next it executes the FORMULA formula and quits. After the macro "quits," it empties the queue, entering X in cell B1.

In other words, when Excel is the active application, no matter where you put the SEND.KEYS formulas within your macro, Excel doesn't execute them until after the macro can accept manual-keystroke entries. This fact offers both advantages and disadvantages to keystroke macros.

The message queue can store eight messages, and each message is the set of keystrokes issued by one SEND.KEYS formula or by some other application. For this reason, SEND.KEYS works well with the dialog box functions (that is, those with question marks in their names): You can bring up the dialog box with certain options preselected and use SEND.KEYS for the remaining options.

Using SEND.KEYS with dialog boxes

An exception to the rule of delaying the processing of SEND.KEYS messages is that Excel accepts such messages when it would also accept manual input in a dialog box. For example, earlier in this chapter we described the use of the following fragment to toggle the Printer Fonts check box off and on.

cmd subr	**PrinterFonts**	Toggles Printer Fonts option.
	=SEND.KEYS("%(TFR)~")	
	=RETURN()	

The dialog box is called up and accepts the message only after the macro has finished executing. However, the following macro fragment performs the same task without needing to halt the macro.

cmd subr	**PrinterFonts2**	Toggles Printer Fonts option.
	=SEND.KEYS("%(R)~")	
	=FORMAT.FONT?()	
	...next formulas to be executed	
	=RETURN()	

This macro calls the Format Font dialog box, and then it pauses to accept keyboard input—but the SEND.KEYS formula has already stored its message in the message queue. Therefore, when FORMAT.FONT requests input, the queue provides it, selecting the Printer Fonts option and doing the equivalent of pressing the Enter key.

After SEND.KEYS cancels the dialog box, the macro continues—exactly as it would have if you had used the dialog box function alone and selected the options manually. Although you used the question-mark form of the FORMAT.FONT function, the dialog box is never actually displayed.

Using SEND.KEYS within a macro

A disadvantage to the way that SEND.KEYS works inside a macro is that sometimes you have to take a few extra steps to get Excel to respond to the messages sent while the macro is running.

For example, suppose you want to create a macro that temporarily switches a PostScript printer to manual feed, prints the document, and then switches back to continuous feed (that is, to using the paper tray). If you did this manually and from the keyboard, you would press Alt-fr; Excel would display the Printer dialog box.

If you then pressed Alt-s, Excel would display this dialog box:

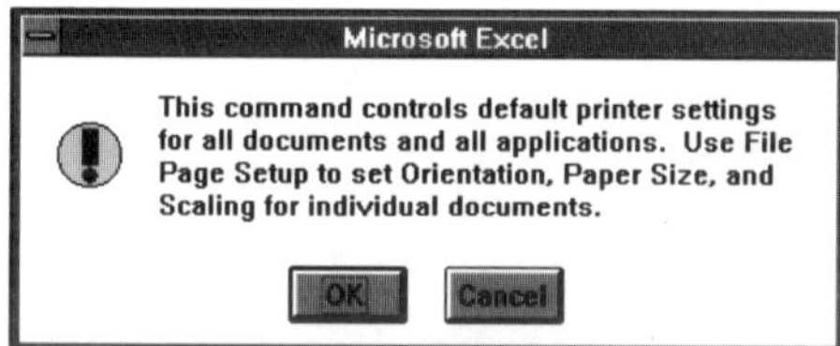

Next you would press Enter to see the dialog box containing options for the current PostScript printer:

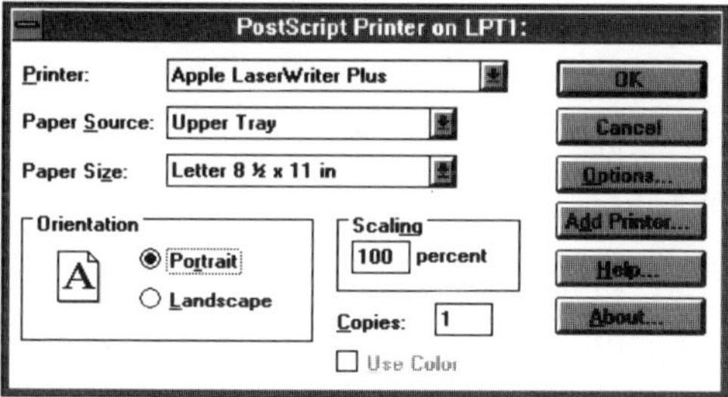

To activate the Paper Source drop-down list, you would press Alt-s again and then press the Down direction key to select Manual Feed. Finally, you would press Enter to dismiss the Printer Options dialog box and press Enter again to dismiss the Printer dialog box.

Because the PRINTER.SETUP function does not offer options beyond merely specifying the name of the printer to which you want to print, to add this feature you'd have to write a macro that uses the SEND.KEYS function.

It's easy to set up individual formulas to make the switch; to set the printer to manual feed, you would use the formula

```
=SEND.KEYS("%(frs){enter}%s{down}{enter 2}")
```

To set the printer back to using the paper tray, you would use the formula

```
=SEND.KEYS("%(frs){enter}%s{up}{enter 2}")
```

Notice that to set the printer back to the paper tray, you use the same series of key-strokes, except you use the Up direction key instead of the Down direction key.

However, consider what happens if you use these formulas in a macro such as the following:

cmd M	**PrintManual**	Prints manual copy.
	=SEND.KEYS("%(frs){enter}%s{down}{enter 2}")	Set to manual feed.
	=PRINT()	Print it.
	=SEND.KEYS("%(frs){enter}%s{up}{enter 2}")	Set to paper tray.
	=RETURN()	

As we've seen, these formulas don't perform their tasks in the order shown, because both key messages are sent after the Print command has been executed. Instead, we need to stop the macro to allow the message queue to empty and then start it back up again to print the sheet and set the printer back to the paper tray, as shown in the following two macros.

cmd M	**PrintManual**	Prints manual copy.
	=SEND.KEYS("%(frs){enter}%s{down} {enter 2}")	Set to manual feed.
	=PauseForKeys(pm.next)	
pm.next	=PRINT()	Print it.
	=SEND.KEYS("%(frs){enter}%s{up}{enter 2}")	Set to paper tray.
	=RETURN()	

cmd subr	**PauseForKeys**	Halts, then continues w/ ref.
	=ARGUMENT("pfk.ref",8)	Ref of next cell to execute.
pfk.doc	=GET.CELL(32,pfk.ref)&"!"	Name of sheet containing ref.
pfk.extRef	=pfk.doc&REFTEXT(pfk.ref,TRUE)	Assemble complete ext. ref.
pfk.keys	="%mr"&pfk.extRef&"{enter}"	Assemble Macro Run cmd.
	=SEND.KEYS(pfk.keys)	Send it.
	=HALT()	

The *PrintManual* macro sends the first key message to set the printer to manual feed, and then it calls the *PauseForKeys* macro, sending it the reference of the cell where execution will begin again.

The *PauseForKeys* macro takes this reference, finds the name of the sheet containing the reference, and constructs an external reference to enter in the Macro Run dialog box. Depending on the speed of your computer, you might or might not see this dialog box come up on the screen; to verify that this is actually happening, try removing the *{enter}* code in cell *pfk.keys*. The effect of *PauseForKeys* is that it adds another message to the queue (after the message that sets the printer) to use the Macro Run command to run the macro starting at the specified cell—in this case, the reference passed as the argument *pfk.ref*.

Although this method of starting and stopping a macro allows you to use SEND.KEYS within a macro while maintaining the desired order of execution, it does have one major disadvantage: You can't use this method within nested subroutines. To see why, suppose that the second version of the *PrintManual* macro were called by another macro. If the HALT function weren't present in *PauseForKeys*, the RETURN formula in *PrintManual* would return control to the calling macro; however, the HALT function cancels all subroutine calls. To get around this, you would have to create a variant form of the RETURN function, which would store a list of the names of each nested subroutine, and use SEND.KEYS or the RUN function to transfer control back up the chain of nested macros.

Looping with SEND.KEYS

Because the macro must stop to force Excel to process your SEND.KEYS formulas, you can't call the *PauseForKeys* macro (or a similar technique) within a FOR-NEXT or WHILE-NEXT loop. To illustrate, suppose you've created a macro in the following form:

numDocs	=COLUMNS(DOCUMENTS())
	=FOR("n",1,numDocs)
	= SEND.KEYS(keys1)
	= PauseForKeys(nextCell)
nextCell	= SEND.KEYS(keys2)
	=NEXT()

If you run this macro, Excel issues an error dialog box when it encounters the NEXT function because Excel has forgotten all about the FOR formula when *PauseForKeys* halts. Therefore, Excel issues the same error that it would have if you had started this macro manually in the cell *nextCell*.

However, the following looping method works well with SEND.KEYS macros.

numDocs	=COLUMNS(DOCUMENTS())
	=SET.VALUE(n,0)
n	=IF(n>=numDocs,GOTO(endFragment),n+1)
	= SEND.KEYS(keys1)
	= PauseForKeys(nextCell)
nextCell	= SEND.KEYS(keys2)
	=GOTO(n)
endFragment	...next formulas

Because GOTO is "hardwired" and doesn't really depend on a formula that starts the loop (as do FOR-NEXT and WHILE-NEXT), Excel continues with the loop until every document has been processed.

Using SEND.KEYS with other applications

One major benefit of using SEND.KEYS is that you can use Excel macros to automate other applications running under Windows or OS/2. However, because you can't simulate mouse activity with macros, you can control only those applications that can be run by using keystrokes rather than a mouse.

To illustrate, let's consider the following macro, which is used for transferring an Excel SYLK file from a Macintosh to a PC over a serial line, using the Windows Terminal application. The *TransferSYLK* macro assumes that you've already started Terminal with a settings document named MACXFER.TRM, that the Terminal window is maximized, and that you've already set up the appropriate communications parameters for sending files over a serial line.

cmd T	**TransferSYLK**	Transfers Excel SYLK document.
curFile	macro1	Default doc name, without extension.
curDir	="c:\excel\xlstart\"	Default pathname.
termTitle	TERMINAL - MACXFER.TRM	Name of application process to activate.
docName	=INPUT("Doc name?",2,,curDir&curFile)	Verify doc name.
	=IF(NOT(docName),RETURN())	Quit if Cancel.
	=APP.MINIMIZE()	Minimize Excel.
	=APP.ACTIVATE(termTitle)	Activate terminal.
	=SEND.KEYS("%tf",TRUE)	Start file transfer.
	=SEND.KEYS(docName&".SLK",TRUE)	Enter filename with path into transfer dialog.
	=SEND.KEYS("~",TRUE)	Send Enter.
	=SEND.KEYS("~",TRUE)	Send Enter again, for Replace dialog, if any.
	=APP.ACTIVATE(,FALSE)	Go back to minimized Excel.
msg	Press Enter when transfer is complete.	
	=ALERT(msg,2)	Wait for transfer to finish.
	=APP.MAXIMIZE()	
	=OPEN(docName&".slk")	Open doc as SYLK.
	=SAVE.AS(docName,1)	Save in Normal format.
	=RETURN()	

The macro starts out by defining text that sets the default document name and pathname; in this case, we're storing the incoming SYLK file in Excel's startup directory. The text in the cell *termTitle* is the exact text that you see if you choose the Windows Control Switch To command and select the name of the application and document representing that task.

The INPUT formula in the cell *docName* proposes the default name and path of the document to which you want to save the incoming file; if the user clicks Cancel or presses Esc, the macro is stopped. At this point in the execution of the macro, the screen looks like the one shown in Figure 18-1.

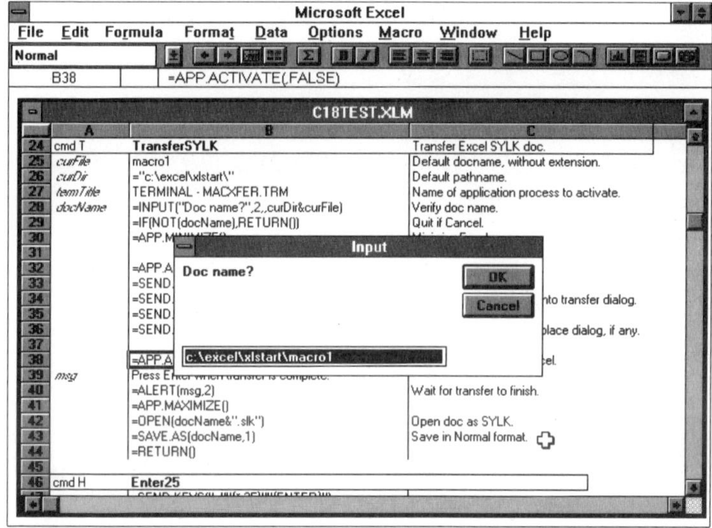

FIGURE 18-1.
The initial Input dialog box, requesting the name of the file to receive.

Next, the APP.MINIMIZE function minimizes the Excel application and activates Terminal with the APP.ACTIVATE formula, which takes the form

APP.ACTIVATE(*titleT,waitL*)

where *titleT* is the exact name of the task you want to switch to, as displayed in the application's title bar; if omitted, Excel switches back to the Excel application. The *waitL* argument determines whether Excel waits to be activated before activating the specified application; if TRUE, Excel waits, and if FALSE or omitted, Excel activates the application even if Excel isn't active. The implication of this is that you can run an Excel macro that uses SEND.KEYS in the background, without activating Excel first.

We use this feature in the SEND.KEYS formulas that follow. The *%tf* keys in the first SEND.KEYS formula correspond to Terminal's Transfers File command, and the next SEND.KEYS formula enters the full pathname of the file to receive. The screen should now look like this:

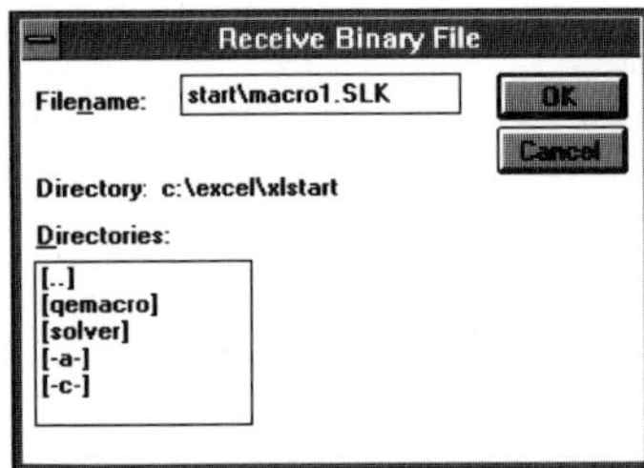

The third SEND.KEYS formula does the equivalent of pressing Enter in the dialog box to start the transfer. If the file already exists, Terminal displays the following dialog box.

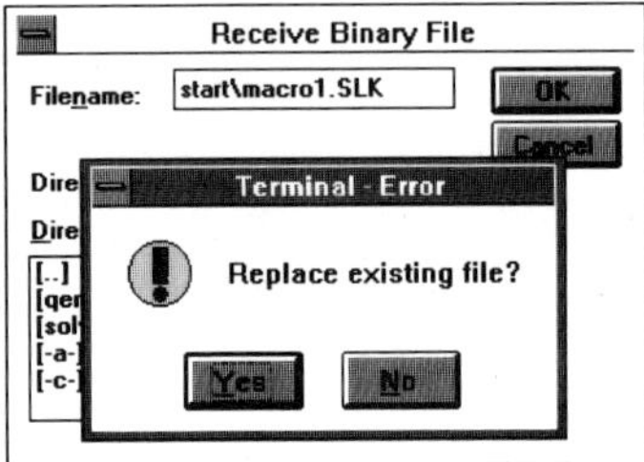

The fourth SEND.KEYS formula does the equivalent of pressing Enter in this dialog box.

The second APP.ACTIVATE formula switches back to Excel in its minimized state and displays the dialog box over the Terminal window. (See Figure 18-2.)

At this point, Terminal receives the file as a background process while the Alert dialog box remains in the foreground. After the transfer is complete, the status bar at the bottom of the Terminal window disappears, and the user can press Enter to continue the macro. Finally, the macro maximizes Excel, opens the transferred document, and saves it in the Normal format.

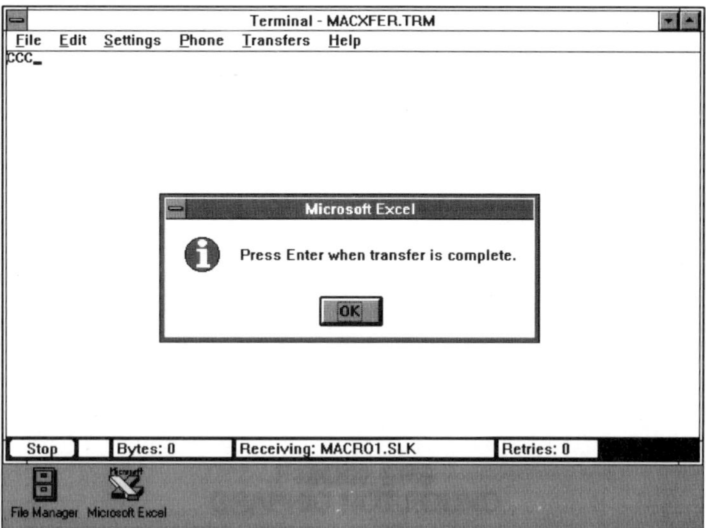

FIGURE 18-2.
Excel displays its Alert dialog box over the Terminal workspace.

Applications for SEND.KEYS

The SEND.KEYS function can perform various tasks that might not be immediately apparent. This chapter concludes with several miscellaneous uses of the SEND.KEYS function.

Logging changes to a worksheet

You can use SEND.KEYS to start the Recorder and record all changes made to a spreadsheet. To start the recorder, you can use the formula

```
=SEND.KEYS("%MC~")
```

To stop the Recorder, you can use the formula

```
=SEND.KEYS("%MC")
```

To record all changes to a worksheet, you can make the macro that contains the first formula an Auto_Open macro and the second one an Auto_Close macro.

Opening password-protected sheets

In Excel, you can password-protect sheets in two ways. With the File Save As command, you can require that a password be entered to open the sheet; using Options Protect Document, you can require that a password be entered before the sheet can be modified. You can use SEND.KEYS to respond to both these requests for passwords.

For example, suppose you save a worksheet as TEST.XLS, specifying the password *secret*. You can open the worksheet using this fragment:

	A	B
2		=SEND.KEYS("secret~")
3		=OPEN("TEST.XLS")

This macro sends *secret* and Enter to the message queue and then opens TEST.XLS. Because TEST.XLS is protected, however, the macro issues a dialog box that asks for the password. At this point, the message queue sends the message containing this information, and the macro continues.

Now, suppose you protect the sheet with the Options Protect Document command, specifying the password *mystery*. After you save the changes, you can open the worksheet and unprotect it with this fragment:

	A	B
2		=SEND.KEYS("secret~")
3		=OPEN("TEST.XLS")
4		=SEND.KEYS("%OPmystery~")

If TEST.XLS is not protected, these macros will enter *secret* in a dialog box or worksheet the first opportunity they get. This can be a problem in a business when a worksheet will sometimes be protected and sometimes not. For example, during a budgeting cycle a worksheet might be open for changes until a certain date, and after that the worksheet is protected from further changes.

The macro shown in Figure 18-3 opens the worksheet, using the password if necessary. Then the macro unprotects the contents of the worksheet if necessary.

If the file is protected, Excel displays a dialog box that requests the password, which is entered by the first SEND.KEYS formula. However, if the file is not protected, the password characters must go somewhere; in such a case, an INPUT formula traps the characters harmlessly. This trick works because when the macro encounters an INPUT formula, Excel pauses the macro execution and waits for keyboard input—in this case, the password.

After the file is open, we can check to see whether its contents are protected. If they are, the macro sends the proper password.

cmd T	**TrapPassword**	Traps password if not needed.
	=SEND.KEYS("secret~")	Send keys to unprotect file.
	=OPEN("TEST.XLS")	Open file.
	=IF(NOT(GET.DOCUMENT(6)))	If file not protected...
	= INPUT(,)	trap unneeded password.
	=END.IF()	
	=IF(GET.DOCUMENT(7))	If sheet protected...
	= SEND.KEYS("%OPmystery~")	unprotect worksheet.
	=END.IF()	
nextTest	=RETURN()	Quit.

FIGURE 18-3.
A macro that opens a file that is sometimes password protected. Sometimes the file's contents are password protected.

Editing formulas

Many users of Lotus 1-2-3 are accustomed to editing formulas by using keystroke macros. In Excel, you can usually perform the same task using other means. However, you can use SEND.KEYS to edit formulas as you do manually or with 1-2-3.

For example, suppose your original formula in cell B1 of a worksheet is

```
=SUM(A1:A3)
```

and you want to edit the formula so that it becomes

```
=3*SUM(A1:A3)
```

The following macro fragment performs this task without using SEND.KEYS.

thisFormula	=GET.FORMULA(!B1)
newFormula	=LEFT(thisFormula,1)&"3*"&MID(thisFormula,2,99)
	=FORMULA(newFormula,!B1)

When you use this macro, however, remember that GET.FORMULA returns the formula in R1C1 style. This fact could affect the spacing for the edits because each cell address in R1C1 style uses more characters than it does in A1 style.

Alternatively, you can use the following macro to edit the cell:

```
=SELECT(!B1)
=SEND.KEYS("{F2}{HOME}{RIGHT}3*~")
```

This macro selects the cell, enters the Edit mode, moves the insertion point to the beginning of the formula and then one character to the right, inserts the new characters, and then sends the Enter key.

APPENDIX A

Excel's Functions, Listed by Category

The following table contains all of Microsoft Excel's worksheet and macro functions, placed in these categories:

- Numeric
- Logical and Lookup
- Value and Conversion
- Financial
- Statistical
- Time and Date
- Text
- Editing
- Names and References
- Navigation and Selection
- Formatting
- Control
- Windows
- Dialog Box
- Events
- File
- Linking
- Menu
- Objects
- Charting
- Outlining
- Printing
- Database and Data Menu
- Dynamic Data Exchange (DDE)
- Dynamic Link Libraries (DLL)
- NewWave

We describe what the function returns—whether it is a command-equivalent (CE) or an action-equivalent (AE)—and the general purpose of the function.

In the first column we indicate standard worksheet (W) functions, and in the second column we indicate macro (M) functions.

•	A bullet means that the function is unchanged from versions of Excel earlier than version 3.0.
✓	A check mark means that the function is in some respect changed from earlier versions.
+	A plus sign means that the function is new in version 3.0.

Some functions are listed in more than one category; the IF function, for example, can be considered both a *logical* function and a *control* function.

Function type W	Function type M	Name	Comments
NUMERIC			
•		ABS	Returns: Absolute value of *n*.
•		ACOS	Returns: Arccosine of *n*.
•		ACOSH	Returns: Inverse hyperbolic cosine of *n*.
•		ASIN	Returns: Arcsine of *n*.
+		ASINH	Returns: Inverse hyperbolic sine of *n*.
•		ATAN	Returns: Arctangent of *n*.
•		ATAN2	Returns: Arctangent of *n*, given Cartesian coordinates.
+		ATANH	Returns: Inverse hyperbolic tangent of *n*.
•		COS	Returns: Cosine of *n*.
+		COSH	Returns: Hyperbolic cosine of *n*.
•		EXP	Returns: Specified number to the *n*th power.
•		FACT	Returns: Factorial of a number.
•		FIXED	Returns: Number rounded to a specified number of decimal places.
•		INT	Returns: Number rounded to nearest integer.
•		LN	Returns: Natural log of a number.
•		LOG	Returns: Log of a number to a specified base.
•		LOG10	Returns: Base-10 log of a number.
•		MAX	Returns: Larger of two numbers.
•		MDETERM	Returns: Determinant of an array.
•		MIN	Returns: Smaller of two numbers.
•		MINVERSE	Returns: Inverse matrix of an array.
•		MMULT	Returns: Product of two arrays.
•		MOD	Returns: Remainder of the division of one number by another.

(continued)

Function type W	Function type M	Name	Comments
NUMERIC, *continued*			
•		PI	Returns: Value of pi.
•		PRODUCT	Returns: Product of a list of numbers.
•		RAND	Returns: A random number from 0 to 0.999…
•		ROUND	Returns: *n* rounded to the indicated number of digits.
•		SIGN	Returns: –1, 0, or 1.
•		SIN	Returns: Sine of *n*.
+		SINH	Returns: Hyperbolic sine of *n*.
•		SQRT	Returns: Square root of *n*.
•		SUM	Returns: Sum of supplied arguments.
+		SUMPRODUCT	Returns: Sum of product of arrays.
•		TAN	Returns: Tangent of *n*.
+		TANH	Returns: Hyperbolic tangent of *n*.
✓		TRUNC	Returns: Truncated number. Accepts *precision* argument to specify number of places to truncate.
LOGICAL AND LOOKUP			
•		AND	Returns: Logical AND of all arguments.
•		CHOOSE	Returns: Chosen value.
•		FALSE	Returns: FALSE.
•		HLOOKUP	Returns: Value in a range that matches a specified value in the range's top row.
•		IF (form 1)	Returns: One of two values depending on whether an expression evaluates to true or false.
•		INDEX (form 1)	Returns: Reference of a cell within a specified range. Reference form.
•		INDEX (form 2)	Returns: Value of an element in an array. Array form.
•		LOOKUP (form 1)	Returns: Value in a range. Vector form.
•		LOOKUP (form 2)	Returns: Value in an array. Array form.
•		MATCH	Returns: Relative position of an element in an array that matches a specified value.
•		NOT	Returns: The logical opposite of a value.
•		OR	Returns: TRUE if either of two values is TRUE.
•		TRUE	Returns: TRUE.
•		VLOOKUP	Returns: Value in a range that matches a specified value in the range's left row.

Function type W	M	Name	Comments
VALUE AND CONVERSION			
•		ISBLANK	Returns: TRUE if value is blank.
•		ISERR	Returns: TRUE if value is an error value other than #N/A.
•		ISERROR	Returns: TRUE if value is an error value.
•		ISLOGICAL	Returns: TRUE if value is a logical.
•		ISNA	Returns: TRUE if value is #N/A.
•		ISNONTEXT	Returns: TRUE if value is not text (including blank cells).
•		ISNUMBER	Returns: TRUE if value is a number.
•		ISREF	Returns: TRUE if value is a reference.
•		ISTEXT	Returns: TRUE if value is text.
•		N	Returns: Value converted to a number.
•		NA	Returns: Error value #N/A.
•		T	Returns: Text referred to by the specified value.
•		TEXT	Returns: Value converted to text in the specified format.
•		TYPE	Returns: Selected value's type (number, text, logical, formula, error, or array).
•		VALUE	Returns: Text converted to a value.
FINANCIAL			
•		DDB	Returns: Depreciation of a fixed asset using the double-declining balance method.
•		DOLLAR	Returns: A dollar amount expressed as text.
•		FV	Returns: Future value of an investment, based on constant periodic payments and a fixed interest rate.
✓		GROWTH	Returns: Finds the best-fit exponential curve that matches specified data. Accepts *constant* argument, so you can force the constant term to 0.
•		IPMT	Returns: Interest payment for a period based on constant periodic payments and a fixed rate.
•		IRR	Returns: Internal rate of return.
•		MIRR	Returns: Modified internal rate of return for a series of periodic cash flows.
•		NPER	Returns: Number of periods for an investment based on constant, periodic payments and a fixed rate.

(continued)

Function type W	Function type M	Name	Comments
FINANCIAL, *continued*			
•		NPV	Returns: Net present value of an investment, based on constant, periodic payments and a fixed rate.
•		PMT	Returns: Periodic payment for an annuity based on constant payments and a fixed rate.
•		PPMT	Returns: Payment on the principal for a specified period, based on constant periodic payments and a fixed rate.
•		PV	Returns: Present value of an investment.
•		RATE	Returns: Interest rate per period for an annuity.
•		SLN	Returns: Depreciation of an asset for any period, using the straight-line method.
•		SYD	Returns: Depreciation of an asset for any period, using the sum-of-the-year's-digits method.
+		VDB	Returns: Depreciation of an asset for any period, using the double-declining balance method.
STATISTICAL			
•		AVERAGE	Returns: Average (mean) of the arguments.
•		COUNT	Returns: Number of numeric entries in a list.
•		COUNTA	Returns: Number of nonblank values in a list.
•		DCOUNT	Returns: Number of cells in a database field that are numeric.
•		DCOUNTA	Returns: Number of cells in a database field that are nonblank.
✓		LINEST	Returns: Regression coefficient *r2*, standard error, sum of squares, F-statistic, and degrees of freedom. Returns additional regression statistics. Also takes additional argument to force constant term to 0.
✓		LOGEST	Returns: Regression coefficient *r2*, standard error, sum of squares, F-statistic, and degrees of freedom. Returns additional regression statistics. Also takes additional argument to force constant term to 0.
+		MEDIAN	Returns: Median of a set of numbers.
•		STDEV	Returns: Standard deviation of a population of numbers based on a sample of that population.

(continued)

Function type W	M	Name	Comments
STATISTICAL, *continued*			
•		STDEVP	Returns: Standard deviation of a population of numbers based on the entire population.
✓		TREND	Projects points along a straight line based on existing points. Accepts *constant* argument, so you can force the constant term to 0.
•		VAR	Returns: Variance of a population of numbers based on a sample of that population.
•		VARP	Returns: Variance of a population of numbers based on the entire population.
TIME AND DATE			
•		DATE	Returns: Serial number of a date.
•		DATEVALUE	Returns: Serial number of a date represented as text.
•		DAVERAGE	Returns: Average of a field in a database.
•		DAY	Returns: Day of the month of a date.
+		DAYS360	Returns: Number of days between two dates based on a 360-day year.
•		HOUR	Returns: Hour of a serial time/date value.
•		MINUTE	Returns: Minute portion of a serial time/date value.
•		MONTH	Returns: Month portion of a serial time/date value.
•		NOW	Returns: Serial time/date value of the present moment. Mac and PC versions use different date systems.
•		SECOND	Returns: Seconds portion of a serial time/date value.
•		TIME	Returns: Serial time value of the present moment. PC and Mac versions use different date systems.
•		TIMEVALUE	Returns: Serial time value of the time represented by a text value indicating time (for example, 11:00 AM).
+		TODAY	Returns: Date serial number of the current day.
•		WEEKDAY	Returns: Day of the week represented by a serial time/date value.
•		YEAR	Returns: Year portion of a serial time/date value.

Function type W	M	Name	Comments
TEXT			
•		CHAR	Returns: Text character corresponding to ASCII code *n*.
•		CLEAN	Returns: Text without non-printable characters.
•		CODE	Returns: ASCII code for first character in text.
•		EXACT	Returns: TRUE if both arguments are exactly the same.
•		FIND	Returns: Position of one string within another.
•		LEFT	Returns: Leftmost characters from specified text.
•		LEN	Returns: Length of specified text.
•		LOWER	Returns: Specified text converted to lowercase.
•		MID	Returns: Series of characters from specified text.
•		PROPER	Returns: Text in which any letter that does not follow a letter is capitalized.
•		REPLACE	Returns: Characters in the specified text replaced with other text.
•		REPT	Returns: Text repeated the specified number of times.
•		RIGHT	Returns: Rightmost characters from specified text.
•		SEARCH	Returns: Number of the specified character in specified text.
•		SUBSTITUTE	Returns: Text with indicated replacements.
•		T	Returns: Text referred to by the specified value.
•		TEXT	Returns: Value converted to text in the specified format.
•		TRIM	Returns: Specified text with extra space characters removed.
•		UPPER	Returns: Specified text in all uppercase characters.
EDITING			
	•	CANCEL.COPY	AE: PC—Esc; Mac—Command-. (period).
	•	CLEAR	CE: Edit Clear.
	+	CONSOLIDATE	CE: Data Consolidate. Consolidates data from multiple worksheets. Three new arguments.
	•	COPY	CE: Edit Copy.
	•	CUT	CE: Edit Cut.

(continued)

Function type W	M	Name	Comments
EDITING, ***continued***			
	+	DUPLICATE	CE: Duplicates the selected worksheet or macro sheet object. Returns #VALUE! if no object was selected.
	•	EDIT.DELETE	CE: Edit Delete.
	•	EDIT.REPEAT	CE: Edit Repeat.
	•	FILL.DOWN	CE: Edit Fill Down.
	•	FILL.LEFT	CE: Edit Fill Left.
	•	FILL.RIGHT	CE: Edit Fill Right.
	•	FILL.UP	CE: Edit Fill Up.
	+	FILL.WORKGROUP	CE: Edit Fill Workgroup. Fills the current selection into the same range in every worksheet in the workgroup.
	•	FORMULA	AE: Entering a formula from the keyboard.
	•	FORMULA.ARRAY	AE: Entering an array formula from the keyboard.
	•	FORMULA.FILL	AE: Entering a formula into a range of cells.
	•	FORMULA.FIND	CE: Formula Find.
	•	FORMULA.FIND.NEXT	AE: PC—F7; Mac—Command-H.
	•	FORMULA.FIND.PREV	AE: PC—Shift-F7; Mac—Shift-Command-H.
	•	FORMULA.REPLACE	CE: Formula Replace.
	•	GET.FORMULA	Returns: Content of a cell as it would appear in the formula bar.
	•	GET.NOTE	Returns: Text from a note.
	+	GOAL.SEEK	CE: Formula Goal Seek.
	•	INSERT	CE: Edit Insert.
	•	NOTE	CE: Formula Note: ? form takes no arguments.
	•	PASTE	CE: Edit Paste.
	+	PASTE.PICTURE	CE: Edit Paste Picture (Shift-Paste).
	•	PASTE.SPECIAL (form 1)	CE: Edit Paste Special. Pastes from worksheet to worksheet.
•		TRANSPOSE	Returns: Specified array with rows and columns switched.
	•	UNDO	CE: Edit Undo.
NAMES AND REFERENCES			
	•	A1.R1C1	Switches between A1 and R1C1 styles of references.
	•	ABSREF	Returns: Absolute reference of the cells that are offset by *refT* from *ref*.
	•	ACTIVE.CELL	Returns: External reference of active cell (as text).

(continued)

Function type W	Function type M	Name	Comments
NAMES AND REFERENCES, *continued*			
•		ADDRESS	Returns: Reference of a specified type to a specific cell or range of cells.
	•	APPLY.NAMES	CE: Formula Apply Names.
•		AREAS	Returns: Number of areas in the reference.
✓		CELL	Returns: Information about a cell.
•		CHOOSE	Returns: Chosen reference.
•		COLUMN	Returns: Column number of reference.
•		COLUMNS	Returns: Number of columns in reference.
	•	CREATE.NAMES	CE: Formula Create Names.
	✓	DEFINE.NAME	CE: Formula Define Name.
	•	DELETE.NAME	AE: Clicking the Delete button in the Formula Define Name dialog box.
	•	DEREF	Returns: Value of cells in a reference.
	+	FORMULA.CONVERT	Returns: Reference in specified format. Converts the references in a formula from A1 to R1C1 style.
	✓	GET.CELL	Returns: Information about a cell.
	✓	GET.DEF	Returns: Name, as text, corresponding to a given definition.
	•	GET.NAME	Returns: Definition of a specified name, as text.
•		INDEX (form 1)	Returns: Reference of a cell within a specified range. Reference form.
•		INDEX (form 2)	Returns: Value of an element in an array. Array form.
•		INDIRECT	Returns: Reference specified by another reference.
	•	LIST.NAMES	CE: Formula Paste Names. Selects the Paste List option.
	✓	NAMES	Returns: Horizontal array of the names defined in a document.
✓		OFFSET	Returns: Reference of a specified height and width offset from the selection by a specified amount. Now works on worksheets.
	•	*reference*	Transfers macro execution to the specified cell, with the supplied arguments.
	•	REFTEXT	Returns: Reference converted to an absolute text reference.
	•	RELREF	Returns: Distance between one reference and another, expressed as an R1C1-text reference.
•		ROW	Returns: Row number of reference.

(continued)

Function type W	Function type M	Name	Comments
NAMES AND REFERENCES, *continued*			
•		ROWS	Returns: Number of rows in a reference or array.
	•	SELECT (form 1)	AE: Selecting cells. Selects cells on a worksheet or macro sheet.
	•	SELECTION	Returns: Reference of selection.
	•	SET.NAME	Defines a name on a macro sheet using the specified value.
	•	SET.VALUE	Sets the value of a cell or cells on a macro sheet without disturbing the formula or formulas contained in the cell or cells.
	•	TEXTREF	Converts text to an absolute reference.
NAVIGATION AND SELECTION			
	•	FORMULA.GOTO	CE: Formula Goto.
	•	HLINE	AE: Clicking on a horizontal scroll arrow.
	•	HPAGE	AE: Clicking in the horizontal scroll bar.
	•	HSCROLL	AE: Dragging the horizontal scroll box.
	•	SELECT.END	AE: PC—Ctrl-(arrow); Mac—Command-(arrow).
	•	SELECT.LAST.CELL	AE: Last Cell option in the Formula Select Special dialog box. Same as SELECT.SPECIAL(11) in Excel version 3.0.
	✓	SELECT.SPECIAL	CE: Formula Select Special.
	•	SHOW.ACTIVE.CELL	CE: Formula Show Active Cell. AE: PC—Ctrl-Backspace; Mac—Command-Delete.
	•	UNLOCKED.NEXT	AE: Tab.
	•	UNLOCKED.PREV	AE: Shift-Tab.
	•	VLINE	AE: Clicking a vertical scroll arrow.
	•	VPAGE	AE: Clicking in vertical scroll bar.
	•	VSCROLL	AE: Dragging the vertical scroll box.
FORMATTING			
	✓	ALIGNMENT	CE: Format Alignment. New Wrap Text option.
	+	APPLY.STYLE	CE: Format Style. Applies a defined style to the selected range. Returns #VALUE! if *styleNameT* isn't defined.
	✓	BORDER	CE: Format Border.
	✓	COLUMN.WIDTH	CE: Format Column Width.
	+	DEFINE.STYLE (form 1)	AE: Define button in the Format Style dialog box. By example.

(continued)

Function type W	Function type M	Name	Comments
FORMATTING, *continued*			
	+	DEFINE.STYLE (form 2)	AE: Define button in the Format Style dialog box. Sets a number format, using arguments from the FORMAT.NUMBER function.
	+	DEFINE.STYLE (form 3)	AE: Define button in the Format Style dialog box. Sets a font format, using arguments from the FORMAT.FONT function.
	+	DEFINE.STYLE (form 4)	AE: Define button in the Format Style dialog box. Sets alignment, using arguments from the ALIGNMENT function.
	+	DEFINE.STYLE (form 5)	AE: Define button in the Format Style dialog box. Sets a border format, using arguments from the BORDER function.
	+	DEFINE.STYLE (form 6)	AE: Define button in the Format Style dialog box. Sets a pattern format, using arguments from form 1 of the PATTERNS function.
	+	DEFINE.STYLE (form 7)	AE: Define button in the Format Style dialog box. Sets cell protection, using arguments from the CELL.PROTECTION function.
	•	DELETE.FORMAT	AE: Clicking the Delete button in the Format Number dialog box.
	+	DELETE.STYLE	AE: Clicking the Delete button in the Format Style dialog box. Deletes a style. Returns #VALUE! if the style name doesn't exist.
	•	FONT	CE: Options Font in Macintosh version 1.5. Included only for macro compatibility; use FORMAT.FONT and DEFINE.STYLE instead.
	•	FORMAT.FONT (form 1)	CE: Format Font. Sets a font for selected cells.
	•	FORMAT.FONT (form 2)	CE: Format Font. Sets a font for specified characters in a text box.
	•	FORMAT.NUMBER	CE: Format Number.
	•	JUSTIFY	CE: Format Justify.
	+	MERGE.STYLES	AE: Clicking the Merge button in the Font Style dialog box. Merges styles from the specified open document into the active document.
	•	PATTERNS (form 1)	CE: Format Patterns. For cells.
	+	PATTERNS (form 3)	CE: Format Patterns. Text boxes, rectangles, ovals, arcs, and pictures.
	•	REPLACE.FONT	For compatibility with Windows version 2.1 or earlier. In 3.0, use FORMAT.FONT instead.
	✓	STANDARD.FONT	Sets the standard font for the worksheet. In 3.0, use DEFINE.STYLE and APPLY.STYLE.
	•	STYLE	Provided for compatibility with Mac version 1.5 or earlier. In 3.0, use FORMAT.FONT instead.

Function type: W	Function type: M	Name	Comments
CONTROL			
	•	ARGUMENT (form 1)	Assigns a value to a name.
	•	ARGUMENT (form 2)	Assigns a value to a named reference.
	•	BREAK	Interrupts a FOR-NEXT, FOR.CELL-NEXT, or WHILE-NEXT loop.
	•	CALLER	Returns: Reference or ID of calling macro or object.
	+	ELSE	Used with IF, ELSE.IF, and END.IF.
	+	ELSE.IF	Used with IF, ELSE.IF, and END.IF.
	+	END.IF	Ends an IF block.
	•	ERROR	Disables display of error messages or specifies a macro to be run when an error is encountered.
	•	FOR	Starts a FOR-NEXT loop.
	+	FOR.CELL	Runs a FOR-NEXT loop once for each cell in the specified range.
	•	GOTO	Transfers macro execution to the specified cell.
	✓	HALT	Halts all macro execution.
•		IF (form 1)	Executes one expression if test is true, another if false.
	+	IF (form 2)	New form of the IF function, used with ELSE, ELSE.IF, and END.IF.
	+	LAST.ERROR	Returns: Reference of cell on a macro sheet in which the most recent error occurred.
	•	NEXT	Ends a FOR-NEXT, FOR.CELL, or WHILE-NEXT loop.
	•	RESTART	Removes specified number of levels of RETURN in an executing macro.
	•	RESULT	Specifies type of value returned by a macro.
	•	RETURN	Ends a macro routine.
	✓	RUN	CE: Macro Run.
	•	STEP	Changes macro execution to one cell at a time.
	+	VOLATILE	Sets a custom function to recalculate each time the worksheet on which it is used is recalculated.
	•	WAIT	Pauses a macro for the specified time.
	•	WHILE	Starts a WHILE-NEXT loop.
WINDOWS			
	•	ACTIVATE	CE: Documents on Window menu. Activates a window or a pane of a window.
	•	ACTIVATE.NEXT	AE: PC—Ctrl-F6; Mac—Command-M. Activates next window.
	•	ACTIVATE.PREV	AE: PC—Ctrl-Shift-F6; Mac—Command-Shift-M. Activates previous window.

(continued)

Function type W	Function type M	Name	Comments
WINDOWS, *continued*			
	•	ARRANGE.ALL	CE: Window Arrange All.
	•	CALCULATE.DOCUMENT	CE: Options Calculate Document.
	•	CALCULATE.NOW	CE: Options Calculate Now, Chart Calculate Now.
	•	CALCULATION	CE: Option Calculation.
	•	CELL.PROTECTION	CE: Format Cell Protection.
	•	CLOSE	CE: PC—Document window Control Close. AE: Mac—Clicking the window's close box.
	•	CLOSE.ALL	CE: File Close All.
	+	COLOR.PALETTE	AE: Choosing a file in the Copy Colors From list box in the Options Color Palette dialog box. Replaces the color palette of the active document with that from another open document.
	✓	DISPLAY (form 1)	CE: Options Display. For controlling screen display in a document.
	•	DISPLAY (form 2)	CE: Info menu. Commands on the Info menu, displayed when Window Show Info has been selected.
	•	ECHO	Turns screen updating on or off.
	+	EDIT.COLOR	AE: Clicking the Edit button in the Options Color Palette dialog box. Sets an existing color to the RGB values specified.
	•	FREEZE.PANES	CE: Options Freeze Panes, Unfreeze Panes.
	•	FULL	AE: PC—pressing Ctrl-F10 (full size) or Ctrl-F5 (previous size), or double-clicking the title bar; Mac—double-clicking the title bar or clicking the zoom box.
	✓	GET.DOCUMENT	Returns: Information about a document.
	✓	GET.WINDOW	Returns: Information about a window.
	✓	GET.WORKSPACE	Returns: Information about the workspace.
	•	HIDE	CE: Window Hide.
+		INFO	Returns: Information about the current operating environment.
	•	MOVE	CE: PC—Control Move (Windows Control menu). Dialog box form available only in PC versions.
	•	NEW.WINDOW	CE: Window New Window.
	•	PRECISION	CE: Options Calculation. AE: Clicking the Precision As Displayed option.
	✓	PROTECT.DOCUMENT	CE: Options Protect Document, Unprotect Document.

(continued)

Function type: W	Function type: M	Name	Comments
WINDOWS, *continued*			
	•	QUIT	CE: PC—File Exit; Mac—File Quit. Quits Excel and closes any open documents.
	✓	ROW.HEIGHT	CE: Format Row Height.
	•	SAVE	CE: File Save.
	✓	SAVE.AS	CE: File Save As.
	•	SAVE.?WORKSPACE	CE: File Save Workspace.
	•	SHORT.MENUS	CE: Options Short Menus or Chart Short Menus.
	•	SHOW.CLIPBOARD	CE: OS/2 and Mac—Window Show Clipboard. In Windows, equivalent to running the Clipboard application from the Control menu.
	•	SHOW.INFO	CE: Window Show Info. Displays the Info window for the selected range.
	•	SIZE	CE: PC—Control Size. AE: Mac—dragging the size box of a window.
	•	SPLIT	CE: Control Split (Windows Control menu). In Windows and OS/2 versions only. AE: Dragging the split bar in the active window.
	•	UNHIDE	CE: Window Unhide.
	•	WINDOWS	Returns: The names of all open (including hidden) windows.
	+	WORKGROUP	CE: Window Workgroup. Creates a workgroup from the specified documents.
	✓	WORKSPACE	CE: Options Workspace.
DIALOG BOX			
	•	ALERT	Returns: TRUE if OK clicked, FALSE if Cancel clicked.
	•	BEEP	Causes a beep.
	•	DIALOG.BOX	Creates a dialog box from a definition table.
	•	INPUT	Returns: Information entered in Input dialog box; FALSE if Cancel clicked.
EVENTS			
	•	CANCEL.KEY	Starts a specified macro when a macro is interrupted, or disables interruption.
	+	DISABLE.INPUT	Blocks all input to Excel from the keyboard and the mouse.
	+	ON.DATA	Runs a macro when data is sent from another application to a specified document.
	•	ON.KEY	Runs a macro when a key is pressed in combination with control keys.

(continued)

Function type W	M	Name	Comments
EVENTS, *continued*			
	+	ON.RECALC	Runs a macro when the document is recalculated.
	•	ON.TIME	Runs a macro at a specified time.
	•	ON.WINDOW	Runs a macro when the specified window is activated.
FILE			
	•	DIRECTORY	Returns: Current directory, as text. Changes the current directory.
	•	DOCUMENTS	Returns: Horizontal array of names of all open documents, in alphabetic order.
	•	FCLOSE	Closes a text file.
	•	FILE.CLOSE	CE: File Close.
	•	FILE.DELETE	CE: File Delete. Deletes the specified file.
	•	FILES	Returns: Horizontal text array of all files in the specified directory or folder.
	•	FOPEN	Returns: File ID of the open file; #N/A if not successful. Opens or creates a file.
	•	FPOS	Returns: Current position in a text file. Sets the current position in a text file.
	•	FREAD	Returns: Characters read from a text file.
	•	FREADLN	Returns: A line of text read from a text file.
	•	FSIZE	Returns: Size of a text file, in bytes (characters).
	•	FWRITE	Returns: Number of characters written to a text file.
	•	FWRITELN	Returns: Number of characters written to a text file.
	✓	NEW	CE: File New. Creates a new document.
	✓	OPEN	CE: File Open. Opens an existing file or workspace.
LINKING			
	✓	CHANGE.LINK	AE: Clicking Change button in the File Links dialog box.
	+	GET.LINK.INFO	Returns: Information about a link.
	✓	LINKS	Returns: Horizontal array of text values: the names of all worksheets used in external references in the specified document.
	✓	OPEN.LINKS	Opens documents linked to a specified document.
	•	PASTE.LINK	CE: Edit Paste Link.
	+	PASTE.PICTURE.LINK	CE: Edit Paste Picture Link (Shift-Paste Link).

(continued)

Function type W	M	Name	Comments
LINKING, *continued*			
	+	SET.UPDATE.STATUS	Sets manual or automatic updating for a link.
	+	UPDATE.LINK	AE: Clicking the Update button in the File Links dialog box. Updates a link to the specified document.
MENU			
	•	ADD.BAR	Returns: Bar ID number. Adds a new menu bar.
	✓	ADD.COMMAND	Adds a command to a menu. Now replaces deleted built-in menu commands.
	•	ADD.MENU	Adds a menu to a menu bar.
	•	CHECK.COMMAND	Adds or removes a check mark before a menu command.
	+	CUSTOM.REPEAT	Creates a custom Edit Repeat command for custom commands.
	+	CUSTOM.UNDO	Creates a custom Edit Undo command for custom commands.
	•	DELETE.BAR	Deletes a menu bar.
	•	DELETE.COMMAND	Deletes a command on a menu.
	•	DELETE.MENU	Deletes a menu.
	•	ENABLE.COMMAND	Dims or undims a menu command. Returns #VALUE! if disabling a built-in command.
	•	GET.BAR	Returns: Number of the active menu bar.
	•	HELP	CE: Help or Window Help.
	•	MESSAGE	Displays a message in the status bar.
	•	RENAME.COMMAND	Renames a menu command.
	•	SHOW.BAR	Displays a menu bar created with ADD.BAR.
OBJECTS			
	+	ASSIGN.TO.OBJECT	CE: Macro Assign to Object. Assigns a macro to the selected object, to be run when the object is clicked. Returns: #VALUE! if no object was selected.
	+	BRING.TO.FRONT	CE: Format Bring To Front. Brings selected object to front. Returns: #VALUE! if the selection isn't one or more objects.
	+	CREATE.OBJECT (form 1)	AE: Clicking an icon in the Toolbar and creating a new line, rectangle, oval, arc, or picture. Creates a new object: line, rectangle, oval, arc, or picture. Returns: Text ID of the object.
	+	CREATE.OBJECT (form 2)	AE: Clicking an icon in the Toolbar and creating a new text box or button. Creates a new object: text box or button. Returns: Text ID of the object.

(continued)

Function type W	Function type M	Name	Comments
OBJECTS, *continued*			
	+	CREATE.OBJECT (form 3)	AE: Clicking an icon in the Toolbar and creating an embedded chart. Creates a new object: embedded chart. Returns: Text ID of the object.
	•	FORMAT.MOVE (form 1)	AE: Moving an object with the mouse. Moves worksheet and macro sheet objects.
	•	FORMAT.SIZE (form 1)	AE: Sizing a selected object with the mouse. Worksheet objects.
	+	GET.OBJECT	Returns: Information about an object.
	+	GROUP	CE: Format Group. Groups currently selected objects.
	+	HIDE.OBJECT	Hides the selected or specified object.
	+	OBJECT.PROTECTION	CE: Format Object Protection. AE: Clicking the Locked check box in the Format Object Protection dialog box. Sets protection options for the selected object.
	+	PLACEMENT	CE: Format Object Placement. Sets alignment of object relative to the grid of cells.
	+	SELECT (form 2)	AE: Selecting objects on a worksheet or macro sheet.
	+	SEND.TO.BACK	CE: Format Send To Back AE: Moving the selected object behind all other objects.
	+	TEXT.BOX	Replaces specified characters in a text box with new text.
	+	UNGROUP	CE: Format Ungroup. Breaks grouped objects into separate objects.
CHARTING			
	•	ADD.ARROW	CE: Chart Add Arrow. Adds an arrow to the active chart.
	•	ADD.OVERLAY	CE: Chart Add Overlay.
	•	ATTACH.TEXT	CE: Chart Attach Text.
	•	AXES (form 1)	CE: Chart Axes.
	+	AXES (form 2)	CE: Chart Axes. For 3D charts.
	•	COMBINATION	CE: Gallery Combination.
	•	COPY.CHART	CE: Edit Copy Chart.
	•	DELETE.ARROW	CE: Chart Delete Arrow.
	•	DELETE.OVERLAY	CE: Chart Delete Overlay.
	+	EDIT.SERIES	CE: Chart Edit Series. Creates, edits, and deletes data series on charts.
	•	FORMAT.FONT (form 3)	CE: Format Font. Sets a font for chart items, including text boxes.
	•	FORMAT.LEGEND	CE: Format Legend.

(continued)

Function type			
W	M	Name	Comments
CHARTING, *continued*			
	+	FORMAT.MAIN	CE: Format Main Chart.
	•	FORMAT.MOVE (form 2)	AE: Moving a chart item with the mouse. Moves chart items.
	+	FORMAT.OVERLAY	CE: Format Overlay.
	•	FORMAT.SIZE (form 2)	AE: Sizing a selected object with the mouse. Worksheet objects and chart items. Returns: TRUE if the object has been sized.
	•	FORMAT.TEXT	CE: Format Text.
	+	GALLERY.3D.AREA	CE: Gallery 3D Area. Creates a 3D chart.
	+	GALLERY.3D.COLUMN	CE: Gallery 3D Column. Creates a 3D column chart.
	+	GALLERY.3D.LINE	CE: Gallery 3D Line. Creates a 3D line chart.
	+	GALLERY.3D.PIE	CE: Gallery 3D Pie. Creates a 3D pie chart.
	•	GALLERY.AREA	CE: Gallery Area. Creates an area chart.
	•	GALLERY.BAR	CE: Gallery Bar. Creates a bar chart.
	•	GALLERY.COLUMN	CE: Gallery Column. Creates a column chart.
	•	GALLERY.LINE	CE: Gallery Line. Creates a line chart.
	•	GALLERY.PIE	CE: Gallery Pie. Creates a pie chart.
	•	GALLERY.SCATTER	CE: Gallery Scatter. Creates a scatter chart.
	•	GET.CHART.ITEM	Returns: Position of a specified chart item.
	✓	GRIDLINES	CE: Chart Gridlines.
	•	LEGEND	CE: Chart Add Legend, Delete Legend.
	•	MAIN.CHART	CE: Format Main Chart in Excel version 2.2 or earlier.
	•	MAIN.CHART.TYPE	CE: Chart Main Chart Type (Macintosh version 1.5). In Excel version 3.0, use FORMAT.MAIN.
	•	OVERLAY	CE: Format Overlay in Excel 2.2 or earlier.
	•	OVERLAY.CHART.TYPE	CE: Mac—Chart Overlay Chart Type. Included for compatibility with Macintosh 1.5 or earlier; in Excel 3.0, use FORMAT.OVERLAY.
	•	PASTE.SPECIAL (form 2)	CE: Edit Paste Special. Pastes from worksheet to chart.
	•	PASTE.SPECIAL (form 3)	CE: Edit Paste Special. Pastes from chart to chart.
	•	PATTERNS (form 2)	CE: Format Patterns. For lines (arrows) on worksheets or charts.
	•	PATTERNS (form 4)	CE: Format Patterns. For chart plot areas, bars, columns, pie slices, text labels.
	•	PATTERNS (form 5)	CE: Format Patterns. For chart axes.
	•	PATTERNS (form 6)	CE: Format Patterns. For chart gridlines and so forth.

(continued)

Function type W	Function type M	Name	Comments
CHARTING, *continued*			
	•	PATTERNS (form 7)	CE: Format Patterns. For chart data lines.
	•	PATTERNS (form 8)	CE: Format Patterns. For picture chart markers.
	•	PREFERRED	CE: Gallery Preferred.
	•	SCALE (form 1)	CE: Format Scale. Category (*x*) axis, 2D chart.
	•	SCALE (form 2)	CE: Format Scale. Value (*y*) axis, 2D chart or *xy* (scatter) chart.
	+	SCALE (form 3)	CE: Format Scale. Category (*x*) axis, 3D chart.
	+	SCALE (form 4)	CE: Format Scale. Series (*y*) axis, 3D chart.
	+	SCALE (form 5)	CE: Format Scale. Value (*z*) axis, 3D chart.
	+	SELECT (form 3)	AE: Selecting a chart object. Selects a chart object as specified by the selection code.
	•	SELECT.CHART	CE: Chart Select Chart. Provided for compatibility with Mac 1.5 or earlier. In Excel 3.0, use SELECT("Chart") instead.
	•	SELECT.PLOT.AREA	Provided for compatibility with Mac 1.5 or earlier. In Excel 3.0, use SELECT("Plot") instead.
•		SERIES	Used only in charts. Cannot be entered in a macro sheet or a worksheet. Use EDIT.SERIES in macros.
	•	SET.PREFERRED	CE: Gallery Set Preferred.
	+	VIEW.3D	CE: Format 3D View. Adjusts the view in a 3D chart.
OUTLINING			
	+	DEMOTE	AE: Clicking the Demote button in the Toolbar. Demotes the selected portion of an outline by one level.
	+	OUTLINE	CE: Formula Outline. Specifies settings for creating or formatting an outline.
	+	PROMOTE	AE: Clicking the Promote icon in the Toolbar. Promotes selected parts of an outline by one level.
	+	SHOW.DETAIL	Expands or collapses the subtopics in an outline.
	+	SHOW.LEVELS	Displays the specified number of row and column levels in an outline.
PRINTING			
	•	PAGE.SETUP (form 1)	CE: File Page Setup. For worksheets and macro sheets.
	•	PAGE.SETUP (form 2)	CE: File Page Setup. For charts.
	✓	PRINT	CE: File Print.

(continued)

Function type W	Function type M	Name	Comments
PRINTING, *continued*			
	+	PRINT.PREVIEW	CE: File Print Preview. Calls up the Print Preview window so that you can view the way the document will be printed.
	•	PRINTER.SETUP	CE: PC only. File Printer Setup.
	•	REMOVE.PAGE.BREAK	CE: Options Remove Page Break.
	•	SET.PAGE.BREAK	CE: Options Set Page Break.
	•	SET.PRINT.AREA	CE: Options Set Print Area.
	•	SET.PRINT.TITLES	CE: Options Set Print Titles.
DATABASE AND DATA MENU			
	•	DATA.DELETE	CE: Data Delete.
	•	DATA.FIND	CE: Data Find.
	•	DATA.FIND.NEXT	AE: Pressing the Down direction key.
	•	DATA.FIND.PREV	AE: Pressing the Up direction key.
	•	DATA.FORM	CE: Data Form.
	•	DATA.SERIES	CE: Data Series.
✓		DGET	Returns: Single record extracted that matches the criteria.
•		DMAX	Returns: Maximum value in database field.
•		DMIN	Returns: Minimum value in database field.
•		DPRODUCT	Returns: Product of values in database field.
•		DSTDEV	Returns: Standard deviation of a population, based on a sample matching database criteria.
•		DSTDEVP	Returns: Standard deviation of a population, based on a population matching database criteria.
•		DSUM	Returns: Sum of the numbers matching database criteria.
•		DVAR	Returns: Variance of a population, based on a sample matching database criteria.
•		DVARP	Returns: Variance of a population, based on a population matching database criteria.
	•	EXTRACT	CE: Data Extract.
	•	PARSE	CE: Data Parse.
	•	SET.CRITERIA	CE: Data Set Criteria.
	•	SET.DATABASE	CE: Data Set Database.
	+	SET.EXTRACT	CE: Data Set Extract. Names the selection Extract.
	•	SORT	CE: Data Sort.
	•	TABLE	CE: Data Table.

Function type W	M	Name	Comments
DYNAMIC DATA EXCHANGE (DDE)			
	✓	APP.ACTIVATE	AE: Activating an application. Windows and OS/2 versions only.
	•	APP.MAXIMIZE	AE: Maximizing the Excel application. Windows and OS/2 versions only.
	•	APP.MINIMIZE	AE: Minimizing the Excel application. Windows and OS/2 versions only.
	•	APP.MOVE	AE: Dragging Excel's workspace with the mouse. Windows and OS/2 versions only.
	•	APP.RESTORE	CE: Control Restore. Restores Excel workspace to previous size and location. Windows and OS/2 versions only.
	•	APP.SIZE	CE: Control Size. Changes size of Excel's workspace window. Windows and OS/2 versions only.
	•	COPY.PICTURE	CE: Edit Copy Picture. AE: Holding down Shift key while choosing the Copy command.
	+	CREATE.PUBLISHER	CE: Edit Create Publisher. Publishes the current selection. (Macintosh with System 7 only.)
	+	EDITION.OPTIONS	Sets options or performs actions relative to a publisher or subscriber. (Mac with System 7 only.)
	•	EXEC (form 1)	Starts a separate program. Windows and OS/2 form.
	•	EXEC (form 2)	Starts a separate program. Mac form.
	•	INITIATE	Returns: Number of open channel. Initiates a channel to another application.
	•	OPEN.MAIL	CE: File Open Mail.
	+	REQUEST	Returns: Array of specified type of information from another application. Requests information from another application.
	•	SEND.KEYS	Sends keystrokes to the active application. Windows and OS/2 versions only.
	•	SEND.MAIL	CE: File Send Mail.
	+	SUBSCRIBE.TO	Returns: TRUE if successful. Subscribes to a previously published document. (Mac with System 7 only.)
	+	TERMINATE	Returns: #VALUE! if not successful. Closes a channel to another application.

Function type W	M	Name	Comments
DYNAMIC LINK LIBRARIES (DLL)			
✓	✓	CALL	Now usable directly on worksheets and with arguments to the REGISTER function, so you can now register a code resource and call its processes at the same time.
	✓	EXECUTE	Returns: Values that reflect the status of the command execution. Sends commands to another active program.
	✓	POKE	Returns: Status of transmission. Sends data to a document in another application.
	✓	REGISTER	Makes a code resource available to Excel. Different forms for PC and Mac platforms.
	✓	UNREGISTER	Removes a code resource from memory.
NEWWAVE			
	+	ATTRIBUTES	CE: File Object Attributes. Sets options in the File Object Attributes dialog box.
	+	SAVE.NEW.OBJECT	CE: File Save New Object. Saves a copy of the object as a new object with the name you specify.
	+	SHARE	CE: Edit Share. Puts on the Clipboard a shared view of the object you specify.
	+	SHARE.NAME	CE: Edit Share. Puts on the Clipboard a shared view of the object you specify.

APPENDIX B

Excel's Functions, Listed Alphabetically

The first three columns describe the type of Microsoft Excel function:

W:	Worksheet
C:	Charting
M:	Macro

Functions identified here as *Worksheet* (non-Macro) functions are not represented in the *Applies To* column, to eliminate clutter. The *?* column indicates whether the function has a dialog box (question-mark) form.

The *Applies To* column uses the following codes:

W:	Worksheets and macro sheets
C:	Charts
CM:	Command macros
FM:	Function macros

The *Environment* column describes which operating environment the function belongs to:

W:	Windows
P:	OS/2
M:	Macintosh

An *N* in the Windows column indicates that the function is used only by the Hewlett-Packard NewWave version of Excel. A 7 in the Macintosh column indicates that Apple System 7 is required for this function in the Macintosh version of Excel. A • means that the function is unchanged, a ✓ means it has changed, and a + means it's a new function. An * following an argument in the *Arguments* column means that the argument is required.

For example, if you refer to the table you can see that ATTACH.TEXT is a macro function that has a dialog box form (that is, ATTACH.TEXT?), applies only to charts, and is available in the Windows, OS/2, and Macintosh versions of Excel.

Function type				Applies to				Environment				
W	C	M	?	W	C	CM	FM	W	P	M	Name	Arguments
		•		•		•		•	•	•	A1.R1C1	L*
•								•	•	•	ABS	N*
		•		•		•	•	•	•	•	ABSREF	refT*, reference*
•								•	•	•	ACOS	N*
•								+	+	+	ACOSH	N*
		•		•	•	•		•	•	•	ACTIVATE	windowT, paneN
		•		•	•	•		•	•	•	ACTIVATE.NEXT	—
		•		•	•	•		•	•	•	ACTIVATE.PREV	—
		•		•		•		•	•	•	ACTIVE.CELL	—
		•			•			•	•	•	ADD.ARROW	—
		•						•	•	•	ADD.BAR	barN
		✓						✓	✓	✓	ADD.COMMAND	barN*, menuNT*, commandRef*, positionNT
		•						•	•	•	ADD.MENU	barN*, menuRef*, positionNT
		•			•			•	•	•	ADD.OVERLAY	—
•								+	+	+	ADDRESS	rowN*, colN*, absN, a1, sheetnameT
		•						•	•	•	ALERT	messageT, typeN
		✓	•	•		•		✓	✓	✓	ALIGNMENT	typeN*, wrapL
•								•	•	•	AND	L1*, L2, ...
		✓						•	•	✓	APP.ACTIVATE	titleT, waitL
		•						•	•		APP.MAXIMIZE	—
		•						•	•		APP.MINIMIZE	—

(continued)

Function type				Applies to				Environment				
W	C	M	?	W	C	CM	FM	W	P	M	Name	Arguments
		•	•					•	•		APP.MOVE	xN, yN
		•						•	•		APP.RESTORE	—
		•	•					•	•		APP.SIZE	xN, yN
		•	•	•		•		•	•	•	APPLY.NAMES	nameArray*, ignoreL, useRowColL, omitColL, omitRowL, orderN, appendLastL
		+	•	•		•		+	+	+	APPLY.STYLE	styleT*
•								•	•	•	AREAS	ref
		•				•	•	•	•	•	ARGUMENT (form 1)	nameT*, dataTypeN
		•				•	•	•	•	•	ARGUMENT (form 2)	nameT, dataTypeN, ref*
		•						•	•	•	ARRANGE.ALL	—
•								•	•	•	ASIN	N*
+								+	+	+	ASINH	N*
		+	•	•		•		+	+	+	ASSIGN.TO.OBJECT	macroRef
•								•	•	•	ATAN	N*
•								•	•	•	ATAN2	xN*, yN*
+								+	+	+	ATANH	N*
		•	•		•			•	•	•	ATTACH.TEXT	attachToN*, seriesN, pointN
		+	•	•		•		N			ATTRIBUTES	commentT, autoShareL
•								•	•	•	AVERAGE	n1*, n2, …
		•	•		•			•	•	•	AXES (form 1)	xMainL, yMainL, xOverL, yOverL
		+	•		•			+	+	+	AXES (form 2)	xMain, yMain, zMain
		•						•	•	•	BEEP	toneN
		✓	•	•		•		✓	✓	✓	BORDER	outlineN, leftN, rightN, topN, bottomN, shadeL, outlineColorN, leftColorN, rightColorN, topColorN, bottomColorN
		•				•	•	•	•	•	BREAK	—
		+		•		•		+	+	+	BRING.TO.FRONT	—
		•		•	•	•		•	•	•	CALCULATE. DOCUMENT	—
		•		•	•	•		•	•	•	CALCULATE.NOW	—
		•	•	•	•	•		•	•	•	CALCULATION	typeN*, iterL, maxN, maxChangeN, updateL, precisionL, date1904L
•		✓				•	•	•	•	•	CALL	registerRef*, arg1, arg2, …
✓		✓				•	•	•	•	•	CALL	moduleT, procT, typeT, regT
✓		✓				•	•	•	•	•	CALL	fileT, resourceT, typeT, argT
		•				•	•	•	•	•	CALLER	—
		•		•		•		•	•	•	CANCEL.COPY	—
		•		•		•		•	•	•	CANCEL.KEY	enableL, macroRef
✓		✓						•	•	•	CELL	infoTypeN*, ref

(continued)

Function type				Applies to			Environment				
W	C	M	?	W	C	CMFM	W	P	M	Name	Arguments
		•	•	•		•	•	•	•	CELL.PROTECTION	lockedL, hiddenL
		✓	•	•		•	✓	✓	✓	CHANGE.LINK	oldT*, newT*, typeOfLinkN
•							•	•	•	CHAR	N*
		•					•	•	•	CHECK.COMMAND	barN*, menuNT*, commandNT*, checkL*
•							•	•	•	CHOOSE	indexN*, value1*, value2, ...
•							•	•	•	CLEAN	T*
		•	•				•	•	•	CLEAR	typeN
		•		•	•	•	•	•	•	CLOSE	saveL
		•		•	•	•	•	•	•	CLOSE.ALL	—
•							•	•	•	CODE	T*
		+	•	•	•	•	+	+	+	COLOR.PALETTE	fileT
•							•	•	•	COLUMN	ref
		✓	•	•		•	✓	✓	✓	COLUMN.WIDTH	widthN, ref, standardL, typeN
•							•	•	•	COLUMNS	array*
		•	•		•		•	•	•	COMBINATION	typeN*
		+	•	•		•	+	✓	+	CONSOLIDATE	sourceRefsT, functionN, topRowL, leftColL, createLinksL
		•		•		•	•	•	•	COPY	—
		•			•		•	•	•	COPY.CHART	sizeN*
		•		•		•	•	•	•	COPY.PICTURE	appearanceN*, sizeN
•							•	•	•	COS	N*
+							+	+	+	COSH	N*
•							•	•	•	COUNT	value1*, value2, ...
•							•	•	•	COUNTA	value1*, value2, ...
		•	•	•		•	•	•	•	CREATE.NAMES	topL, leftL, bottomL, rightL
		+		•		•	+	+	+	CREATE.OBJECT (form 1)	objectTypeN*, ref1*, xOffset1N, yOffset1N, ref2*, xOffset2, yOffset2
		+		•		•	+	+	+	CREATE.OBJECT (form 2)	objectTypeN*, ref1*, xOffset1N, yOffset1N, ref2*, xOffset2, yOffset2, text
		+		•		•	+	+	+	CREATE.OBJECT (form 3)	objectTypeN*, ref1*, xOffset1N, yOffset1N, ref2*, xOffset2, yOffset2, xySeriesN
		+		•	•	•			7+	CREATE.PUBLISHER	filenameT*, appearanceN, sizeN
		+					+	+	+	CUSTOM.REPEAT	macroT, repeatT, recordT
		+					+	+	+	CUSTOM.UNDO	macroT*, undoT
		•		•		•	•	•	•	CUT	—
		•	•	•		•	•	•	•	DATA.DELETE	—
		•		•		•	•	•	•	DATA.FIND	L*
		•		•		•	•	•	•	DATA.FIND.NEXT	—

(continued)

Function type				Applies to			Environment				
W	**C**	**M**	**?**	**W**	**C**	**CMFM**	**W**	**P**	**M**	**Name**	**Arguments**
		•		•		•	•	•	•	DATA.FIND.PREV	—
		•		•		•	•	•	•	DATA.FORM	—
		•	•	•		•	•	•	•	DATA.SERIES	rowCol, typeN, dateN, stepValueN, stopValueN
•							•	•	•	DATE	yearN*, monthN*, dayN*
•							•	•	•	DATEVALUE	dateT*
•							•	•	•	DAVERAGE	database*, field*, criteria*
•							•	•	•	DAY	serialN*
+							+	+	+	DAYS360	startDate*, endDate*
•							•	•	•	DCOUNT	database*, field, criteria*
•							•	•	•	DCOUNTA	database*, field*, criteria*
•							•	•	•	DDB	costN*, salvageN*, lifeN*, periodN*, factorN
		✓	•	•		•	✓	✓	✓	DEFINE.NAME	nameT*, refersTo, macroTypeN, shortcutT, hiddenL
		+		•		•	+	+	+	DEFINE.STYLE (form 1)	styleT*, numberL, fontL, alignmentL, borderL, patternL, protectionL
		+		•		•	+	+	+	DEFINE.STYLE (form 2)	styleT*, attributeN*, formatT
		+		•		•	+	+	+	DEFINE.STYLE (form 3)	styleT*, attributeN*, nameT, sizeN, boldL, italicL, underlineL, strikeL, colorL, outlineL, shadowL
		+		•		•	+	+	+	DEFINE.STYLE (form 4)	styleT*, attributeN*, typeN, wrapL
		+		•		•	+	+	+	DEFINE.STYLE (form 5)	styleT*, attributeN*, outlineN, leftN, rightN, topN, bottomN, shade, outlineColorN, leftColorN, rightColorN, topColorN, bottomColorN
		+		•		•	+	+	+	DEFINE.STYLE (form 6)	styleT*, attributeN*, aAutoN, aPatternN, aForeN, aBackN
		+		•		•	+	+	+	DEFINE.STYLE (form 7)	styleT*, attributeN*, lockedL, hiddenL
		•			•		•	•	•	DELETE.ARROW	—
		•					•	•	•	DELETE.BAR	barN*
		•					•	•	•	DELETE.COMMAND	barN*, menuNT*, commandNT*
		•		•		•	•	•	•	DELETE.FORMAT	formatT*
		•					•	•	•	DELETE.MENU	barN*, menuNT*
		•		•		•	•	•	•	DELETE.NAME	nameT*
		•			•		•	•	•	DELETE.OVERLAY	—
		+		•		•	+	+	+	DELETE.STYLE	styleT*
		+	•	•		•	+	+	+	DEMOTE	rowColN

(continued)

Function type				Applies to				Environment				
W	C	M	?	W	C	CM	FM	W	P	M	Name	Arguments
		•		•		•	•	•	•	•	DEREF	reference*
✓								•	•	•	DGET	database*, field*, criteria*
		•						•	•	•	DIALOG.BOX	dialogRef*
		•		•		•		•	•	•	DIRECTORY	pathT
		+						•	•	+	DISABLE.INPUT	L
		✓	•	•		•		✓	✓	✓	DISPLAY (form 1)	formulasL, gridlinesL, headingsL, zerosL, colorN, reserved, outlineL, pageBreaksL, objectN
		•		•		•		•	•	•	DISPLAY (form 2)	cellL, formulaL, valueL, formatL, protectionL, namesL, precedentsN, dependentsN, noteL
•								•	•	•	DMAX	datebase*, field*, criteria*
•								•	•	•	DMIN	datebase*, field*, criteria*
		•				•	•	•	•	•	DOCUMENTS	typeN
•								•	•	•	DOLLAR	N*, decimalsN
•								•	•	•	DPRODUCT	database*, field*, criteria*
•								•	•	•	DSTDEV	database*, field*, criteria*
•								•	•	•	DSTDEVP	database*, field*, criteria*
•								•	•	•	DSUM	database*, field*, criteria*
		+		•		•		+	+	+	DUPLICATE	—
•								•	•	•	DVAR	database*, field*, criteria*
•								•	•	•	DVARP	database*, field*, criteria*
		•				•		•	•	•	ECHO	L
		+	•	•		•		+	+	+	EDIT.COLOR	colorN*, redValueN, greenValueN, blueValueN
		•	•	•		•		•	•	•	EDIT.DELETE	shiftN
		•		•	•	•		•	•	•	EDIT.REPEAT	—
		+	•		•			+	+	+	EDIT.SERIES	seriesN, nameRef, xRef, yRef, zRef, plotOrderN
		+		•	•	•				7+	EDITION.OPTIONS	editionTypeN*, editionNameT*, ref, optionN*
		+				•	•	+	+	+	ELSE	—
		+				•	•	+	+	+	ELSE.IF	logicalTestL
		•						•	•	•	ENABLE.COMMAND	barN*, menuNT*, commandNT*, enableL*
		+				•	•	+	+	+	END.IF	—
		•				•	•	•	•	•	ERROR	enableL*, macroRef
•								•	•	•	EXACT	text1*, text2*
		•				•		•	•		EXEC (form 1)	programT*, windowN
		•				•				7+	EXEC (form 2)	programT*, backgroundL, preferredSizeN
		✓				•		•	•	7+	EXECUTE	channelN*, executeT*

(continued)

Function type				Applies to				Environment				
W	C	M	?	W	C	CM	FM	W	P	M	Name	Arguments
•								•	•	•	EXP	N
		•	•					•	•	•	EXTRACT	uniqueL
•								•	•	•	FACT	N
•								•	•	•	FALSE	—
		•						•	•	•	FCLOSE	fileN*
		•						•	•	•	FILE.CLOSE	saveL
		•	•					•	•	•	FILE.DELETE	fileT*
		•						•	•	•	FILES	directoryT
		•		•		•		•	•	•	FILL.DOWN	—
		•		•		•		•	•	•	FILL.LEFT	—
		•		•		•		•	•	•	FILL.RIGHT	—
		•		•		•		•	•	•	FILL.UP	—
		+	•	•		•		+	+	+	FILL.WORKGROUP	typeN*
•								•	•	•	FIND	findT*, withinT*, startAtN
•								•	•	•	FIXED	N*, decimalsN
		•	•	•		•				•	FONT	nameT*, sizeN*
		•						•	•	•	FOPEN	fileT*, accessN
		•				•	•	•	•	•	FOR	counterT*, startN*, endN*, stepN
		+		•		•		+	+	+	FOR.CELL	refNameT*, areaRef, skipBlanksL
		•	•	•		•		•	•	•	FORMAT.FONT (form 1)	nameT, sizeN, boldL, italicL, underlineL, strikeL, colorN, outlineL, shadowL
		•	•	•		•		•	•	•	FORMAT.FONT (form 2)	nameT, sizeN, boldL, italicL, underlineL, strikeL, colorN, outlineL, shadowL, objectIDT, startN, charN
		•	•		•			•	•	•	FORMAT.FONT (form 3)	colorN, backgdN, applyL, nameT, sizeN, boldL, italicL, underlineL, strikeL, outlineL, shadowL
		•	•		•			•	•	•	FORMAT.LEGEND	positionN
		+	•		•			+	+	+	FORMAT.MAIN	typeN*, viewN, overlapN, gapWidthN, varyL, dropL, hiloL, angleN, gapDepthN, chartDepthN
		•	•	•		•		•	•	•	FORMAT.MOVE (form 1)	xPosN*, yPosN*, ref
		•	•	•	•	•		•	•	•	FORMAT.MOVE (form 2)	xPos*, yPos*
		•	•	•		•		•	•	•	FORMAT.NUMBER	formatT*
		+	•		•			+	+	+	FORMAT.OVERLAY	typeN*, viewN, overlapN, gapWidthN, varyL, dropL, hiloL, angleN, seriesDistN, seriesN
		•	•	•		•		•	•	•	FORMAT.SIZE (form 1)	xOffN, yOffN, ref
		•	•	•	•	•		•	•	•	FORMAT.SIZE (form 2)	widthN, heightN

(continued)

Function type				Applies to				Environment				
W	C	M	?	W	C	CM	FM	W	P	M	Name	Arguments
		•	•	•	•	•		•	•	•	FORMAT.TEXT	xAlign, yAlign, orientN, autoTextL, autoSizeL, showKeyL, showValueL
		•		•	•	•		•	•	•	FORMULA	formulaT*, ref
		•		•		•		•	•	•	FORMULA.ARRAY	formulaT, ref
		+		•		•		+	+	+	FORMULA.CONVERT	formulaT*, fromA1L*, toA1L, toRefTypeN, relToRefR
		•		•		•		•	•	•	FORMULA.FILL	formulaT*, ref
		•	•	•		•		•	•	•	FORMULA.FIND	text*, inN*, atN*, byN*, dirN, matchCaseL
		•		•		•		•	•	•	FORMULA.FIND.NEXT	—
		•		•		•		•	•	•	FORMULA.FIND.PREV	—
		•	•	•		•		•	•	•	FORMULA.GOTO	ref, cornerL
		•	•	•		•		•	•	•	FORMULA.REPLACE	findT*, replaceT*, lookAt, lookBy, currentCell, matchCaseL
		•						•	•	•	FPOS	fileN*, positionN
		•						•	•	•	FREAD	fileN*, numChars*
		•						•	•	•	FREADLN	fileN*
		•		•		•		•	•	•	FREEZE.PANES	logical*
		•						•	•	•	FSIZE	fileN*
		•		•	•	•		•	•	•	FULL	logical*
•								•	•	•	FV	rateN*, PerN*, pmtN*, pvN, typeN
		•						•	•	•	FWRITE	fileN*, text*
		•						•	•	•	FWRITELN	fileN*, text*
		+	•		•			+	+	+	GALLERY.3D.AREA	typeN*
		+	•		•			+	+	+	GALLERY.3D.COLUMN	typeN*
		+	•		•			+	+	+	GALLERY.3D.LINE	typeN*
		+	•		•			+	+	+	GALLERY.3D.PIE	typeN*
		•	•		•			•	•	•	GALLERY.AREA	typeN*, deleteOverlayL
		•	•		•			•	•	•	GALLERY.BAR	typeN*, deleteOverlayL
		•	•		•			•	•	•	GALLERY.COLUMN	typeN*, deleteOverlayL
		•	•		•			•	•	•	GALLERY.LINE	typeN*, deleteOverlayL
		•	•		•			•	•	•	GALLERY.PIE	typeN*, deleteOverlayL
		•	•		•			•	•	•	GALLERY.SCATTER	typeN*, deleteOverlayL
		•		•		•		•	•	•	GET.BAR (form 1)	—
		•		•		•		•	•	•	GET.BAR (form 2)	barN*, menuNT*, commandNT*
		✓		•		•		✓	✓	✓	GET.CELL	typeN*, ref
		•			•		•	•	•	•	GET.CHART.ITEM	xyIndex*, pointIndex, itemT
		✓		•		•	•	✓	✓	✓	GET.DEF	defT*, documentT, typeN
		✓		•	•	•	•	✓	✓	✓	GET.DOCUMENT	typeN*, nameT

(continued)

Function type				Applies to				Environment				
W	C	M	?	W	C	CM	FM	W	P	M	Name	Arguments
		•		•	•	•	•	•	•	•	GET.FORMULA	reference*
		+		•	•	•	•	+	+	+	GET.LINK.INFO	linkT*, typeN*, typeOfLinkN, ref
		•		•		•	•	•	•	•	GET.NAME	nameT*
		•		•		•	•	•	•	•	GET.NOTE	cellRef, startCharN, charsN
		+		•		•	•	+	+	+	GET.OBJECT	typeN*, objectIDT, startN, countN
		✓		•	•	•	•	✓	✓	✓	GET.WINDOW	typeN*, windowT
		✓					•	✓	✓	✓	GET.WORKSPACE	typeOfInfo*
		+	•	•		•		+	+	+	GOAL.SEEK	targetCellR*, targetValueN*, variableCellR*
		•		•		•	•	•	•	•	GOTO	ref
		✓	•		•			✓	✓	✓	GRIDLINES	xMajor, xMinor, yMajor, yMinor, zMajor, zMinor
		+		•	•	•		+	+	+	GROUP	—
✓								•	•	•	GROWTH	knownYs*, knownXs, newXs, const
		✓				•	•	✓	✓	✓	HALT	cancelCloseL
		•						•	•	•	HELP	fileName!topicN
		•		•	•	•		•	•	•	HIDE	—
		+		•		•		+	+	+	HIDE.OBJECT	objectIDT, hideL
		•		•		•		•	•	•	HLINE	columnsN*
•								•	•	•	HLOOKUP	lookupValue*, tableArrayR*, rowIndexN*
•								•	•	•	HOUR	serialN*
		•		•		•		•	•	•	HPAGE	windowsN*
		•		•		•		•	•	•	HSCROLL	positionN*, colL
•								•	•	•	IF (form 1)	logicalTestL*, trueValueN, falseValueN
		+				•	•	+	+	+	IF (form 2)	logicalTestL*
•								•	•	•	INDEX (form 1)	reference*, rowN*, colN*, areaN
•								•	•	•	INDEX (form 2)	arrayRef*, rowN, colN
•								•	•	•	INDIRECT	refT*, a1L
+								+	+	+	INFO	typeN*
		•						•	•	7+	INITIATE	appT*, topicT*
		•						•	•	•	INPUT	messageT*, typeN, titleT, defaultValue, xPosN, yPosN
		•	•	•		•		•	•	•	INSERT	shiftN
•								•	•	•	INT	N*
•								•	•	•	IPMT	rateN*, perN*, nPerN*, pvN*, fvN, typeN
•								•	•	•	IRR	valuesAR*, guessN
•								•	•	•	ISBLANK	valueN*

(continued)

Function type				Applies to				Environment				
W	C	M	?	W	C	CM	FM	W	P	M	Name	Arguments
•								•	•	•	ISERR	valueN*
•								•	•	•	ISERROR	valueN*
•								•	•	•	ISLOGICAL	valueN*
•								•	•	•	ISNA	valueN*
•								•	•	•	ISNONTEXT	valueN*
•								•	•	•	ISNUMBER	valueN*
•								•	•	•	ISREF	valueN*
•								•	•	•	ISTEXT	valueN*
		•		•		•		•	•	•	JUSTIFY	—
		+				•	•	+	+	+	LAST.ERROR	—
•								•	•	•	LEFT	T*, nChars
		•			•			•	•	•	LEGEND	logical
•								•	•	•	LEN	text*
✓								•	•	•	LINEST	knownYs*, knownXs, constL, statsL
		✓		•		•		✓	✓	✓	LINKS	documentT, typeN
		•		•		•		•	•	•	LIST.NAMES	—
•								•	•	•	LN	N*
•								•	•	•	LOG	N*, baseN
•								•	•	•	LOG10	N*
✓								•	•	•	LOGEST	knownYs*, knownXs, constL, statsL
•								•	•	•	LOOKUP (form 1)	lookupValueN*, lookupVectorR*, resultVectorR*
•								•	•	•	LOOKUP (form 2)	lookupValueN*, array*
•								•	•	•	LOWER	text*
		•	•		•			•	•	•	MAIN.CHART	typeN*, stackL, 100L, varyL, overlapL, dropL, hiloL, overlap%N, clusterN, angleN
		•			•			•	•	•	MAIN.CHART.TYPE	typeN*
•								•	•	•	MATCH	lookupValueN*, lookupArrayR*, matchTypeN
•								•	•	•	MAX	n1*, n2, ...
•								•	•	•	MDETERM	array*
+								+	+	+	MEDIAN	num1*, num2, ...
		+		•		•		+	+	+	MERGE.STYLES	documentT*
		•						•	•	•	MESSAGE	logical*, text
•								•	•	•	MID	text*, startN*, nChars*
•								•	•	•	MIN	num1*, num2, ...
•								•	•	•	MINUTE	serialN*
•								•	•	•	MINVERSE	array*

(continued)

Function type				Applies to				Environment				
W	C	M	?	W	C	CM	FM	W	P	M	Name	Arguments
•								•	•	•	MIRR	values*, financeRateN*, reinvestRateN*
•								•	•	•	MMULT	array1*, array2*
•								•	•	•	MOD	N*, divisorN*
•								•	•	•	MONTH	serialN*
		•	•	•	•	•		•	•	•	MOVE	xPos, yPos, windowT
•								•	•	•	N	value*
•								•	•	•	NA	—
		✓		•		•	•	✓	✓	✓	NAMES	documentT, typeN
		✓	•	•	•	•		✓	✓	✓	NEW	typeN*, xySeriesN
		•		•		•		•	•	•	NEW.WINDOW	—
		•				•	•	•	•	•	NEXT	—
•								•	•	•	NOT	logical*
		•	•	•		•		•	•	•	NOTE	addT, cellRef, startCharN, charsN
•								•	•	•	NOW	—
•								•	•	•	NPER	rateN*, pmtN*, pvN*, fvN, typeN
•								•	•	•	NPV	rate*, value1*, value2, ...
		+		•		•		+	+	+	OBJECT.PROTECTION	lockedL, lockT
✓				•		•	•	•	•	•	OFFSET	ref*, rowsN*, colsN*, heightN, widthN
		+		•	•	•		•	•	7+	ON.DATA	documentT, macroT
		•		•	•	•		•	•	•	ON.KEY	keyT*, macroT
		+		•	•	•		+	+	+	ON.RECALC	sheetT, macroT
		•		•	•	•		•	•	•	ON.TIME	time*, macroT*, waitTimeN, insertL
		•		•	•	•		•	•	•	ON.WINDOW	windowT, macroT
		✓	•					✓	✓	✓	OPEN	fileT*, updateLinksN, readOnlyL, formatN, protPwdT, writeResPwdT, ignoreRORecL, fileOriginN
		✓	•	•		•		✓	✓	✓	OPEN.LINKS	document1T*, document2T, ..., readOnlyL, typeOfLinkN
		•	•							•	OPEN.MAIL	subjectT, commentsT
•								•	•	•	OR	logical1*, logical2, ...
		+		•		•		+	+	+	OUTLINE	autoStylesL, rowDirL, colDirL, createN
		•	•		•			•	•	•	OVERLAY	typeN*, stackL, 100L, varyL, overlapL, dropL, hiloL, overlap%N, clusterN, angleN, seriesN, autoL
		•			•			•	•	•	OVERLAY.CHART.TYPE	typeN*

(continued)

Function type				Applies to				Environment				
W	C	M	?	W	C	CM	FM	W	P	M	Name	Arguments
		•	•	•		•		•	•	•	PAGE.SETUP (form 1)	headT, footT, leftN, rightN, topN, botN, headingL, gridL, hCenterL, vCenterL, orientationN, paperSizeN, scalingN
		•	•		•			•	•	•	PAGE.SETUP (form 2)	headT, footT, leftN, rightN, topN, botN, sizeN, hCenterL, vCenterL, orientationN, paperSizeN, scalingN
		•	•					•	•	•	PARSE	text*
		•		•	•	•		•	•	•	PASTE	—
		•		•		•		•	•	•	PASTE.LINK	—
		+		•		•		+	+	+	PASTE.PICTURE	—
		+		•		•		+	+	+	PASTE.PICTURE.LINK	—
		•	•	•		•		•	•	•	PASTE.SPECIAL (form 1)	pasteN*, operationN*, skipBlanksL*, transposeL*
		•	•		•			•	•	•	PASTE.SPECIAL (form 2)	rowColN*, seriesL*, categoriesL*, replaceL*
		•	•		•			•	•	•	PASTE.SPECIAL (form 3)	pasteN*
		•		•		•		+	+	+	PATTERNS (form 1)	aPatternN, aForeN, aBackN
		•		•	•	•		•	•	•	PATTERNS (form 2)	lAutoN, lStyleN, lColorN, lWtN, hWidthN, hLengthN, hTypeN
		+		•		•		+	+	+	PATTERNS (form 3)	bAutoN, bStyleN, bColorN, bWtN, shadowL, aAutoN, aPatternN, aForeN, aBackN, roundedL
		•		•	•	•		•	•	•	PATTERNS (form 4)	bAutoN, bStyleN, bColorN, bWtN, shadowL, aAutoN, aPatternN, aForeN, aBackN, invertL, applyL
		•			•			•	•	•	PATTERNS (form 5)	lAutoN, lStyleN, lColorN, lWtN, tMajorN, tMinorN, tLabelN
		•			•			•	•	•	PATTERNS (form 6)	lAutoN, lStyleN, lColorN, lWtN, applyL
		•			•			•	•	•	PATTERNS (form 7)	lAutoN, lStyleN, lColorN, lWtN, mAutoN, mStyleN, mForeN, mBackN, applyL
		•			•			•	•	•	PATTERNS (form 8)	typeN, pictureUnitsN, applyL
•								•	•	•	PI	—
		+		•		•		+	+	+	PLACEMENT	typeN
•								•	•	•	PMT	rateN*, nPerN*, pvN*, fvN, typeN
		✓						•	•	7+	POKE	channelN*, itemT*, dataRef*
•								•	•	•	PPMT	rateN*, perN*, nPerN*, fvN, typeN

(continued)

Function type				Applies to				Environment				
W	C	M	?	W	C	CM	FM	W	P	M	Name	Arguments
		•		•		•		•	•	•	PRECISION	logical*
		•			•			•	•	•	PREFERRED	—
		✓	•	•	•	•		✓	✓	✓	PRINT	rangeN, fromN, toN, copiesN, draftL, previewL, printWhatN, colorL, feedN
		+		•	•	•		+	+	+	PRINT.PREVIEW	—
		•	•					•	•		PRINTER.SETUP	printerT*
•								•	•	•	PRODUCT	num1*, num2, ...
		+	•	•		•		+	+	+	PROMOTE	rowColN
•								•	•	•	PROPER	T*
		✓	•	•	•	•		✓	✓	✓	PROTECT.DOCUMENT	contentsL, windowsL, passwordT, objectsL
•								•	•	•	PV	rateN*, perN*, pmtN*, fvN, typeN
		•						•	•	•	QUIT	—
•								•	•	•	RAND	—
•								•	•	•	RATE	nPerN*, pmtN*, pvN*, fvN, typeN, guessN
		•				•	•	•	•	•	REF	argument1, argument2, ...
		•				•	•	•	•	•	REFTEXT	reference*, a1L
		✓				•	•	✓	✓	✓	REGISTER	moduleT*, procedureT*, typeT*, functionT, argumentT
		•		•		•	•	•	•	•	RELREF	reference*, relToRefR*
		•		•		•		•	•	•	REMOVE.PAGE.BREAK	—
		•						•	•	•	RENAME.COMMAND	barN*, menuTN*, commandTN*, nameT*
•								•	•	•	REPLACE	—
		•		•		•		•	•	•	REPLACE.FONT	fontN*, nameT*, sizeN, boldL, italicL, underlineL, strikeL, colorN, outlineL, shadowL
•								•	•	•	REPT	text*, nTimes*
		+		•		•		•	•	7+	REQUEST	channelN*, itemT*
		•				•	•	•	•	•	RESTART	levelN
		•				•	•	•	•	•	RESULT	typeN
		•				•	•	•	•	•	RETURN	value
•								•	•	•	RIGHT	text*, nChars
•								•	•	•	ROUND	N*, nDigits*
•								•	•	•	ROW	ref
		✓	•	•		•		✓	✓	✓	ROW.HEIGHT	heightN, ref, standardHeightL, typeN
•								•	•	•	ROWS	array*
		✓	•			•	•	✓	✓	✓	RUN	ref, stepL

(continued)

Function type				Applies to			Environment				
W	C	M	?	W	C	CMFM	W	P	M	Name	Arguments
		•		•	•	•	•	•	•	SAVE	—
		✓	•	•	•	•	✓	✓	✓	SAVE.AS	documentT, typeN, protPwdT, backupL, writeResPwdT, readOnlyRecL
		+	•	•		•	N			SAVE.NEW.OBJECT	objectNameT*
		•	•				•	•	•	SAVE.WORKSPACE	nameT
		•	•		•		•	•	•	SCALE (form 1)	crossN, catLabelsN, catMarksN, betweenL, maxL, reverseL
		•	•		•		•	•	•	SCALE (form 2)	minN, maxN, majorN, minorN, crossN, logarithmicL, reverseL, maxL
		+	•		•		+	+	+	SCALE (form 3)	catLabelsN, catMarksN, reverseL, betweenL
		+	•		•		+	+	+	SCALE (form 4)	seriesLabelsN, seriesMarksN, reverseL
		+	•		•		+	+	+	SCALE (form 5)	minN, maxN, majorN, minorN, crossN, logarithmicL, reverseL, minL
•							•	•	•	SEARCH	findT, withinT*, startNum
•							•	•	•	SECOND	serialN*
		•		•		•	•	•	•	SELECT (form 1)	selectionR, activeCellR
		+		•		•	+	+	+	SELECT (form 2)	objectIDT*, replaceL
		+			•		+	+	+	SELECT (form 3)	itemT*, singlePointL
		•			•		•	•	•	SELECT.CHART	—
		•		•		•	•	•	•	SELECT.END	directionN*
		•		•		•	•	•	•	SELECT.LAST.CELL	—
		•			•		•	•	•	SELECT.PLOT.AREA	—
		✓	•	•		•	✓	✓	✓	SELECT.SPECIAL	typeN*, valueTypeN, levelsN
		•		•		•	•	•	•	SELECTION	—
		•					•	•		SEND.KEYS	keyText*, waitL
		•							•	SEND.MAIL	recipientT*, subjectT, returnReceiptL
		+		•		•	+	+	+	SEND.TO.BACK	—
•					•		•	•	•	SERIES	nameRef, categoriesN, valuesN*, plotOrderN*
		•		•		•	•	•	•	SET.CRITERIA	—
		•		•		•	•	•	•	SET.DATABASE	—
		+		•		•	+	+	+	SET.EXTRACT	—
		•				•	•	•	•	SET.NAME	nameT*, value
		•		•		•	•	•	•	SET.PAGE.BREAK	—
		•			•		•	•	•	SET.PREFERRED	—
		•		•		•	•	•	•	SET.PRINT.AREA	—

(continued)

Function type				Applies to				Environment				
W	C	M	?	W	C	CM	FM	W	P	M	Name	Arguments
		•		•		•		•	•	•	SET.PRINT.TITLES	—
		+		•	•	•		+	+	+	SET.UPDATE.STATUS	linkT*, statusN*, typeOfLinkN
		•				•		•	•	•	SET.VALUE	ref*, values*
		+				•		N			SHARE	—
		+				•		N			SHARE.NAME	rangeName*
		•						•	•	•	SHORT.MENUS	logical*
		•		•		•		•	•	•	SHOW.ACTIVE.CELL	—
		•						•	•	•	SHOW.BAR	barN
		•						•	•	•	SHOW.CLIPBOARD	—
		+		•		•		+	+	+	SHOW.DETAIL	rowColN*, rowColNumN*, expandL
		•						•	•	•	SHOW.INFO	logical*
		+		•		•		+	+	+	SHOW.LEVELS	rowLevelN, colLevelN
•								•	•	•	SIGN	N*
•								•	•	•	SIN	N*
+								+	+	+	SINH	N*
		•		•	•	•		•	•	•	SIZE	widthN*, heightN*, windowT
•								•	•	•	SLN	costN*, salvageN*, lifeN*
		•	•	•		•		•	•	•	SORT	sortByN*, key1R*, order1N*, key2R, order2N, key3R, order3N
		•		•		•		•	•	•	SPLIT	colSplitN, rowSplitN
•								•	•	•	SQRT	N*
		✓		•		•		+	•	•	STANDARD.FONT	fontT, sizeN, boldL, italicL, underlineL, strikeL, colorN, outlineL, shadowL
•								•	•	•	STDEV	num1*, num2, ...
•								•	•	•	STDEVP	num1*, num2, ...
		•				•	•	•	•	•	STEP	—
		•	•	•		•		•	•	•	STYLE	boldL, italicL
		+		•		•				7+	SUBSCRIBE.TO	fileT*, formatN*
•								•	•	•	SUBSTITUTE	T*, oldT*, newT*, instanceN
•								•	•	•	SUM	n1*, n2, n3, ...
+								+	+	+	SUMPRODUCT	array1*, array2*, ...
•								•	•	•	SYD	costN*, salvageN*, lifeN*, perN*
•								•	•	•	T	N*
		•	•	•		•		•	•	•	TABLE	rowRef, columnRef
•								•	•	•	TAN	N*
+								+	+	+	TANH	N*
		+						•	•	7+	TERMINATE	channelN*
•								•	•	•	TEXT	value*, formatT*
		+		•		•		+	+	+	TEXT.BOX	addT*, objectIDT*, startN, charsN
		•				•	•	•	•	•	TEXTREF	text*, a1L

(continued)

Function type				Applies to				Environment				
W	C	M	?	W	C	CM	FM	W	P	M	Name	Arguments
•								•	•	•	TIME	hourN*, minuteN*, secondN*
•								•	•	•	TIMEVALUE	timeText*
+								+	+	+	TODAY	—
•								•	•	•	TRANSPOSE	array*
✓								•	•	•	TREND	knownYs*, knownXs, newXs, const
•								•	•	•	TRIM	text*
•								•	•	•	TRUE	—
✓								•	•	•	TRUNC	N*, precisionN*
•								•	•	•	TYPE	value*
		•		•	•	•		•	•	•	UNDO	—
		+		•		•		+	+	+	UNGROUP	—
		•		•	•	•		•	•	•	UNHIDE	windowT*
		•		•		•		•	•	•	UNLOCKED.NEXT	—
		•		•		•		•	•	•	UNLOCKED.PREV	—
		✓		•		•	•	+	+	•	UNREGISTER	registerT*
		+		•		•		+	+	+	UPDATE.LINK	linkT, typeOfLinkN
•								•	•	•	UPPER	text*
•								•	•	•	VALUE	text*
•								•	•	•	VAR	num1*, num2, ...
•								•	•	•	VARP	num1*, num2, ...
+								+	+	+	VDB	costN*, salvageN*, lifeN*, startPeriodN*, endPeriodN*, factorN, noSwitchL
		+	•		•			+	+	+	VIEW.3D	elevationN, perspectiveN, rotationN, axesL, height%N
		•		•		•		•	•	•	VLINE	rowsN*
•								•	•	•	VLOOKUP	lookupValue*, tableArray*, colIndexN*
		+				•	•	+	+	+	VOLATILE	—
		•		•		•		•	•	•	VPAGE	windowsN*
		•		•		•		•	•	•	VSCROLL	positionN*, rowL
		•				•		•	•	•	WAIT	serialN*
•								•	•	•	WEEKDAY	serialN*
		•				•	•	•	•	•	WHILE	testL
		•		•	•	•	•	•	•	•	WINDOWS	typeN
		+		•		•		+	+	+	WORKGROUP	nameArray
		✓	•			•		✓	✓	•	WORKSPACE	fixedL, decimalsN, r1c1L, scrollL, statusL, formulaL, menuKeyT, remoteL, enterMoveL, underlinesN, toolsL, notesL, navKeysL, menuKeyActionN
•								•	•	•	YEAR	serialN*

Index

D

G

H

I

K

L

M

N

T

More Titles from Microsoft Press

MICROSOFT PRESS® COMPUTER DICTIONARY

Microsoft Press

More than 5000 comprehensive entries make this the standard microcomputer dictionary for classrooms, libraries, and individual computer users. This dictionary especially appeals to users who are involved with personal computers but who are not computer sophisticates. Each entry is written in clear, standard English, and each goes beyond mere definition to provide context. Compiled by a distinguished board of advisers drawn from the computer, business, and academic communities.

400 pages, softcover $19.95 ($24.95 Canada)   Order Code PRCODI

THE MICROSOFT® VISUAL BASIC™ WORKSHOP

John Clark Craig

Create Windows applications quickly with Microsoft Visual Basic and THE MICROSOFT VISUAL BASIC WORKSHOP. Whether you're a new or experienced Windows programmer, you'll find this book-and-disk package invaluable. It includes dozens of ready-to-use Visual Basic routines and applications that can be easily incorporated into your Windows programming projects. The author provides helpful overviews of both Visual Basic and event-driven programming. Also covered are advanced programming concepts—using Dynamic Data Exchange using the Windows Applications Programming Interface, creating Dynamic Link Libraries, and using Windows graphics.

NOTE: Both executable and source-code files are included so you can preview Visual Basic if you don't already own it!

320 pages, includes one 5.25-inch 1.2 MB disk $34.95 ($44.95 Canada)   Order Code VIBAWO

The Waite Group's MICROSOFT QUICKBASIC™ PRIMER PLUS

The Waite Group: Stephen Prata with Harry Henderson

This is the ideal introduction—and more—for anyone eager to explore the Microsoft QuickBASIC programming environment. Covering Microsoft QuickBASIC version 4.5, this book provides step-by-step instructions, clear and helpful explanations, superb programming examples, and expert advice. You'll also find detailed information on topics not fully covered in standard introductions—graphics, debugging, sound, error trapping, interaction with DOS, and mixed-language programming. In addition, each chapter includes a series of review questions and answers so that you can chart your progress.

624 pages $24.95 ($32.95 Canada)   Order Code QBPRPL

MICROSOFT® MOUSE PROGRAMMER'S REFERENCE, 2nd ed.

This is the official documentation for programming the Microsoft Mouse. It provides all the software and how-to information you need to incorporate a sophisticated mouse interface for MS-DOS operating system-based programs. Fully updated to cover Microsoft BallPoint mouse and the mouse driver version 8, this new edition includes: sample programs that demonstrate mouse programming in six PC programming languages; a complete reference to all mouse function calls; an overview of mouse programming; detailed information about writing and using mouse menu programs; comprehensive index; and much more. The two 5 1/4-inch companion disks include sample mouse menus, MOUSE.LIB and EGA.LIB, and a collection of valuable programming examples in interpreted Basic, Microsoft QuickBasic, Microsoft C, Microsoft QuickC, Microsoft Macro Assembler, FORTRAN, and Pascal.

352 pages with two 5.25-inch disks $34.95 ($44.95 Canada)   Order Code MOPRR2

Microsoft Press books are available wherever quality computer books are sold. Prices subject to change.
Or call **1-800-MSPRESS** for ordering information or placing credit card orders.
Please refer to **BBK** when placing your order.

In Canada, contact Macmillan Canada, Attn: Microsoft Press Dept., 164 Commander Blvd., Agincourt, Ontario, Canada M1S 3C7. 416-293-8141
In the U.K., contact Microsoft Press, 27 Wrights Lane, London W8 5TZ.

Move Up to Microsoft® Word for Windows™ and Microsoft PowerPoint®

MICROSOFT® WORD STEP BY STEP (Word for Windows™ Edition)

Microsoft Corporation

Tried and tested, this book and disk package is the official Microsoft courseware for Microsoft Word for Windows version 2.0. It's an excellent, self-paced study course for anyone using Word for Windows. Similar in format to *Microsoft Excel Step by Step*, the lessons in this edition are progressive yet modular so the novice can advance from one lesson to the next, and the intermediate user can jump in at any point. The package comes complete with disk-based tutorials, seventeen follow-along lessons, and practice exercises.

220 pages, softcover with one 5.25-inch disk $29.95 ($39.95 Canada) Order Code WOWIST

RUNNING WORD FOR WINDOWS™

Russell Borland

This example-rich book is an outstanding reference for intermediate and advanced users. Now completely updated (formerly *Working with Word for Windows*), it highlights all the new document-processing, desktop publishing, and WYSIWYG features of Word for Windows version 2.0. Russell Borland, a former member of the Microsoft Word for Windows development team, has included scores of insights and power tips not found in the documentation or in other Word for Windows books.

700 pages, softcover $24.95 ($32.95 Canada) Order Code RUWDWI

(Available January 1992)

WORD FOR WINDOWS™ COMPANION, 2nd ed.

The Cobb Group: Mark W. Crane

A wealth of useful information for users at any level of experience. This comprehensive resource is both an exceptional tutorial for new Word users and a master reference guide for experienced users. You'll learn basic concepts of word processing, typography, and design so that you'll be able to create professional-looking documents with confidence and ease. In addition to detailed explanations, the book offers scores of illustrations, examples, and tips to enhance your productivity. An extensive index and side-margin headings make information readily accessible. Covers version 2.0.

896 pages, softcover $27.95 ($34.95 Canada) Order Code WDWIC2

(Available March 1992)

POWERPOINT® PRESENTATIONS BY DESIGN

Roger C. Parker

A superb introduction to Microsoft's popular desktop presentation software program. You get an information-packed overview of every PowerPoint tool and feature, accompanied by expert advice on designing and preparing slides and overheads. Covers both the Windows and the Apple Macintosh versions of PowerPoint.

400 pages, softcover $24.95 ($34.95 Canada) Order Code POPRDE

Microsoft Press books are available wherever quality computer books are sold. Prices subject to change.
Or call **1-800-MSPRESS** for ordering information or placing credit card orders.
Please refer to **BBK** when placing your order.

In Canada, contact Macmillan Canada, Attn: Microsoft Press Dept., 164 Commander Blvd., Agincourt, Ontario, Canada M1S 3C7. 416-293-8141

In the U.K., contact Microsoft Press, 27 Wrights Lane, London W8 5TZ.

Great Resources for the Microsoft® Excel User

RUNNING MICROSOFT® EXCEL, 2nd ed.

The Cobb Group

No matter what your level of expertise—longtime Lotus® 1-2-3® user, veteran Microsoft Excel user, beginning or occasional Microsoft Excel user—this will be your primary source of information, advice, and solid tutorial. RUNNING MICROSOFT EXCEL is packed with step-by-step instruction, superb examples, and dozens of screen illustrations to help you understand and use every function and command of the program. In addition, special "Excel Tips" throughout the book spotlight effective shortcuts. New information covers version 3.

848 pages, softcover $27.95 ($36.95 Canada) Order Code RUEX2

MICROSOFT® EXCEL STEP BY STEP (PC Edition)

Microsoft Corporation

The official Microsoft Excel courseware. Learn to create useful, error-free spreadsheets with Microsoft Excel for Windows the most effective and timesaving way—by combining self-paced lessons and disk-based practice files. The lessons are progressive yet modular, so the novice can advance from one lesson to the next, and the intermediate user can step in at any point to learn specific skills. Each of the seventeen lessons includes clear objectives, step-by-step instructions, real-world business examples (on disk and in the book), review exercises, and summaries. An ideal training guide for business, classroom, or home use.

286 pages, softcover with one 5.25-inch disk $29.95 ($39.95 Canada) Order Code EX3STP

RUNNING WINDOWS™

Craig Stinson and Nancy Andrews

"RUNNING WINDOWS does not skirt a subject, but instead dives right in....The text is clear and concise....Its detailed explanations will save you much more time than it takes to read it." ***PC Magazine***

Build your confidence and enhance your productivity with the Microsoft Windows—quickly and easily—using this hands-on introduction. This Microsoft-authorized, bestselling volume provides detailed coverage of every aspect of installing and using Windows 3, incorporating real-world examples to help you optimize Windows' performance.

522 pages, softcover $24.95 ($32.95 Canada) Order Code RUWI2

WINDOWS™ 3 COMPANION

The Cobb Group: Lori Lorenz and Michael O'Mara

"An excellent reference featuring dozens of live examples of how different functions work." ***PC Magazine***

This resource covers everything from installing and starting Windows to using all its built-in applications and desktop accessories. Novices will value the book for its step-by-step tutorials and great examples; more experienced users will turn to it again and again for its expert advice, tips, and information. The authors detail the features and use of Windows' Program Manager, File Manager, and Printer Manager so that you'll be able to expertly maneuver through Windows, control the environment, and easily manage files, disks, and printers.

536 pages, softcover $27.95 ($36.95 Canada) Order Code WI3CO

Microsoft Press books are available wherever quality computer books are sold. Prices subject to change.
Or call **1-800-MSPRESS** for ordering information or placing credit card orders.
Please refer to **BBK** when placing your order.

In Canada, contact Macmillan Canada, Attn: Microsoft Press Dept., 164 Commander Blvd., Agincourt, Ontario, Canada M1S 3C7. 416-293-8141

In the U.K., contact Microsoft Press, 27 Wrights Lane, London W8 5TZ.